W9-CLQ-130

This Book Comes With Lots of
FREE Online Resources

Nolo's award-winning website has a page dedicated just to this book. Here you can:

KEEP UP TO DATE. When there are important changes to the information in this book, we'll post updates.

GET DISCOUNTS ON NOLO PRODUCTS. Get discounts on hundreds of books, forms, and software.

READ BLOGS. Get the latest info from Nolo authors' blogs.

LISTEN TO PODCASTS. Listen to authors discuss timely issues on topics that interest you.

WATCH VIDEOS. Get a quick introduction to a legal topic with our short videos.

And that's not all. Nolo.com contains thousands of articles on everyday legal and business issues, plus a plain-English law dictionary, all written by Nolo experts and available for free. You'll also find more useful **books, software, online apps, downloadable forms,** plus a **lawyer directory.**

With
Downloadable
FORMS

NOLO
LAW for ALL

Get forms and more at
www.nolo.com/back-of-book/ML.html

9th Edition

Music Law

How to Run Your Band's Business

Attorney Richard Stim

NINTH EDITION	SEPTEMBER 2018
Editor	ELIZABETH GJELTEN
Cover Design	SUSAN PUTNEY
Book Production	SUSAN PUTNEY
Proofreading	ROBERT WELLS
Index	ACCESS POINTS INDEXING
Printing	BANG PRINTING

Names: Stim, Richard, author.
Title: Music law : how to run your band's business / attorney Richard Stim.
Description: 9th edition. | Berkeley, California : Nolo, 2018. | Includes index.
Identifiers: LCCN 2018011629 (print) | LCCN 2018013934 (ebook) | ISBN 9781413325614 (ebook) | ISBN 9781413325607 (pbk.)
Subjects: LCSH: Band musicians--United States--Handbooks, manuals, etc. | Band musicians--Legal status, laws, etc.--United States--Popular works. | Performing arts--Law and legislation--United States--Popular works.
Classification: LCC KF390.E57 (ebook) | LCC KF390.E57 S87 2018 (print) | DDC 344.73/097--dc23
LC record available at https://lccn.loc.gov/2018011629

This book covers only United States law, unless it specifically states otherwise.

Please note

We believe accurate, plain-English legal information should help you solve many of your own legal problems. But this text is not a substitute for personalized advice from a knowledgeable lawyer. If you want the help of a trained professional—and we'll always point out situations in which we think that's a good idea—consult an attorney licensed to practice in your state.

Acknowledgments

Thanks to those who provided me with helpful information in various chapters: Craig Leon, Kathryn Roessel, George (area 51) Earth, Frank Gallagher, Andrea Ross, Andy Olyphant, Lindsay Hutton, Howard Thompson, Don Ciccone, and Marc Weinstein.

And thanks to Nolo Legal Editor Elizabeth Gjelten, who edited the 9th edition.

This book is for Bruce Anderson and Andrea Ross, my two favorite bandleaders.

About the Author

Richard Stim is a lawyer, musician, and the author of several books including *Getting Permission* (Nolo), *Profit From Your Idea* (Nolo), and *Patent, Copyright & Trademark: An Intellectual Desk Reference* (Nolo).

Table of Contents

Your Legal Companion

When we asked musician and producer Steve Albini for a forward to this book, he wrote, "The conventional wisdom in the music industry is to 'get a good lawyer.' My advice to the contrary would be to have no truck with lawyers at all."

Steve has engineered over a thousand records—many on his own record label—with international sales in the millions. As musicians, he and his band mates in Big Black and Shellac have toured the world and sold hundreds of thousands of records of their own. What sets Albini apart from lots of other musicians in bands is that he's reached success on his own terms—which, in most of his business dealings, involves no lawyers or written contracts. Rather than relying on legal protections in the music industry, Albini's strategy is to be careful to work only with trustworthy people.

To some extent, Steve's approach regarding lawyers is similar to that of Nolo, the company that publishes this book. Nolo was founded on the idea that many legal tasks can be performed without the aid of an attorney. At the same time, Nolo recognizes that there are some tasks that will require a lawyer's help.

In other words, as much as we admire Steve's career and work, this book does not shun written agreements or attorneys. Instead, we recommend easy-to-understand written contracts for your business agreements, and we attempt to make the law (and dealing with lawyers) easy to manage.

We do agree with Steve's advice that the trustworthiness of the parties is the most important aspect of any working relationship. A contract, no matter how carefully drafted, cannot completely insulate you from the dishonest acts of an individual or company. As you proceed through this book, keep in mind that the key to a satisfying and successful music career is not on the dotted line, but in the company you keep.

Get Forms, Updates, and More at This Book's Companion Page

You can download any of the forms and agreements in this book at:

www.nolo.com/back-of-book/ML.html

When there are important changes to the information in this book, we'll post updates on this same dedicated page as well as podcasts and videos from author Rich Stim.

Yes, Your Band Is a Business!

"It's very easy in this business to find people who are willing to put their arm around you and tell you how great you are. Unfortunately, their other hand is in your pocket."

—Paul Stanley of KISS

Lou Reed once told an audience, "Give me an issue and I'll give you a tissue." Many music business executives have a similar attitude—they have little sympathy for the moral, business, or ethical issues faced by a band competing in the music business. The sole concern for most music industry companies is whether or not the band will make a lot of money. Therefore, bands should not expect much help (or sympathy) from their label, distributor, or booking agent when dealing with common problems. Even if your band can afford accountants, business managers, and lawyers to help you with problems, you'll save considerable time and money by making your band as self-sufficient as possible.

Taking On the Music Industry

Some people perceive the music industry as a bunch of conniving executives who steal artists' songs and recordings. Popular films and books reinforce these stereotypes. Why? Is the music business more unethical than other industries?

No, the music industry is probably not that much different from others. All businesses are opportunistic. If there is an opportunity to get ahead, then you can bet someone will take advantage of it. The problem in the music industry is that getting ahead often means taking advantage of musicians who aren't experienced in the business side of music. But if a musician learns the basics about business and law, there is less of an opportunity for that type of abuse. That's what this book is about: protecting yourself and minimizing your damages.

This isn't to say that you can always avoid getting screwed. Be prepared for some setbacks. In this chapter we'll ease you into the different aspects of your band's business, and we'll try to help you decide on the business form that is best for your band.

Your Band Is a Business

The first and most important step in running your band's business is to accept the fact that it *is* a business. Producing music is your band's creative work, and selling that music is a business venture. As long as your band is interested in profiting from its music, business knowledge is as essential to your success as musical creativity!

You may be surprised to learn that taking care of business actually involves creativity and is not quite as boring as you may believe (ask Mick Jagger—a business school graduate). In fact, your band may well enjoy the power that comes with understanding how to run a business—and to do it successfully. This doesn't mean your band must micromanage every detail of its business. As your band develops, you will delegate power and responsibilities. But, especially at the beginning, it's important for you to understand basic contract and accounting principles in order to make smart decisions and avoid the many pitfalls that often trap bands and their members.

Apathy Is Not the Answer

There is a joke that asks for the definition of "apathy." The answer: "I don't know and I don't care." Unfortunately, many musicians take this attitude toward the business dealings of their band. Don't be one of them.

The "I Don't Know" Excuse

Some musicians believe that they are unable to understand business principles. This is *not* a valid excuse. Scientific studies have shown that many of the same cognitive skills that are used in music are used in mathematics and business. That is, if you can mix eighth and sixteenth notes and still land on the downbeat, then you probably possess the skills necessary to understand a spreadsheet.

The "I Don't Care" Excuse

It only takes getting burned once before a musician realizes, "I *do* care about business." Most musical careers are relatively short, and the only way to make a career last longer is to devote equal time to music and business. Without business knowledge, you may soon find that the glory days have ended and you're broke.

Cutting Through the Legal Jargon

Sometimes, failing to understand business principles is really nothing more than not knowing the language. As in many other industries, the music industry often uses a smokescreen of strange terms (such as "compulsory license" and "mechanical royalties") and legalese (such as "the band hereby indemnifies") that can make otherwise simple concepts incomprehensible. In this book, we'll discuss business and legal issues without relying on jargon, plus we'll introduce you to the terms you need to know.

Common Band Issues

Performing in a band can be so much fun that sometimes you can't believe you get paid to do it. Then, unfortunately, sometimes you don't get paid … and it's not so much fun. Suddenly, you're anxious about your relationship with a club owner, a manager, or maybe even your own band mates.

Having been in a few bands myself, I can feel your pain. Hopefully this book can steer you through some of the common crises experienced by most musicians. And even if you must hire a lawyer (sorry!), this book should save you time and money by educating you as to your options. Below are some of the problems addressed in *Music Law*.

- **Disputes between band members.** Sometimes the only harmony within a band is provided by the backup singers. Sure, confrontations may spark the band creatively, but most of the time, they distract you from making great music. This book includes a simple band agreement that can prevent some disputes over money, ownership of the band name, and ownership of band equipment. We also have suggestions for avoiding disputes in the recording studio, over song ownership, and about division of song income.

- **Management issues.** A good manager can be an excellent buffer between your band and the business. A bad manager can be a major disaster. Within this book, you will find some common ways that managers screw bands and how to avoid it.

- **Lawyers.** There are occasions when your band must hire an attorney—for example, to negotiate a major contract, or to sue or to defend your band in a lawsuit. This book provides detailed discussions about when a lawyer might be necessary, suggestions on how to choose the right lawyer, and tips on how to avoid being overbilled.

- **Song ownership and music publishing.** Ownership and publishing of songs results in substantial music business revenue. For that reason, it is potentially explosive territory for bands and often members can't seem to agree on who wrote a song or how to split the revenue. You'll find plenty of information on these issues and some practical alternatives on how bands can divide songwriting income.

- **The making and selling of your band's recordings.** Some bands make a comfortable living without ever signing with a label. They perform for years, surviving on the sale of their own recordings. It's not that hard to master the business of making and selling band recordings. You will find recording tips and methods of distributing and selling your music online and off. In addition, we have included a chapter on licensing your band's music for use in film, TV, and advertisements.

- **Record companies and distribution.** Many bands are surprised to find that their troubles really begin once they get signed to a record company. As Kurt Neuman of the BoDeans put it, "We had it made and then we got a record deal." This book addresses most of the important issues for an independent record deal, and explains the principles of independent distribution.

CAUTION

Major label agreements are outside the scope of this book. If your band has been offered a major label recording contract—that is, an agreement with Universal, Sony, Warners, or EMI—you'll need an attorney or an experienced manager to help you negotiate the deal.

- **Taking your band online.** It's easy to bring your band to a global audience without leaving home. This book explains the issues involved with taking your band online.
- **Band names.** In this book, you will find plenty of information on trademarks and other band name issues as well as an explanation of how to research and register your band's name with the federal government.

Written Agreements: Your First Line of Defense

A contract sets up rules for doing business and makes it easier for your band to go after people who have ripped you off. This book provides samples of several common agreements such as partnership agreements, compulsory licenses, and independent record contracts. Whenever a sample agreement is provided, we explain how to fill it out and modify it to fit your needs.

Below are some of the agreements you'll find in this book:

- **Partnership agreement:** for all band members; covers how to divide expenses and profits, rights to songs, rights to the band name, and related issues.
- **Management agreement:** for your band and your manager; covers commissions, length of representation, and post-termination issues.
- **Label-shopping agreement:** for your band and your attorney (or whoever is shopping your band to record companies); covers issues such as the extent and length of payment for the representation.
- **Performance agreement:** for your band and the venue that is booking your band; covers the payment and other performance details.
- **Model release agreement:** for your band and any person whose image is used on band artwork or merchandise; covers the extent of the use and the payment.
- **Artwork agreement:** for your band and those providing artwork for recordings or merchandise; covers the extent of the artwork use and payment.
- **Musician release agreement:** for your band and any nonband musician providing a performance for recordings; covers the extent of the musical use and payment.

- **Compulsory license agreement:** for your band and any nonband songwriter or copyright holder; deals with the right to "cover" that person's song on your band's recording.
- **Simple Master/Sync License:** for basic licensing of music for use in a film or video and when the songs and recordings are owned by the same entity.
- **Sync License:** for licensing songs for use in films or TV; this can be modified for other sync rights—for example, for use in advertisements.
- **Master Use License:** for licensing sound recordings for use in films or TV.
- **Independent label recording and license agreements:** for your band and an independent record label; covers the details of ownership and making of recordings.

By the way, if you have a question that's not addressed in the book, you may want to consult my blog (www.dearrichblog.com).

Band Partnerships and Beyond

Okay, you've accepted the fact that your band is a business. But what kind of business is it? Every business has a legal structure, which we refer to as a business form. You've probably heard of most of the common ones:

- **Sole proprietorship.** In a sole proprietorship, you own and operate the band by yourself and are personally liable for business debts. You pay the other band members, either as employees or as independent contractors. You don't file a separate business tax return. You report business income on your individual tax return. (This type of arrangement is referred to as a "pass-through" entity because the income passes through the business to the owners before it is taxed.)

- **Partnership.** If you form a partnership, your band splits the profits and losses among the band members, and each member is personally liable for all partnership debts. The partnership is also a pass-through tax entity (see above).

- **Limited liability company (LLC).** To form an LLC, your band must file papers with the state government. The LLC operates like a partnership— profits and losses are shared, and income is reported on each partner's individual tax return. But, unlike a partnership, each band member is shielded from personal liability for many business debts—a legal theory known as "limited liability."

- **Corporation.** To create a corporation, the band must file papers with the state government. Your band will have to file a corporate tax return (and pay taxes at corporate tax rates). (A corporation is not a pass-through entity.) The band members (who are shareholders in the corporation) have limited liability for band-related debts.

That's a snapshot of the various business entities. Later in this chapter, more information is provided on each entity's advantages and disadvantages. By default, most bands qualify as partnerships—an informal business entity that's easy to form and manage.

Since your band is likely to be a partnership, most of this chapter is geared toward creating a band partnership agreement (a BPA). A BPA defines the rights and obligations of the band members. Think of it as the band's business rule book. While there's no requirement that your band must have a written BPA, it's recommended. As with any type of venture, it's always best to make sure everyone is clear on the arrangement and that everyone knows their rights and responsibilities, which reduces the chances of a dispute later. And if a dispute does erupt, it will be easier to solve if you have a written agreement as a guide.

In this chapter, you'll find two types of band partnership agreements: a short-form agreement that establishes some basic rules, and a long-form partnership agreement that is more comprehensive and deals with more contingencies. A bare-bones agreement might be fine in the beginning, but as the stakes grow, so should your BPA.

It's also possible that your band business has progressed beyond the partnership stage. Perhaps you are touring regularly or have experienced a serious increase in band income. As a result, band members may be concerned about personal liability. We will help you analyze which business form is best for your band. In the event your band wants to limit personal liability, the most common approach is to convert the band partnership to a band limited liability company (LLC). The conversion process is discussed at the end of this chapter.

Who Needs a Band Partnership Agreement?

Any business that operates as a partnership is advised to execute an agreement among all the partners to make sure that everyone understands and agrees to certain terms, such as shares of ownership, shares of profit distribution, and rules for joining or leaving the partnership. A band partnership agreement (BPA) is simply a partnership agreement that is tailored to the needs of a band. Typically, a BPA:

- provides a method for resolving disputes
- sets standards for firing and hiring band members
- creates a system for dividing band income and expenses, including future royalties
- establishes guidelines for when members depart or the band breaks up, and
- defines who may use the band name and songs.

> ⓘ **CAUTION**
> **BPAs are used only for bands that operate as partnerships.** If your band is operating as a sole proprietorship, corporation, or limited liability company (LLC), you should not use a BPA.

Many bands get along fine without a written BPA, especially small bands that play just as much for fun as for business. They have adopted commonsense principles and work out business deals as they go along. Some bands wait until they have a record deal before formalizing their arrangements with a written BPA.

But while winging it might work for a while, forging ahead without an agreement can be risky. Countless bands have been unpleasantly surprised at how an unforeseen conflict can suddenly swoop in and cause chaos, or even destroy a band. Putting your agreement in writing sooner rather than later helps to avoid such disputes, because it forces you to deal with issues before they become threatening problems.

Besides the common wisdom that a written agreement is always a good idea among business partners, another reason to enter into a BPA with your bandmates is that if you don't, the laws of your state will have the final word on how your partnership is run. All states except Louisiana have adopted the Uniform Partnership Act (UPA) in some form, which provides standard, default rules for partnerships that haven't executed their own agreements. In the absence of your own agreement, for example, the UPA says that profits must be shared equally and that each member has an equal voice in running the business. If that's not the arrangement you and your bandmates want, you won't want to be caught without a written agreement.

Aren't Oral Agreements Valid?

Oral contracts and agreements—including oral BPAs—are legally binding. But without a written document, band members may have different recollections of the terms of the oral agreement. Especially in the heat of a dispute, different memories and misunderstandings among band members will leave an oral agreement meaningless and unenforceable. Keep in mind the old saying that an oral agreement isn't worth the paper it's written on.

What If You're Not a *Typical* Band?

What if you're not a typical band? For example, what if you are a vocalist and a DJ, or what if your group consists of two people behind computers who swap files until they've produced the ideal dance tracks? Should you still use the band partnership agreement?

Assuming that you all contribute and work regularly toward a joint goal of success, then the agreement should work. In other words, it's not important whether you think of yourselves as a traditional band with drums, bass, guitars, and vocals; what matters is that you think of yourselves as partners in a musical venture.

So, regardless of your style or method of collaboration, use the BPA to establish the important rules for revenue and responsibilities, as well as to determine the ownership of property. If you don't consider yourself a traditional band, feel free to change the wording of the agreement to reflect your group's status. For example, you can strike the word "band" throughout the agreement and instead substitute another term for your relationship—perhaps the name of your musical collaboration. Also, not only will the partnership agreement work for various types of musical collaborations, the advice in this chapter regarding forming an LLC or other business form also applies to most musical collaborations.

The abbreviated short-form agreement is quite simple and easy to complete. If your band is just starting out, or is undecided on whether to use a BPA, take a look at the short-form agreement. It's not very complex and will provide a minimal, but significant, level of protection for band members. Even if you decide not use it, your band should at least discuss some of the issues raised in it, such as who owns the band name or what type of vote is necessary to kick out a band member.

The second (or full-length) agreement is more complex and covers a wider range of potential problems. If your band is growing as a business—such as earning regular income of more than $3,000 a month—you should consider adopting the long BPA. As your revenues increase, the long BPA is designed to preserve each band member's rights. You should also use the long BPA if your band is preparing to sign a record deal, because the agreement will safeguard each member's right to royalties, even after a member leaves the group. (See Chapter 14 on independent record deals.)

> ⓘ **CAUTION**
> **Get professional help with major-label record deals.** Signing a record deal with a major label is beyond the scope of this book. If you're being offered a deal with a major label (Sony, Universal, Warners, and EMI), you'll need a lawyer or sophisticated manager to negotiate the contract. See Chapter 4 for information on hiring and working with lawyers, and Chapter 14 on independent record deals versus major-label deals.

Using a BPA to Avoid Getting Screwed

Most of the chapters in this book describe how a band gets screwed by forces outside the band such as a record company, manager, retail store, or music publisher. In this chapter, however, we deal with situations in which the band can be harmed by internal forces—that is, by a band member or ex-member. The following situations are unfortunately all too common:

- An ex-band-member claims a right to use the band name or band logo.
- The band breaks up and there is a dispute about dividing the assets.
- A dispute between the band and an ex-member results in a costly lawsuit.

Thankfully, you can help avoid these and most other ugly situations by covering them in your BPA.

Situation #1:
An ex-band-member claims a right to use the band name or logo.

A band can get screwed when ex-members begin using the band's name or a substantially similar name. The similarly named band confuses fans, dilutes the strength of the original band's drawing power, and may generate merchandise sales that are not shared with other members of the original band. For example, ex-members of Creedence Clearwater Revival used the name Creedence Clearwater Revisited—without the consent or participation of founder John Fogerty. He sued to prevent the band's use of the name but lost the case on appeal. Other bands such as Ratt, Queensryche, Talking Heads, Megadeth, and the Doors have run into similar problems. If these bands had agreed on ownership of the name, a great deal of litigation (and aggravation) could have been avoided.

How to avoid getting screwed:
In your BPA, be sure to cover two things concerning your band's name:
- whether the band as a whole owns the name, or whether specific individuals in the band own it, and
- which band members (if any) can continue to use the name of the band in the event that the band splits up or members leave the band.

Dealing with this issue in your BPA will help to avoid disputes over who owns the name and will help prevent unauthorized—and potentially damaging—use of the name by former band members.

Situation #2:
The band breaks up and there is a dispute about dividing the assets or debts.

Bands have a notoriously difficult time staying together. But common as they are, band breakups can be complex. The band may be earning record royalties or have outstanding debts. When there is no BPA and the band members cannot agree how to divide the assets and debts, an ugly breakup can quickly go from bad to worse. If there are assets, they may be held by the courts until the matter is resolved—which sometimes can take months or years.

How to avoid getting screwed:
Establish a system in your BPA for dividing assets and debts. The most common arrangement is for a band to split the band's assets (usually equipment) after paying off people to whom the band owes money (referred to as creditors). The sample long BPA at the end of this chapter provides a common asset and debt division system for your band to adopt.

Situation #3:
An ex-band-member sues the band.

There are a variety of reasons why an ex-band-member might sue the band. Take the case of Guns 'N' Roses drummer Steve Adler. The band asked Adler to sign an agreement terminating his partnership interest in the band and agreeing to a lump sum as settlement for leaving. Slash, the guitarist for Guns 'N' Roses, later testified that Adler was strung out on heroin when Adler signed the termination agreement. Adler sued, claiming that the termination agreement was invalid because he was not mentally capable at the time he signed it. He claimed that the band owed him money and drum equipment. To avoid a court judgment, the band settled with Adler, agreeing to pay him $2.5 million. The band also had to pay its own legal costs.

Whatever the dispute, fighting it out in court is the most expensive and time-consuming way to resolve disputes. Paying legal fees, even for a relatively short case, can quickly put a band into bankruptcy. The Guns 'N' Roses dispute might have been avoided, for example, if the band had established a system for distributing income to terminated members in their BPA.

How to avoid getting screwed:

A BPA can avoid disputes in the first place by establishing the rules of the band at the outset. A thorough, written agreement is often enough to resolve a conflict before it gets ugly and ends up in court. Even if a dispute does arise, a BPA can help the band avoid a lawsuit by establishing a method for resolving disputes such as arbitration or mediation.

What About Songwriting?

Under our model BPA, each songwriter owns their own songs. However, many bands decide to share songwriting income in some way. The long-form BPA below includes two optional provisions that can be inserted if your band wants to share songwriting income. We provide more information about dividing songwriting income in Chapter 7.

Abbreviated Band Partnership Agreement

If your band is just starting out or not earning much income (say, under $3,000 a month), or if you're just not ready to deal with a long agreement, we recommend you execute at least a basic BPA covering the essentials. In this section, we'll walk you through the simple task of putting together a short BPA. A sample form appears below. You can modify the form to fit your needs, though if many modifications are necessary you may want to use the long form that is covered in the next section.

 FORMS
You can download this form (and all other forms in this book) from Nolo.com; for details, see "Get Forms, Updates, and More at This Book's Companion Page," in the appendix.

Names of Partners

Enter the names of the band members who will be included in your partnership. You should include the names of only those members who will actually be full partners who will share band profits and debts. Other musicians who may sometimes play with your band, but to whom you don't intend to give an ownership interest in your band, should not be included.

Partnership Name

You will need to create a name for your band partnership. Most bands usually use the band name and add the word "partnership" at the end (for example, "The Imagine Dragons Partnership").

Band Name and Ownership

Enter the name of your band as you will use it in public. If you haven't already discussed ownership of the band name, now is the time. See instructions for the long BPA later in this chapter, or refer to Chapter 9 on protecting your band name. Depending on how your band wants to deal with name ownership, choose one or more of the alternative provisions, or create your own. If one person owns the name, enter that person's name.

Profits and Losses

This clause establishes that band members will share all profits equally. If you want a different arrangement, you should use the long BPA, below.

Partnership Voting

Indicate whether a unanimous vote or just a majority vote is required to expel a band partner, to add a new band partner, and to enter the band into an agreement that will last longer than one year.

Tie-Breaker

This is an optional provision in which you can name one band member whose vote will have the power to break a tie. (In essence, that member's vote would count twice.) If you do not want to name a tie-breaker, enter "none."

Addition of Band Partner

This clause simply states that any new band members will be bound by the terms of this agreement.

Leaving Members

This clause establishes that the partnership will stay in effect when a member leaves. It also says that a band member may voluntarily quit the band, and that a leaving member is entitled to her share of the net worth of the partnership as well as her share of royalties. Any payments will be made only after the band has actually received the income and deducted expenses.

Mediation; Arbitration

Under this clause, if a dispute arises, the band members agree to try to resolve it through mediation or, if that fails, binding arbitration, rather than going to court. On the one hand, mediation and arbitration can be expensive, because you must pay for the mediator or arbitrator. On the other hand, these methods may save thousands of dollars in legal fees and may resolve the dispute with a less contentious method. (For more information on these methods, see the discussion of mediation and arbitration later in this chapter, with the explanation of the full-length partnership agreement.) Enter the location where you agree to mediate, most likely the city where you all live. If you don't want this provision, delete it.

Signatures

Have all band members sign and date the agreement, and enter their personal addresses and Social Security numbers.

> **CANADIAN RULES**
> **If you are a Canadian resident,** any reference to "state" or "county" in the model agreement should be changed to "province." Occasionally, Canadian contract and partnership laws differ from American law, and when that occurs, we provide an explanation for the difference.

[Abbreviated] Band Partnership Agreement

Band Partners

Names of band members ("Band Partners"): _____

_____

_____

Partnership Name

The Band Partners establish themselves as a general partnership (the "Band Partnership") known as the _____ .

Band Name

The Band Partnership will do business under the name _____

_____ (the "Band Name").

Each Band Partner acknowledges that (*check appropriate box*):

☐ Band Partners who leave the band will have no interest in the Band Name.

☐ No individual member will have a right to use the Band Name in the event the band breaks up.

☐ The Band Name is the exclusive property of _____

_____ .

Profits and Losses

The Band Partners will share equally in all payments that are paid to the Band Partnership or to any Band Partner as a result of Band Partnership activities. After deducting Band Partnership expenses (for example, reasonable salaries, rent, promotional costs, travel costs, office expenditures, telephone costs, and accounting and legal fees), these payments will be distributed in cash to the Band Partners.

Partnership Voting

Check either "unanimous vote" or "majority vote" for each issue.

	Unanimous Vote	Majority Vote
Expelling a Band Partner (unanimous except for party to be expelled)	☐	☐

Admission of a new Band Partner	☐	☐
Entering into any agreement that binds the Band Partnership for more than one year	☐	☐
Dissolving the Band Partnership	☐	☐

Tie-Breaker (*optional*)

In the event that a majority cannot be achieved, the decision of _____ _____ will prevail.

Addition of a Band Partner

Each new Band Partner must agree to be bound by all of the provisions in this Agreement. The addition of a new Band Partner will not end the Partnership, which will remain in full force.

Leaving Members

A Band Partner may leave the Band Partnership (a "Leaving Member") voluntarily (by resignation) or involuntarily (by reason of death, disability, or being expelled). A Leaving Member is entitled to a proportionate share of the net worth of the Band Partnership as of the date of leaving, and to the Leaving Member's share of any future royalties or fees earned from sound recordings that include the Leaving Member's performance. These payments will be made when actually received by the Band Partnership and after subtracting a proportionate deduction of expenses. If a member leaves, the Band Partnership will remain in full force among the remaining members.

Mediation; Arbitration

If a dispute arises under this Agreement, the parties agree to first try to resolve the dispute with the help of a mutually agreed-on mediator in _____ _____ . Any costs and fees other than attorney fees will be shared equally by the parties. If it proves impossible to arrive at a mutually satisfactory solution, the parties agree to submit the dispute to binding arbitration in the same city or region, conducted on a confidential basis under the Commercial Arbitration Rules of the American Arbitration Association, or the rules of _____ .

Amendments

This agreement may not be amended except in writing signed by all Band Partners.

Band Member Signature _____

Address _____

_____

Date _____ Soc. Sec. # _____

Band Member Signature _____

Address _____

_____

Date _____ Soc. Sec. # _____

Band Member Signature _____

Address _____

_____

Date _____ Soc. Sec. # _____

Band Member Signature _____

Address _____

_____

Date _____ Soc. Sec. # _____

Band Member Signature _____

Address _____

_____

Date _____ Soc. Sec. # _____

Full-Length Band Partnership Agreement

Use the long-form BPA if your band income is growing or if your band has signed a publishing or record company deal and the members are comfortable discussing and negotiating the details. The following instructions explain how to fill out the BPA and what the various clauses mean. Many clauses have alternative provisions for you to choose from, which are explained in the instructions. Some clauses, as noted in the instructions, are optional altogether. A sample appears below. You can modify the form agreement to fit your needs.

FORMS
You can download this form (and all other forms in this book) from Nolo.com; for details, see "Get Forms, Updates, and More at This Book's Companion Page," in the appendix.

In the Introduction clause, fill in the names of the band members who will be included in the partnership. Don't include any musicians to whom you don't want to give an ownership interest in the band.

The Band Partnership

You will need to create a name for your band partnership. Most bands usually use the band name and add the word "partnership" (for example, "The Radiohead Partnership"). You also need to insert the state or province in which the band resides. If different members live in different areas, choose the state or province in which the band meets to practice. Finally, insert the location for the band's headquarters (usually an address where the band gets its mail).

Band Partner Services

This provision explains what types of services are expected from the band members. The "merchandising rights" section refers to the band partnership's right to use the band member's name and picture on products such as T-shirts.

Nonband Partnership Activities

Under this provision, band members can participate in side projects such as solo recordings or playing in other bands, provided that these activities don't interfere with the band. The obligations of being in this band must take priority over all other activities. Without this essential commitment, it will be difficult to coordinate touring and recording.

Band Name, Domain Name, and Logo

This provision deals with ownership of the band's name and, if you have them, your band's domain name and logo. Enter the band's name. If you don't have a domain name or logo, don't check those sections—leave them blank. If you do have a domain name for your band, enter it. If you have a logo, enter "see attached." Then be sure to attach a copy of the logo to the completed agreement. Staple a clean, final version of the logo to the agreement.

If you haven't already discussed ownership of the band name (see Chapter 9), now is the time. Any logo and domain name should also be considered when determining ownership rights. The person in the band who thought up the name does not get any special ownership rights. As we explain in Chapter 9, the primary issues are whether the band or specific individuals in the band own the name, and which band members (if any) can continue to use the name of the band in the event that the band splits up or if members leave the band. Sometimes (particularly in the event of band names that feature one performer, such as the Jimi Hendrix Experience or Jon Spencer Blues Explosion), the name of the band may be owned and controlled by one member.

TIP

If one person owns the domain name, have that person listed as owner and contact person with the domain name registry. Domain name registries issue domain names and manage domain name renewals. Therefore, if your band agrees that one person is the owner, that person should be listed with the registry. Otherwise, the owner may have difficulty transferring and renewing the domain name.

Depending on your band's determination, choose one of the alternative provisions or create your own. The three alternatives given are:

1. The band owns the name even if members leave; if the band breaks up, no member may use the band name.
2. The band owns the name but only if certain members remain in the band. If the band breaks up, no member may use the band name.
3. One person in the band owns the name and controls its use.

Warranties

Warranties are contractual promises. If a band member breaks one of these promises (for example, by driving drunk to a gig), that can be the basis for expulsion. You can add other promises if you want. For example, "... will appear punctually for all performances, recording sessions, and rehearsals."

The last sentence of this provision ("Each Band Partner indemnifies each other Band Partner from all claims...") refers to a legal principle known as indemnification. If a band partner breaks one of the promises—for example, by getting in a fist fight with a club manager—and the band partnership is sued, partnership law says that every partner of the band is liable for any damages awarded. If each band partner indemnifies the other partners, however, then ultimately only the band partner who caused the problem will pay the damages and legal fees by paying back the others. Of course, this clause must be considered in a real-world perspective. A partner may be "judgment proof"—that is, the band member may not have the ability to pay. In that case, the indemnity clause will fail to shield innocent band members.

Profits and Losses

This provision includes a standard definition of net profits. It provides that before the band members are paid, the band's debts and other reasonable expenses must be deducted.

Practically, the issue of profits and losses is a matter of maintaining a bank account and making regular accountings of expenses and income. Bands that can afford it hire an accountant to handle these details and to make the payments to the band partners. If you cannot afford an accountant, there are many popular accounting programs (such as *Quicken*, *QuickBooks*, and Mint.com) that make managing your band's money quite easy.

Ownership of Recorded Compositions

If your band wants to create its own publishing company and share songwriting income, check "will" in this clause to create a band partnership publishing company. If you don't want to share songwriting income or create a publishing company, check "will not" or delete the language. This clause and the next two ("Division of Publishing Revenue" and "Publishing Administration") only affect songs written by band members that are recorded and released under the band name.

The issue of whether to share songwriting income is sometimes controversial for band members, and we have devoted Chapter 8 to this issue. You should review that chapter prior to making a decision. If an agreement on songwriting cannot be reached right now, leave this and the next two provisions blank or remove them from your BPA.

Division of Publishing Revenue

If you did not create a publishing company with the previous clause, this provision will not apply to you. You can delete the language altogether.

When your band shares song income through a publishing company, there are many ways to divide the money. You can choose from three alternatives, or create your own. Your three alternatives in the agreement are:

- all money divided equally
- writers split writer share, and band splits publisher share, or
- a compromise system in which band members receive one credit for performing a song, and two credits for both writing and performing a song.

We have provided a detailed explanation of dividing song income in Chapter 8.

Publishing Administration

If you did not create a publishing company, this provision will not apply to you. You can delete the language altogether if you use the form on the companion page to this book.

This provision permits the band's publishing company to "administer" the songs. Administration is explained in Chapter 8, but generally it means the band has the right to enter into contracts regarding the songs, make decisions about the use of the songs, collect royalties for the songs, and sue infringers of the songs. This provision also guarantees that the band can continue to administer the songs even after a member departs, and establishes the publishing rights for the departing member.

Meetings and Voting

This provision establishes the type of vote—majority or unanimous—that is required for different band actions. You are free to decide which issues require a majority or unanimous vote. However, we recommend that the first one (expelling a band partner) be done by unanimous vote. A unanimous vote should also be required to dissolve the band partnership. It's also wise to require at least a majority vote for purchases above a certain amount. Purchases between $200 and $500—depending on your band's financial situation, of course—typically warrant a majority vote.

Your band is also free to "skew" the voting. That is, one member may be granted two or three votes for every other member's one vote. This may be the case, for example, in a band that is centered around one founding individual. This can be accomplished with the optional statement, by filling in the name(s) of who gets extra voting power and how many votes they get. If you don't want to skew the voting, leave the clause blank or delete the clause.

In addition, in the event that the band partners cannot reach a majority agreement on a band partnership issue, you may choose an individual who acts as the tie-breaker. Often this is a founding member, but it can be any band partner—or it can be a nonpartner such as a manager or advisor. Enter the name of the tie-breaker in the blank, or if you don't want to designate one, either leave it blank or delete the clause.

Books of Account and Records

This accounting provision sets out some rules for band bookkeeping. The fiscal year is based on a calendar year. However, you may want to consult with your tax preparer or accountant in case there is an advantage for having a fiscal year that ends on another date (for example, April 15). The accounting statement that must be furnished to band members is just a spreadsheet that details the band's income minus the band's expenses during the preceding period.

Ending the Partnership

Without a written BPA, a partnership would end if one of the members quit or died. This clause establishes that your partnership will not terminate simply because a member leaves (or when a new member joins). The language referring to "operation of law" simply reaffirms the power of any other partnership laws to terminate your partnership in certain situations (such as a lawsuit being filed), depending on the laws of your state.

If your band is built around a key performer, the partnership can also provide for termination if that member departs. If you wish to use such a provision, fill in this section. Otherwise, leave it blank or delete the language.

Distribution of Band Assets After Termination

This provision explains how the band's money is used to pay off debts and obligations before repaying band partners. It is divided into three sections, which deal with current assets and debts, band equipment, and future income and royalties. This pay-off system is based on partnership laws that require that creditors get paid before partners. It is standard for all forms of partnerships and should not be changed. The term "capital contributions" refers to the contributions that band partners make, usually when they join the band partnership. For example, members may contribute money or equipment.

Addition of a Band Partner

This establishes the obligations of a new band partner. Generally, the new band partner cannot share in previously acquired assets or property and has no share in any recordings (or their royalties) created prior to joining the band.

Leaving Members

This provision helps to head off problems by providing a system to deal with band members who leave. It provides for a 30-day notice period for leaving members (whether expelled or quitting) and gives the band the option to exclude the leaving member from performances during the notice period.

A leaving member, whether expelled or quitting, is entitled to a payment. If the leaving partner has an interest in song ownership, then you will have to pay the share of the income earned from those songs. The amount you pay depends on the partner's proportionate share.

If you want to list reasons that justify expelling a member from the band, note them in this optional section. If you don't want to specify reasons for firing a member, either leave the section blank or remove the language altogether. You can choose one or both of the reasons supplied in the agreement, or you can write in your own. The ones we've supplied are all financial. Under many state partnership laws, a partner's personal bankruptcy causes the partnership to dissolve. Therefore, some partnerships like to include a provision that provides for immediate expulsion in the event of financial problems such as bankruptcy or insolvency. If you add your own specific criteria, be careful not to be too specific, as this may limit your ability to fire someone. We suggest you include general language such as: "or for any reason that appears sufficient to the remaining Band Partners."

Determination of Net Worth

This provision provides a method of paying off the ex-band partner. Usually the band partnership cannot afford to pay off large sums at one time, so payments above $10,000 are staggered over several years.

Band Partnership Bank Account

Your band will need to decide who has "signing power." This is who has the authority to sign checks to buy things, to endorse checks for deposit, and to sign for withdrawals from the partnership account. Insert the name or names of the band partners who will be allowed to sign band partnership checks. Sometimes two signatures are required, or required on checks over an amount like $500.

Mediation; Arbitration

This provision gives alternatives to resolving your dispute in court that may be more private, and potentially less expensive. (See "What Are Mediation and Arbitration?" below.) We generally recommend you include this provision in most, if not all, of your contracts.

We recommend that you choose the county, province, or city in which the band resides for arbitration. If all the members do not reside within one area, choose a place that is convenient. Enter your location of choice in the first blank.

What Are Mediation and Arbitration?

In mediation, a neutral third party, called a mediator (usually an attorney or expert in the music business), helps the parties reach a solution. The mediator is trained in getting parties to discuss issues that are in dispute and to reach mutually satisfactory agreements. Arbitration is a similar process, except that while a mediator is only a facilitator for the parties who ultimately reach their own agreement, an arbitrator actually decides how the case should be resolved. The decision of the arbitrator is "binding" and is as enforceable as a court judgment. Unlike a court judgment, an arbitrator's decision normally cannot be appealed by the loser. Keep in mind that some attorneys don't like these alternatives because the mediator and arbitrator must be paid, and the arbitration decision usually cannot be appealed (also because attorneys are often not required).

In several states there are organizations that specialize in arbitration for people in the arts, such as California Lawyers for the Arts (www.calawyersforthearts.org) and Volunteer Lawyers for the Arts (in New York at www.vlany.org, as well as in other cities and states). You can substitute the rules of one of these organizations for those of the American Arbitration Association in your agreement. If your band is based in Canada, you can still use the AAA's rules, as they perform arbitration in all major Canadian cities. Check one of the choices or delete the unwanted alternative.

General

This section contains standard contractual provisions (called "boilerplate") that appear in most contracts, regardless of the subject matter. Boilerplate provisions are explained in "What Do These Boilerplate Provisions Mean?" below.

In the blank space, insert the state of residence for the band partners (Canadian bands should enter their province). In the event of a dispute, this determines which law will govern the arbitration or lawsuit.

We have included language advising each band partner to hire an attorney. It's unlikely that each band partner will do this, but the language reminds the partners they have a right to have the agreement independently evaluated.

Signatures

Have all band members sign and date the agreement, and enter their personal addresses. The birthdates of band members are optional. A person under the age of majority is considered a minor and lacks the ability to enter into a binding contract. The age of majority varies from state to state but is usually 18 years old. If a minor signs an agreement and later wants to get out of it (referred to as "disaffirming the agreement"), a court will usually permit the minor to do that. Therefore, if one of the band partners is under 18, it is wise to have both parents or a guardian sign on behalf of the minor. In some states—California, New York, Tennessee, and Massachusetts, for example—if the parents sign the agreement, the minor is prohibited by law from disaffirming it.

What Do These Boilerplate Provisions Mean?

Standard, or "boilerplate," provisions in contracts establish important rules and can affect how disputes are resolved and how the contract is enforced by a court. Here's an explanation of some of the most common boilerplate provisions you'll find in contracts:

- The sentence that begins "The Agreement may not be amended ..." establishes that the agreement is the final version and that any further change must be in writing.
- The sentence dealing with "waiver of any right" allows a band partner to permit something that is otherwise prohibited by the agreement without permanently giving up that right. For example, say your BPA establishes that each band member has an equal vote in all important matters. Under the waiver provision, if a member misses a vote, that doesn't mean that she has lost her voting power under the agreement.
- The sentence that starts "If a court finds any provision of this Agreement invalid..." permits a court to delete an invalid provision and still keep the rest of the agreement legal and intact.
- The sentence dealing with "successors and assigns" provides that if a band member's interest is transferred to someone else (for example, a band member dies and his interest goes into an estate), then whoever acquires that interest must abide by the terms of this agreement.

Band Partnership Agreement

Introduction

This Band Partnership Agreement (the "Agreement") is made by and between _____
_____ , (collectively
referred to as "Band," individually referred to as "Band Partners"). This agreement will
be effective as of the date of the last signature below (the "Effective Date"). The Band
Partners agree as follows:

The Band Partnership

The Band Partners establish themselves as a general partnership (the "Band
Partnership") to be known as _____ under the laws of
_____ for the purposes of musical and related entertainment
activities. The Band Partnership will commence on the Effective Date and will
continue until it is ended according to this Agreement. The principal place of
business of the Band Partnership will be at _____
or at any other place the Band Partners determine.

Band Partner Services

In order to fulfill the Band Partnership purposes, each Band Partner will contribute
musical entertainment services to the Band Partnership. Such contributions will
include, but not be limited to, services:
- as a recording artist with respect to sound recordings
- as a musical performer in all media and on the live stage, and
- related to merchandising rights solely with respect to activities as a member
  of the Band.

Nonband Partnership Activities

Each Band Partner is permitted to engage in one or more businesses, including other
musical entertainment efforts, but only to the extent that such activities do not
directly interfere with the business and obligations of the Band Partnership. Neither
the Band Partnership nor any other Band Partner will have any right to any income
or profit derived by a Band Partner from any nonband Partnership business activity
permitted under this paragraph.

Name and Logo

The Band Partnership will do business under the name _____
_____ (the "Band Name")
as an assumed name and as its trademark and service mark.

(*Check if applicable and fill in*)

☐ The Band also uses the following logo (the "Band Logo") as a trademark and service mark: _____
_____ .

☐ The Band also owns and uses the following domain name: _____
_____ .

Each Band Partner acknowledges that the Band Name as well as any Domain Name and Logo the Band may have are (select one):

☐ the exclusive property of the Partnership and not owned by any individual member, and, unless otherwise authorized in writing, departing Band Partners will have no interest whatsoever in the Band Name, Domain Name, and Logo, apart from the limited right to be known as an ex-member of the Band. If the Partnership dissolves, no individual member will have a right to use the Band Name, Domain Name, and Logo, apart from the limited right to be known as an ex-member of the Band.

☐ the exclusive property of the Partnership and not owned by any individual member, except that if _____
and _____ cease to be members of the Partnership, the Partnership will cease use of the Band Name, Domain Name, and Logo (including "formerly [Band Name]" or similar references) in connection with any offering of entertainment services. Departing Band Partners will have no interest whatsoever in the Band Name, Domain Name, and Logo, apart from the limited right to be known as a former member of the Band. In the event that the Partnership dissolves, no individual member will have a right to use the Band Name, Domain Name, and Logo, apart from the limited right to be known as an ex-member of the Band.

☐ not assets of the Band Partnership, but rather are the sole and exclusive property of _____ [*name of person who owns Band Name, Domain Name, and Logo*] and, unless otherwise authorized in writing, will remain that person's sole and exclusive property during and after the term of this Agreement. The other Band Partners will have no interest whatsoever in the Band Name, Domain Name, and Logo, apart from the limited right to be known as former members of the Band.

Warranties

Each Band Partner warrants that the Band Partner:

- is free to enter into this Agreement
- is under no restriction that will interfere with this Agreement
- has not done nor will do any act or thing that might hurt the Band Partnership
- will not sell or transfer any interest in the Band Partnership without the prior written consent of the other Band Partners, and
- will refrain from activities that could prohibit the Band Partner from performing.

Each Band Partner indemnifies each other Band Partner from all claims that may arise from any breach of these warranties.

Profits and Losses

Unless agreed otherwise in writing by the Band Partners, the Band Partners will share equally in all of the Net Profits, losses, rights, and obligations of the Band Partnership. "Net Profits" will mean all payments that are paid to the Band Partnership or to any Band Partner as a result of Band Partnership activities, after deducting Band Partnership expenses (that is, reasonable salaries, rent, promotional costs, travel costs, office expenditures, telephone costs, and accounting and legal fees). The Net Profits will be distributed in cash to the Band Partners.

Ownership of Recorded Compositions

The Band Partners ☐ will ☐ will not create a publishing entity (the "Band Partnership Publishing Company") that will own all rights to "Recorded Compositions." Recorded Compositions are songs:

- recorded by the Band
- released for sale on sound recordings under the Band Name, and
- that were written or cowritten in whole or in part by one or more Band Partners.

Each Band Partner agrees to assign any ownership interest in each Recorded Composition to the Band Partnership Publishing Company and to sign any documents necessary to show the transfer of ownership to the Band Partnership Publishing Company.

Division of Publishing Revenue

Revenue from the Band Partnership Publishing Company, if such publishing company has been created, will be distributed as follows:

- ☐ All music publishing income derived from Recorded Compositions, including both writer's and publisher's shares, will be divided equally among the Band Partners.

- ☐ The Band Partners will share equally in the publishing income from all Recorded Compositions. The writers of each Recorded Composition will receive an equal pro rata share of the songwriters' income with respect to each Recorded Composition. By way of example, if two Band Partners write a Recorded Composition, each will share equally in the songwriters' income from that song. The publishing income from that song will be distributed equally to all Band Partners.

- ☐ All revenue derived from Recorded Compositions will be pooled (whether it is characterized as publishing or songwriter revenue). Each Band Partner will receive one credit for performing on each Recorded Composition. The writers of each Recorded Composition will receive one credit for writing each Recorded Composition. Each Band Partner's total number of credits equals the numerator (top number of a fraction). The total number of credits equals the denominator, or bottom number of a fraction. Each Band Partner then receives this fraction of the song income. By way of example, if all four Band Partners perform on a song and one Band Partner has written that song, the songwriter Band Partner would receive two-fifths of the revenue, and the other three band members would each receive one-fifth of the revenue.

Publishing Administration

The Band Partnership Publishing Company, if such company has been created, will have the worldwide, exclusive right to:

- administer and control the copyright ownership to the Recorded Compositions
- designate all persons to administer the copyrights to the Recorded Compositions, and

- enter into agreements to copublish, subpublish, or otherwise deal with the copyrights in the Recorded Compositions.

In the event that one of the Band Partners leaves the Band Partnership (a "Leaving Member"), the control of the jointly owned copyrights will vest exclusively in the remaining Band Partners for the term of this Band Partnership.

The Leaving Member's interest in the Band Partnership Publishing Company will extend only to those Recorded Compositions that were commercially released for sale during the Leaving Member's period as a Band Partner ("Leaving Member Recorded Compositions"). The Leaving Member will receive semiannual accountings and payments with respect to any income due on Leaving Member Recorded Compositions.

Meetings and Voting

Each Band Partner has the right to participate in the business of the Band Partnership. Meetings of the Band Partners can be called by any member of the Band Partnership on reasonable notice.

(*Check either "unanimous vote" or "majority vote" for each issue.*)

	Unanimous Vote	Majority Vote
Expelling a Band Partner (unanimous except for party to be expelled)	☐	☐
Admission of a new Band Partner	☐	☐
Entering into any agreement that binds the Band Partnership for more than one year	☐	☐
Additional capital contributions by any Band Partner	☐	☐
Receipt of any bonus or goods or other assets of the Band Partnership in excess of that received by any other Band Partner	☐	☐
Any expenditure in excess of $ _____	☐	☐
Incurring any major obligation such as borrowing or lending money	☐	☐

	Unanimous Vote	Majority Vote
Selling, leasing, or transferring any Band Partnership property	☐	☐
Entering into any contract that takes less than a year to complete	☐	☐
Check-signing rights	☐	☐
Amendment of this Agreement	☐	☐
Dissolving the Band Partnership	☐	☐

(*Check and fill in blanks if applicable*)

☐ In matters that require a majority vote, _____
_____ shall be entitled to extra voting power, in the
amount of _____ votes for every other Band Partner's single vote.

☐ In the event that a majority cannot be achieved, the decision of _____
_____ shall prevail.

Books of Account and Records

The books of the Band Partnership and all other documents relating to the business of the Band Partnership will be maintained at its principal place of business and be available for inspection at reasonable times by any Band Partner (or any designated representative of any Band Partner). The fiscal year of the Band Partnership ends on December 31. The Band Partnership will provide an accounting statement to each Band Partner twice a year, at the end of June and December.

Ending the Partnership

This Agreement and the Band Partnership will not terminate if a Band Partner leaves the Partnership. If a member leaves, the Band Partnership will remain in full force among the remaining members.

This Agreement will terminate, and the Band Partnership will end, on the first to occur of the following events:

- the written agreement of the Band Partners to end the Band Partnership, or
- by operation of law, except as otherwise provided in this Agreement.

(*Check and fill in blank if applicable*)

☐ If _____ leaves the Band Partnership, the Band Partnership shall end. The addition of a new Band Partner shall not end the Partnership, and it shall remain in full force among the remaining Band Partners.

Distribution of Band Assets After Termination

Income and Debts. After termination of the Band Partnership, any income that is owed to the Band Partnership will be collected and used first to pay off debts to people outside the Band (creditors), and any remaining money will be used to pay debts (loans in excess of capital contributions) to Band Partners. If money remains after paying off these debts to Band Partners, it will be distributed equally to the Band Partners.

   Band Property. Any property owned or controlled by the Band Partnership (for example, musical equipment) will not be sold but will be evaluated, by an accountant if necessary. The property will then be distributed, as nearly as possible, in equal shares among the Band Partners.

   Royalties and Future Income. If, at the time of termination, the Band is entitled to royalties or owns property that is generating income or royalties, the Band Partnership will vote to either establish an administrative trust or designate an individual (for example, an accountant) to collect and distribute the royalties on an ongoing basis to the Band Partners according to their respective interests.

Addition of a Band Partner

Each new Band Partner must agree to be bound by all of the provisions in this Agreement. A new Band Partner has no rights to the Band Partnership property or assets existing at the time of admission to the Band Partnership ("Existing Property") or in any of the proceeds derived from the Existing Property (for example, revenue or royalties generated by recorded compositions, sound recordings, or other materials created prior to the new Band Partner's admission).

Leaving Members

A Band Partner may leave the Band Partnership (a "Leaving Member") voluntarily (by resignation) or involuntarily (by reason of death, disability, or being expelled). A Band Partner who resigns must give thirty (30) days' prior written notice. The Band Partnership will provide thirty (30) days' written notice if it expels a Partner. The Band has, at its option, the right to immediately exclude any expelled partners from live or recorded performances during this 30-day notice period. A Leaving Member is entitled to:

- the Leaving Member's proportionate share of the net worth of the Band Partnership as of the date of disassociation
- the Leaving Member's share of any royalties, commissions, or licensing fees earned from sound recordings that include the Leaving Member's performance. These payments will be made when actually received by the Band Partnership and after subtracting a proportionate deduction of expenses. The Leaving Member's record royalties will be paid only after the record company has recouped the band's recording costs for the respective recording.

An expelled Partner will be entitled to receive the value of his or her interest in the partnership according to the provisions of this Agreement.

(Check and fill in blank if applicable)
A Band Partner may be expelled from the Partnership if:

☐ the Band Partner seeks protection under the federal bankruptcy code

☐ the Band Partner makes an assignment for the benefit of creditors, or

☐ _____
_____ .

Determination of Net Worth

If the Leaving Member and the Band Partnership cannot agree on the net worth of the Band Partnership, then it will be determined by a mutually agreed-on accountant. The net worth will be determined as of the date thirty (30) days after receipt of the written notice of leaving, whether voluntary or involuntary. The Leaving Member's share will be paid in installments starting one month after determining the net worth and be payable as follows:

- If the share is less than $10,000, it will be paid in 12 monthly installments.
- If the share is more than $10,000 but less than $25,000, it will be paid in 24 monthly installments, or
- If the share is more than $25,000, it will be paid in 36 monthly installments.

The share payments will include interest at the prime interest rate.

Notices

All accountings and notices required under this Agreement will be given in writing by personal delivery, mail, or fax at the addresses of the Band Partners set forth below (or at any other addresses designated by a Band Partner).

Band Partnership Bank Account

A Band Partnership bank account may be opened by the Band Partners. _____
_____ has the right to sign any checks drawn on the Band Partnership bank account, endorse checks for deposit, or make any withdrawals from the Band Partnership bank account.

Mediation; Arbitration

If a dispute arises under this Agreement, the parties agree to first try to resolve the dispute with the help of a mutually agreed-on mediator in _____ .
Any costs and fees other than attorney fees will be shared equally by the parties. If it is impossible to arrive at a mutually satisfactory solution within a reasonable time, the parties agree to submit the dispute to binding arbitration in the same city or region, conducted on a confidential basis pursuant to:

- ☐ the Commercial Arbitration Rules of the American Arbitration Association, or

- ☐ the rules of _____ .

Any decision or award as a result of any arbitration proceeding will include the assessment of costs, expenses, and reasonable attorneys' fees and a written determination by the arbitrators. Absent an agreement to the contrary, any such arbitration will be conducted by an arbitrator experienced in music industry law. An award of arbitration will be final and binding on the Band Partners and may be confirmed in a court of competent jurisdiction. The prevailing party has the right to collect from the other party its reasonable costs and attorney fees incurred in enforcing this Agreement.

General

This Agreement may not be amended except in a writing signed by all Band Partners. No waiver by any Band Partner of any right under this Agreement will be construed as a waiver of any other right. If a court finds any provision of this Agreement invalid or unenforceable as applied to any circumstance, the remainder of this Agreement will be interpreted to best carry out the intent of the parties. This Agreement is governed by and interpreted in accordance with the laws of _____ .
The provisions of this Agreement are binding on the successors and assigns of the Band Partners. In the event of any dispute arising from or related to this Agreement, the prevailing party is entitled to attorney fees.

Signatures

MY SIGNATURE BELOW INDICATES THAT I HAVE READ AND UNDERSTOOD THIS
AGREEMENT AND HAVE BEEN ADVISED OF MY RIGHT TO SEEK INDEPENDENT
LEGAL REPRESENTATION REGARDING THIS AGREEMENT.

Band Member Signature _____

Address _____

_____

Date _____ Soc. Sec. # _____

Band Member Signature _____

Address _____

_____

Date _____ Soc. Sec. # _____

Band Member Signature _____

Address _____

_____

Date _____ Soc. Sec. # _____

Band Member Signature _____

Address _____

_____

Date _____ Soc. Sec. # _____

Band Member Signature _____

Address _____

_____

Date _____ Soc. Sec. # _____

What's the Right Business Entity for Your Band?

Most of this chapter focuses on the band partnership—the most common type of business entity for musical groups. But there is a world beyond partnerships and your band may want to explore some of the alternatives.

There are three important factors in choosing a business form: personal liability, taxes, and the relative difficulty and expense of formation. Below, we discuss personal liability and difficulty of formation. The tax issues regarding business forms are discussed in Chapter 17. If your band doesn't choose a business form, it's probably a partnership by default.

> **SEE AN EXPERT**
>
> **Talk with an expert.** An accountant or tax preparation expert can best advise you on the tax pros and cons of sole proprietorships, corporations, partnerships, and LLCs.

Personal Liability: Can They Take My Amplifier?

Liabilities are debts, or money, that you owe. Most band businesses carry some liabilities—for example, monthly rent for rehearsal space, installments due on a band van, or payments due to a recording studio. Additional liabilities may arise if your band is devastated by theft, if a fire or flood ruins your band equipment, or if you are the victim of a lawsuit—for instance, because someone is injured in your rehearsal studio and sues you (as well as the building owner) for damages.

If you operate your band business as a partnership—the most common business form for bands—then each partner will be personally liable for all band business debts. In other words, a creditor can collect a partnership debt against any band partner, regardless of which partner incurred the debt. That means that if your guitarist orders $50,000 worth of sound equipment for the band partnership without telling you and then moves to Venezuela, you could be on the hook. You can create a partnership agreement in which the partners apportion or share their potential liability—for example, the agreement may state that each partner is liable only for certain debts. But this agreement is enforceable only among the partners; it won't eliminate your personal liability to people outside the band who are owed money.

Limited liability companies (LLCs) and corporations are created to shield band members from personal liability. In theory, forming an LLC gives its owners "limited liability." This means that the band members/owners are not personally liable for business debts or lawsuits. The main reason most bands go to the trouble of forming LLCs and corporations is to get this limited liability. But that's not to say you should rush out tomorrow and turn your band partnership into one of these entities. As explained below, limited liability can sometimes be more of a myth than a reality for most bands. For practical reasons, you may not get the benefits you want from the LLC or corporate form of business, so it's often not worth the time, trouble, and expense of converting to an LLC or incorporating.

 TIP
Many major-label bands create subsidiary companies that deal with specific business issues. For example, to limit its liability, a band may create an LLC solely for touring or selling merchandise. Consult an attorney and tax expert if you want to form an LLC or corporation for these specific purposes.

Business Debts

LLCs and corporations were created to help people invest in a business without risking all their personal assets if the business failed or was unable to pay its debts. In an LLC or corporation, musicians may lose what they invested in the band, but band creditors can't go after personal assets such as band members' bank accounts or homes.

This theory may not work for your band, especially if you're just starting out. Major creditors such as banks don't want to be left holding the bag if your band business goes under. To help ensure payment, they will want to be able to go after your personal assets as well as your business assets. If your band forms an LLC or corporation, creditors may demand that one of the band partners *personally guarantee* business loans, credit cards, or other extensions of credit by signing a legally enforceable document pledging your personal assets to pay the debt if your business assets fall short. This means that the band member who gives the personal guarantee will be personally liable for the debt, just as if he or she were a sole proprietor or partner. In that case, the so-called protections of limited liability are irrelevant.

> **EXAMPLE:** The members of the band Faith & Sadie form an LLC to run their band business. When the band applies for a business credit card from the bank, they learn that the application contains a clause providing that the signatories—the people who sign the application—will be personally liable for the credit card balance, even though the credit card will be in the LLC's name. When the band asks the bank to remove the clause, the bank refuses, stating that its policy is to require personal guarantees from all small businesses. Two band members sign the application. Now, if the band LLC fails to pay off the credit card, the bank can go after the signatories personally and collect against their personal assets, such as personal bank accounts.

Lawsuits

Forming an LLC or corporation can shield you from personal liability from many business-related lawsuits. That's one of the main reasons for choosing these types of entities. As explained below, however, the members of a band LLC or corporation won't be shielded from some suits.

Corporation and LLC Owners Are Personally Liable for Their Own Negligence: Band members who have an ownership interest in a band corporation or LLC are personally liable for any damages caused by their own personal negligence or intentional wrongdoing in carrying out band business. If your band forms a corporation or an LLC, and it doesn't have the money or insurance to pay a claim, the lawyer suing the band will seek a way to collect against your personal assets. Here are some ways that may happen:

- A visitor slips and falls at your rehearsal space and breaks his hip. His lawyer sues the band LLC and the members personally for negligence claiming the band members failed to keep the premises safe.

- Your band LLC hires a driver to take you on a tour. The driver accidentally injures someone while running an errand for you. The injured person sues the band LLC and you personally for damages claiming you negligently hired, trained, and/or supervised the driver.
- Your band creates an album and licenses it to a record label. Another musician claims that a song on the album infringes on her copyright. Even if you've formed a corporation or an LLC, the copyright holder can sue you personally for causing copyright infringement. This is so even though your corporation or LLC owns the copyright, not you personally.

Piercing the Corporate Veil: Another way that the band members can be personally liable even though you've formed an LLC or a corporation is through a legal doctrine called "piercing the corporate veil." Under this legal rule, courts disregard the corporate entity and hold its owners personally liable for any harm done by the corporation *and* for corporate debts.

Generally, the courts say that corporate limited liability protection will be disregarded—that is, the owners will be held personally liable for business debts and claims—only in extreme cases. Most typically this occurs when owners fail to respect the separate legal existence of their LLC or corporation, but instead treat it as an extension of their personal affairs, for example, if band members fail to follow routine corporate formalities, such as adequately investing in or capitalizing (putting money in) the business. You can avoid this result by taking the following actions:

- **Act fairly and legally.** Do not conceal or misrepresent material facts or the state of your finances about your band to other businesses, creditors, or outsiders. Or put more bluntly, don't engage in fraud.
- **Fund your LLC or corporation adequately.** You don't have to invest a lot of money in your band business, but do try to put in enough cash or other liquid assets (assets that can be readily converted to cash) at the beginning so your band will be able to meet foreseeable expenses and liabilities. If you fail to do this, it is possible that a court faced with a balance sheet that shows a very minimal investment may disregard your limited liability protection. This is particularly likely if you engage in a risky venture that everyone knows needs a large investment.

- **Keep band business and personal business separate.** Get a federal Employer Identification Number for your LLC or corporation and open up a separate band checking account. (For an explanation of EINs and how to get one, see Chapter 18.) As a routine business practice, write all checks for business expenses or payouts of profits out of this account, and deposit all revenue into it. Keep separate accounting books for your band—these can consist of a simple single-entry system, such as your check register and deposit slips, but a double-entry system will serve you better when it comes time to prepare your end-of-year income tax returns. Lastly, you should keep written records of all major LLC and corporate decisions.

Liability and Bankruptcy

In olden days (the 19th century and earlier), a musician who owed large sums of money could lose everything he owned and even be thrown in debtor's prison by creditors. In our modern society, however, there is no such thing as unlimited liability. First of all, some of your personal property is always safe from creditors' reach. How much depends on the state in which you live. For example, creditors may not be allowed to take your car, your business tools (musical equipment), or your home and furnishings, depending on how much each is worth.

Moreover, bankruptcy is always an option if your debts get out of control. By filing for bankruptcy, you can partly or wholly wipe out your debts and get a fresh financial start. Since a partnership is a separate entity for bankruptcy purposes, a partner's personal bankruptcy doesn't bankrupt the partnership, and vice versa.

The Role of Insurance

If incorporating or forming an LLC won't always relieve the band members of personal liability—except perhaps in the event of bankruptcy—what else can you do to protect your band and yourself from business-related lawsuits and some band debts? We advise you to consider insurance. Insurance protects your band from typical (and some atypical) dilemmas. For example, if you are sued for certain claims, not only will the insurer pay damages but the insurer may step in to pay the lawyer who defends your band.

Before purchasing insurance, consider the likelihood of a lawsuit. Most bands rarely get sued unless an awful event has occurred, for example, an accident on the way to a gig. Therefore, one way to keep costs down is to maintain insurance for the most likely liabilities—for example, be sure to have vehicle insurance for your van. The trick with insurance is to get only the coverage you really need—and to pay as little as possible for it. We'll explain the basic principles, below.

Below are a few choices of some common insurance protections.

Key Insurance Terms	
Policy	Your policy is the written document or contract between you and the insurance company.
Premium	The premium is the periodic payment you pay to the insurance company for the benefits provided under the policy.
Rider	A rider is a special provision attached to a policy that either expands or restricts the policy.
Claim	A claim is your notification to an insurance company that you believe a payment is due to you under the terms of the policy.
Commission	This is a fee or percentage of the premium you pay to an insurance broker or agent.
Deductible	The deductible is the amount of out-of-pocket expenses that you must pay before the insurance payment begins. For example, if your deductible for business equipment loss is $1,000 per year and you suffer $1,000 in damages in one year, there will be no payment under the policy.
Endorsement	An endorsement is paperwork that is added to your policy and that reflects any changes or clarifications in the policy.
Exclusions	Exclusions are things your insurance policy will not cover.
Underwriter	This is the person or company that evaluates your business and determines what insurance you may qualify for.

Property Insurance

Business property insurance compensates you for damage or loss of your band property—both the physical space where you practice (if you operate a home practice space, for example) and the equipment and other supplies used by your band. If you rent commercial space—for example a practice studio— your lease may require you to carry a specified amount of property insurance.

A "named peril" policy protects against only the types of damage listed in the policy—typically, fire, lightning, vehicles, vandalism, storms, smoke, and sprinkler leaks. A "special form" policy offers broader coverage, commonly against all but a few excluded risks (often including earthquakes), and is more expensive.

If your band buys property insurance, you'll have a choice between an actual cash value policy, which pays you whatever your damaged equipment is actually worth on the day it is damaged, or a replacement cost policy, which pays to replace your equipment at current prices. A replacement cost policy is always more expensive, but it's often worth the extra money. Band equipment, particularly computers, mixers, and so on, lose their value quickly. And if you're like most bands, you're probably using some equipment that's already out of date. If you suffer a loss, you'll need to replace this equipment and get back to jamming—and you won't have much to spend if all you get is the $100 your insurance company gives you for your vintage Marshall amp.

Liability Insurance

Liability insurance covers damage to other people or their property for which you are legally responsible. This includes, for example, injuries to the A&R scout who trips on your guitar cord at your studio, as well as, in some cases, any injuries caused to fans at a show. Liability insurance policies typically pay the injured person's medical bills and other out-of-pocket losses, any amount you are ordered to pay in a lawsuit for a covered claim, and often the cost of defending you in such a lawsuit.

Car Insurance

If you have a car or van, you probably already have insurance that covers your personal use. However, your personal insurance policy may not cover business use (remember, your band is a business). If your personal coverage doesn't cover band use, you'll want to get business coverage to protect against lawsuits for damage you cause to others or their vehicles while on band business.

If you don't do much band business driving—and particularly if you don't often have band business passengers—then you can probably get coverage simply by informing your insurance company of your planned business use (and paying a slightly higher premium). Many insurance companies simply factor in occasional business use of a vehicle, along with commuting miles, driver experience, and many other factors, in setting your insurance premium. If you use a commercial vehicle (such as a van or delivery truck) or put most of the miles on your car while doing business, you will probably have to get a separate business vehicle insurance policy.

Even if auto insurance is mandatory in your state, you may want to check with your insurance agent to be sure that your policy covers your vehicle for band business use. If the vehicle is owned by the band, make sure that you have discussed the possible contingencies—uses of the vehicle, passengers, and traveling out of state—with your insurance agent.

Business Interruption Coverage

If your band business becomes your primary source of income, you may want to obtain business interruption insurance—a policy that replaces the income you won't be able to earn if you must temporarily shut down or relocate your band due to a covered event, such as a fire or storm. These policies typically provide both money to replace your lost profits, based on your band's earnings history (as shown by its financial records), and money to pay the operating expenses you still have to pay even though you can't do business (like studio rent and overhead). If you are not dependent on your band business, you probably don't need this type of policy.

When you're shopping for this type of insurance (or any other, for that matter), always check the exclusions and coverage. For example, some policies may provide an "extended period of indemnity," which kicks in after you start performing again, to cover your continuing losses until you are earning the same income as you were before the interruption. If your fans and booking agents don't immediately flock back to your band, your policy will pay for the business you're still not getting during this transition period.

Package Deals

Your band may want to consider a business owners' policy or BOP. These packages typically include business property insurance, liability protection, and some business interruption protection. An annual BOP premium ranges from $500 to $3,500, with an average cost of $1,200.

Typically, a BOP policy does not provide coverage for employment practices liability (often referred to as EPLI) to protect you from lawsuits brought by current or former employees, workers' compensation, or other employee benefits (health or disability insurance, for example).

RESOURCE

If you're looking for insurance for musicians, review the information at MusicPro Insurance (www.musicproinsurance.com) or Clarion Associates, Inc. (www.clarionins.com) and Production Insurance (www.productioninsurance.com) where your band may be able to obtain insurance for instrument and equipment loss, tour liability, composer's liability, and travel and accident insurance, health insurance, or term life insurance.

Finally, keep in mind that sometimes your band must get insurance— for example, if you have employees, state laws may require that you obtain workers' compensation coverage. A good insurance agent can help you make the right decisions. If you do acquire insurance, here are some additional tips:

- Maintain enough property and liability coverage to protect your band from common claims—for example, fire, theft, or accidental injury.
- When possible, keep insurance costs down by selecting high deductibles.

- Do your best to reduce hazards or conditions that can lead to insurance claims.

If you are concerned about being sued over band debts—for example, you fail to pay back a credit card or a loan, or you default on a lease—note that insurance won't protect you from liability for these business debts.

Expense and Difficulty of Forming Your Band Business

Another factor that may affect your choice of business structure is how hard it is to form that type of business. For example, creating and maintaining a corporation requires some diligence and paperwork. Creating and maintaining an LLC is quite a bit easier. Creating a sole proprietorship or partnership is the easiest; just start performing or selling your CDs and you've done it.

You can create each type of business without the help of an attorney. Nolo (www.nolo.com), the publisher of this book, offers online assistance in forming LLCs and corporations, as well as books on forming partnerships, corporations, nonprofits, and LLCs. Generally, if you're confused, too busy, or unsure of how to form a business entity, see an attorney and a tax consultant. Even if you decide to use an attorney's services, continue reading this section to inform yourself on what you're getting into.

Required Paperwork for All New Businesses

If you're starting a new business from scratch, you'll have to take care of some paperwork no matter what business form you choose. Many businesses will need to obtain one or more of the following:

- **EIN.** A federal Employer Identification Number (known as an FEIN, or simply an EIN) is required for partnerships, LLCs, and corporations. (If you're a sole proprietor without employees, you can use your Social Security number.) An explanation how to obtain an EIN is provided in Chapter 17.
- **DBA.** If you're doing business under an assumed name (that is, the band is not named after the members ala Crosby, Stills & Nash), local governments require that you file a DBA ("doing business as") statement. You can find out the details from the county clerk at your local courthouse.

If you're doing band business as a sole proprietorship under your own name (that is, your last name—for example, The Charlie Daniels Band), you won't need to file. (For more information on band names, read Chapter 9.)

- **Local permits.** In addition to filing a DBA, your local or state government may have other permit or licensing requirements. You can usually find out those details at your county clerk's office.

> **CAUTION**
>
> **Business names versus trademarks.** Registering your business name as a DBA with your county clerk or filing incorporation papers does not guarantee your right to use your name in business or to use that name to identify your products. Before choosing a name for your band business, review the rules regarding trade names and trademarks in Chapter 9.

How to Create a Sole Proprietorship

Forming a sole proprietorship is effortless. If you're running your band business by yourself—that is, without anyone sharing the expenses and profits—you've already created a sole proprietorship.

How to Create a Partnership

Like a sole proprietorship, you don't have to do anything (other than sell your band's music) to create a partnership. No written agreement is required among the partners—although a written agreement is strongly recommended. One reason for using a band partnership agreement (BPA) is to establish each partner's share of the income; another is to guarantee the continued existence of the partnership in the event one partner leaves or dies. Without a BPA, the departure of a partner ends the band partnership.

How to Create a Limited Liability Company

You can form an LLC in every state. Creating an LLC requires formal filing procedures, and the rules differ from state to state.

Creating an LLC requires filing a document—called Articles or Certificate of Organization—with the state's corporate filing office, usually the Secretary of State. The owners (known as members) can manage the business or designate others to do so. In general, there is far less formality to maintaining an LLC than a corporation.

RESOURCE
Nolo, the publisher of this book, offers incorporation and LLC formation services at its website, www.nolo.com.

Honey, I Incorporated the Kids: Family-Owned Bands

If you're one of the many family-owned band businesses, you may wonder how your family fits into the world of business forms. Here are some things to consider.

If a band consists solely of a husband and wife and they operate their band business in a community property state (Arizona, California, Idaho, Louisiana, Nevada, New Mexico, Texas, Washington, or Wisconsin), they can operate as a sole proprietorship for federal-tax-filing purposes. They can report all band income and expenses on Schedule C (*Profit or Loss From Business*), which is then attached to their Form 1040. If a band comprises a husband and wife and they operate their band business in a non-community-property state, or if a husband and wife have a band with others in any state, then these bands should form a partnership and file a partnership return (IRS Form 1065) that lists the partnership's income and deductions and each partner's share of partnership profits or losses. (This form is more commonly known as Schedule K-1.) The partners use this information to report partnership income or losses on their personal tax return (IRS Form 1040). The same rule holds true if other relatives join in the musical effort: They should also be made partners and given Schedule K-1s.

Family members can also operate as an LLC or corporation. One of the advantages of the corporate business form is that the family can provide and fully deduct employee health benefits.

How to Create a Corporation

Each state's incorporation laws may differ. Therefore, providing detailed instructions for incorporating in your state is beyond the scope of this book. However, here are the basic rules followed in most or all states.

One person, or many, can incorporate a band business. The process starts when an incorporator—any of the owners—prepares and files Articles of Incorporation with the state's corporate filing office, usually the Secretary of State. Bylaws—rules that establish the voting, directors, equity, and other rules—must be prepared (but not filed).

Once the state certifies the Articles of Incorporation, the corporation's board of directors is chosen, the bylaws are adopted, and stock is issued to the owners (one person can own 100% of the stock). The directors manage the business and choose officers who manage the day-to-day operations.

What's Right for Your Band?

In general, we recommend the following approach to choosing a business form:

- **Single owner—keep it simple.** If liability is not a major concern and one person runs the band, keeps all the money, and pays salaries, then maintain the arrangement as a sole proprietorship. Each salaried band member is either an employee or an independent contractor. Salaried musicians who are paid to practice and perform are probably classified as employees. Musicians who are added just to play an occasional gig are probably classified as independent contractors. This classification can make a big difference when it comes time to pay taxes.
- **Band members share expenses and profits—keep it simple.** If liability is not a major concern and the members share in expenses and profits, keep things simple as a partnership. For most bands, a partnership arrangement works fine, because you don't have to do anything to exist as a partnership (although we recommend creating a band partnership agreement). Some bands are partnerships that employ side musicians. For example, the three core members of a band may be a partnership, and the hired drummer and bass player may be employees of the partnership.

- **Getting bigger or incurring liability is a concern—consider an LLC or a corporation.** If your band is signing a major label agreement or touring regularly and has serious concerns about taxes and liability, you should look into insurance and/or forming an LLC or a corporation.

Converting From a Partnership to an LLC

During the years that this book has been available, one business form—the LLC—has grown in popularity. The popularity of the LLC is due to the fact that it allows all owners of the business to quickly and easily achieve the dual goals of "pass-through" tax treatment (the same tax treatment sole proprietors and partnerships receive) and limited personal liability protection (which means owners aren't personally liable for business debts and claims).

As a result of its ease of formation and liability shield, many bands have converted from partnership status to an LLC. If you want to convert your band partnership to an LLC, you'll need to transfer the assets of the band partnership to the LLC, and you should consult with a tax advisor as to state tax rules.

It's possible to accomplish the conversion on your own. But if you prefer making music to filling out legal and tax forms, then leave these tasks to a professional.

Factors to Consider Before Converting

Below is a checklist, borrowed from Anthony Mancuso's *Form Your Own Limited Liability Company* (Nolo), that can help you decide whether your band should make the conversion to an LLC:

- **Is your band involved in extensive touring or is it incurring business debts and claims that could threaten personal assets?** If your band is at a higher risk for lawsuits and claims, consider limiting personal liability by forming an LLC.
- **Do you own sufficient personal assets that would be at risk (such as equity in a house) if a band lawsuit resulted in a judgment that could be collected from your personal assets?** If the answer is yes, an LLC may be the proper route for your band.

- **How much does your state charge for creating an LLC?** Does your state also charge an annual fee? This information can be located at your state government website. High fees may dissuade you from forming an LLC.
- **How are LLCs taxed in your state?** Again, the information is located at your state government website. A tax advisor may help you determine if the conversion is worthwhile.
- **(Optional) Have you consulted with an accountant or lawyer on any complex tax and legal issues surrounding your band's business formation?** If you haven't, you may want to seek some consultation before proceeding. For help in dealing with attorneys, see Chapter 4.

What's Involved in Converting From a Partnership to an LLC?

A band partnership can convert to an LLC in most states with a modest amount of paperwork and fees, and with no change to income tax treatment and filing requirements. That said, as with all legal and tax rules, there are numerous exceptions and strategies that affect a partnership's conversion to an LLC.

Legal Considerations

In order to change a general partnership to an LLC, the partners must take the following action:

- **Terminate the partnership and convert to an LLC.** Your BPA probably requires the unanimous consent of all partners to dissolve or change the form of the business. Even if your BPA states a lesser vote requirement, it's probably best to get everyone on board by obtaining unanimous approval. (You don't want to drag a reluctant band member into your new LLC.) Additional paperwork may be required to legally terminate a partnership when it is converted to an LLC. For example, your state may require a notice of dissolution of partnership to be published in a newspaper of general circulation in the county where the principal office of the band partnership was located—a routine filing that most newspapers are set up to handle for a modest fee. A phone call to the legal notice departments of your local newspapers should tell you whether this procedure is required in your state and, if so, how much you have to pay to publish this notice.

- **File Articles of Organization.** Your band must file LLC Articles of Organization with the state filing office (typically, the Corporations Division of the Secretary of State's office handles LLC filings). Many states provide an online LLC Articles form specifically designed to handle the conversion of a partnership to an LLC.

- **Prepare Operating Agreement.** The band members should create an LLC Operating Agreement similar to a band partnership agreement. This documents ownership interests, profits, losses, voting and liquidation rights, and other rights and responsibilities of the members. Most bands, when converting to an LLC, set up an LLC that will be managed by all band members (owners), in a system known as member-management (versus management by a select LLC management team, which is called manager-management). Although the LLC Operating Agreement usually contains many of the same provisions found in the BPA, some fine-tuning of the LLC operating agreement may be appropriate to reflect the nuances of LLC tax treatment. This is true even though co-owned LLCs generally are treated the same as partnerships under federal and state law. For that reason, it's best to check with a tax advisor when making the conversion.

- **Revise licenses, permits, and registrations.** Your band LLC should obtain new permits, licenses, and registrations in the name of the band LLC and should cancel old licenses and permits taken out in the name of the now defunct band partnership. If the LLC will do business under a name different from the name of the LLC specified in its Articles of Organization, it should file a fictitious business name statement with the county clerk.

- **Get an EIN.** If the band partnership had an EIN, the band LLC can continue to use it. Otherwise, the band must obtain an EIN to prepare its annual IRS and state information returns.

> ### States May Impose Special LLC Tax Return Filing Requirements and Fees
>
> Most states treat LLCs the same as the IRS—that is, they treat them either as a sole proprietorship (if an LLC has one owner) or a partnership (if it has more than one owner). However, some states may impose special LLC tax return and LLC annual tax and/or annual fee requirements. In other words, if you convert a partnership to an LLC in some states, your annual state tax or fee payments can change. For example, the California Franchise Tax Board requires LLCs that are formed or earn income in California to file Form 568, *Limited Liability Company Return of Income*, and pay an $800 minimum tax each year, plus an additional annual fee if gross receipts exceed certain thresholds. Check with your tax advisor to find out whether special LLC fees and tax information apply in your state and whether your state imposes a separate entity-level tax or fee on LLCs.

Income Tax Consequences of Conversion

Generally, there are no income tax consequences when a band partnership is changed into a band LLC, provided that the band members keep the same capital, profits, loss, and liability sharing ratios in the band LLC that they had in the band partnership. There may be variations in some state laws regarding the tax consequences of forming an LLC, and your band should speak with a tax professional before making the conversion.

Tax Filing Procedures

After your band partnership is converted to a band LLC, you continue to file a partnership tax return, IRS Form 1065, *U.S. Return of Partnership Income,* at the end of each tax year. (There are no special LLC federal tax forms— LLCs use federal partnership tax forms. An explanation for tax-filing requirements is provided in Chapter 17.) The LLC also continues to prepare a 1065 Schedule K-1, *Partner's Share of Income, Credits, Deductions, etc.,* for each LLC member. The K-1 shows the amount of band LLC income or loss, deductions, and credits each band member must report on their individual 1040 tax returns. The basic income tax treatment of profits earned in the business remains the same after the conversion to an LLC. Band members continue to report and pay income tax on all profits earned each year in the business, whether or not profits are actually paid out in cash by the business to the members.

Band members who receive a share of the LLC profits are not considered employees for payroll tax purposes. However, payroll taxes must be withheld and paid for anyone who receives a salary or other type of guaranteed payment from the band LLC. In other words, if you not only pay out profits to a member, but also employ a member and pay for actual services performed for the LLC, payroll taxes must be withheld from (and paid) on the salary amount.

Beware of Securities Laws

Normally, a member-managed band LLC does not have to be concerned with federal and state securities laws. (A "security" is defined as a sale of an interest with the expectation of earning profits from the efforts of others.) However, if the band creates a manager-managed LLC, the sale of LLC interests probably will be considered a sale of securities under the federal and state rules. That's because the nonmanaging members are investing with the expectation of earning profits from the efforts of others—the classic definition of a "security." In that case, you will need the assistance and advice of an attorney.

Resources for Forming an LLC

The prospect of forming an LLC can be a challenging experience; many people find the legal paperwork less than thrilling. Fortunately, there are plenty of resources available to you to help you handle some, most, or all of the legal paperwork necessary to form your own LLC. In this section, we will list several of the most helpful of these resources.

State Websites

Each state office that accepts LLC filings maintains a website. One way to locate the state filing office is to go to the website for the National Association of Secretaries of State (NASS) (www.nass.org), select "Business Services" (under the "Initiatives" tab near the top of the page), then select "Corporate Registration." This will take you to the page for the section or division that handles LLC and corporate filings in the state, where you should be able to find more information and the appropriate official state forms.

Most states provide downloadable standard "Articles of Organization" to form LLCs. Download the form, fill it in on your computer according to the instructions provided with the form, then print and mail the form together with the required filing fee to the office for filing. The turnaround time in most states to process and file Articles is one to two weeks.

States also are starting to provide online filing services. If your state provides this service, just fill in the appropriate form within your browser and submit it for filing. The filing fee is charged to your credit card. Typically, online filing is accomplished on the same day or within a few days, and you'll receive a filing receipt from the office either by email or by snail mail within a week of the submission date.

Legal and Business Self-Help Books and Software

There are several publishers of books and software that give you background information on LLCs, plus the forms necessary to organize your own business entity. Nolo (www.nolo.com), the publisher of this book, is a leading source of self-help business formation and operation books and software. Below is a partial list from their catalog of business entity formation and operation resources (see additional Nolo catalog and ordering information at the back of this book).

- *Form Your Own Limited Liability Company*, by Anthony Mancuso. This national title shows you how to form this newest type of business entity under each state's LLC law and the latest federal rules. If you don't need the formality of the corporate form, but would like to have limited personal liability for business debts, this book is for you. Includes instructions for preparing Articles of Organization plus Operating Agreements for member-managed and manager-managed LLCs.

- *Your Limited Liability Company: An Operating Manual*, by Anthony Mancuso. This book provides ready-to-use minutes forms for holding formal LLC meetings; it also contains resolutions to insert in your minutes to formally approve standard legal, tax, and other important business decisions that arise in the course of operating an LLC.

Business Entity Formation and Compliance Services

If you're one of the many entrepreneurs who prefer to handle the big decisions and delegate the routine paperwork to others, you may prefer to pay a business formation service to form your LLC or corporation. A leading business entity service provider is Nolo, the publisher of this book, at www.nolo.com, which can handle the formation of an LLC or corporation.

Management

n the motion picture *Stardust*, a British band hires an American manager who tells them they need never worry about business again. It's a jungle out there, explains the new manager, "and I'm the biggest ape in the jungle." For many bands, this is the ideal image of a manager: an assertive, aggressive "ape" who intimidates everyone around him. We will see, however, that managers come in various forms, and a manager's effectiveness is not always related to shouting power.

In this chapter, we offer information about hiring (and firing) a manager. We'll provide an explanation of what a manager does and how to avoid the problems created by handshake deals or management agreements that last too long. We will examine the manager's commission payments and advise how to avoid getting screwed by deductions or commission payments that continue after the management agreement is over. In addition, we provide two sample management agreements: a short-form agreement and a long agreement with more options.

What Is a Manager?

A manager (often referred to as a "personal manager") secures opportunities for earning money, develops a career plan for the band, acts as a liaison between record companies and the band, and shields the band from business pressures.

The arrangement between the manager and the band is known as the management agreement (or management deal). The management agreement is usually a written document, but it can be oral. As with other agreements, we recommend that you put your agreement in writing. We'll go through the provisions of a sample agreement in this chapter.

A band's arrangement with the manager is almost always exclusive. That is, you can sign with only one manager at a time. Managers, on the other hand, can—and often do—represent more than one band. If you're concerned that a manager might not be loyal to your band or might have a conflict of interest, you'll need to use your best judgment as to whether to hire that manager. (Conflicts of interest are also discussed in Chapter 4.)

The manager's compensation (known as a commission) is negotiated at the beginning of the relationship between the band and the manager. Most managers earn a commission of between 10% and 15% (sometimes as high as 20%) of the band's income after certain deductions have been subtracted. Many management agreements state that the commission is a percentage of "gross revenues," which is slightly misleading. The term "gross revenues" usually refers to total income with no deductions taken out. However, in management agreements with bands, the term "gross revenues" often refers to band income *after* deductions. We'll discuss the intricacies of gross revenues later in this chapter.

A personal manager is generally one person. However, sometimes a manager works for a management company that consists of many personal managers. If a band signs with a management company, it can preserve its relationship with an individual manager through a contract provision known as a "key person" provision. We'll discuss key person provisions when we go through the long-form sample agreement.

Personal Managers, Road Managers, and Business Managers

Personal managers should be distinguished from business managers and road managers. A personal manager is the mastermind behind the band's business, developing a career plan for the band and acting as a liaison between record companies and the band. The business manager (usually an accountant or tax attorney) handles only finances and investments. For example, the business manager does the band's tax returns and distributes income to the band members and the personal manager. The road manager travels with the band and supervises the day-to-day activities of touring. In the early stages of a band's development, when there is not much income and the band has not signed a record deal, the personal manager may perform all three jobs. We discuss road managers in Chapter 6, and we discuss business managers throughout this chapter.

Avoiding Common Management Problems

There are innumerable ways that managers have screwed bands; we highlight some of the most common examples below.

Situation #1:
There's no written agreement.
A handshake deal is an oral agreement with no written contract. Although at one time handshake deals were standard, that's no longer the case. As we've said before, oral agreements are an invitation to trouble, particularly with important deals like your management agreement. Written management contracts are now the standard in the music business, and we recommend that you use one.

If you have a dispute with your manager, the details of a handshake deal may be difficult and time-consuming to prove in court. If you need convincing, ask Bruce Springsteen. He planned to record his fourth album but ran into a problem after a falling-out with his manager, Mike Appel. It took lawyers over a year to disentangle the artist and the manager. At one point in the legal mess, Springsteen was so frustrated he jumped on a table in a law office and began screaming at the lawyers. Finally, after his record company stepped in to help negotiate, a settlement was reached.

How to avoid getting screwed:
If you are dealing with an inexperienced manager, you will have more bargaining power and should insist on a written agreement.

Unfortunately, you may find yourselves dealing with an experienced manager who may insist on a handshake deal. If your band can't persuade the manager to sign a written agreement, you should write down the key terms of the deal on a piece of paper and keep that paper as a record of the agreement. You should also confirm the details of the arrangement in a letter to the manager (for example, "Dear Tom: Our band wanted to summarize the terms of our oral agreement with you. We agreed that … and so on"). Keep a copy of this letter. In addition, you should make an effort ahead of time to understand basic management principles such as gross revenues and the length of the agreement. Be sure to read the sample agreements (below) and review the commentary, which explains the most common provisions of a management deal.

Situation #2:
The management agreement lasts too long.

The length of the management deal—how long the manager will manage the band—is referred to as the term of the agreement. The band and manager can always extend the term if they mutually agree to do so. But the term can be shortened only if there is a method provided in the agreement for early termination. Agreements usually run from one to three years, and often there is an option for the agreement to be extended for an additional two-year period.

Often, a band finds itself unhappy with its manager well before the term of management is over. If, for instance, a manager with a three-year term does a lousy job for a year and fails to bring the band any opportunities, the band might want to find a different manager. However, if the band fires the manager after only one year, the manager can sue the band for damages for the band's breach of the three-year contract.

How to avoid getting screwed:

If possible, try to limit the length of the term to one or two years. You can always renew it if everybody's happy with the arrangement. If your manager insists on three years (or longer), try to establish money standards—also known as earning plateaus—for each year. If the manager doesn't generate a certain amount of money for the band during a specific year, then the band can terminate the arrangement. For example, you can include in your agreement that if the band earns less than $50,000 during the second year, the manager can be fired.

Another solution is to require the band to obtain a record deal by a certain date. If the goal is not reached, the band can fire the manager. Keep in mind, though, that a manager might take *any* record deal in order to meet this requirement. However, this isn't terribly likely because a manager is interested in making money, and if the record deal is bad, the manager won't earn much. In addition, if the band is unable to attract a deal, the manager will probably want out of the arrangement as well.

Situation #3:
The manager's commission is calculated from too much income.

A manager is paid by commission, which is a percentage of the band's income. For example, if a band earns $100,000 in one year and the manager earns a 20% commission, the manager would receive $20,000. Often the commission is calculated after certain deductions have been subtracted from the band's income, such as tour expenses or promotion costs. The deductions that are taken from the band's income before the commission is calculated will depend on your agreement with the manager. The more deductions that are taken, the less money gets paid to the manager and the more money your band gets to keep.

An Unusual Definition of "Gross Income"

The terms "gross income" and "gross revenue" usually mean income before any deductions have been taken. However, in music management deals, these terms are typically used even though they often refer to band income after deductions have been made. Since you can't rely on these terms having their usual meaning, it's doubly important that everyone understands what they mean before you enter into a management deal.

A manager should not take a commission on money that is used to pay for crucial band services, such as recording expenses. A band can be screwed when its manager takes a commission "off the top" without permitting the band to first deduct or exclude certain payments or expenses. These amounts, sometimes referred to as "pass-through" income, should be deducted before the manager takes a commission. Including or excluding certain money when calculating a manager's commission can make a big difference in the band's income.

EXAMPLE 1: **Manager Takes It Off the Top**

Total Earnings	$	100,000
Manager's commission	–	20,000
(20% of $100,000)		
Recording Expenses	–	50,000
Band's income	= $	30,000

EXAMPLE 2: **Manager Takes Commission After Deductions and Expenses**

Total Earnings	$	100,000
Recording Expenses	–	50,000
Earnings after expenses	=	50,000
Manager's commission	–	10,000
(20% of $50,000)		
Band's income	= $	40,000

As you can see, the band takes home a lot more money if it pays its bills before the manager takes a commission. By taking the money off the top, the manager is unjustly enriched, because the manager is in effect getting a cut of the recording budget. This leaves the band with less money to pay its operating expenses.

How to avoid getting screwed:

In your management agreement, don't let the manager take a commission on income off the top. Instead, try to have some (or all) of the following sums deducted before the manager takes a commission:

- Recording funds advanced by a record company to pay for making recordings
- Money paid by the record company to make videos
- Payments for roadies, sound, and light services
- Payments to record producers, mixers, remixers, engineers, or others who are employed in the production of the band's records

- Payments to cowriters or copublishers who are not members of the band
- Tour support
- Booking agent fees
- Payments to musicians who are not members of the band
- Payments to acts that open for your band
- Expenses in connection with promotional and marketing activities
- Any reimbursements received by your band for expenses paid out of gross income. These occur when you are paid back for something you didn't have to pay in the first place. For example, if your band paid for the shipping of master tapes, which was supposed to be paid by your record company, you may receive reimbursement later. The manager should not receive a commission on this payback.
- Income from recording studios, acting, or other entertainment or music sources. The manager should not receive a payment when band members earn money from nonband sources of income.
- Packaging income. The manager receives income directly from the ticket sales for a show that the manager is presenting.
- Songwriting income (music publishing).

If you have an oral agreement, make sure that the band and manager have agreed on what can or cannot be included in the band's commissionable income, and keep a record of this list.

When Does the Manager Get Paid?

As a practical matter, the calculation of the manager's commission is usually done by the band's accountant or business manager on a monthly basis. In other words, the manager does not simply deduct a percentage from any check that arrives for the band. Instead, all checks for the month are deposited in an account, and the band's business manager or accountant then subtracts those amounts that the manager cannot commission. The manager receives a percentage of the remaining money, and the band receives the rest.

Situation #4:

Commission payments continue too long after the management term ends.

A manager will often get continued commission payments *after* the management deal has ended. These payments are referred to as "post-term commissions." Most managers believe that post-term commissions are fair compensation because they negotiated the original deals that earned—and continue to earn—the income. Sometimes these post-term commissions continue *forever* (in legal lingo, "in perpetuity"). For example, Pink Floyd's ex-manager received a commission from some of Pink Floyd's income (income from deals he negotiated) for over 30 years.

There are two common ways that post-term commissions are calculated. In one, the manager gets a post-term commission from all albums created during the time when he or she was manager. In the other scenario, the manager gets a commission on all albums recorded under a record deal negotiated by the manager—no matter when the albums are created. In other words, if the manager negotiates a three-record deal, the manager would get a cut of the income from all three record deals, even if the management agreement ended after only one album was recorded and the other two were recorded a year or more after the manager left.

As you can see, these types of deals can be quite expensive for a band. If a band is paying a 20% post-term commission to an ex-manager and a 20% commission to a new manager, then 40% of the band's income is being paid out before the band gets its cut.

How to avoid getting screwed:

If possible, limit post-term commissions to *only* albums created during the term. That way, the manager gets paid only for records that are created while the manager is actually performing services. Second, try to negotiate a decreasing percentage after termination. For example, if the manager's commission was 20%, it could decrease in 5% increments over a two-year period as follows: 20% for the first six months after the termination, 15% for the next six months, 10% for the next six months, and 5% for the last six months. After that, the manager receives no more income. How many managers will accept this? Many bands have been happily surprised to learn that it is often not too difficult to obtain this concession, particularly if the manager does not have a major label track record (that is, the manager does not represent any major label artists).

Situation #5:
The band pays too many of the manager's expenses.

A personal manager will require that the band reimburse the manager for certain management expenses, such as traveling on behalf of your band to meet with record company executives. It is standard to reimburse the manager for all reasonable expenses. It is also standard that the manager must obtain the band's consent before incurring any single expense above a certain amount (say, $200).

Bands can easily get screwed when their manager's expenses get out of control. Sometimes a manager runs up a tab for many smaller expenses that don't each require band approval. Many bands have been shocked to learn how quickly small expenses can add up to several thousand dollars. A manager may travel to a music convention on behalf of two bands he represents and bill one band for the entire trip (or worse, bill both bands for the entire trip). The manager may bill the band for expenses even when the band has no income, creating a personal debt.

How to avoid getting screwed:

Establish rules in your management agreement for which expenses the band will cover. The manager should obtain the band's written approval of either any expense over $200 *or* any total expenses over $1,000 in any month. If the manager has expenses involving two bands or more, those expenses should be prorated. That is, if 30% of the manager's time on a trip to Los Angeles was for your band and 70% was for another band, then the expenses should be split 30-70 between the two bands. Expenses should be paid only when the band earns money and actually receives payment, and band members should never have to dig in their own pockets to pay management expenses. Much of this is monitored by the business manager, who reviews expenses and income and pays the band and manager accordingly.

Situation #6:

The band wants to fire the manager.

If your manager isn't working hard enough for your band (for example, the manager is devoting more time to another band), or your manager has made offensive career choices (for example, booking your band on a one-year tour of Alaska opening for a polka trio), then you need to consider your options. Firing a manager is a last resort and should be considered only after you have exhausted every other option, such as discussing the problem with the manager, amending the agreement, attending mediation, and so on. Consider your decision carefully, because firing a manager is usually a messy and contentious procedure that can disrupt band activities for several months or even much longer. The Jefferson Airplane had a particularly nasty dispute with a former manager that lasted 21 years, during which time the band received no record royalties.

How to avoid getting screwed:

Review your management agreement and consult with a music business attorney to determine if there is a legitimate basis for termination (Chapter 4 provides information on finding an attorney). For example, your band may have the right to fire the manager because the manager failed to achieve a certain earnings plateau. Before making a final decision to fire the manager, your band should also consider the following:

- **Dispute resolution procedures.** Your agreement may provide for a method of resolving disputes, such as mediation or arbitration. You will have to pursue those dispute resolution methods before terminating the manager. We discuss dispute resolution in the sample management agreement.

- **Post-term commissions.** Even if your band has the legal right to terminate the manager, your band will still be on the hook for post-term commissions (as discussed above). If you hire a new manager, you will have to pay both the old and new manager.

- **The term.** If several years are left on the term, the fired manager may claim more than post-term commissions. The manager may claim that there are two or three additional years of future records, concerts, and other possible band income that have been denied to the manager. In other words, the more time that is left on the agreement, the more damages the fired manager may claim.

Dear Rich: How Do I Invest in a Band?

A partner and myself are considering investing in a band. The band is pretty far along, playing 2,000-seat venues, recording their first album, and seemingly taking success very seriously. They need funds to go to the next level and we are comfortable getting involved. However, the zillions of music industry contracts/guides out there do not touch on contracts protecting an investor buying a percentage of the band's entire business. Can you steer me toward something like this? I am looking for specific contract templates, along with what-to-watch-out-for insight.

Investing in a band is the same as investing in any other business (which is why you're probably not finding paperwork specifically geared to bands). So let's take a look at the three things required to invest in a business: (1) a formal business entity—that is the band must be a partnership, LLC, or corporation (preferably one of the latter two), and (2) an agreement between the owners of the entity formalizing your investment (for example, a stock agreement), and (3) some knowledge of the industry in which you are investing.

LLC or corporation. We recommend that the band form an LLC or corporation, because investors in those entities have limited liability. That way, investors will be shielded if the band throws a TV out of their hotel window and it lands on someone's Ferrari. These entities are also better suited for making investments than a partnership. There are plenty of self-help books and forms, and online programs that explain how to form and invest in LLCs and corporations, though our hearts are with the Nolo products.

Why it matters that you learn about the industry. Every industry has its quirks and the music industry has more than most. You should take a basic primer in music copyrights and trademarks because the assets of the band are concentrated in those intangibles. You'll probably want the songwriters in the band to contribute their songwriting copyrights to the band entity. However, that's not something they're obligated to do. So, before you drop your money into the band's piggy bank, you should probably be sure that the assets placed into the entity reflect the moneymaking features of the band. And of course, it's probably in everyone's best interests for you and your partner to have your own attorney and the band to have different representation. That will go a long way to prevent a post-breakup challenge to the agreement.

These contract provisions will affect your decision to fire the manager and your bargaining power if you want to negotiate a termination. Consider that most managers don't go willingly and that it is likely your manager will seek additional compensation. Even so, it's possible to work out a termination without resorting to litigation. In order to do this, you will have to negotiate with the manager and reach a settlement of your differences. Usually this means some form of payment or promise of payment in the future. You should document this termination in some way, possibly by a letter in which you list the terms of the settlement. If you are having trouble reaching a decision, consult a music business attorney. It may be expensive, but it will guarantee that your arrangement is terminated properly.

Abbreviated Management Agreement

This section walks you through the simple task of putting together an abbreviated (or short-form) management agreement. The short-form agreement has mostly fixed terms without much choice. It is suitable if you want to work with a new or inexperienced manager, if you want to have a one-year trial arrangement with a manager, or if you're just not ready to use the long agreement. Keep in mind, though, that the more detailed and customized your agreement, the more protection your band will have. (The long agreement is covered in the next section.) A sample appears below.

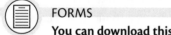

FORMS
You can download this form (and all other forms in this book) from Nolo.com; for details, see "Get Forms, Updates, and More at This Book's Companion Page," in the appendix.

CANADIAN RULES
If you are a Canadian resident, any reference to "state" or "county" in the model agreement should be changed to "province." Occasionally, Canadian contract and partnership laws differ from American law, and when that occurs, we provide an explanation for the difference.

Introduction

Insert the name of the manager and, if applicable, the management company. You should also insert the type of business form and address of the manager or management company (for example, "Mary Smith and Mental Midget Management, a New York corporation, with its address at 47 Prospect Street, Huntington, NY 11743"). If you are signing *only* with a management company and not a specific manager, insert only the name of the company.

Insert your band's name, business form, and address (for example, "Petty Larceny, a general partnership, with its address at 5678 Hempstead Turnpike, Wantagh, NY 11793"). If you are unsure of your business form, review Chapter 2. After that, insert the names of the band members.

Obligations of Manager

This section lists the manager's obligations. The obligations listed in this short agreement are standard for managers. Your band may not like the idea of someone providing "guidance and advice" as to the proper method of presenting the band's music, but this is exactly what a manager is supposed to be doing: studying your band's performance and the audience's reaction to determine how to make your band more successful. A band's arrangement with the manager is almost always exclusive. That is, you can sign with only one manager at a time, and the band cannot make music business deals without the manager.

The Term

This provision (the "term") establishes how long the manager has the job with your band, which in this case is one year. If your band and the manager want to renew at the end of the year, you can do so on the same terms for additional one-year periods. If you want to change the terms, you should execute a new agreement—most likely a longer, more customized one, such as the long-form agreement discussed below.

Commission During the Term

In the blank, enter the commission percentage your manager will receive. The standard commission percentage is between 10% and 15% (sometimes as high as 20%). A manager who demands 20% should have a successful track record—otherwise your band is paying too much. This provision establishes a number of deductions that must be made before a manager can calculate his or her cut. If the manager will not agree to one or more of these, you may cross them out and have each person who signs the agreement initial each cross-out.

Note that, in this provision, songwriting income is not deducted from the manager's commission. If you do not want your manager to be able to commission songwriting income, or if you want different deductions to be taken from the band's income before the manager's commission is calculated, you should use the long agreement, which is covered in the next section.

Commission After the Term

Managers typically earn post-term commissions—income from the band *after* their job as manager has ended. This provision allows the manager to receive post-term commissions on income from only those records created during the management term. The manager may not receive any commissions on income from records created before or after the term.

Earlier in this chapter, we suggested a descending system for post-term commissions. This provision allows you to choose the descending rate (such as 20%, 15%, 10%, 5%) and the periods that each rate will be paid (usually three- or six-month terms). You can negotiate the numbers according to your bargaining power. We have given space for up to four periods over which to lower your commission rate. If you do not use all four, just cross out the remaining language, enter "N/A," or remove the language altogether. After the last period is over, no more payments are due to the manager.

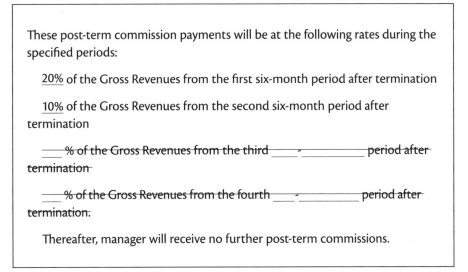

These post-term commission payments will be at the following rates during the specified periods:

20% of the Gross Revenues from the first six-month period after termination

10% of the Gross Revenues from the second six-month period after termination

~~——% of the Gross Revenues from the third ——-———— period after termination~~

~~——% of the Gross Revenues from the fourth ——-———— period after termination.~~

Thereafter, manager will receive no further post-term commissions.

Sample Clause

Manager's Expenses

Bands are usually obligated to pay their manager's reasonable expenses in promoting the group. This provision sets limits on how much the manager can spend before getting the band's permission. This provision also prevents the band members from becoming personally obligated for management expenses. Feel free to adjust any of the figures in this provision.

Mediation; Arbitration

Mediation and arbitration are more efficient and often less expensive methods of resolving disputes than filing a lawsuit. (See Chapter 2 for an explanation of mediation and arbitration.) If you don't want mediation and arbitration, we recommend that you delete this provision.

We suggest that you choose the county, province, or city in which the band resides for arbitration. If all the members do not reside within one area, choose a place that is convenient. Enter your location of choice in the blank.

[Abbreviated] Management Agreement

Introduction

This Management Agreement is between _____ ("Manager") and _____ ("Band"), comprising the following members: _____ ("Band Members"). Band agrees to have Manager serve as its exclusive personal manager.

Obligations of Manager

Manager will guide and advise Band in the music business. Manager will serve as Band's exclusive agent for the exploitation and promotion of Band's music services and products throughout the world. Manager will work in association with Band in the negotiation of recording, merchandising, or other agreements affecting Band.

The Term

The term of this agreement will continue for one year after the date of execution of this agreement and may be renewed by mutual consent of the parties on the same terms for subsequent one-year terms.

Commission During the Term

Manager is entitled to _____ % of Gross Revenues received by Band during the term. "Gross Revenues" are all moneys, including advances and fees, received by Band in connection with Band's entertainment-related activities, but excluding recording funds advanced by a record company, money paid to make videos, payments to record producers, musicians, mixers, remixers, directors, engineers, or any other individuals involved in the creation of audio or audiovisual recordings, payments to nonband-member cowriters or copublishers, tour support, and any reimbursements received by Band for expenses paid out of Gross Revenues.

Commission After the Term

Unless Manager has been terminated for a material breach of this Agreement, Manager is entitled to post-term commission payments derived from master recordings created during the Term. Under no circumstances will Manager be entitled to income from albums created before or after the Term. These post-term commission payments will be at the following rates during the specified periods:

_____% of the Gross Revenues from the first _____ period after termination

_____% of the Gross Revenues from the second _____ period after termination

_____% of the Gross Revenues from the third _____ period after termination

_____% of the Gross Revenues from the fourth _____ period after termination.

Thereafter, Manager will receive no further post-term commissions.

Manager's Expenses

Band will pay documented reasonable and necessary costs incurred by Manager in connection with Manager's duties on behalf of Band. Band will pay such expenses only out of Gross Revenues commissionable under this Agreement, and no members of Band will be personally liable for any such expenses. Manager will not incur expenses in excess of $200 in any single transaction, or $1,000 during any calendar month, without Band's prior written consent.

Mediation; Arbitration

If a dispute arises under this Agreement, the parties agree to first try to resolve the dispute with the help of a mutually agreed-on mediator in _____ .
Any costs and fees other than attorney fees will be shared equally by the parties. If it is impossible to arrive at a mutually satisfactory solution within a reasonable time, the parties agree to submit the dispute to binding arbitration in the same city or region, conducted on a confidential basis under:

☐ the Commercial Arbitration Rules of the American Arbitration Association, or

☐ the rules of _____ .

General

This Agreement may not be amended except in a writing signed by all parties. If a court finds any provision of this Agreement invalid or unenforceable as applied to any circumstance, the remainder of this Agreement will be interpreted so as best to effect the intent of the parties. This Agreement will be governed by and interpreted in accordance with the laws of the State of _____ . This Agreement expresses the complete understanding of the parties with respect to the subject matter and supersedes all prior proposals, agreements, representations, and understandings.

Band Members

Band Member Signature _____

Address _____

_____

Date _____ Soc. Sec. # _____

Band Member Signature _____

Address _____

_____

Date _____ Soc. Sec. # _____

Band Member Signature _____

Address _____

_____

Date _____ Soc. Sec. # _____

Band Member Signature _____

Address _____

_____

Date _____ Soc. Sec. # _____

Band Member Signature _____

Address _____

_____

Date _____ Soc. Sec. # _____

Manager

Band Manager Signature _____

Address _____

_____

Date _____ Soc. Sec. # _____

In several states, there are organizations that specialize in arbitration for people in the arts, such as California Lawyers for the Arts (www.calawyersforthearts.org) and Volunteer Lawyers for the Arts (in New York at www.vlany.org, as well as in other cities and states). You can substitute the rules of one of these organizations for those of the American Arbitration Association in your agreement. If your band is based in Canada, you can still use the AAA's rules, as they perform arbitration in all major Canadian cities. Check one of the choices or delete the unwanted alternative.

General

The following provisions are standard contractual provisions referred to as boilerplate. Boilerplate provisions are explained in Chapter 2.

Insert the state (or province, in the case of Canadian bands) of residence for the Band Partners. In the event of a dispute, this determines which state law will govern the arbitration or lawsuit.

Signatures

Have all band members and the manager fill in the signature section with signatures, addresses, and dates. Enter the same address for all the band members: the mailing address for the band. Be sure to use an address that will be able to receive mail for two to three years. If there is no such address, use a post office box or an address for the parents of one of the members.

Full-Length Management Agreement

The long-form agreement below covers many more details than the abbreviated form. It includes options and alternatives to deal with most of the situations that may arise between a band and manager. A sample appears below. The following instructions explain how to fill out the form and what the various clauses mean. Many clauses have alternative provisions for you to choose from, which are explained in the instructions. Some clauses, as noted in the instructions, are optional altogether.

FORMS
You can download this form (and all other forms in this book) from Nolo.com; for details, see "Get Forms, Updates, and More at This Book's Companion Page," in the appendix.

Introduction

Insert the name of the manager and, if applicable, the management company. You should also insert the type of business form and address (for example, "Mary Smith and Mental Midget Management, a New York corporation, with its address at 47 Prospect Street, Huntington, NY 11743"). If you are signing only with a management company and not a specific manager, insert only the name of the company. You will not need the optional "Key Person Provision."

Insert your band's name, business form, and address (for example, "Petty Larceny, a general partnership, with its address at 5678 Hempstead Turnpike, Wantagh, NY 11793"). If you are unsure of your business form, review Chapter 2. After that, insert the names of the band members.

Obligations of Manager

This section lists the manager's obligations. These include:

- **Guidance and advice.** Your band may bristle at the idea of someone providing "guidance and advice" as to the proper method of presenting the band's music, but this is exactly what a manager is supposed to be doing—studying your band's performance and the audience's reaction to determine how to make your band more successful.
- **Engagement of services.** A band's arrangement with the manager is almost always exclusive. That is, you can sign with only one manager at a time, and the band cannot make music business deals without the manager. Your band cannot hire another manager until you terminate this relationship. Many managers handle more than one band, and this provision guarantees the manager's right to represent a "stable" of artists.

- **Negotiation and execution of agreements.** This provision provides that the manager oversees every band contract. It does not mean that the manager can sign agreements without your consent. That depends on the "power of attorney" provision, which appears later in the sample agreement.
- **Other obligations.** If your band wants specific tasks to be listed, you can add them here (for example, "Manager will perform regular radio promotion at regional college radio stations for all band recordings").

Key Person Provision

This is an optional provision. If a band prefers to work with only one manager at a management company, that arrangement is sometimes known as a "key man" or "key person" relationship. This provision allows your band to terminate the relationship with the management company (including post-term commissions) if your personal manager is no longer associated with the management company. If you want to name a key person, check the box and fill in that person's name. Otherwise don't check the box and leave the clause blank, or delete the clause altogether.

The Term

This provision (the "term") establishes how long the manager has a job. We recommend that you keep it as short as possible—perhaps one or two years. You can always renew it if the manager is performing successfully. Most managers want a minimum of three years.

As mentioned earlier in this chapter, your band can establish some criteria for keeping the manager. Choose one of the options for the term of the management agreement. Either check the option you want and fill in the blanks or delete the other, unwanted options and fill in the blanks of your choice.

- **Option 1** simply establishes a fixed term for the agreement. Enter the number of years it will last if you choose this option.
- **Option 2** gives the parties a one-year period to determine if the relationship is working before continuing for the full term, which is

presumably longer than one year (most likely three years). Enter the full term in the blank if you choose this option.

- **Option 3** establishes one earning goal that must be reached before renewal. Enter the earning goal if you choose this option.
- **Option 4** sets two yearly earning goals in order for the manager to continue. If you choose this option, enter the earning goals.
- **Option 5** sets a "signing" goal. The manager must obtain a recording contract in order for the manager to continue. Enter the time limit for the manager to secure a record deal if you choose this option.
- **Option 6** is similar to Options 4 and 5. In Options 4 and 5, if the goal is not reached, the agreement is terminated. Option 6 is a "flip" version, using a record deal as a goal. If the goal is reached, then the management agreement is renewed. That is, instead of using the goal as a basis for termination, it's used as a basis for renewal.

Commission During the Term

The standard commission percentage is between 10% and 15% (sometimes as high as 20%). A manager who demands 20% should have a successful track record—otherwise, your band is paying too much. In this agreement, the manager cannot commission the band's income "off the top." Certain payments—generally income that "passes through" the band and is used to pay for crucial band services such as recording expenses—are excluded before the manager gets a cut. Check the exclusions that your band has negotiated.

- **Recording funds advanced by a record company.** A manager should never commission the money received to pay for making recordings (the "recording fund" or "recording advance"). Sometimes the band does not use all of the recording fund to make the recording and the manager may try to commission the surplus. If you decide to allow the manager to commission the surplus, change the language to read as follows: "recording funds advanced by a record company and actually used to create master recordings."
- **Money paid to make videos.** This is "pass-through" income, and it would be unfair for the manager to obtain a commission on it. This should not be commissioned, since the band cannot keep this money.

- **Payments to record producers, website developers, musicians, and so on.** Same as above.

- **Payments to nonband member cowriters or copublishers.** A manager should not commission payments to nonband members who collaborate on songs (see Chapter 7).

- **Tour support.** These payments, made by a record company, are to assist the band in meeting cash shortages while touring. A manager should not commission these payments.

- **Booking agent fees.** Many managers will not agree to this, as they prefer to commission gross revenue before booking agent fees are paid.

- **Payments to opening acts.** Your band, as the headlining act, usually pays the opening band when touring. A manager should not commission these payments.

- **Expenses in connection with promotional and marketing activities and so on.** We recommend that the manager should not commission these independent promotion payments, because promotion is for the benefit of both the band and manager.

- **Income from music publishing and songwriting.** If you have the power to exclude this income from a manager's commission, check this exclusion. If a manager insists on receiving some income from music publishing and songwriting, look at the optional compromise provision below ("Commission on Publishing Income"). Note: If you fill in the optional provision below, you should *not* check this exclusion.

- **Income from any entertainment presentations which manager packages and so on.** We recommend that a manager should not commission income from a manager-owned or controlled production (for example, a packaged tour) as the manager would be paid twice (referred to as "double-dipping"): once from ticket revenues, and once from your band's show income.

- **Payments to nonband member musicians.** This is "pass-through" income, and it would be unfair for the manager to obtain a commission on it.

- **Reimbursements received by band for expenses paid out of gross revenues.** Sometimes, a band must pay for expenses out of its own pocket (such as artwork for an album) and is later reimbursed by the record company. We recommend that the manager not commission these reimbursements.

- **Expenses in connection with establishing a band website.** A band's website is a promotional and communication tool. As such, it benefits both band and manager. If possible, expenses for creating and maintaining the site should not be commissioned.
- **Income from recording studios, acting, and so on.** Band members who earn income from another entertainment source should not allow the manager to commission this income. For example, if a member works as an actor or author, owns a recording studio or a music label, or performs in a side project or produces other artists, that income should not be commissioned.

Commission on Publishing Income

Band members often believe that the success of songwriting has nothing to do with the manager's work. Many managers, on the other hand, believe that songs become popular partly through their work. One possible compromise is to set a management goal. If the manager achieves that goal, then the band will permit the manager to take a commission on the music publishing income. If the manager does not achieve the goal, the band retains all of the publishing income. This way, the manager must prove himself before getting publishing income. If you want to do this, check this provision and fill in the goals and commission rate you and your manager agree to. Note: If you use this provision, you should *not* check the exclusion "income from music publishing and songwriting" in the "Commission During the Term" section above. If you do not use this clause, either leave it blank or delete the clause. For more on music publishing, see Chapter 8.

Commission After the Term

Managers typically earn income from the band *after* their job as manager has ended (sometimes referred to as post-term commissions).

Earlier in this chapter, we suggested a descending system for post-term commissions. This provision allows you to choose the descending rate (such as 20%, 15%, 10%, and 5%) and the periods that each rate will be paid (usually three- or six-month terms). You can negotiate the numbers according to your bargaining power. We have given space for up to four periods over which to descend your commission rate. If you do not use all four, just cross out the remaining language, enter "N/A," or remove the language altogether. After the last period is over, no more payments are due to the manager.

These post-term commission payments will be at the following rates during the specified periods:

    <u>20%</u> of the Gross Revenues from the first <u>six-month</u> period after termination

    <u>10%</u> of the Gross Revenues from the second <u>six-month</u> period after termination

    ~~____% of the Gross Revenues from the third ____-_____ period after termination~~

    ~~____% of the Gross Revenues from the fourth ____-_____ period after termination.~~

    Thereafter, manager will receive no further post-term commissions.

These post-term commission payments will be at the following rates during the specified periods:

    <u>20%</u> of the Gross Revenues from the first <u>three-month</u> period after termination

    <u>15%</u> of the Gross Revenues from the second <u>three-month</u> period after termination

    <u>10%</u> of the Gross Revenues from the third <u>three-month</u> period after termination

    <u>5%</u> % of the Gross Revenues from the fourth <u>three-month</u> period after termination.

    Thereafter, manager will receive no further post-term commissions.

Leaving Member

In Chapter 14, we discuss the "leaving member" provision. If the band breaks up or a member leaves, this provision gives the manager the right to manage the leaving members under the same terms and conditions.

> **EXAMPLE:** Dawn and Joanna leave the group The Bird Feeders. The "leaving member" provision allows their manager to continue managing either of them in their solo career or new musical ventures. In other words, the manager can still earn a percentage of Dawn and Joanna's income.
>
> In order to put some restrictions on the manager's leaving member rights, this member provision is "tied" to the band's recording agreement, if any. That is, if you don't have a record deal or if the record deal doesn't include a leaving member provision, your band would have no obligations.
>
> If any band members are uncomfortable with this provision, they should attempt to strike it completely or have themselves excluded from this provision. Generally the manager seeks to latch on to the songwriter and vocalists in the group, as they tend to be the ones with the most earning potential.

Manager's Expenses

The band is usually obligated to pay the manager's reasonable expenses in promoting the group. This provision sets limits on how much the manager can spend before getting the band's permission. This provision also prevents the band members from becoming personally obligated for management expenses. Feel free to adjust any of the figures in this provision.

Business Manager

The business manager is usually an accountant who acts as a neutral party, dividing up band income and paying band members and the manager.

Mediation; Arbitration

Mediation and arbitration are more efficient and often less expensive methods of resolving disputes than filing a lawsuit. (See Chapter 2 for an explanation of mediation and arbitration.) If you don't want mediation and arbitration, we recommend that you delete this provision.

We suggest that you choose the county, province, or city in which the band resides for arbitration. If all the members do not reside within one area, choose a place that is convenient. Enter your location of choice in the blank.

In several states, there are organizations that specialize in arbitration for people in the arts, such as California Lawyers for the Arts (www.calawyers forthearts.org) and Volunteer Lawyers for the Arts (in New York at www. vlany.org, as well as in other cities and states). You can substitute the rules of one of these organizations for those of the American Arbitration Association in your agreement. If your band is based in Canada, you can still use the AAA's rules, as they perform arbitration in all major Canadian cities. Check one of the choices, or delete the unwanted alternative.

General

The following provisions are standard contractual provisions referred to as boilerplate. Boilerplate provisions are explained in Chapter 2.

In the blank space, insert the state (or province, in the case of Canadian bands) of residence for the band partners. In the event of a dispute, this determines which state law will govern the arbitration or lawsuit.

Signatures

Have all band members and the manager sign and date the agreement. Enter the same address for all the band members: the mailing address for the band. Be sure to use an address that will be able to receive mail for two to three years. If there is no such address, use a post office box or an address for the parents of one of the members.

Tips for Finding an Experienced Manager

- If you open for a popular band and hit it off with the band members, ask them about their management. They may recommend you to their manager.
- If you have a booking agent or attorney, ask them about managers. Music attorneys and booking agents deal with managers on a daily basis and may be able to do some matchmaking.
- If you plan on emailing music tracks to a manager, you should first determine which managers accept unsolicited material. You can find lists of band managers and band management companies on the Internet (type "band management," "band managers directory," or "band managers list" into your search engine). Often these lists indicate which managers accept unsolicited material. Attempt to match your band with a manager who handles similar acts.
- If you are an aggressive, extroverted person, you should consider attending one of the numerous regional industry conventions. Find out which managers will be at the convention and which ones handle bands similar to yours. A listing of industry personnel is often published by the convention, or the managers may be speaking at a special management seminar. You can find lists of music business conferences and conventions on the Internet (type "music industry conference," "music business conference," or "music seminar list" into your search engine).

Management Agreement

Introduction

This Management Agreement is between _____ ("Manager") _____and ("Band"), comprising the following members: _____ ("Band Members"). Band agrees to have Manager serve as its exclusive personal manager.

Obligations of Manager

Manager will use its best efforts to perform the following services:

- **Guidance and Advice.** Manager will give guidance and advice in order to enhance Band's career in the entertainment, music, and related industries. This guidance and advice includes methods of presenting Band's music and talents and the selection and coordination of business managers, accountants, and booking agents who may obtain employment for Band.
- **Engagement of Services.** Manager will serve as Band's exclusive agent for the exploitation and promotion of Band's music services and products throughout the world. Nothing contained in this Agreement limits Manager's right to represent other musicians, bands, or entertainers.
- **Negotiation and Execution of Agreements.** Manager will work in association with Band in the negotiation of recording, merchandising, or other agreements affecting Band.
- **Other Obligations.** *(optional)* _____.

Key Person Provision *(Check if applicable and fill in blank)*

☐ _____ ("Key Person") of Manager's company will directly oversee the day-to-day performance of its services under this Agreement. In the event that Key Person is not directly involved in the day-to-day activities, Band is entitled to terminate the management relationship.

The Term

The term of this Agreement will continue for *(check one)*:

☐ _____ years after the date of execution of this Agreement.

☐ _____ years after the date of execution of this Agreement, except that either party may terminate the Agreement within one year of the date of execution by sending written notice to the other party.

☐ _____ years after the date of execution of this Agreement, except that Band may terminate this Agreement at the end of any year if the Band fails to earn gross income (as defined in this Agreement) of at least $_____ during that year.

☐ _____ years after the date of execution of this Agreement, except that Band may terminate this Agreement at the end of any year if the Band fails to earn gross income (as defined in this Agreement), according to the following schedule: (a) at least $_____ during the first year of the Management Agreement; or (b) at least $_____ during the second year of the Management Agreement.

☐ _____ years after the date of execution of this Agreement, except that Band may terminate this Agreement if the Band has failed to sign a record agreement with a major label within _____ years of signing this Agreement.

☐ _____ years after the date of execution of this Agreement, and Band agrees to renew the Agreement under the same terms and conditions for an additional two years if the Band has signed a recording agreement with a major label within _____ years of the execution of this Agreement.

Commission During the Term

Manager is entitled to _____ % of Gross Revenues received by Band during the term. "Gross Revenues" is all money including advances and fees received by Band in connection with Band's entertainment-related activities, but excluding:

(Check if excluded)

☐ recording funds advanced by a record company

☐ money paid to make videos

☐ payments to record producers, musicians, mixers, remixers, directors, website developers, engineers, or any other individuals involved in the creation of audio or audiovisual recordings

☐ payments to nonband-member cowriters or copublishers

☐ tour support

- ☐ booking agent fees
- ☐ payments to opening acts
- ☐ expenses in connection with promotional and marketing activities and independent promotion, marketing, or publicity
- ☐ income from music publishing and songwriting
- ☐ income from any entertainment presentations that Manager packages or presents and for which Manager receives a portion of the ticket revenues for packaging or presenting the event
- ☐ payments to nonband-member musicians
- ☐ any reimbursements received by Band for expenses paid out of Gross Revenues
- ☐ payments for Band website creation and maintenance
- ☐ income from recording studios, acting, or other entertainment or other nonband sources of revenue.

Commission on Publishing Income (*Check if applicable and fill in blanks*)

☐ Manager is not entitled to commission on revenue from music publishing in any year of the Term unless Band has received Gross Revenues in that year in excess of $_____ (the "Publishing Cap"). In the event the Publishing Cap is reached, Manager is due _____ % of the Band's publishing income paid that year. In no event shall Manager take a commission on: (a) what is commonly known as the "writer's share" of the songwriting; (b) performance royalties from BMI or ASCAP; (c) any royalties from synchronization rights other than for Band videos; or (d) cover recordings by other artists.

Commission After the Term

Unless Manager has been terminated for a material breach of this Agreement, Manager is entitled to post-term commission payments on any type of income that was subject to commission during the term. Under no circumstances is Manager entitled to income from albums or videos created before or after the Term.

These post-term commission payments will be at the following rates during the specified periods:

_____% of the Gross Revenues from the first _____ period after termination

_____% of the Gross Revenues from the second _____ period after termination

_____% of the Gross Revenues from the third _____ period after termination

_____% of the Gross Revenues from the fourth _____ period after termination.

Thereafter, Manager will receive no further post-term commissions.

Leaving Member

The terms and conditions of this Agreement will continue to apply only for the remainder of the Term and only with respect to the services of any member of Band whose recording services are retained by a record company under the "leaving member" provisions of any recording contract entered into by Band during the Term.

Manager's Expenses

Band will pay documented reasonable and necessary costs incurred by Manager in connection with Manager's duties on behalf of Band. Band will only pay such expenses out of Gross Revenues subject to commission under this Agreement, and no member of Band is personally liable for any such expenses. Manager must not incur expenses in excess of $200 in any single transaction, or $1,000 during any calendar month, without Band's prior written consent. If Manager's expenses are incurred in connection with its services to other clients of Manager, the expenses must be prorated between Band and Manager's other clients based on the amount of time Manager rendered its services on behalf of Band and other clients. Under no circumstances will Manager's overhead be characterized as expenses reimbursable by Band.

Business Manager

All Gross Revenues subject to commission under this Agreement will be collected by an accountant or business manager experienced in the music business and designated by Band after consultation with Manager.

Power of Attorney

During the Term, Manager will have a special power of attorney to execute standard performance contracts relating to any live performance agreement during any touring period approved in writing by Band, provided that Manager uses reasonable good faith efforts to submit these contracts to Band for execution.

Not Theatrical or Talent Agency

It is understood and agreed that Manager is not licensed as a theatrical artist agency or talent agency and will not perform services that require a professional license.

Mediation; Arbitration

If a dispute arises under this Agreement, the parties agree to first try to resolve the dispute with the help of a mutually agreed-on mediator in _____.
Any costs and fees other than attorney fees will be shared equally by the parties. If it is impossible to arrive at a mutually satisfactory solution within a reasonable time, the parties agree to submit the dispute to binding arbitration in the same city or region, conducted on a confidential basis under:

☐ the Commercial Arbitration Rules of the American Arbitration Association, or

☐ the rules of _____ .

Any decision or award as a result of any such arbitration proceeding will include the assessment of costs, expenses, and reasonable attorneys' fees and a written determination by the arbitrators. Absent an agreement to the contrary, any arbitration will be conducted by an arbitrator experienced in music industry law. An award of arbitration is final and binding on the Band Partners and may be confirmed in a court of competent jurisdiction. The prevailing party has the right to collect from the other party its reasonable costs and attorney fees incurred in enforcing this agreement.

General

Nothing contained in this Agreement is meant to establish either Manager or Band a partner, joint venturer, or employee of the other party for any purpose. This Agreement may not be amended except in a writing signed by both parties. No waiver by either party of any right will be construed as a waiver of any other right. If a court finds any provision of this Agreement invalid or unenforceable as applied to any circumstance, the remainder of this Agreement will be interpreted to best carry out the intent of the parties. This Agreement is governed by and interpreted in accordance with the laws of the State of _____ . This Agreement expresses the complete understanding of the parties with respect to the subject matter and supersedes all prior proposals, agreements, representations, and understandings. Notices required under this Agreement can be sent to the parties at the addresses provided below. In the event of any dispute arising from or related to this Agreement, the prevailing party is entitled to attorneys' fees.

If these terms and conditions are agreeable, please sign and execute both copies of this Agreement and return one copy to Manager.

Band Members

Band Member Signature _____

Address _____

_____

Date _____

Soc. Sec. # _____

Band Member Signature _____

Address _____

_____

Date _____

Soc. Sec. # _____

Band Member Signature _____

Address _____

_____

Date _____

Soc. Sec. # _____

Band Member Signature _____

Address _____

_____

Date _____

Soc. Sec. # _____

Manager

Band Manager Signature _____

Address _____

_____

Date _____

Soc. Sec. # _____

Variations on Management Arrangements

There are many variations on management agreements. For example, Jon Landau, who manages Bruce Springsteen, is also Springsteen's record producer and is personally involved in what ends up on his albums. Sometimes a band member manages the band. For example, Elvis's first manager was a member of his backup band. Below, we discuss some of the variations on management agreements.

Member-Managed Bands

Except for a major label signing, a band does not have to hire a manager and can probably manage itself (we will refer to this situation as a "member-managed" band). The difficulty with member-management is usually finding someone in the band who is willing to handle the business side of things (it's probably the person who is reading this book!). The member-manager carries a double load—performing and managing—and is usually not compensated for management duties.

Here are some suggestions for a member-managed band:

- Have only one member-manager, because, as a general rule, having several persons in the band handling business doesn't work.
- Provide incentives for member-management, such as offering 5% or 10% of show income for booking gigs.
- Have regular meetings to discuss current band business; otherwise, band members may feel out of the loop.
- Hire a manager if member-management is not working out. It's better to pay someone 15% than have your band break up over member-management problems.

Producer/Manager Deals

Some bands sign production company/management agreements or production company/management/music publishing arrangements. Under these arrangements, the band signs with a company that manages the band, produces recordings, and also owns a piece of the band's music publishing. This "Swiss Army knife" approach, in which your band puts three different functions in the hands of one company, was initially popular in country and rap music but now includes all genres of music (and is sometimes referred to as a "360 deal"). It is also used by successful record producers who have a knack for producing popular recordings and want a piece of the resulting publishing income.

These agreements require an enormous amount of trust, because the band is picking a manager, a producer, and a music publisher all in one shot. As a rule of thumb, you should disregard the deal completely if the production/management company has not had any previous success (for example, has never placed a record on the *Billboard* charts). You should also attempt to speak with any other artists handled by the same production/management company to find out what it's like working with the company.

Attorney/Management Deals

If your manager is an attorney, there is a potential problem if the manager is giving you legal advice such as reviewing your band's recording agreement. The attorney/manager's advice may be influenced by the potential commission, not by a desire to protect the band. For example, an attorney/manager may agree to less favorable terms and conditions in order to get the deal done quickly—that is, to receive the management commission. It is always better to have an attorney who is not your manager (or your manager's attorney) look over your band's recording agreement.

4

Attorneys

Locating, Hiring, and Firing an Attorney

The first step in finding an entertainment attorney is to be sure you know what you want to accomplish. "This sounds obvious," said one music business attorney, "but every lawyer has had the experience of being interviewed by a band that has heard that they need an entertainment lawyer, but have no idea what they want that lawyer to accomplish." Therefore, before you begin your search, have a discussion with your band members as to exactly why you need an attorney.

> **RESOURCE**
>
> **When you have a legal question (such as whether a minor can sign a contract or whether you can deduct the cost of driving to a gig), you can often get a fast and inexpensive (sometimes free) answer by using an ask-a-lawyer service.** Some of these providers, like JustAnswer (www.justanswer.com), are only in the business of answering questions. Others, like Avvo (www.Avvo.com) and Justia (www.justia.com), use a "free" Q&A process to connect lawyers with potential client leads. Whichever service you use, make sure the company only uses lawyers. (The home page should have a link or disclaimer explaining how the service works and who answers the questions.) If you want to keep your Q&A confidential, you'll probably have to pay for the answer, because nonfee services typically post the questions and answers.

Locating an Attorney

The best way to locate an attorney is through referrals from other bands. It is also possible to locate, interview, and hire a music attorney through the many online legal directories. Nolo (www.nolo.com), the publisher of this book, operates a directory, as does Avvo (www.avvo.com), LegalMatch (www.legalmatch.com), and many other online services. Many of these directory services permit you to interview two or three attorneys for free or at a reduced hourly rate.

The Volunteer Lawyers for the Arts in New York City (www.vlany.org) maintains a national directory of various organizations offering legal assistance for musicians. You should always be aware that directories, referral services, and bar associations cannot guarantee the quality of the attorney's services.

How to Interview an Attorney

"Once you know what you need," a music business attorney told us, "then, the first questions you will ask prospective lawyers will have to do with the specific job at hand." For example, do you need advice reviewing and negotiating a contract, protecting the band name or song copyrights, or shopping a tape to managers or to record companies? "Unless the attorney has a solid reputation in the music community as an entertainment lawyer," the attorney told us, "ask whether he is experienced in that specific type of work. Get a feeling for his experience level by asking what other bands in your genre he represents, and what he has done for them. If you are determined to achieve a specific result (for example, changing the seven-record deal you've been offered into a two-record deal), discuss whether he believes your expectations are realistic. If you are looking for someone to shop your tape, ask which bands he has succeeded in placing. Also ask questions such as 'Will you return all of our phone calls personally?' 'What record executives or record labels do you represent?' 'Do you represent other bands on the label that wants to sign us?' 'How long will it take you to get us a first draft of a contract?' 'Have you listened to the tape we sent you?'"

Talking About Money

After you have discussed the legal tasks required, it's time to start talking about money. You should understand up front that most attorneys bill an hourly fee of $200 to $400 an hour and send a bill at the end of each month. Some attorneys bill on a fixed-fee basis in which your band pays a set fee for services (expect to pay $5,000 to $25,000 to negotiate a major label deal). Most attorneys ask for a retainer, which is an advance payment for legal work (see "What Is a Retainer?" below). The amount of the retainer is included in the attorney-client fee agreement.

You and your lawyer will negotiate the fee agreement, which establishes the payments and the lawyer's responsibilities. Read it and understand your rights as a client. If you sign a fee agreement, be sure to include a provision stating you have the right to drop your attorney at any time. (In many states, such as California, a client always has the right to terminate the attorney for any reason or no reason.)

Don't be shy about billing. It's important for all concerned to know whether you can afford the services. Ask how charges are calculated, and what the estimated cost for the job at hand will be. Is a retainer required? If the lawyer bills by the hour, ask if you can get a cap on the price in case negotiations are unusually protracted. Find out if you can use a credit card, or pay over several months, and whether interest will be charged if your payments are late. Be sure you will be provided with a written retainer letter outlining payment terms.

Beware, however: Some attorneys in the music business use unique billing systems. An attorney may, for example, charge the band a percentage of the "value" of a deal. This "value billing" system is an unpredictable combination of hocus-pocus and greed. Only the powerhouse firms engage in value billing. Beware of attorneys who may attempt to switch to value billing during the period of legal representation. Every lawyer should provide a retainer letter up front saying how charges will be calculated.

Below are some billing tips that will help protect your band:

- **Understand exactly how you're being billed.** In your initial meeting with the attorney, ask how you are being billed. If you are billed on an hourly system, find out the increments. For example, some attorneys charge a minimum of one-quarter of an hour (15 minutes) for a phone call, no matter how short the conversation.

- **Watch out for hidden expenses.** Find out what costs and expenses you must pay other than the fees for the lawyer's work, such as costs for copies or faxes, travel expenses, or court costs. Watch out if your attorney wants to bill for services such as "word processing" or "administrative services." This often means you will be paying the administrative assistant's salary.

- **See if you can avoid hourly rates.** If you can, get your attorney to agree to fixed fees for certain work rather than hourly billings. For example, if your attorney is negotiating a merchandising deal, get a flat rate for the whole job. That way you'll know exactly what to expect. If you can't get fixed billings, ask your attorney to estimate fees for work and ask for an explanation if the bill exceeds the estimate.

- **Review billings carefully.** Billings should be prompt and clear. Do not accept summary billings (for instance, one sentence such as "litigation work"). Every item should be explained with rate and hours worked, including fractions. Late billings are not acceptable, especially in litigation. When you get bills you don't understand, ask the attorney for an explanation—and request that the attorney not bill you for the explanation.

What Is a Retainer?

A retainer is an advance payment to an attorney. The attorney places the retainer in a bank account (in some states, this must be an interest-bearing account) and deducts money from the account at the end of each month to pay your bill. When the money is depleted, the attorney may ask for a new retainer. If the retainer is not used up at the end of the services, the attorney must return what's left. The amount of the retainer usually depends on the project.

For example, retainers for litigation are typically between $2,000 and $5,000. Some attorneys use the term "retainer" to refer to a monthly fee that the attorney gets regardless whether any legal services are performed. In other words, you are paying a monthly fee just to keep the attorney available to you. We recommend you avoid this type of arrangement.

Power of Attorney

When your band grants a "power of attorney" to the manager, the manager has legal authority to act on your behalf. A "special power of attorney" (also known as a "limited power of attorney") allows the manager to handle specific tasks incurred in the daily business, such as signing booking contracts and endorsing checks. A "general power of attorney" is much broader and allows the manager to sue people on your behalf or bind the band to long-term contracts.

We recommend that you grant the manager only a special power of attorney and list the activities that are permitted. This provision allows the manager to sign touring contracts and requires that the manager make a good faith effort to show the contract to the band for its signature first. In addition, the manager cannot book the band until the band has designated the periods when it will tour.

Not Theatrical or Talent Agency

This provision is primarily for the benefit of the manager. Four states—California, Florida, New York, and Massachusetts—have laws known as "talent agent laws" that require a license for anyone who obtains employment for an entertainer. For example, a booking agent who obtains a series of concerts for a band or a talent agent who obtains a movie part for a band would have to be licensed under these laws. Other state laws may govern the activities of an agent—see the NAPAMA website (www.napama.org).

There are some exceptions. For example, in California, a person does not need a license to obtain a record deal on behalf of a musician. In New York, a person does not need to be licensed to perform incidental booking (for example, a special record company showcase). Because these laws vary and the exceptions are not always interpreted in the same manner, most managers want to make it clear that they are not acting as talent agents. That's why this provision is inserted. Regardless of the contract provision, if a manager violates the law and engages in the booking business, the manager would be subject to the talent agency laws.

Attorney Style

Choosing an attorney is also a matter of style. Your band may prefer to be represented by an attorney whose style and demeanor correspond with the band's approach. Among those factors that a band may consider when determining style are whether the attorney has clout in the industry; whether the attorney understands the band's music; whether the attorney is aggressive, ethical, knowledgeable, affordable, and impresses friends or terrifies adversaries. After you talk to a number of different lawyers, you can take a band vote on which feels the most right for you. You'll probably wind up hiring the one with whom you obviously click.

Three Tips for Saving Money With Your Attorney

It's common for a band to feel overwhelmed by a lawyer's bill. Often, that's because the band is not using the attorney's services efficiently. To get the most bang for your legal buck, you need to be organized. Disorganization is unprofessional and can kill careers. Here are some tips for saving money with an attorney:

- **Elect a contact person.** Elect one member to be the "contact person" with the attorney, to ask questions and relay information to the rest of the band. Lawyers charge for telephone time, so don't duplicate your effort. The contact person should keep a written list of "questions for the lawyer," ask them all in one telephone call, and take notes on the answers. Because many lawyers charge in 15-minute increments, five three-minute questions will cost the same as one five-minute question.
- **Keep track of documents.** Documentation is the heart of legal work, and your band needs to have a system to keep track of the papers. Buy a filing cabinet or accordion folder just for band business. Put that folder in the hands of the person in the band who has the neatest bedroom. Place all important papers in this file and nowhere else. Put a copy of all lawyer correspondence, copyright registration papers, and contracts in the file in a well-organized manner, where you can refer to them or produce them if a new lawyer ever needs them. Duplicating records costs money.

- **Prepare for attorney meetings.** Have a band meeting an hour before a meeting at the lawyer's office. Make a written list of any questions or problems you need to cover during the meeting. Travel to the meeting together, so that you aren't billed for time spent reexplaining things to the band member who arrives a half-hour late.

Evaluating Your Attorney's Services

How do you know if your lawyer is doing a good job? Generally the measurement of a professional's performance (whether it is a doctor, lawyer, or dentist) is that he or she:

- provides you with accurate and understandable advice
- permits you to make informed decisions as to how to proceed, and
- works with you to efficiently resolve conflicts and solve problems.

If your attorney is not fulfilling all three of these requirements, then there is a problem in the attorney-client relationship. For example, there is generally a problem if:

- your attorney is not returning phone calls within 48 hours
- your bills are disproportionate to what the attorney predicted and there is no plausible explanation, or
- you are unable to understand why your attorney is doing things or your attorney talks down to you.

As a general rule, if you leave the lawyer's office confused or unclear of your course of action, there is a problem. After all, the primary purpose of an attorney is to counsel you as to your legal options. If you don't understand these options, the attorney has failed. This doesn't mean that the lawyer will always present a black-and-white explanation. There are many gray areas in the law. For example, the law regarding band names is often murky. However, a good attorney will explain this murkiness and evaluate your chances if there is a dispute over the use of a name.

It's sometimes hard to judge the quality of the work an attorney is doing. However, at a minimum, your lawyer should return your phone calls (or have an associate or an assistant deal with them) within one business day, or two at the most. If the lawyer doesn't, you should get a new lawyer. Your attorney should be taking the time to carefully explain the deals you are signing in language that you can understand. You should also receive regular progress reports on your band matters, if you ask for them. If weeks are passing without any apparent progress, there should be a legitimate explanation for the delay. "I've been too busy to get to it" is not a legitimate explanation.

Firing Your Attorney

A band doesn't have to love its attorney, but the members should respect and trust the attorney's abilities as a hired professional. As a general rule, you should switch attorneys if you are unhappy with your lawyer's services. Switching attorneys means that you fire one attorney and hire another. However, since switching attorneys is a nuisance and your band may lose time and money, you should carefully discuss the situation with your band.

How do you fire an attorney? You should notify the attorney by letter that you are terminating services and that you want your files returned. The attorney will probably retain a copy of your files and return the originals to you. You may be asked to pay any outstanding bills. However, an attorney cannot withhold your files because you have failed to pay your bills.

If your attorney is representing you to a third party (for example, to a record company), you should notify the third party that you are no longer working with the attorney and that future correspondence should be sent to you (at least until you retain a new attorney).

The easiest way to switch attorneys is to find a new attorney and ask the old attorney to send the file to the new attorney. In that case, before terminating your current attorney you would have another attorney prepared to take over any outstanding legal work.

How to Avoid Getting Screwed by Your Attorney

Sadly, there are a number of common situations that result in disputes between bands and their lawyers. The best way to protect yourself from an ugly dispute with an attorney is to approach all relationships with lawyers carefully and anticipate problems before they catch you.

Situation #1:
A contract negotiation goes on forever.
Lawyers' fees can quickly get out of control if negotiations for recording or other contracts drag on too long. During this time a band may be missing other, better opportunities or simply paying too much for legal fees.

How to avoid getting screwed:
It's normal for recording contracts to go through many drafts to correct errors and ensure the language is exactly how everyone wants it. While it would be foolish to rush into signing a contract without examining it carefully and making appropriate changes, you also don't want the revision process to go on forever. As long as you and your attorney are conscientious, the fewer drafts, the better. It is common for major label record deals to take three to four months to negotiate. Indie deals should take less—usually under two months.

Make sure your band and the attorney are in agreement as to the goals of the contract negotiation. For example, if getting a guaranteed two-record deal is most important, tell your lawyer that is your number-one priority. Once you have achieved most or all of your goals, then be flexible on remaining issues so that you can save time.

Situation #2:
A lawsuit goes on forever.
If you are involved in a dispute that's made it to litigation, it may take months or years to resolve. Some lawsuits, such as the Jefferson Airplane's dispute with its former manager, can go on for decades. During the dispute, the Airplane's record company, RCA, refused to pay over $1.3 million in royalties and $700,000 in interest to the band, claiming it could not make the payment unless the management problems were resolved. After 20 years, a San Francisco judge finally ended the lawsuits, and the record company was required to make the payment. As you can imagine, bands can easily get buried in legal fees during even a medium-length lawsuit. Plus, during the period of the dispute the band may be under legal restrictions that cut into its profit-making ability—such as a ban on using a name or releasing a new recording.

How to avoid getting screwed:

Beware of litigation! One lawsuit can easily cost $10,000 to $50,000, and often the only ones who profit are the lawyers. If you're in a dispute, before screaming "I'll see you in court!" ask your attorney for a realistic assessment of your odds and the potential costs. The assessment and underlying reasoning should be in plain English. If a lawyer can't explain your situation clearly to you, he or she won't be able to explain it clearly to a judge or jury.

Also ask your attorney about alternative dispute resolution methods such as arbitration and mediation. Often these procedures can save money and are generally much faster than litigation. Mediation is a procedure in which a neutral person, experienced in resolving disputes, helps the parties find a solution. The mediator doesn't make a decision or ruling; the mediator only helps the parties settle their controversy. Arbitration is similar to mediation except that the arbitrator makes a decision that is binding on the parties. In some states there are organizations that specialize in these alternative dispute resolution procedures, such as California Lawyers for the Arts and the Volunteer Lawyers for the Arts.

Situation #3:
Your lawyer represents both sides in a negotiation and you feel like you got screwed.

Lawyers are bound by ethical rules to disclose if there is a potential conflict of interest. A conflict of interest occurs whenever the lawyer represents adverse interests—for example, if your attorney also represents your record company or manager. When there is a conflict of interest, there is the potential that your attorney may not battle as forcefully for your position. For example, if the attorney represents you and a record label, it is possible that the attorney will be apprehensive of endangering a lucrative relationship with the record label for the sake of your band. Another danger is that the attorney you use may enter into an unethical relationship with a band's manager or record company. For example, Billy Joel sued his former attorneys, alleging that the attorneys gave his manager payoffs and kickbacks. Evidence surfaced that the attorneys had loaned money to Joel's manager to buy a racehorse (which allegedly was killed to recover insurance money). The attorneys denied all of Joel's allegations, and the case was eventually settled.

How to avoid getting screwed:

Attorneys should disclose a conflict without being asked, but they don't always do so. Always ask your attorney if there is a potential conflict. Always investigate possible conflicts. If there is a conflict, discuss the matter with bandmates. It's possible that an attorney can vigorously represent both your interests despite a potential conflict of interest. This is a judgment call that should be made based on your feeling for the attorney and any other information you have obtained, such as references from other clients.

Many bands proceed in the face of a potential conflict because they have faith in their attorney's ability to protect the band's interests and perhaps because they believe that such so-called conflicts can be helpful. Keep in mind that many people shop for a lawyer because he or she has conflicts (also known in our business as "relationships"). These relationships can be great and provide otherwise unavailable access, until they become a double-edged sword.

If your band wants to proceed, your attorney may furnish you with a waiver in which the band gives up any right to complain about the situation later. The waiver is used to protect the attorney from a malpractice claim. You don't have to sign the waiver, but the attorney will probably not go ahead if you don't sign it. If your band does not want to sign, find a different attorney.

Having an Attorney Shop Your Music

Some entertainment attorneys shop the band's music to record labels and music publishers. (Nonattorneys also shop music; see "Label-Shopping Agreements and Lawyers," below.) These "shoppers" use their industry connections to obtain deals for the band and are paid with a percentage of the band's income from the deal (typically 5% to 10%). This is referred to as a label-shopping deal, and the income may continue for the life of the deal, or for a limited period of time, depending on the arrangement with the attorney.

For example, an attorney may shop your band's music around and draft your contract in return for a percentage of the band's income from that deal. The attorney may charge $5,000 plus 5% of your record deal. Every time your band receives a payment from the record deal, the attorney would receive 5%. Your band may have to continue paying this percentage even after you switch attorneys.

Label-Shopping Agreements and Lawyers

You might wonder why we discuss "label-shopping agreements" only with reference to lawyers, when in fact nonlawyers can—and often do—perform the task of shopping your band's music for you. The answer is really just a matter of terminology. When a nonattorney manager shops your tapes, that's just part of his job, so the band doesn't execute a specific label-shopping agreement for that job. A separate agreement isn't usually necessary, because shopping music is most likely part of the management agreement, and is probably one of the main reasons the band hired the manager in the first place. But while it's at the heart of a manager's job to try to secure record deals for your band, attorneys usually have a different role with a band. Shopping music isn't generally part of an attorney's job description, so separate shopping agreements are necessary.

You may wonder why attorneys shop music. After all, this is not a task that requires a legal education—managers and bands themselves often perform the same function. The reason is that attorneys have assumed a unique position of power in the music business: They're well connected and have knowledge about contracts. Since many labels are run by attorneys, this creates a situation that many musicians find very depressing—attorneys shopping music to other attorneys. After all, where are the people who are passionate about music? Unfortunately, you will have to put aside such concerns and accept music shopping by attorneys as a business reality.

On the other hand, some attorneys report that less importance is now placed on music-shopping arrangements. That's because, as one lawyer told us, "[Labels] have discovered what pathetic taste most lawyers have. Therefore, they don't pay much attention to the music that lawyers send in unless there's some other evidence that the band has something going for it."

What Should You Pay for Label Shopping?

There are several important variables when determining how much to pay a label shopper:

- the size of the percentage
- what deductions are made before the percentage is calculated, and
- whether there is a limit as to how much the shopper receives.

Shoppers traditionally receive 5% to 10% of the record deal, with most deals closer to 10%. Sometimes (but usually not often) a band can make certain deductions before the percentage is calculated. For example, if the label is advancing $50,000 to the band to make a video, the band should try to exclude such payments from the shopper's income. As you can see, the issue of deductions and commissions affects label-shopping agreements in the same way that it affects management agreements (see Chapter 3).

The total amount to be paid to the shopper is also an important factor. Many shopping arrangements are for the length of the record deal. Therefore, if you sign a six-record contract, each time your band receives an advance, the person who shopped the music would get a cut. For that reason, some bands attempt to limit the total payments by placing a limit or "cap" on the money paid to the shopper. For example, your agreement could give the attorney 5% of the income from the record deal up to $20,000. After that, the attorney would receive no more of the payments.

Sometimes the decision of how much is fair is based on the band's circumstances. As one attorney explained, "If a band has never played anywhere besides the drummer's garage and they find a lawyer who procures a major label deal based on a demo, I would say that 5% over the life of the deal would be a bargain. On the other hand, if they've already sold 5,000 units of their [do-it-yourself] record in their hometown, it's a complete rip-off."

Potential Pitfalls of Label-Shopping Arrangements

Label shopping used to be a function of the band's manager, but the lines between managers and attorneys have blurred in the past two decades. There is often a large gray area between managers and attorneys—some managers are lawyers, and some lawyers perform management functions. In the past, when the functions were always separate, a band could use the attorney and the manager as a system of checks and balances. That is, the attorney could review the management agreement on behalf of the band, or the manager could advise the band when to switch attorneys.

Whether the same person should perform both functions is a matter that your band must decide based on your knowledge of—and trust in— the attorney. It can be a boon for musicians who can save money on legal bills, but it can also be a risky proposition, particularly when the manager/ attorney is getting a percentage of a record deal. Why? Because whenever the manager/attorney is getting a percentage of the deal, there is always the possibility that the band won't get the same impartial legal advice as they would if they retained a separate attorney who was paid on an hourly basis. As is often the case in the music industry, it comes down to greed. An attorney who is getting a percentage of a record deal may forgo other contract considerations (such as length of the contract or song ownership) in order to get the highest possible payments.

As you can see, potentially sticky issues may arise when an attorney shops a demo. Consider the following potential situations:

- **The attorney does not take a personal interest in your band's career.** Sometimes, an attorney who shops music does not use discretion. The attorney simply dumps demos with many record companies in the hopes that one of them connects.

- **The attorney has a conflicting interest.** Since the attorney is earning a percentage from the deal, it is possible that the attorney's major concern is the size of the advance. Your band may have other priorities, such as obtaining a higher royalty rate, getting a guaranteed second record, or getting a good royalty rate for songs written by the band (referred to as "controlled compositions" and discussed in Chapters 8 and 14).

- **The attorney mixes business and legal services.** When an attorney performs nonattorney services, such as shopping music, the attorney is mixing legal and nonlegal services. In some states, such as California, the law requires that before an attorney enters into such a relationship, the client must be advised in writing to seek the advice of another (independent) attorney and that the terms of the business arrangement must be in writing and should be in a manner which "should reasonably have been understood" by the client. In other words, you should understand everything you sign and, if necessary, seek independent advice.

- **The band overpays for the shopping services.** The attorney may continue to earn a percentage of the band's income for years—even after the band breaks up. This sum may be unfair in proportion to the services performed by the attorney.

Musicians should also be aware that most states have rules that prohibit attorneys from "soliciting" business. "So if a lawyer calls you, or comes charging into the dressing room after a gig with a fist full of business cards, check him out carefully," warns one attorney we spoke with. "Interview a few other attorneys before you make up your mind. By the time that happens, you will have come too far to risk trusting your progress to someone unsavory."

Despite these potential problems, attorney-shopping agreements are still common in the record business. It is difficult for bands to obtain access to record companies, and an attorney may be the only available means of entry.

Label-Shopping Agreement

We have drafted a model label-shopping agreement that includes some provisions that will protect your band. The agreement we have provided can also be used if someone besides an attorney is shopping your music. For that reason we have chosen to use the term "representative" rather than attorney.

The following instructions explain how to fill out the label-shopping agreement and what the various clauses mean. Many clauses have alternative provisions for you to choose from, which are explained in the instructions. Some clauses, as noted in the instructions, are optional altogether. A sample appears below. You can modify the form agreement to fit your needs.

 FORMS

You can download this form (and all other forms in this book) from Nolo.com; for details, see "Get Forms, Updates, and More at This Book's Companion Page," in the appendix.

Introduction

Insert the name and address of the representative. If the representative is an attorney, you can also indicate where the attorney is licensed to practice (for example, "Gilbert Grand, an attorney licensed to practice in the State of California, whose address is 34 West Pier #103, Sausalito, California").

Insert your band's name, its business form and mailing address, and the names of all the members.

Obligations of Representative

This section establishes some basic responsibilities of the representative.

- **Representation.** Most representatives will want the exclusive right to solicit on behalf of your band. This is reasonable so the representative doesn't have to worry about being undermined by another representative.
- **Solicitations and Reports.** This clause establishes that the representative must give you written reports on whom he or she has solicited. *It is crucial that the representative furnishes your band with proof of each solicitation.* As you will see later in this agreement, the proof of solicitation may make a difference as to whether your band has to pay the representative. For example, say this label-shopping agreement ends and, on your own, your band solicits and obtains a deal with a record company. If your former representative suddenly appears and claims a piece of the deal, you could quickly find yourselves in an ugly dispute. Under a later provision in our label-shopping agreement, the representative would be entitled to a cut only if he or she could prove a direct solicitation with the record company *and* that your new deal occurred within a specific number of months after the end of the agreement. *Watch out for language that allows the representative to get a cut of any deal regardless of whether the representative solicited the company.*

Percentage Payments and Cap

This section establishes the payment structure between the band and the representative. We strongly recommend using Alternative A, which caps the payment at a specified amount. Many representatives, however, will not accept that provision and will insist instead that the representative should be entitled to income from any deal that is made during the six-month term of the label-shopping agreement. If the representative refuses to agree to a payment cap, use Alternative B, with a lower percentage commission. Check and fill in the alternative you want to use, or delete the unwanted alternative altogether.

- **Alternative A—Payment Cap.** Under this payment system, the representative's payment is capped. A payment cap prevents the rep from earning an unfair amount, because after a certain amount (the "Representative Band Income Cap"), the payments will stop. We recommend a commission percentage of 10% or less, and a cap somewhere between $10,000 to $20,000. The exact numbers you're able to negotiate will depend on the bargaining power of your band and the representative.
- **Alternative B—Continuing Payments.** If the representative is unwilling to agree to the payment cap, you may agree to pay the representative a continuing payment, in which case you should use Alternative B. In the case of continuing payments with no cap, 5% is a typical and fair amount.

Exclusions From Representative Band Income

The representative should not get a percentage of certain band income that is categorized as "pass-through income." Generally speaking, pass-through income is money that the band uses for crucial expenses such as recording costs or payments to nonband musicians. These costs should be subtracted from the band's income before the representative takes his or her commission. Check the costs that will be deducted from the band's income before the representative calculates a commission. The number of exclusions you're able to get the representative to agree to will depend on your bargaining power.

Payments to Business Manager

If your band has a business manager, that person will be in charge of receiving money on behalf of the band and distributing it to the appropriate people. This clause simply notes that a business manager may be in charge of collecting income from record labels and making payments to the representative. Check this clause if you have a business manager; otherwise leave it blank or delete it altogether.

Costs and Expenses

The band is usually required to pay the representative's reasonable expenses. This provision sets limits on how much the representative can spend before getting the band's permission.

Disclaimer

This is a standard disclaimer telling the band that the representative can't guarantee a deal.

Term

We recommend a six-month term, as that should provide sufficient time for a representative to contact music companies. You may, however, enter a different term length.

Termination

Either party can terminate the agreement, but there are financial consequences for the band if it terminates prior to the end of the term—specifically, that the band will have to pay the value of the representative's services.

- **Termination by Representative.** If the representative terminates, your band has no obligation to pay for his or her services.
- **Termination by the Band.** If your band terminates the agreement early, you'll have to pay the "value of his or her services." If a representative

At some point in your band's career, you may find yourself sitting in an attorney's waiting room preparing to hire someone who charges more per hour than your band earns in one night. Perhaps your band has been threatened with a lawsuit, or perhaps you need help negotiating a contract.

How do you choose an attorney? And if things don't work out, how do you fire one? In this chapter we will prepare you for dealing with attorneys. We will help you find, evaluate, and fire an attorney, and we will also discuss what to do about issues such as large legal bills, unending lawsuits, and terminal contract negotiations.

Entertainment Attorneys

When it comes to music attorneys, one size does *not* fit all. Your band's choice of an attorney usually depends on the situation. The most common reason that a band hires a lawyer is to review, draft, or negotiate a contract. To some extent, we have made that task easier by providing you with background contract information in this book. However, there may be situations where your band needs more legal help—and in that case you would seek an attorney knowledgeable in negotiating entertainment contracts. This type of attorney is often referred to as an entertainment attorney or a music attorney.

However, there are different types of entertainment lawyers. Some of them only negotiate contracts; some only handle lawsuits between entertainers and companies; and some are in the business of shopping music. (Shopping is the process of soliciting labels on behalf of a band.) Some attorneys perform all of these functions and more. We will walk you through the procedure of finding the entertainment attorney that is right for your band.

Often a band maintains an ongoing relationship with an entertainment lawyer (much like a patient with a family doctor), and if special problems arise, such as tax problems, criminal charges, or bankruptcy, the entertainment attorney will help the band find a specialist. For example, if a band faces a lawsuit, the entertainment attorney can help the band find a lawyer who specializes in litigation (a litigator).

is an attorney, that person may wish to set the value of those services at his or her usual hourly billing rate—which for attorneys is often between $200 and $400. We recommend establishing a lower rate in the agreement if possible, since an attorney is not providing legal services when sending music to A&R representatives.

Agreements Not Resulting From Representative Solicitation

This clause establishes that your representative will not receive any income from a deal in which a record company contacts your band independently, without having been solicited by the representative.

Agreements Occurring After Termination

Under this provision, if you enter into an agreement within a certain number of months (we recommend six months) of termination, you will have to pay the representative a fee if the representative had solicited the company during the term of the label-shopping agreement and reported the solicitation in a monthly report.

Dissolution of the Band

This provision protects band members by preventing the representative from getting rights over members after the band dissolves.

Mediation; Arbitration

This provision provides a private and typically less-expensive method of resolving disputes than filing a lawsuit. (See Chapter 2 for an explanation.)

We suggest that you choose the county, province, or city in which the band resides for arbitration. If all the members do not reside within one area, choose a place that is convenient. Enter your location of choice in the blank.

Label-Shopping Agreement

Introduction

This Management Agreement is between _____
("Representative") and _____ ("Band"),
comprising the following members: _____
_____ ("Band Members").

The Band owns certain musical recording, songwriting, and related rights referred to in this Agreement as "Band Rights." The Band desires to have Representative "shop" the Band to companies in the music business.

Obligations of Representative

Representative shall perform the following services:

- **Representation.** Representative will contact and solicit potential licensees or music industry companies on behalf of the Band. This representation is solely for the purpose of soliciting agreements for the Band in the music business (referred to in this Agreement as "Band Agreements"). During the term of this Agreement, Representative will have the exclusive right to solicit on behalf of the Band.
- **Solicitations and Reports.** Representative will, on a monthly basis, provide to Band a list of companies solicited by Representative, the name of the person to whom the solicitation was made, the manner of solicitation, and follow-up ("Monthly Reports"). Monthly Reports will also provide an estimate of time spent and expenses.

Percentage Payments and Cap

As compensation for the services provided above, Representative will receive (*check one and fill in blanks*):

- ☐ **Alternative A.** _____ percentage of income from each Band Agreement (the "Representative Band Income") up to a total of $ _____ (the "Representative Band Income Cap"). Once the Representative has received total payments equaling the Representative Band Income Cap, the Band will have no further payment obligations to Representative from that Band Agreement.
- ☐ **Alternative B.** _____ percent of income from Band Agreements (the "Representative Band Income").

Exclusions From Representative Band Income

Representative Band Income shall not include the following payments made under a Band Agreement:

Check if excluded

☐ video production costs

☐ tour shortfall advances

☐ union or guild payments

☐ nonband songwriter or cowriter payments

☐ payments to other musicians performing with Band

☐ pension or health contributions

☐ other: _____

Payments to Business Manager (*Check if applicable*)

☐ All advances must be paid directly to a mutually agreed-on business manager or accountant, who will issue payments to Representative within thirty (30) days of receipt of Representative Band Income along with any accountings as provided by the licensee, music publisher, or record company.

Costs and Expenses

Regardless of whether a Band Agreement is secured, the Band will pay all reasonable costs incurred by Representative in pursuit of Band Agreements. Such expenses do not include travel and living expenses unless they were incurred at the Band request or approved by Band. Representative will not incur any individual expense in excess of $50 without prior approval of the Band. The Band will promptly pay Representative costs and expenses on receipt of Representative invoice and itemized statement reflecting such costs and expenses.

Disclaimer

Representative makes no guarantee as to the likelihood of success regarding exploitation of the Band Rights. Representative is free to conduct business other than on the Band's behalf including relationships with third parties in the same field as the Band.

Term

The term of this Agreement shall be for _____ months unless terminated earlier, as provided below.

Termination

This Agreement may be terminated at any time at the discretion of either the Band or Representative, provided that written notice of such termination is furnished to the other party thirty (30) days prior to termination.

- **Termination by Representative.** If this Agreement is terminated by the Representative, the parties will have no further obligation to each other, and the Band is free to contract with any third party without any obligation of payment of any fees to Representative.
- **Termination by the Band.** If this Agreement is terminated by the Band, the Band agrees to pay to Representative the reasonable value of any services rendered by Representative. The parties agree that Representative's hourly rate for rendering services shall be _____ .

Agreements Not Resulting From Representative Solicitation

If a potential licensee or music company contacts the Band without any direct or indirect solicitation by the Band or Representative, then Representative shall have no rights to any income resulting from any agreements resulting from that unsolicited contact.

Agreements Occurring After Termination

If within _____ months of termination of this Agreement, the Band enters into an agreement to exploit any Band Rights with any company directly contacted by Representative and included in a Monthly Report, the Band agrees to pay the fees established in the "Percentage Payments and Cap section," above.

Dissolution of the Band

If, during the term of this Agreement, the Band dissolves and determines not to continue as a performing or recording entity, this Agreement shall terminate, and no Band Member shall be personally bound or personally liable to Representative for work performed.

Mediation; Arbitration

If a dispute arises under this Agreement, the parties agree to first try to resolve the dispute with the help of a mutually agreed-on mediator in _____ . Any costs and fees other than attorney fees will be shared equally by the parties. If it proves impossible to arrive at a mutually satisfactory solution within a reasonable time, the parties agree to submit the dispute to binding arbitration in the same city or region, conducted on a confidential basis pursuant to:

☐ the Commercial Arbitration Rules of the American Arbitration Association, or

☐ the rules of _____ .

Any decision or award as a result of any such arbitration proceeding will include the assessment of costs, expenses, and reasonable attorneys' fees and a written determination of the arbitrators. Absent an agreement to the contrary, any arbitration shall be conducted by an arbitrator experienced in music industry law. An award of arbitration is final and binding on the Band Partners and may be confirmed in a court of competent jurisdiction. The prevailing party has the right to collect from the other party its reasonable costs and attorney fees incurred in enforcing this Agreement.

General

Nothing contained in this Agreement is meant to establish either Representative or Band a partner, joint venturer, or employee of the other party for any purpose. This Agreement may not be amended except in a writing signed by both parties. No waiver by either party of any right shall be construed as a waiver of any other right. If a court finds any provision of this Agreement invalid or unenforceable as applied to any circumstance, the remainder of this Agreement shall be interpreted to best carry out the intent of the parties. This Agreement is governed by and interpreted in accordance with the laws of the State of _____. This Agreement expresses the complete understanding of the parties with respect to the subject matter and supersedes all prior proposals, agreements, representations, and understandings. Notices required under this agreement can be sent to the parties at the addresses provided below. In the event of any dispute arising from or related to this Agreement, the prevailing party is entitled to attorneys' fees.

If these terms and conditions are agreeable, please sign and execute both copies of this Agreement and return one copy to Representative.

Band Members

Band Member Signature _____

Address _____

_____

Date _____   Soc. Sec. # _____

Band Member Signature _____

Address _____

_____

Date _____   Soc. Sec. # _____

Band Member Signature _____

Address _____

_____

Date _____   Soc. Sec. # _____

Band Member Signature _____

Address _____

_____

Date _____   Soc. Sec. # _____

Manager

Band Manager Signature _____

Address _____

_____

Date _____   Soc. Sec. # _____

Representative

Representative Signature _____

Address _____

_____

Date _____   Soc. Sec. # _____

In some states there are organizations that specialize in arbitration for people in the arts, such as California Lawyers for the Arts (www.calawyersforthearts.org) and Volunteer Lawyers for the Arts (in New York at www.vlany.org, as well as in other cities and states). You can substitute the rules of one of these organizations for those of the American Arbitration Association in your agreement. If your band is based in Canada, you can still use the AAA's rules, as they perform arbitration in all major Canadian cities. Check one of the choices or delete the unwanted alternative.

General

The following provisions are standard contractual provisions referred to as boilerplate. Boilerplate provisions are explained in Chapter 2.

In the blank space, insert the state (or province, in the case of Canadian bands) of residence for the band partners. In the event of a dispute, this determines which state law will govern the arbitration or lawsuit.

Signatures

You may wish to have an attorney review this agreement before you and your band signs it. That may seem odd, since the other party is an attorney/representative. However, as we mentioned earlier, an attorney who is shopping your music may have interests adverse to your band.

Once you're satisfied that you want to proceed, have all band members and the representative sign and date the agreement. Enter the same address for all the band members: the mailing address for the band. Be sure to use an address that will receive mail for two to three years. ●

Band Equipment

I f you're in a band, then you know musical equipment is often the number-one topic backstage. Musicians love to swap details about the virtues of their guitars, amps, and effects pedals. When they have a day off, many musicians spend their free time at local music shops hunting for a great deal. This chapter provides information about your legal rights when buying new or used equipment. We will also discuss how to insure band equipment against theft and explain how to keep an inventory of band equipment.

Equipment Ownership

Ownership of musical equipment can be confusing in a band, particularly if the group has failed to establish ownership principles in a partnership agreement. Below we will discuss how to determine ownership and some of the differences between group and individual ownership.

Band Ownership of Equipment

Band equipment is owned either by the band or by an individual member. If equipment is owned by the band, then:

- The equipment stays with the band even if an individual member leaves. (However, the band agreement may provide for a method of reimbursing leaving members for a percentage of the value of the equipment.)
- The cost (or a portion of the cost) of the equipment is deducted from the group's partnership income tax form, and all of the band partners can claim the deduction on their individual returns.
- If the band breaks up, the equipment is divided among band members according to the partnership agreement.

Equipment Contributed by a Member

There are two ways a band acquires equipment: The band purchases it with band money (for example, with income from a show), or an individual member gives equipment to the band. Often when a band uses a member's equipment, it's not clear whether the equipment has actually been "donated" or whether it still belongs to the band member. When using equipment purchased individually by a band member, you should try to establish who officially owns the equipment. If the band member is okay with the band keeping it, then that member has contributed something of value to the band, which may affect his or her rights if the member leaves or if the group breaks up. That's why it's important to keep track of band equipment with a band inventory form (a sample is provided below).

> EXAMPLE: All of the band members have contributed equally to the group, except that the bass player also contributes a P.A., valued at $5,000, to the band. Therefore, the bass player has given $5,000 more to the band than the other band members and (depending on the partnership agreement) would be entitled to be repaid the value of the P.A. equipment at the time the bass player left or the band broke up. **Note:** The P.A. system's value decreases or depreciates over time.

When Should Bands Own Equipment?

We recommend band ownership of equipment if the equipment will be used by all members (for example, a P.A., van, or recording equipment) *or* if the band is filing a partnership tax return. Group ownership of P.A.s and vans is a good idea, because this equipment stays with the band even though individual band members come and go. However, a departing member may claim a right to be repaid for any ownership interest in band property.

> EXAMPLE: Four band members are equal partners in a band, which means they share equally in the band's income and expenses. The band pays $5,000 for a P.A., and the bass player is fired a week later. Under the band partnership agreement, the bass player is owed $1,250 (a payment equal to one-quarter of the value of the P.A.).

Buying Band Equipment

Buying band equipment can be tricky. Many musicians, particularly guitarists, favor vintage equipment rather than a newly made instrument. They may appreciate the sound of the guitar or may buy it as an investment (rare guitars increase dramatically in value). When buying equipment, whether new or used, your band should consider some of the legal issues related to equipment purchases. For example, some purchases come with warranties; some do not. And you may run into legal problems if the equipment you are purchasing is stolen.

Legal Protection When Buying Equipment

There are various laws protecting your band when it purchases equipment.

- **New products.** As a general rule, almost all new musical equipment comes with a full or limited warranty from the manufacturer that covers the property for a specified time period (the "warranty period"). Under most state laws, you are entitled to see the warranty before purchasing the equipment. A *full warranty* provides that the product will be repaired or replaced for free during the warranty period. A *limited warranty* places restrictions on repair and replacement (for example, you may have to pay for labor costs). *You do not have to return a warranty card to assert your rights (no matter what the warranty card may say).* In addition to the manufacturer's warranty, in most states new merchandise is covered by an *implied warranty*. This means that regardless of the manufacturer's warranty, the store or manufacturer must repair or replace the equipment if it is defective. The implied warranty lasts as long as the manufacturer's warranty period. If the manufacturer has not provided a warranty period, the implied warranty is for one year. Some retailers offer—for a price—extended warranties, which increase the time period for protection. Because of the price, fine-print limitations, and the general reliability of musical equipment, consumer advocates maintain that extended warranties are not worth the cost.

- **Used equipment.** Generally there are no warranties for used or secondhand equipment sold "as is." For example, if you buy a secondhand amplifier, you won't have a legal right to return it unless the seller gave you a warranty in writing or as a matter of store policy. Even if the seller didn't guarantee the equipment, you would have a legal right to return it if the seller deliberately deceived you—for example, by switching the amplifier you purchased with a different one before delivering it to your practice space.

- **Credit card purchases.** We recommend using a credit card to make purchases and to pay for repairs. If you use a bank credit card such as Visa, MasterCard, American Express, or Discover to purchase equipment within your home state or within 100 miles of your residence, and the purchase is for more than $50, you can refuse to pay for it if the company won't repair or replace defective merchandise. In other words, the charge will be reversed until the dispute is resolved. However, in order to use this system, you should notify your credit card company promptly when the charge first appears on your bill. Usually, the credit card company prints a telephone number for reporting such problems on the back of the bill. Some credit card companies also insure new purchases made using the card (see below).

- **Online purchases.** If you purchase equipment online (or by mail order), the equipment must be shipped within the time promised at the time of ordering. If no time was promised, the company must ship the item within 30 days. If the item can't be shipped to you within the promised time or 30 days, then you have the right to cancel the order and get a refund or agree to a new delivery date. If the item is not in stock, find out if your credit card will be charged *before* the item is shipped. If you have the option, we recommend that you not be charged until the item is shipped. The company's return policy is usually printed in the company's catalog or is posted on their website.

- **Retail store purchases.** What if you purchase some musical equipment that works fine, but you're just not happy with it and you want to return it? A store does not *have* to give you a refund or a credit for an item (although most stores do). In some states, the store can simply refer you to the manufacturer for repair or replacement. Rules on refunds vary from state to state. In 14 states, including California and New York, a store can maintain a "no-refund" policy only if that policy is posted at the sales counter or on order forms. In many of those states, if the policy isn't posted, you have the right to return merchandise within 30 days.

Stolen Equipment

If you buy, trade, or receive property that you suspect is stolen, you could be liable for a crime known as "receiving stolen merchandise." In California, for example, if you acquire stolen merchandise worth more than $950, you could be sentenced to more than a year in prison. In order to be convicted of the crime of receiving stolen property, you must know (or have a good reason to believe) that the equipment you are acquiring is stolen. If you have a suspicion it's stolen but you're not sure, then you have an obligation to investigate.

One common indicator that equipment is stolen is when it is offered at a ridiculously low price. If suspicious, ask the seller to furnish you with valid photo identification such as a driver's license. A dealer in stolen merchandise will generally not be willing to do so. In many states, dealers in used merchandise have the same obligation to investigate ownership. That's why pawn shop owners routinely require valid identification before taking items.

Insurance, Maintenance, and Inventory of Your Equipment

A few years ago, the only musicians who had instrument insurance were classical players seeking to protect their 100-year-old cellos and violins. Nowadays, with the proliferation of musical equipment theft (see below), insurance is common among all types of musicians. Below we provide some background on insuring your equipment and protecting it while under repair. We also provide a method of keeping track of your equipment inventory.

Equipment Insurance

Most insurance companies offer insurance, known as business insurance, that covers your band property. Talk to an insurance broker and find out what type of protection is available. Make sure that the coverage includes protection of your property wherever you perform, including out-of-state locations. Online, consider Music Pro Insurance (www.musicproinsurance. com). The rates are reasonable—for example, expect to pay approximately $250–$400 a year to insure $20,000 worth of equipment.

There are other insurance possibilities. Some credit card companies offer theft insurance for equipment that was purchased using the card. Check your credit card agreement to see if this type of coverage is available to you. It's also possible that individual band members' homeowner's insurance or rental insurance will cover the theft of equipment. For example, a homeowner's policy may cover equipment stolen from a band member's home or vehicle. Check your homeowner's or renter's policy to determine if it extends to stolen equipment used for a business.

Valuing Music Equipment

The Internal Revenue Service usually discounts one-seventh of the purchase price of equipment each year over a seven-year period. (Note that in many cases, you can deduct the whole price of some equipment from your income tax in one year. See Chapter 17 for more information.) Many insurance companies use the same system. For example, if a band bought a $700 amplifier, then each year it would lose one-seventh of its value, $100. If the band kept it for two years, then it would be valued at $500. To determine the value of your equipment for inventory purposes, you can either apply the depreciation value (deduct one-seventh of the price for each year of use) or have the band reach an agreement as to the equipment's value.

Repair Shops

Here are three basic rules for repair shops:

- *Always* obtain a claim check or repair invoice with the repair shop's name and address when dropping off equipment for repair.
- *Always* obtain a repair estimate.
- *Always* request that if the work exceeds the estimate by a certain amount (for example, more than $50 over the estimate, or more than 10% over the estimate), your approval must be obtained before proceeding.

Have the repair shop write the estimate and approval information on your check or invoice.

Sample Band Inventory

As part of your equipment maintenance and protection program, your band should create an equipment inventory. If all that your band owns is a P.A. system, then your task is fairly simple: Keep track of the receipt for the purchase of the P.A. However, if your band owns more equipment or has invested in a vehicle such as a van, you should keep an inventory of all equipment and keep the inventory updated and filed in the band business folder. The following sample band inventory contains all the important information about band equipment.

In the Equipment/ID column, give a brief but clear description of the equipment. In the Value column, insert the value of the equipment as of the date that the band acquired it. This will be either the price paid by the band for the equipment (whether new or used), or the value of the equipment as of the date that it was contributed by a band member. Also indicate whether it was bought new or used. In the How & When Band Acquired column, be sure to enter the date that the band acquired the equipment. You need a date to correspond with the value in order to keep track of the equipment's depreciation. Finally, enter the serial number for each piece of equipment.

Sample Band Inventory			
Equipment/ID	**Value**	**How & When Band Acquired**	**Serial Number**
Alessis RA-100 power amp	$410 new	Band purchased 12/15/18 at Lucky Music	AL22-789
Peavey bass cabinet	$450 used	Contributed by John on 4/1/18	HB25436
2 JBL 15-inch 2-way PA speakers	$800 used	Band purchased 1/22/18 at used equip. sale at Rocket Studios	LO91084 LO61743
2 Shure 58 microphones	$210 new	Band purchased 5/1/18 from The Musician's Friend (online)	SH4567 & SH4536

Preventing and Dealing With Theft

In 2013, the band Flock of Seagulls had their equipment van stolen outside a motel in Downey, California. Fortunately, the theft was captured on video surveillance, and the thieves were apprehended. Minneapolis rock band Cold Kingdom, weren't so lucky when $33,000 worth of band equipment was stolen in 2015. Whether you are a regional group or a national touring band, the theft of band equipment can be traumatic financially and otherwise, and may even lead to the breakup of a band.

Generally, there isn't much to do after your equipment is stolen. Stolen equipment is difficult to recover, and the only thing that will assist in recovery is equipment serial numbers and proof of ownership. For that reason, it helps to inventory your equipment and to keep track of sales receipts. Also, it's wise to label your equipment with a stencil or engraving tool. This may not prevent a theft from your van, but it can deter "stage thefts" when a member of another band attempts to walk off with your equipment.

Some bands maintain insurance for their musical instruments. While insurance compensation can certainly help your band get back on its feet, the insurance payout may not reflect the full value of the stolen instruments—especially in the case of vintage equipment—and it may take several months to get the payout.

Frank Gallagher is a former tour manager and sound engineer who worked with a wide range of bands including the Talking Heads and Buddy Guy. According to Gallagher, most equipment theft is not planned, but done by opportunists—unscrupulous people who simply take advantage of a situation. He offers the following tips to prevent losses from theft:

- **Avoid thefts from vans.** Since most musical equipment is stolen from vans, you can take some commonsense precautions. Gallagher's number one rule is *never* leave your van unattended while loading in or out. If possible, use a van that allows you to load only out the back, and, if you must store equipment overnight, back the van against a building or wall so that the rear doors are inaccessible.

- **Hang on to the small stuff.** According to Gallagher, many thieves won't steal anything big because they can't carry it. "Cymbals and microphones are stealable and expendable. Write your name on [the bottom of] your cymbals with a magic marker. Keep an inventory of all equipment. Stencil and identify every case." Gallagher also advises staying overnight outside the city you are playing. "Don't stay downtown. *Never!* After your gig, get on the highway in the direction you're headed for the next day and find a motel out of town. Get a room on street level and back your van up to the door. Stay on the highway. It's cheaper than downtown, too."

- **After the theft.** After equipment is stolen, you should contact the local police and file a police report. If you have insurance, a police report is usually a requirement for you to recover. Gallagher advises calling the local radio stations. In addition, you should contact local pawn shops and used music equipment stores to determine if any of your equipment has been offered for sale. And of course, check eBay, Craigslist, and used music equipment sites in case the thief is attempting to unload the purloined instruments.

Be Careful in Church and School

Gospel bands should take note: More musical equipment is stolen from churches than from clubs or concert halls. For this reason, musicians should be careful leaving instruments unattended in houses of worship. The same is true at schools.

Performance and Touring

E very band loves the thrill of performing. Unfortunately, the business of performing is not as exciting. For every hour a band spends on stage, it probably spends at least five to ten hours getting the gig, promoting the show, loading and moving equipment, doing sound checks, and waiting to get paid and load out. On top of this, club owners may not pay your band, and sound and light people may make your band sound and look terrible. If you're on tour, the daily grind can break your band's spirit and bankbook.

The information in this chapter will help make your live performances and tours both profitable and enjoyable for your band. We will review the procedure of getting gigs and getting paid, and provide you with information regarding some of the business issues that may arise at shows. We will also provide a sample performance agreement and offer advice on preparing a tour budget.

Getting Gigs and Getting Paid

It's getting harder and harder for a local band to land a gig. The number of live music venues that feature unsigned artists is decreasing, and competition for bookings among bands is fierce. Since it's a buyer's market, many club owners pay tiny sums (under $100) for a band's performance. Some clubs have even instituted a demeaning "pay to play" system in which the band must buy a block of tickets and attempt to sell them themselves. Under these circumstances, it is easy to understand why new bands feel that live performing is a rip-off. On the other hand, established musical groups are relying more on touring and merchandise income in order to make up for diminished recording sales, Below, we provide some background information on getting gigs and protecting your band's interests.

Getting Gigs

Getting a gig is a matter of luck, timing, and making the right impression. You'll also need patience, persistence, and a good demo.

Never booked a show before? First, you must identify the person who makes the booking decisions at the venue. Then, learn the procedure for dealing with the booker. Every experienced booker has some system for submitting music.

Obviously, your band's style of music should match the genre or types of bands that are commonly booked at the club. Beware: Sometimes a band's music remains unheard for weeks or months. A manager with connections may help to open the door for you, or, if you have friends in another band, they may be able to help get the booker's attention.

If a national touring band is headlining in your town, the booker at the club usually doesn't have the freedom to choose an opening act. The touring band either brings the opening act or chooses the opener. If the booker does have the freedom to choose the opener, then you need to somehow demonstrate that your band's music complements the music of the headliner without getting in the way. In addition, the simpler the setup and breakdown for an opening act, the easier it is to get the gig.

If you're trying to get a headlining gig at a local club, then your task is simple, though not necessarily easy: You have to demonstrate that your band is a money-maker—that is your band packs them in, and your fans buy lots of drinks.

How Bands Get Paid

Bands are commonly paid in four ways:
1. a percentage of the gate
2. a flat fee with no percentage
3. a guaranteed fee or a percentage of the gate, whichever is higher, or
4. a guaranteed fee plus a percentage of revenues above the guarantee.

The percentage of the gate may be a percentage of the gross revenue or net revenue. Gross revenue is all of the money paid for tickets, and net revenue is the amount left over after certain deductions have been taken. If the percentage is of net revenue, you should know the deductions that are made by the club in determining net profits.

Performance Agreements

The performance agreement offers a short summary of the terms so that there will be no disagreements about how much the band is paid and how long the band must play. Most promoters and club owners are legitimate, and they will honor the terms of these agreements. However, performance agreements (like all agreements) are only as reliable as the people making them. Therefore, don't assume that an agreement will protect your rights when dealing with an unsavory promoter. It's true that if a club owner disregards the terms of an agreement, your band can sue—but, realistically, most bands don't want to get involved in a lawsuit. Therefore, use common sense when booking. If you've been burned by a club before, you're likely to get burned again. Don't count on an agreement to protect you.

When Your Band Does Not Get Paid

After the applause dies down and the equipment is packed up, the band's manager (or someone from the band) walks into a funky office where the club owner is counting the evening's receipts. If all goes well, the owner reaches into the metal cash box and pays the band according to the agreed terms.

Sometimes, however, a club owner or concert promoter may refuse to pay your band, or pay only a portion of the fee, claiming that ticket sales were below expectations. It's often difficult to avoid being ripped off, particularly if your band is on tour. If you have the bargaining power, request half or all of the guarantee before the gig (a common practice among union musicians and established acts). If you are a member of the musicians' union and have signed a union contract (known as a "Federation Contract"), you can file a dispute with your local union representative or with a union rep in the town of the performance. (The musicians' union is discussed below.)

Some bands obtain their shows through booking agents. These agents earn a fee for each performance they book for the band (see "Booking Agents," below). If your band obtained the show through a booking agent and the band is stiffed, notify your agent immediately and ask the agent to pressure the club owner. After all, the booking agent got the gig and expects to earn a percentage of the fee.

If you are ripped off locally, you can consider filing a small claims case. However, most bands don't want to bother with this because they are afraid that if they assert legal rights, they will have trouble getting gigs in the future. Unfortunately, this can be a very real concern for bands that need exposure. If your band does intend to pursue legal rights, the limit for small claims cases ranges from $2,500 to $25,000, depending on the state. And remember: Winning the case doesn't mean you will obtain the money. Enforcing the judgment can be difficult.

To prove the amount you are owed or to increase your chances of victory in small claims court, it helps to have a written performance agreement. The next section discusses these agreements. Practically, however, many small clubs refuse to sign a written performance agreement. If you can't get a signed agreement, try to get any sort of documentation, such as a handwritten letter or a fax confirming the booking.

American Federation of Musicians

When you hear people talk about the musicians' union, they're talking about the American Federation of Musicians (AFM) (www.afm.org). The AFM is the union for U.S. and Canadian musicians, with local offices throughout the United States and Canada. Major labels (EMI, Warners, Universal, and Sony) typically require that band members join the AFM. Even if you're not signed to a major label, it's a good idea to join the union if you tour a lot. The AFM guarantees minimum compensation for union contract shows and recording jobs. It also provides group insurance plans, including medical, liability, personal accident, term life, and equipment insurance. Another benefit for American musicians traveling to Canada is that they can avoid "work permit" hassles at the border through a union procedure that is arranged with their local union 30 days prior to the gig.

Keep in mind, however, that not all clubs have relationships with the AFM, and for that reason, many clubs do not sign union contracts or pay union wages. To join the AFM, a musician must complete a form and pay an initiation fee (usually $100, though it may vary depending on the local) and annual local and national dues (from $100 to $175 total). Union musicians also pay the union a percentage of income from union performance and recording jobs (usually 2% to 4%).

Performance Agreement

Many bands and venues use a one-page contract that lists the basic arrangements, such as the date of the show and payment. These may vary in appearance and content, but they usually contain the information provided in the sample performance agreement, below. Sometimes, however, a band or a venue may have more detailed requirements than payment and booking times. Requirements such as backstage food and drinks, merchandise rights, lights and sound, or insurance are included in a document called a "rider" that is attached to the one-page contract. That is, the one-page contract establishes the essentials while the rider sets forth the detailed information about what color M&Ms are required backstage. If your band is looking for a simple agreement, then just use the one-page contract. But if your band has the bargaining power, you might include a detailed rider.

This section provides instructions on how to complete a performance agreement and rider and what the provisions mean.

It's possible that a venue may provide you with a performance agreement that differs from our version. If so, you can use our agreement for comparison purposes and to help you understand what the clauses mean. The agreements do not have to be identical. As long as you can understand the venue's agreement and it basically covers the same issues as our agreement, it's probably fine.

Finally, be aware that some club agreements require your band to post a bond, or to assume all liability for damages (if, for instance, someone is hurt during your show). Your band should approach these kinds of provisions carefully, as they have the potential for a heavy financial burden.

FORMS
You can download this form (and all other forms in this book) from
Nolo.com; for details, see "Get Forms, Updates, and More at This Book's Companion
Page," in the appendix.

Basic Terms

The "Basic Terms" section is completed by simply filling in the requested
information. Most of the basic terms are self-explanatory. The term "purchaser"
is often used to refer to the promoter or club owner. A promoter is a person
who organizes events and may or may not own the venue.

Enter the date and time of the gig. It may seem too obvious, but you
wouldn't be the first band to show up on the wrong day, or show up on the
right day to find another band booked. Also be sure to insert the number
of sets and their length (for example: "One 25–30 minute set at 9 p.m."),
as this will determine your work schedule at the venue. The requirements
regarding load-in and sound check are usually furnished by the venue.

Under "Total compensation," insert the method of payment and the
amount. Bands are usually paid in one of four ways: a percentage of the gate;
a flat fee with no percentage; a guaranteed fee or a percentage of the gate,
whichever is higher; or a guaranteed fee plus a percentage of revenues above
the guarantee. Enter any deposit paid or due before the show, and when it
was paid or is due.

If the band has a partnership tax number or EIN (see Chapter 17),
insert that number. Otherwise, insert one of the band members' Social
Security numbers.

Names of Musicians and Tax Information

Some venues may require the names and Social Security numbers of each
musician. This is most likely if the venue plans to pay any of the musicians
directly rather than through a manager of some sort. Fill in any information that
the venue requires. If a musician will receive pay directly, enter the amount
under "Direct Pay" and enter that musician's Social Security number. The
space marked "Local" is a reference to the number of the local musicians' union.

Artist's Right to Terminate

This allows the Artist to terminate the agreement if the deposit has not been paid as promised. It's possible that if a venue furnishes the performance agreement, this provision will not be in it. Even without this provision, however, your band would have a legal right to cancel if you don't receive the deposit on time and the venue fails to respond to your written requests for the deposit.

Rider and Attachments

This provision is simply a statement that the rider and any other attachments to the agreement are legally binding.

General

The following provisions are standard contractual provisions referred to as boilerplate. Boilerplate provisions are explained in Chapter 2.

In the blank space, insert the state (or province, in the case of Canadian bands) of residence for the Band Partners. In the event of a dispute, this determines which state law will govern the arbitration or lawsuit. Like the "termination" provision, these general or boilerplate provisions are often missing from performance agreements furnished by a venue.

Signatures

The band's manager or one of the band members should sign. Indicate the name and title of the person signing for the Band under "Artist Name and Title." Also enter the band's mailing address. The Purchaser signature should be made by a person authorized to sign, such as the club's owner or an authorized booker. To help ensure that the person signing for the purchaser is actually authorized to sign, have the person signing for the purchaser indicate his title (for example, "Miguel Corrigan, Owner," or "Dana Burgy, Booking Agent").

The rest of the provisions are optional rider provisions. If your band has the bargaining power (for example, you're a popular headlining act), you may be able to obtain most of the provisions in the rider. However, most bands lack the clout to obtain many of these provisions. Include as many of them as you can. Provisions that you don't want to (or can't) include should be struck out and initialed by both parties signing the agreement, or deleted altogether.

Merchandise and Performance

According to industry estimates, successful rock bands often earn $5 per concert fan in merchandise sales (punk and metal bands often earn $8 per person).

When booking, find out each venue's merchandise policy and whether the club will provide personnel to handle sales. Arrange with your T-shirt manufacturer or LP or CD duplicator to ship your merchandise to a venue or hotel so that you can obtain additional products on the road. Some bands even take silk-screening materials with them and make T-shirts on the road. Also find out from the venue about any requirements for local taxes or fees for merchandise sales.

Merchandise Rider Provision

Venues usually want to receive 15% to 40% of gross sales from merchandise. Enter the amount your band and the venue agree on. Some riders state that the venue will handle the sales, in which case you will deliver the merchandise and have the venue sign a receipt indicating the count for all merchandise before sales begin. At the end, the band inventories the remaining merchandise and is owed money for the number of items sold or missing.

Tickets and Ticket Sales Rider Provision

While major label headliners often travel with tour accountants who audit all ticket sales, many bands lack the resources to do so. This provision guarantees the band some basic oversight of ticket sales. Enter the ticket prices, and the maximum number of free admissions that may be allowed as a percentage of total ticket sales. The purpose of limiting free admissions is to prevent unscrupulous concert promoters from taking free tickets themselves, then selling or bartering them and keeping the money.

Dressing Room Rider Provision

This is a basic "clean and safe" dressing room provision. (Depending on how much clout they have, some bands make more elaborate requests such as green ceilings, floor lamps, and carpeted floors.) Enter the number of locked dressing rooms you will get. Enter any special arrangements the venue agrees to make for you, or enter "none."

Complimentary Tickets Rider Provision

Enter the number of free tickets per band member that will be allowed, and the maximum total number for the band. Most venues allow one or two free tickets per band member up to a maximum of 20 for the whole band.

Security Rider Provision

This provision guarantees basic security measures to protect your band and the audience. Your security request can be more specific, depending on your needs and what the club will agree to. For instance, you might request a specific number of security persons or indicate where you want them stationed. If you have no special requests, enter "none."

Hospitality Rider Provision

Hospitality refers to the food and drinks provided backstage. This is a bare-bones hospitality provision. Some artists may make more elaborate requests: Michael Bolton includes a special requirement that backstage coffee be fresh and from a local independent coffee shop. If you don't have any special requests, enter "none."

Background Music Rider Provision

For some bands, the choice of introductory background music is very important. Headlining bands usually have an easy time of getting the background music they want. These bands supply a CD to the sound man. This provision establishes that the music must meet your approval.

Clippings and Posters Rider Provision

This allows your band to review the press generated before and after your show. It may be a measure of how well the club promoted the show.

Insurance Rider Provision

Most legitimate venues have adequate insurance. That is, the club pays an insurance company, and if someone is injured, the insurance company pays for the damage. Therefore, most clubs will permit a national touring band to include this provision in the rider. The real benefit to the band of including this provision is that if the club does not have insurance and signs the agreement, and there is a disaster, the band has a basis to sue the club because it relied on the club owner's promise of insurance.

Cancellation Rider Provision

If you have the bargaining power, you can still get paid for your gig even if the venue cancels the show. The closer the cancellation is to the show date, the larger the payment. Popular groups ask for 50% at four weeks away and 100% at two weeks. Enter the percentage of the payment that you and the venue agree you will be paid in the event of cancellation.

Sound System Rider Provision

Some bands attach a separate "Sound Reinforcement Rider" that includes all the details of the band's public address, speaker, mixer, and personnel requirements. This is done to guarantee that the venue's sound system meets the band's requirements. Enter any requirements about your sound system here.

Pyrotechnic Devices Rider Provision

For obvious reasons, venues are wary of pyrotechnics, and most require a provision such as this to limit damages and to comply with local laws.

Video and Audio Recording Rider Provision

This is your band's antibootlegging provision, preventing the venue from recording or broadcasting the performance without your consent.

Performance Agreement

Basic Terms

Name of band ("Artist"): _____

Name of venue: _____

Person booking performance ("Purchaser"): _____

Date(s) and time(s) of performance: _____

_____

Number of sets and duration: _____ Time for load-in: _____

Time for sound check: _____ Total compensation: _____

Deposit payment: _____ Date deposit payment to be paid: _____

Band's Social Security # or Fed. Tax ID #: _____

Names of Musicians and Tax Information (*optional*)

Name of Musician	Direct Pay	Soc. Sec. #	Local Musicians' Union #
_____	_____	_____	_____
_____	_____	_____	_____
_____	_____	_____	_____
_____	_____	_____	_____
_____	_____	_____	_____

Artist's Right to Terminate

If Artist is entitled to a deposit payment as provided in the Payment section of this Agreement, and the deposit has not been paid within the time specified, Artist shall have the right to terminate this Agreement without any further obligation.

Rider and Attachments

Any attached Performance Agreement Rider (the "Rider") and any other attachments or exhibits to this Agreement are incorporated in this Agreement by reference.

General

Nothing contained in this Agreement or the accompanying Rider constitutes either Purchaser or Artist a partner or employee of the other party. This Agreement and the accompanying Rider and exhibits express the complete understanding of the parties and may not be amended except in a writing signed by both parties. If a court finds any provision of this Agreement or the accompanying Rider invalid or unenforceable, the remainder of this Agreement will be interpreted so as best to effect the intent of the parties. This Agreement shall be governed by and interpreted in accordance with the laws of _____ . In the event of any dispute arising from or related to this Agreement, the prevailing party is entitled to attorneys' fees.

Signatures

Artist Name and Title: _____

Artist Signature: _____

Address: _____

_____

Date: _____

Purchaser Name and Title: _____

Purchaser Signature: _____

Address: _____

_____

Date: _____

[*Optional*] Performance Agreement Rider
Additional Terms and Conditions

Merchandise

A fee of _____ % of gross sales will be paid to Purchaser by Artist for all merchandise sold before, during, or after the performance at the Venue. This fee will be paid to Purchaser on completion of selling.

Purchaser will not permit any other sale or distribution of merchandise bearing Artist's trademarks or image. Purchaser will provide:

☐ a six-foot table and two chairs and two people for merchandise sales in a prominent area of the foyer or lounge leading to the performance area, or

☐ _____ .

Tickets and Ticket Sales

Purchaser agrees that tickets will be consecutively numbered and shall be available at the following prices: _____ . Artist's representative has the right to inspect all ticket records and to be present in the box office prior to and during the performance. Free admission will not exceed _____ % of total tickets.

Dressing Room

Purchaser will provide _____ safe, clean dressing room(s) with _____ lock(s). Purchaser will provide backstage security to prevent unauthorized personnel from having access to the dressing area. Special arrangements will include: _____ .

Complimentary Tickets

Unless otherwise agreed, Purchaser will allow _____ guest(s) per band member, with a maximum of _____ tickets.

Security

Purchaser will provide adequate security so as to guarantee the safety of the audience and the Artist. Special arrangements will include _____ .

Hospitality

Unless otherwise indicated, Purchaser will provide an allowance of hot and cold beverages in the dressing rooms for the sole use of band and crew members. Special arrangements include: _____ .

Background Music

Artist will approve all background music played before and after the Artist's performance.

Clippings and Posters

Purchaser will forward copies of all clippings, reviews, and posters to Artist.

Insurance

Purchaser will obtain and maintain, at its own expense, adequate personal injury and property damage liability insurance coverage. This coverage will extend to all activities related to Artist's engagement and performance. Except for claims arising from Artist's willful or intentional acts, Purchaser will indemnify Artist for any third-party claims.

Cancellation

If Purchaser cancels the performance less than four weeks before the performance, Purchaser will pay Artist ____% of the guaranteed fee for the performance. If Purchaser cancels the performance less than two weeks before the performance, Purchaser will pay Artist ____% of the guaranteed fee for the performance. The parties agree that such payments are reasonable in light of anticipated or actual harm caused by the cancellation and the difficulties of proving the actual damages to Artist.

Sound System

Purchaser agrees to provide a sound system meeting the following requirements:

_____ .

Pyrotechnic Devices

Artist will get Purchaser's approval for any pyrotechnic device used by Artist. Any such device is subject to applicable fire laws and will be administered by a person with professional experience in pyrotechnics.

Video and Audio Recording

Purchaser will not arrange for video or audio recording or live broadcast without first receiving written approval from Artist.

Touring

Touring can be exciting, but it's also expensive. If your band has never traveled beyond your hometown, then get ready for sticker shock. Successful bands know how to travel light and cut costs in order to stay on the road. We'll help you do the same by highlighting common touring expenses and showing you ways to stretch your dollars.

Common Touring Expenses

Below are explanations for some of the common touring expenses.

Salaries

The road manager (referred to as a "tour manager" when the tour is big budget) handles the day-to-day tour details; some road managers also drive the van and operate the P.A. Expect to pay a road manager $1,000 to $2,000 a week. A tech is a professional roadie who manages band equipment and directs the setup and breakdown. Some techs also drive the van. Expect to pay a tech $500 to $1,500 a week. If you hire someone as a driver, expect to pay $500 to $1,000 a week. Hired musicians usually want a salary of $1,000 to $2,000 a week. If you are hiring a union musician, you may be required to sign a special union contract and pay minimum wages established by the national headquarters. If possible, the rest of the band should be paid a salary as well. Unfortunately, there is often not enough tour income to pay band members a salary on the road. However, if there are profits from merchandise, band members often split them at the end of each week.

Per Diems

Per diems (which means "by the day") are payments to the band and crew for daily living expenses such as food. Expect to pay at least $25 to $150 a day for per diems for each person.

Van Expenses

Expect to pay $70 to $200 a day for a passenger van rental (a van with seats) and $65 to $200 a day for a two-seater cargo van. To determine gas expenses, calculate your total mileage and divide it by the van's estimated miles per gallon (you find that information at sites like www.mpgbuddy.com).

In this budget, insurance is included in the price of the rental. However, you may be entitled to more insurance if you pay with certain credit cards or if your personal auto insurance also covers rentals. Some states charge sales tax on rentals, often as high as 8% or 10%. Estimate $30 to $50 a week for tolls. Many tour managers recommend obtaining road service coverage (for flat tires and towing) from AAA or other insurance companies.

Checking Gear on Airlines

Under a Federal Aviation Administration (FAA) uniform national standard, any musical instrument that can be safely stowed either in an overhead bin or under an airline seat may be carried aboard for domestic airline travel.

Airfare and Air Freight

If you are flying, you have two additional expenses: the cost of the airfare for band and crew, and the cost of airfreighting your equipment. As you are probably aware, you can obtain excellent airline prices using online services such as Expedia (www.expedia.com) and Orbitz (www.orbitz.com). Travel agents, especially those that specialize in planning tours for musicians, can also aid in finding excellent rates. Air freight rates for your equipment vary, and you can expect to pay $2 to $10 per pound. If you are using air freight there may be additional costs related to delivering and picking up the equipment at the airport.

Hotels and Airbnb

If your band plans to stay in hotels, we recommend using a travel agent, particularly someone who has experience with bands. If you don't use a travel agent, use a travel site such as Expedia, Kayak, Priceline, or Orbitz, and filter your search for hotels within your budget. You will usually get better rates at musician-friendly hotels. Expect to pay $50 to $300 a night for a double room. Most hotels also charge a special hotel tax, so estimate an additional 5% over the room costs. Pay hotel bills with credit cards, as your credit card contract may provide a method for resolving problems in the event of a dispute.

Alternatively, bands can take advantage of short-term rental services, such as Airbnb and VRBO, that offer a range of temporary housing from single rooms to whole houses. Some listings even cater to traveling musicians. Many bands have ditched the hotel/motel paradigm (and the hassles of crashing on a friend's couch) in favor of the less-expensive and homier aspects of short-term rentals.

Carnets: When Touring Outside the United States and Canada

If your band is traveling out of the country, you may want to use an ATA Carnet, which is the equivalent of a passport for your equipment. The ATA Carnet system is accepted in 50 countries and facilitates movement of equipment through customs and avoids the payment of value added taxes (VATs) and duties that are charged by some foreign customs agents. You must complete an application, post a bond (a payment that will be refunded after the tour), and pay a fee based upon the value of your equipment. All of this must be completed several weeks prior to your departure.

For more information—and to apply for a Carnet online—visit the U.S. Council for International Business website (www.uscib.org) and click the "Trade Services" tab, or try one of the Carnet application services available online, such as www.ATAcarnet.com.

Equipment Rental

If your band chooses to rent equipment, the expenses vary depending on the equipment and the region. Check the yellow pages for musical equipment rental companies in the cities in which you are touring. Expect to pay at least $250 or more per week for amplifier rentals.

Other Insurance

In addition to auto insurance (see above), some bands carry liability insurance (in case someone is injured) and equipment insurance (see Chapter 5).

Sound and Light Expenses

If you are taking sound and light personnel or equipment, you will need to estimate those costs. If you're not taking sound and lights, be aware that some venues charge for supplying these services.

Booking Agent Commissions

Expect to pay 10% or more of your tour income if you use the services of a booking agent (see below).

Miscellaneous

Estimate phone and Internet charges for planning the tour and while on the road. These costs depend on the length and location of the tour. Your band should set aside $100 per week for batteries, strings, drumheads, and other miscellaneous items. Some bands also budget for tips, laundry, and photocopying.

Booking Agents

A booking agent arranges the tour and negotiates payments with the venues. A booking agent usually receives 10% of your income from live performances (referred to as "concert grosses"). In some states, booking agents are regulated, and in California they must be licensed. Normally, a band signs an exclusive arrangement with a booking agent. That is, only *that* booking agent can book the band as long as that agent represents the band. We recommend limiting the arrangement to five years or less.

5% Contingency

Most tour managers recommend including a 5% contingency fee for overruns. That is, estimate your total tour expenses and then add an additional 5% for breathing room in case your estimates are low or there is an emergency.

Touring Expenses: Some Tips for Balancing the Budget

If your band is facing losing money on tour—referred to as a tour shortfall—you've got a couple of options. If you are signed to a record label or a music publisher, you may be able to get tour support, which is financial help from the company to supplement the tour shortfall. Any money you get is deducted from future royalties. Sometimes, tour support payments are part of the recording or publishing agreement. That is, the contract provides for specific tour support payments. Sometimes, however, the record company may simply decide, after discussions with the band or manager, that the company will advance some support for a specific tour.

Without tour support, you'll need to cut expenses. Most bands start with salaries, cutting the road manager, the tech, or both. The second cut is usually hotel costs. The band either sleeps in the van, shares one motel room, or stays with friends. The third cut is probably van rental. If they have them, the band members will use their own vehicles.

Unfortunately, the problem with cutting the road manager, tech, and hotel is that the band can suffer from overwork and sleep deprivation. Despite these dangers, cost-cutting may be your only option if you want your tour to go forward. Lots of bands have successfully toured this way through the United States and Canada.

Frank Gallagher, who has worked as tour manager for many rock and pop bands, offers a few simple money-saving tour tips. "Travel with as little crew as possible. It's ideal to have your own soundman, but usually it's the most expensive item," says Gallagher. He advises working with the local sound person. "A lot of them do a good job and they know the room, so try to defer to the house soundman's advice. If one of your roadies knows how to do monitors, then use that person to handle your monitor mix."

As for your food budget, you can save money as an opening act on a big tour because "they feed you every day and you get the bare minimum of refreshments in your dressing room," says Gallagher. For bands on club tours, George Earth, a prominent touring guitarist, offers a simple tip: "Buy a cooler and use it to save the backstage refreshments you don't drink at night. You'll be glad you had them on the road the next day."

Sample Tour Budget

In order to survive on tour, you should prepare a tour budget. We have provided two sample tour budgets below. One is for a fictional band and demonstrates how the budget is completed. The other is a blank form for you to use with your band.

Fictional Tour Budget

The following sample tour budget is for a fictional band. Imagine this as a first draft of the budget. The fictional band has booked 14 shows. The band has four members, and they want to hire a road manager and tech. The band also wants to rent a van and stay in hotels. The band will need three hotel rooms a night. The estimate for the band's total expenses is approximately $13,000.

If the band were earning $1,000 a night for the 14 shows, they could break even. However, the band expects to earn $300 a night. Therefore, the total band income (not counting merchandise sales) is $4,200—creating a loss of $8,000. What will the band do? Like most bands on a shoestring touring budget, they will forget about the road manager and tech and consider borrowing a van, rather than renting.

Sample Budget Blank Form

The following blank form is for your band to use.

 FORMS

You can download this form (and all other forms in this book) from Nolo.com; for details, see "Get Forms, Updates, and More at This Book's Companion Page," in the appendix.

Tour Budget
17 Days/14 Shows/16 Nights

Salaries	Road mgr 17 days @ $1,250 per week	$ 3,035.00	
	Backline tech 17 days @ $800 per week	1,942.00	
	Salaries Total		$ 4,977.00
Per Diems	Road mgr 17 days @ $25 per day	425.00	
	Backline tech 17 days @ $25 per day	425.00	
	Band member #1	425.00	
	Band member #2	425.00	
	Band member #3	425.00	
	Band member #4	425.00	
	Per Diems Total		$ 2,550.00
Van	Van rental (17 days)	1,200.00	
	Insurance ($1,000 deductible w/rental)	00.00	
	State tax	56.00	
	Transport fees	35.00	
	Gas (1,600 miles x ($2.89 per gallon ÷ 25 mpg))	185.00	
	Total Transportation		$ 1,476.00
Hotel	Road mgr/tech double rm 16 nights @ $60	960.00	
	2 band double rms 16 nights @ $60	1,920.00	
	Hotel tax, etc.	300.00	
	Total Hotel		$ 3,180.00
Misc.	Supplies (drum heads, strings, etc.)	200.00	
	Parking and tolls	200.00	
	Printing/copying (itinerary)	20.00	
	Tips	50.00	
	Laundry	50.00	
	Advance phone and fax charges	30.00	
	Road phone and fax	50.00	
	Misc. Total		$ 600.00
Totals	**Total Tour Expenses**		12,783.00
	5% Contingency		614.15
	Total Estimated Tour Budget		$ 13,397.15

Tour Budget

_____ Days/ _____ Shows/ _____ Nights

Salaries	Road mgr _____ days @ $_____ per week	$	
	Tech _____ days @ $_____ per week		
	Salaries Total		$
Per Diems	Road mgr _____ @ $_____ per day		
	Tech _____ @ $_____ per day		
	Band member #1 _____ @ $_____ per day		
	Band member #2 _____ @ $_____ per day		
	Band member #3 _____ @ $_____ per day		
	Band member #4 _____ @ $_____ per day		
	Per Diems Total		$
Van	Van rental _____ @ $_____ per day		
	Insurance		
	State tax		
	Transport fees		
	Gas (_____ miles x ($_____ per gallon ÷ _____ mpg))		
	Total Transportation		$
Hotel	Road mgr/tech: double rm _____ days @ $_____ per day		
	Band: two double rms _____ days @ $_____ per day		
	Hotel tax, etc.		
	Total Hotel		$
Misc.	Supplies (drum heads, strings, etc.)		
	Parking and tolls		
	Printing/copying (itinerary)		
	Tips		
	Laundry		
	Advance phone and fax charges		
	Road phone and fax		
	Misc. Total		$
Totals	Total Tour Expenses		
	5% Contingency		
	Total Estimated Tour Budget		$

Copyright and Song Ownership

This chapter and the next (Chapter 8) both deal with songwriting. This chapter discusses song ownership—essentially, who owns the rights to a song—that is, the musical composition performed by the band. Ownership is important because it directly affects who earns money from the song. Chapter 8 is about music publishing, which is the method by which songs earn money through record sales, motion pictures, or radio or TV play. (In later chapters, we discuss a second musical copyright—the sound recording copyright—that applies to the recording of the song, not its composition.)

It's easy to determine song ownership if one person writes a song. However, if more than one person contributes to writing a song, as in many band situations, there may be confusion as to ownership. In this chapter, we'll explain the principles of cowriting songs and evaluating songwriter contributions. We'll also talk about what happens when someone claims that you ripped off their song (that is, "infringed" their copyright), or if you believe someone infringed your copyright. Finally, we'll explain how to complete a copyright application and register your song.

Copyright Basics

You may have heard a musician say he or she has "copyright" in a song. This means the musician, as the author of the song, is protected under federal copyright laws. These laws protect the creators of music, literature, visual arts, or other art forms. The creator of a song is the original copyright owner. However, over time the copyright may be bought or sold, which transfers ownership of the rights to the song to other people. For example, Michael Jackson once owned a 50% stake in the copyright to 250 Beatles songs.

CANADIAN RULES

Canadian and American copyright laws are not identical. We'll alert you to the major differences between the two countries' laws. Otherwise, you can apply most of the principles in this chapter to songs written by Canadian citizens.

Copyright Ownership

Copyright literally refers to the "right to copy." The owner of a song controls this right (as well as a number of other rights, discussed below). The owner grants others permission to use the song and can sue anyone who uses the song without permission.

With one important exception (addressed below), the first owner of a song is the songwriter (the "author" under copyright law). The songwriter may then sell the copyright to a music publisher in return for cash payments and continuing royalties. In this way, a song copyright is like other forms of property: It can be bought and sold. When there is more than one writer, there are special rules regarding dividing income and selling song copyrights. These "joint ownership" rules are discussed below.

An Exception to the First-Owner Rule

There is one situation where the writer of a song is not the first owner. This is when a person is employed as a songwriter. In that case, the employer owns the song. Under copyright law, an employee who creates a work such as a song or a magazine article in the course of their employment does not own copyright in the work; the employer does. If a member of your band is employed to write music or has signed an agreement to write a song (or songs) for payment, you should visit the Copyright Office website (www.copyright.gov) and download Circular 9, *Work-Made-for-Hire Under the 1976 Copyright Act*.

A Copyright Is a Bundle of Rights

In addition to preventing unauthorized copying of the song, the owner controls the sale, use, or public performance of the song. This means that unless the song owner gives permission (referred to as a "license") or unless a law permits the use, no other person can record, sell, copy, or publicly perform the song. The owner of the song also controls the right to modify or make "derivative" versions of the song. Derivative versions may include parodies, translations, or abbreviated versions of the song.

> ### To Perform a Song
>
> A song is publicly performed whenever it is heard by the public, whether at a live show, on a television broadcast, over the radio, on YouTube, or on a supermarket loudspeaker. For purposes of defining public performance, it doesn't matter if the performance is free (for example, an open concert in the park) or nonprofit (for example, a charity benefit). In the next chapter, we explain how songwriters are compensated when their song is performed.

How Do You Obtain a Copyright?

Musicians often believe that you can't have a copyright without obtaining a copyright registration. However, for most countries, including the United States and Canada, no registration is necessary. All that is required to copyright your song is that it be original and fixed. "Original" means that the song is original to the writer and that it was not copied from another source. A work is "fixed" when it exists in some tangible manner such as sheet music or a tape recording, or saved onto a computer disk. A work is *not* fixed if it is sung live and never put into sheet music or otherwise recorded. For example, many great American blues artists who only performed live would not have copyright protection for their songs. Lucky for many of these artists, they were recorded by bluesaholic Alan Lomax, who captured legends such as Leadbelly and Muddy Waters on tape. If it weren't for these recordings, these songs would be free for anyone to copy—and sell.

Despite the fact that registration isn't technically necessary, we recommend registering your works. Why? Because registration establishes your claim to ownership, places your song in Copyright Office records, gives you special rights in a dispute, and is required before filing a lawsuit. Later in this chapter we discuss some of the advantages of registration, and we explain how to file a copyright application for registration.

CANADIAN RULES

Canadian copyright includes moral rights. One major difference between U.S. and Canadian copyright laws is a principle known as "moral rights." Under the law of moral rights, the author of a song is considered to have some "moral" claim to what happens to the song. That is, in Canada, even if you sell your song to a music publisher, you can still prevent anyone from distorting or modifying your song or prevent anyone from using your song in connection with a product or service that is prejudicial to your honor or reputation. In other words, if you sold your song, you could still prevent the new owner from using the song in a beer commercial if that commercial would make your fans think less of you. This rule does not apply to American songwriters under American copyright law, but it is an important standard that is also common in Europe.

Licenses and Sales: Transferring Rights

Song owners earn money when people pay for the right to use the song, such as including a song in a movie or recording a cover version of the song. In exchange for a payment, song owners give permission in the form of a written agreement known as a "license." Licenses are generally made by negotiating with the owner. For example, if a movie company wants to use a song, the company would negotiate a license with the song owner.

There is a special license called a compulsory license that applies when you want to cover a copyrighted song for a recording. In that case, you don't need to ask for permission. Congress has established a uniform price for the license, and you do not have to negotiate with the song owner. All you have to do is to pay the amounts required under law and follow a few other rules. For example, if your band wants to sell its cover version of "Knocking on Heaven's Door," you would have to pay about 9 cents per CD or digital download to the owners of the song. Compulsory licenses apply only in the case of covering someone else's song for a recording. (The rules governing compulsory licenses are discussed in more detail in Chapter 8.)

A license is a temporary grant of permission. The owner of the song keeps all copyright ownership. In this way, a license is different than a sale of the copyright. In a sale (sometimes referred to as an "assignment"), the seller permanently gives up some or all of the ownership rights to another. Generally, the assignment is considered a permanent transfer of rights, although copyright law provides a method for the author or the author's heirs to reclaim rights after a period of 35 years.

Many songwriters sell their songs to music publishing companies. Music publishers are companies that exploit songs and collect revenues. Selling to a music publisher doesn't mean that the songwriter stops earning money from the song. Usually the songwriter continues to receive royalties under the terms of a music publishing contract. In the next chapter we discuss the basics of these publishing deals.

Did You Assign Rights 35 Years Ago?

If you or your band assigned a copyright in 1982 (or soon afterwards), you may be eligible to terminate that assignment and reclaim all of the rights. This applies to song copyrights (musical works) or to sound recording copyrights, discussed in Chapter 11. The principle is simple—assignments made after 1977 can be terminated after 35 years. The rules and regulations to make the termination are more complex and can be found in Section 203 of the Copyright Act. Because of their complexity, the advice of an attorney is recommended when seeking to terminate.

To give you an idea of what's required, the Copyright Office has published rules stating that notices of termination may be served no earlier than 25 years after the execution of the grant or, if the grant covers the right of publication (which most music assignments include), no earlier than 30 years after the execution of the grant or 25 years after publication under the grant (whichever comes first). However, termination of a grant cannot be effective until 35 years after the execution of the grant or, if the grant covers the right of publication, no earlier than 40 years after the execution of the grant or 35 years after publication under the grant (whichever comes first). Notices of termination must comply in form, content, and manner with requirements in a regulation issued by the Register of Copyrights, and you can find these regulations online (www.copyright.gov/docs/201-10-final.pdf).

What Can't You Copy?

The purpose of copyright law is to prevent copying—but what exactly does "copying" mean? After all, nobody writes in a vacuum, and every songwriter borrows something from others. How do you know if you borrowed too much? Unfortunately, there's no fixed standard for what is "too much" copying. This can be very frustrating for a musician who wants to borrow from another song, because determining whether there is an infringement is a subjective decision.

Courts sometimes rely on a "lay observer" approach that asks whether an average listener (not a musical expert) hearing both songs would believe that the similarities could result only from copying, not from coincidence. Another rule of thumb is that you can't just borrow well-known parts of music if the result could fairly be said to compete with the original. A good way to approach this as a songwriter is to ask yourself, if you were the *other* songwriter, would you feel ripped off? If the answer is yes, then you shouldn't be surprised if you get a nasty letter from the other band's lawyers when you go ahead with your song.

Avoid Infringement Disputes

When trying to determine whether your song infringes somebody else's copyrighted material, keep in mind that your goal should be to avoid a lawsuit altogether—not to win or lose in court. If you think that the two songs are close enough to spark a lawsuit but you're convinced you would win the case, don't take that as a sign that you should proceed. Copyright infringement lawsuits are expensive to defend and can easily bankrupt your band. It's much better to play it safe and stay out of the courtroom.

When Copying Is Okay

Not all copying is prohibited. Generally speaking, you're allowed to copy anything in the public domain, and you can make limited use of copying under rules of fair use.

The Public Domain

Music that isn't protected by copyright is said to be in the "public domain" and is free for anyone to copy. All songs published before 1923 (and some published after 1923) are in the public domain and can thus be copied freely. For example, the music for "Love Me Tender" was taken from a public domain song called "Aura Lee."

Under a similar principle, you are also free to copy familiar chord progressions or drum or bass patterns. These common elements (for example, a boogie-woogie piano riff) are considered to be the "language" of music and are free for all to use. Think of these elements in the way that words are used in books. By themselves, words or common phrases are not protectable. Everyone is free to use them. But the unique way that these elements are combined (or expressed) is what makes the song protectable.

For example, in a songwriting lawsuit, John Fogerty successfully proved he did not infringe a copyright by demonstrating that the only similarities between the two songs were elements common to all rock and roll songs—simple and common riffs and arrangements. The same rules would apply for common lyric lines such as "got my mojo working" or "baby, be mine."

In a 2018 lawsuit, a judge ruled that Taylor Swift's lyrics, "Playas gonna play" and "haters gonna hate" did not infringe a 2001 song with similar lyrics, because the short phrases weren't protected under copyright law.

Note, however, these rules may not apply when sampling a distinctive drumbeat or distinctive vocal rendition—for example, the opening drum line of "Love to Love You Baby" or James Brown singing "Give It Up." In that case, you may be infringing a second type of copyright known as a sound recording copyright. Sound recording copyrights follow many of the same principles that we discuss in this chapter, but have special rules specific to sound recordings. We discuss sampling and sound recording copyrights in Chapter 11.

Song titles are also not protected under copyright law. That is, anyone is free to use a similar song title—and in fact, many hit songs have identical titles, such as "Wild Thing." Beware, however, that using identical titles might, in rare cases, raise trademark issues. Trademark law is discussed in Chapter 9.

From Public Domain to *Public Domain*

Musician Dave Alvin and his brother used to collect old blues, folk, rhythm and blues, and country recordings, including many long-out-of-print reissue albums on obscure labels. When looking for material for a solo album in 2000, Alvin decided to use many of these public domain songs. The result was *Public Domain*, a recording released by Oakland's Hightone Records. Among the songs recorded by Alvin were "Shenandoah," "Walk Right In," "Short Life of Trouble," "What Did the Deep Sea Say," "Engine 143," "Delia," and "The Murder of the Lawson Family." Because the songs were in the public domain, Hightone Records didn't have to pay any mechanical royalties to use them.

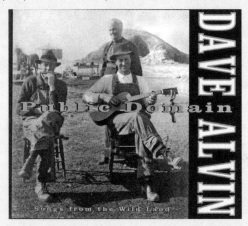

Public Domain, Dave Alvin, ℗ © copyright Hightone Records

RESOURCE

Recommended reading on public domain rules. For an excellent explanation on how to identify public domain music, see *The Public Domain*, by Stephen Fishman (Nolo).

Fair Use

You are also free to copy a portion of a copyrighted work if your copying qualifies as a fair use. Fair use of copyrighted works includes commenting on, criticizing, or parodying the works. For example, a newspaper can freely copy a portion of your song lyrics in a music review. Fair use can apply in songwriting when a writer borrows a phrase or riff from another source. For example, the rap group 2 Live Crew borrowed the opening bass riff of the song "Pretty Woman" and the words (but not the melody) from the first line of the song ("Oh pretty woman walking down the street"). The rest of the lyrics and the music were different. The U.S. Supreme Court permitted it as a fair use because the 2 Live Crew song was a parody, holding the original song up to ridicule.

The difficulty of applying fair use is that the standard is often subjective. That is, you can't guarantee that your band's use is a fair use until a judge makes a determination in a lawsuit—at which point your band may be bankrupt from legal fees. As with other copyright issues, the problem with suing people about fair use claims is that you can't tell ahead of time whether you'll win, and astronomical legal bills often make "winning" not even worth it.

 CANADIAN RULES

Fair use principles differ in the United States and Canada. The standards for the American principle of fair use are defined in the federal copyright law. In Canada, a related principle known as "fair dealing" is used, although it is not explicitly defined in the Canadian law. U.S. rules of fair use may not be the same as Canadian fair dealing principles. For more information on Canadian Copyright law, visit the Canadian Intellectual Property Office (CIPO) website (www.cipo.ic.gc.ca). The site has downloadable forms and circulars about various copyright subjects as well as copyright applications and forms. Circular 2, *Musical Works and Mechanical Contrivances*, is particularly helpful. The site includes information on copyright, online registration, and other electronic services.

Dear Rich: Can We Arrange Elvis Songs?

I'm planning to create an arrangement of Elvis Presley tunes for string quartet. Do I need permission to just use these arrangements for my own string quartet? What if I want to sell the arrangements to others?

You're probably fine arranging and performing a few Elvis songs for private performances. That's because the owners of the music are unlikely to notice (or to care if they do find out). If you plan to perform the music publicly, the venue would need to pay for public performance royalties. If you were to record and release the music, you'd need to pay mechanical royalties.

What if you want to do more? You will need permission if you plan on promoting sales or distribution of sheet music arrangements to other quartets (or seek to stop others who copied your arrangement). That's because the making of sheet music requires authorization whether it is a straight reproduction of the sheet music or an "arrangement" or "orchestration" that qualifies as a derivative work. In other words, you can't reproduce the underlying work—for example, "Heartbreak Hotel"—in a printed arrangement, without the publisher's permission. You can usually find the music publisher's contact information at the following sites: Harry Fox, BMI, ASCAP, or Easy Song Licensing. Also, the National Association for Music Education website has an example of a request form for permission to create musical arrangements.

Coauthorship and Co-Ownership of Songs

When a song or other creative work is created by more than one person, the issue of copyright ownership becomes more complex. This section will discuss how to figure out who owns copyright to a song written by more than one person.

Cowriters Are Co-Owners

When a song has more than one writer, the writers are known as co-owners. This is true whether the songwriters made equal or unequal contributions to the song. (Respective shares of contributions are discussed below.)

The co-owners share the legal rights to the song in the absence of an agreement to the contrary. Joint copyright owners can separately grant permission (a license) for someone to use the song in a movie, provided you share the income with the other. Similarly, either one of you could sue someone who illegally copied your song, provided that you share the financial recovery with your fellow writer.

When it comes to assignment (selling) of copyright, co-owners must jointly agree to sell rights to the whole song, or they can sell their individual share of the ownership. Before a song can be recorded for the first time, we recommend that you obtain the consent of all cowriters. Although copyright law does not explicitly require all writers to consent to the first recording, we recommend this approach since, after the first recording, anyone can record the song as long as payments are made according to compulsory license rules (explained in Chapter 12).

Although each co-owner is entitled to receive money from the song, this doesn't mean that the two writers have to share money from the song equally. One writer may receive 30% of the income and the other may earn 70%. Each writer's share is usually based on the value of their contribution. This is a matter that is agreed on by the two writers. If the writers do not agree and the issue turns into a lawsuit, then a court will decide on the value of each writer's contribution. Courts often start with the presumption that all songwriters contributed equally.

Evaluating Songwriting Contributions

Sometimes, cowriters have a difficult time evaluating their relative contributions. Songwriting credit is one of the touchiest subjects among band members. The following scenario is a common one: The guitar player creates a song structure—some chord changes over a rhythm. The singer adds words and a melody. The bass player figures a bass part. The keyboard player improvises a solo. The problem begins when all four believe they should be listed as cowriters of the song. The internal dispute distracts the band from its music and disrupts band business.

Traditional Methods of Determining the Songwriter

Historically, the creators of the "lead sheet"—the words, melody, and harmonic chord structure—were considered the songwriters. That's because the words, music, and chord changes (along with the tempo) were traditionally the only elements necessary for sheet music. The creation of a solo or a supporting bass or drum part was usually *not* considered an element of songwriting for two reasons: (1) These parts, although they enhance the recorded performance, are not considered essential to the structure of the song; and (2) solos and rhythm parts are usually derived from a limited language of musical parts, and this limited language is not protected by copyright law. For many bands, the old rule still holds true: The creators of the words, melody, and chords are the songwriters.

Exceptions to the Traditional Approach

As songwriting has evolved, exceptions have developed to traditional rules. For example, in rock, pop, and dance music, it's possible that a bass or drum part is so integral to the song that it becomes as important as the melody—for example, the memorable bass riffs on "Come Together" or "White Lines," or the drum solo on "Wipeout." In that case, the members of the band may determine among themselves that the contributor of the riff be included as a songwriter.

How can you tell if a part is important enough to become an element of the song? One way is to ask yourself if another artist covered your song, would the other artist want to duplicate this part? Almost every artist who covers the song "Satisfaction" includes the opening guitar/bass riff. As a general rule, if the part is an indispensable element of the song, then the creator of the part should be considered a songwriter.

> **RESOURCE**
> **"A Whiter Shade of Pale."** An interesting case of songwriter credit arose in the case of the song "A Whiter Shade of Pale" by the '60s group Procol Harum. For an analysis of the songwriting credits for the haunting organ part, see www.procolharum.com/awsopcomp.htm.

Sometimes Rules Don't Matter

It's possible that a band can ditch these evaluation rules and decide on its own method of evaluating songwriter contributions. It's even possible that a person who made no contribution to a song can be listed as a writer. For example, Elvis Presley's manager often demanded that songwriters give Elvis a cowriting credit if they wanted him to perform a song. Songwriters, eager to have a song on an Elvis recording, sometimes shared the credit and partial ownership interest.

It is also important to remember that a person can earn money from a song even if not listed as a songwriter. As we explain in the next chapter, a band member can earn money from a song even if not listed as a writer. If the band earns money from publishing songs, all band members can receive income from band songs if the band partnership agreement provides for sharing songwriting income.

> **EXAMPLE:** The Smokers is a group consisting of four members: songwriters Sasha and Gompers, as well as nonwriters Cherry and Ratgirl. The group has decided to share songwriting royalties. The songs written by Sasha and Gompers are published by their band publishing company. Under their band partnership agreement, the income from the published songs is split equally among the four members.

If You Don't Come Up With a System, Someone Else Will

If you do not have a system for allocating songwriting contributions and a dispute about distributing profits ends up in court, the court will presume that each songwriter contributed equally. For example, if three people wrote a song and there was no agreement among them, a court, unless faced with contrary evidence, would presume that each writer owned a one-third interest. If you want to make ownership decisions yourselves rather than letting a court decide, work out an agreement early on.

Partnership and Collaboration Agreements

Songwriting ownership among joint owners is usually addressed in two types of agreements. One is a collaboration or cowriter agreement; the other is the band partnership agreement. If your band does not have a partnership agreement or does not intend to address songwriting ownership in your partnership agreement, the songwriters should enter into a collaboration agreement.

The collaboration agreement is usually used when two or more people write together. The agreement can be used for one song or for many songs, and it sets forth the percentages and rights of the songwriters. A collaboration agreement can be as simple as a statement of the percentage interests and the name of the song, signed by all writers.

If songs are written jointly by band members, the ownership rights are expressed in the band's partnership agreement (BPA) rather than a collaboration agreement. As discussed in Chapter 2, you can use customized clauses in your BPA to establish exactly the division of songwriting rights and income among band members. For example, if there are four members in a band, but all songs are written by two of the members, the partnership agreement can establish a system dividing up songwriting income as follows:

- songwriting band members earn 60%,
- nonsongwriting band members earn 40%.

In Chapter 8 we offer several alternative systems for dividing up band songwriting income.

Copyright Infringement

Copyright infringement occurs when a song is copied, modified, or performed without authorization of the song owner(s). If the owner did not authorize the use, and if no legal principle such as fair use permitted it (discussed above), then the infringer can be sued for damages to the copyright owner.

Is There Damage?

There are various standards and tests for determining infringement. However, these tests and standards are often less important than a very basic issue: Has the song owner been injured? That is, has the song owner suffered some financial damage because of the infringement? The purpose of an infringement lawsuit is to provide a remedy for the copyright owner's injury. Without a real injury (that is, lost revenue), the issue of infringement is academic and one for which judges have little patience. Even if the songwriter who is suing can claim a minimum amount of damages established by law, a judge will still fashion an award that reflects the true injury.

For example, in one famous case the composer of a song called "Dardanella" sued Jerome Kern, the composer of "Kahlua." The melodies of the songs were different, but the composer of "Dardanella" claimed Mr. Kern had copied part of the *ostinato,* an eight-note pattern that repeated within the background accompaniment. The *ostinato* was not a particularly important aspect of either work, and the owner of "Dardanella" could not prove any injury from the infringement. The judge presiding over the trial, the famous Judge Learned Hand, was annoyed. "This controversy is a mere point of honor of scarcely more than irritation, involving no substantial interest. Except that it raises an interesting point of law, it would be a waste of time for everyone concerned." Judge Hand awarded the plaintiff the minimum amount possible: $250. This case is a reminder that copyright claims should not be filed on principle, but only if actual damages exist. Similarity of works is important, but only if it is closely related to proving an injury.

A large damage payment was justified in a 1994 case involving the singer Michael Bolton. The court in this case ruled that one of Bolton's biggest hits, "Love Is a Wonderful Thing," infringed a song by the Isley Brothers. A jury awarded the Isley Brothers $5.4 million. The verdict was upheld on appeal.

In one of the most surprising music infringement decisions, a jury determined in 2015 that "Blurred Lines," written by Pharrell Williams and Robin Thicke, infringed Marvin Gaye's song "Got to Give It Up" and awarded $7.4 million. (See "Five Lessons From the 'Blurred Lines' Case," below).

Five Lessons From the "Blurred Lines" Case

In 2015, a jury determined that the song, "Blurred Lines," written by Pharrell Williams and Robin Thicke, infringed Marvin Gaye's song "Got to Give It Up." The jury awarded Marvin Gaye's heirs $7.4 million, reflecting the profits earned by "Blurred Lines," which (hard as it may be for some to believe) was the longest running number-one single of the entire decade (racking up sales of 14.8 million copies). Because of the dissimilarity of the songs, the case's outcome is dumbfounding for musicians. Hindsight, affording us excellent vision, reveals five lessons.

- Declaratory actions don't always succeed. The Gaye family didn't file the lawsuit; it was Thicke and Williams who filed, using a procedure known as a declaratory action (used when a party has been threatened with a lawsuit and seeks a preemptive ruling). The procedure has its advantages—Thicke and Williams got to pick the location for the case—but the procedure can also backfire, as some legal experts believe happened here. By initiating the lawsuit, Williams and Thicke may have ruined the chances of a quiet resolution before the song became a super mega hit.

- Don't bother with the "high as hell" defense. Sometimes, one party to a lawsuit is perceived as a villain, and it's all downhill from there. Thicke admitted during the trial that he wasn't present when the song was written and was too high on Vicodin and alcohol to compose anything, anyway. That testimony painted him unfavorably as a lying pop star who wanted credit when the song was a hit but who denied liability when accused of infringement. Character judgment shouldn't be a factor when determining substantial similarity ... but any case can get derailed when one party's veracity is put into question.

- Don't announce you want to copy someone's song. Thicke told GQ Magazine, "Pharrell and I were in the studio and I told him that one of my favorite songs of all time was Marvin Gaye's 'Got to Give it Up.' I was like, 'Damn, we should make something like that, something with that groove." Similar comments were made to other publications. Later when asked by the Gaye family lawyers what he meant, Thicke's defense was that his comments couldn't be trusted because he was "high and drunk" when he did interviews.

Five Lessons From the "Blurred Lines" Case, continued

- Don't prevent jurors from hearing both versions. Many music listeners don't hear much similarity—aside from the uncopyrightable "live party" elements—when comparing the recording of "Blurred Lines" with Gaye's performance of "Got to Give It Up." But the jury never got the chance to make a similar comparison because they never heard Gaye's version. Lawyers for Thicke and Williams argued that Gaye deposited sheet music when he registered his copyright back in 1977 (standard operating procedure for the time) and therefore, the Gaye family's claim could only be limited to the elements in the sheet music. In hindsight, limiting Gaye's claim to the sheet music may have worked against the "Blurred Lines" crew because it allowed the family's lawyers to take a nonholistic approach to the songs. Instead of getting a total feel for each song, the lawyers disassembled the sheet music and focused on eight distinct notated similarities.
- Juries are unpredictable. 'Nuff said.

Of course, many copyright infringement lawsuits are brought out of spite or revenge, or just on principle. When copyright cases are brought for reasons other than money, it's usually because at least one of the participants can afford to slug it out in court.

Substantial Similarity

The standard for copyright infringement is whether the songs are "substantially similar." For purposes of determining infringement, unprotectable similarities such as similar tempos or use of common song forms are generally disregarded. Other similarities may be evaluated by themselves, but the final decision is always based on comparing the complete songs.

There is a common myth among musicians that four bars of music may be copied without infringing copyright. Like most myths, this one's not true. The standard to determine whether infringement has occurred is not the *amount* taken, but the *importance* of the portion taken. If the copied portion of a song is quantitatively small, the court will determine the importance of that portion to the original song. For example, the copying of two bars of music in one song was held to be an infringement, while the copying of six bars of music in another song was not an infringement. Unfortunately, there is no formula that establishes how much taking equals substantial similarity. Below, we briefly discuss some of the common issues that arise regarding song infringement.

All Access: Proving an Infringer Heard Your Song

If you're trying to prove that your song was copied, you won't be able to make that claim unless you can prove two things: that the works are substantially similar, and that there is evidence that the alleged infringer listened to your tune (known as "access").

If there is no access, there is no infringement. For example, in a case involving the Britney Spears song, "What U See is What U Get," two men alleged that they had sent their version of a song to a talent scout representing Spears. However, the court ruled for Spears because the evidence at trial showed that she had recorded her version several months before the two men had even submitted their composition.

The more popular your song is, the easier it is for you to prove access. For example, the copyright owner of the hit song "He's So Fine" sued the late George Harrison, alleging that Harrison's song "My Sweet Lord" infringed copyright. It was proven that Harrison had access to "He's So Fine," since the song was on the British pop charts in 1963 (while a song by the Beatles was also on the British charts). The court concluded Harrison had access—that is, a reasonable opportunity to hear the plaintiff's song—and awarded the defendant $1.6 million.

Conversely, if a song was never released, the copyright owner has a much harder time proving access. For example, an unknown songwriter mailed a demo copy of his song to publishers and record companies listed in an industry songwriter book. Later, the songwriter claimed that two songs performed by Celine Dion infringed his song. The evidence demonstrated that the songwriter's demo never made it past the corporate mailrooms of the companies being sued. The court concluded that "bare corporate receipt" of a song generated by an unsolicited mass mailing was inadequate, by itself, to show access.

When two songs in question are identical, access may be presumed and does not need to be proven. That's because in cases of verbatim copying, it is virtually impossible that two songs could have been independently created. In situations such as this, the burden is on the defendant, the alleged infringer, to disprove access.

Pursuing an Infringer

If you think someone is stealing your song, you will have to prove that the other artist had access to your song (see "All Access: Proving an Infringer Heard Your Song," above) and copied it (or a portion of it), and that the portion that was copied is protected under copyright. If you win your lawsuit, you are entitled to money damages: either the infringer's profits or the fair market value of the use of the song (or special statutory damages; see below). That is, you are entitled to the amount of money that the infringer received for sales of the record, or to the amount you would have received for licensing the song *minus* gross expenses.

If you registered your song prior to the infringement, you may choose to receive special damages, known as statutory damages, instead. These can range up to $150,000 for willful infringements. The actual amount is determined by a judge. Regardless of whether you registered the song prior to the infringement, you can also stop the infringer from any further uses of the infringing song. You should also note that songs are ripped off in many ways. Several advertising companies have been sued for using popular songs in TV commercials without a license.

When considering the strength of your case and deciding whether or not to pursue it, an equally important issue is whether it's worth it even if you win. If the infringing song has not earned money or if the person you are suing has no assets (or if they declare bankruptcy), you will have spent a lot of money for an empty victory. And few copyright infringement cases are assured of victory; they're notoriously difficult to predict. The only general rule is that the more successful your band, the better your chances.

EXAMPLE: **John Fogerty and "The Old Man Down the Road."** Can an author infringe his own work? This may seem like an academic question, but it had a very real application for songwriter John Fogerty when he was sued in 1985. Many of the songs written by Fogerty and popularized by his group Creedence Clearwater Revival were owned by Fantasy Records, a California company. Fantasy sued Fogerty, claiming that one of his newer songs, "The Old Man Down the Road," infringed a 1970 song, "Run Through the Jungle," also written by Fogerty and owned by Fantasy. Fogerty brought his guitar into court, sang both songs for the jury and demonstrated that the elements common to both songs were unprotectable and common to many rock and roll songs. Fogerty won this novel lawsuit (*Fantasy, Inc. v. Fogerty*, 510 U.S. 517 (1994)) and in the process established that a person defending an infringement lawsuit, like the person bringing the suit, is also entitled to the awarding of attorney fees.

Defending Against an Infringement Claim

There are two common reasons why someone may threaten to sue your band over a song:

- A songwriter claims that your song (or a portion of your song) is taken from his copyrighted song.
- A songwriter claims that your song uses a sample from his copyrighted recording. (A "sample" is a portion of a recording that is digitally copied and mixed into your song.)

In the first situation—a songwriter claims you have stolen a song—you will be subject to the copyright infringement standards expressed previously in this chapter. That is, did your band have access to the song, and are the two songs substantially similar? The second situation—sampling—is more complex. We discuss sampling issues in Chapter 11.

As in the case of pursuing an infringer, you need to ask yourself: Regardless of whether any copyright law has actually been violated, how much will it cost to fight? The unfortunate fact is that most working bands can't spare the money necessary to defend a lawsuit. They usually settle the dispute in the cheapest manner possible. Sometimes this means that the band changes the song or stops using the song altogether. For the sake of your band's business, you need to carefully evaluate your course of action with an attorney.

How to Avoid Getting Screwed in Conflicts Over Songs

There are several ways in which bands get into conflicts over band songs. With a basic understanding of copyright law and a willingness to deal with it, these types of disputes can usually be avoided.

Situation #1:
There is a dispute among your band members as to who wrote a song.

Many bands neglect to hammer out song ownership shares before they begin to perform or record a song. If the song becomes popular and the band has not established who will receive songwriting credit, a nasty dispute can ensue, which can seriously harm the band's business.

How to avoid getting screwed:

The best way to deal with a songwriting dispute within your band is to avoid it in the first place. Besides educating yourself about how songs can be jointly owned (discussed earlier in this chapter), it's important to be up front about what each band member wants and expects. If the songwriters in the band do not want to share income from songs with nonsongwriters, they need to clearly say so. It's an understandable and common position among songwriters; after all, songwriting is a special talent that can catapult a good band into a best-selling band. The songwriters, like star athletes on a team, may want to receive a reward for their special talents. If this is the case in your band, it's important to deal with it before releasing a record or preparing to sign a record deal. Band discussions about songwriting can become heated, but don't let that dissuade you from having the discussion if it's time. Avoiding the issue can only cause problems later.

Situation #2:
Your band is sued on an infringement claim.

Bands get screwed in two ways when they are sued over songwriting: (1) A band is pressured into giving up rights because it can't afford to fight the lawsuit; or (2) a band spends too much money and time fighting a lawsuit, even if it ultimately wins.

How to avoid getting screwed:

If your band is threatened with a lawsuit over a song, you need to first evaluate your band's song. Determine whether the song is important enough for your band that it's worth fighting over. For example, if you created a song that borrows a great deal from "Communication Breakdown," and the owners of the Led Zeppelin song threaten to sue your band, your first decision is whether you care enough about your song to fight over it. If you don't, it's easiest (and cheapest) to agree to stop using and selling the song. We are not recommending that you always give up when threatened. We are suggesting, however, always to keep in mind that lawsuits do not always resolve "Who is right?" but rather, "Who has more money?"

If you *do* care about the song and it is important to your band, then you should seek professional help *pronto!* Take your dispute to an attorney (see Chapter 4 for information on dealing with attorneys) and get an assessment of your chances of success in the lawsuit. Do this *immediately* after receiving the threat of the lawsuit—any delay may affect your ability to settle the suit. No lawyer can guarantee whether you'll win or lose, but an experienced copyright attorney can assess your chances of success.

Only if your odds are better than 75% should your band think about fighting. It's possible in some cases that an attorney can deal with the matter for between $1,500 and $5,000, and you won't have to be bullied into a settlement. It's also possible that if the claim against your band is completely worthless (referred to as a frivolous claim), a court may award you an amount to cover your attorney fees. However, don't count on this, as attorney fees awards are rare.

Situation #3:
Your band wants to sue another band for infringement.
A band hears a song with some chords and riffs that are somewhat similar to one of its songs. The band gets angry and hires an attorney. If it loses the case, it gets buried in legal fees. It may even be required to pay the other side's legal fees. Or it may win the case but fail to recover any money from the other band (which has no real assets) and still end up buried in legal fees.

How to avoid getting screwed:
It's a mistake to hire an attorney and go after a potential infringer without thoroughly reviewing the case and determining whether any money can be recovered. In order to avoid getting screwed, your band needs the opinion of a copyright attorney. If an attorney doesn't believe that your band will win a lawsuit or recover any money, then it's probably a good idea to give up on the matter. You may feel that you have been cheated, but don't confuse your moral outrage with your legal rights.

If your attorney feels you have a good case of copyright infringement and that money can be recovered, you need to figure out how you will pay your lawyer. Perhaps your attorney will take the case on a contingency basis, in which case the attorney usually receives one-quarter to one-third of any money recovered. If you lose, you don't have to pay any attorney fees. Note, however, that even if you use a contingency arrangement, your band will probably have to pay nonattorney legal costs such as document fees or court costs, which can quickly add up to hundreds (or thousands) of dollars. (See Chapter 4 for information about hiring attorneys.)

What About Song Parodies?

In order to parody or satirize a song, it's necessary to borrow a portion of the song. For example, Weird Al Yankovic's "Like a Surgeon" wouldn't be an effective parody of "Like a Virgin" if the melody was not borrowed from the original. Therefore, all parodies borrow or modify the original songs. Since only the copyright owner is allowed to modify the song without authorization, the makers of parodies must either get permission or prove that their parody is excused under the principle of fair use.

Judges understand that, by its nature, parody demands some taking from an original work, and a more extensive use of a copyrighted work is permitted, therefore, in order to "conjure up" the original. At issue is often the effect on the potential market—or as it is sometimes phrased in legalese, whether the parodist's result had the intent or the effect of fulfilling a demand for the original work.

This determination is often tricky. For example, in the 1986 case of *Fisher v. Dees*, the composers of the song "When Sunny Gets Blue" claimed that their song was infringed by "When Sonny Sniffs Glue," a 29-second parody that altered the original lyric line and borrowed six bars of the plaintiff's music. The copyright owner argued that the parody reflected negatively on the original song and therefore affected its marketability. The court responded that: "[T]he economic effect of a parody with which we are concerned is not its potential to destroy or diminish the market for the original—any bad review can have that effect—but whether it *fulfills the demand for the original.*" In other words, the important factor is whether the market for the original will be reduced due to people buying the parody instead of the original. The court permitted "When Sonny Sniffs Glue" as a fair use.

What About Song Parodies?, continued

A similar result was reached in a 2003 case involving a rap song entitled "The Forest." The rap song borrowed the first three lines of "What a Wonderful World" ("I see trees of green, red roses too/I see them bloom for me and you/ And I think to myself, what a wonderful world") and ridiculed the description of beauty and optimism by changing the lyrics into an invitation to get high on marijuana ("I see buds that are green, red roses too/I see blunts for me and you/And I say to myself, what a wonderful world"). The lyrics in the rap song borrowed three lines from "Wonderful World," used them once at the beginning of the song, and did not borrow any other music or lyrics or sample the original recording. On that basis a court determined that the use was a parody and permitted under fair use principles.

Borrowing a complete song (not merely 29 seconds or the first three lines) and modifying the lyrics is, however, unlikely to be excused as fair use or parody. Performers such as Weird Al Yankovic who earn a living by humorously modifying hit songs seek permission of the songwriters before recording their parodies.

When Your Song Insults Someone

Occasionally, songwriters are sued if a song makes disparaging remarks about a person, character, or product. For example, John Fogerty wrote a song critical of a record company owner and got sued. (He eventually changed the lyrics.) This type of lawsuit is not based on infringement of copyright. Instead it is based on libel and slander law, which may prohibit you from making untrue statements that cause the public to think less of someone or some product. The standards for libel and slander vary considerably from situation to situation. If you are threatened with such a lawsuit, you should consult an attorney or someone knowledgeable as to the libel laws in your state.

What If Your Song Parodies a Doll?

What if your song isn't a parody of another song, but instead parodies a famous brand name such as the Barbie Doll? In 1997, the Danish group Aqua had a hit with their song "Barbie Girl," in which a singer impersonating Barbie in a high-pitched, doll-like voice chanted, "Life in plastic, it's fantastic." The band did not take any copyrighted material—that is, they did not copy words, music, or images owned by Mattel, the maker of Barbie Doll. Instead, the band only borrowed the famous "Barbie" trademarked name. Mattel sued for trademark infringement and for trademark dilution, a claim that someone is blurring or tarnishing a famous trademark (see Chapter 9). This type of lawsuit differs from copyright infringement because it raises the issue of how the parody affects consumers. For example, would consumers be confused that Mattel sponsored or supported the song? Fortunately, in 2002, a federal judge stepped in to protect the free speech rights of the band and its label, declaring that consumers were not likely to be confused by the band's use of "Barbie." Demonstrating the resilience of the Barbie trademark to such uses, the judge (referring to Mattel as "Speech-Zilla") declared, "Over the years ... Barbie has been labeled both the ideal American woman and a bimbo. She has survived attacks both psychic (from feminists critical of her fictitious figure) and physical (more than 500 professional makeovers)."

Before your band rushes out to parody famous trademarks, keep in mind that Aqua had the legal resources of one of the world's largest record labels, MCA, to fight Mattel. Most bands faced with a lawsuit from the owner of an internationally known trademark will have a difficult time battling—even if legally in the right—against corporate suits. This isn't to say that you should shy away from using your free speech rights, but choose your parodies carefully and, when in doubt, seek the advice of an entertainment lawyer.

Copyright Preregistration

Copyright law gives songwriters (and other copyright owners) the ability to preregister their works. This was done in order to deal with a digital-age problem: prerelease infringement. Songwriters or musicians whose works are prone to infringement before release may preregister their work by filling out an online application at the Copyright Office website. A copy of the unpublished work need not be provided.

The copyright owner of an unpublished work that has been preregistered may file a copyright infringement suit without having to register the work with the Copyright Office. This allows a lawsuit to be filed quickly and may help the owner obtain court action to prevent distribution of the work.

Even more important, the copyright owner may obtain statutory damages and attorney fees in a successful infringement suit against anyone who pirated the unfinished work after the preregistration was made, provided that the work is fully registered with the Copyright Office during the earlier of the following times:

- three months after the first publication of the work, or
- one month after the copyright owner learned of the infringement.

For the vast majority of musicians, preregistration is a waste of money. Few songs or recordings are infringed before they are published or otherwise distributed. This type of thing usually occurs with popular songs recorded by superstar artists. However, you may benefit by preregistering your work if you think it's likely someone may infringe your unfinished song or recording before it is released.

You can preregister your song only if:

- it is unpublished
- its creation has begun, and
- it is being prepared for commercial distribution.

You preregister by completing an online application at the Copyright Office website (www.copyright.gov). You must provide the following information:

- the work's title (a working title may be used)
- the names of the author and copyright claimant
- the date the actual writing of the song began and the date you anticipate completing it, and
- a description of the work—for example, that it is a song, and any other details that may help identify the work in published form.

Copyright Preregistration, continued

You need not provide the Copyright Office with a copy of your unpublished song or make any other deposit. The nonrefundable filing fee for preregistration is $140.

If you fill out the application correctly, the Copyright Office will email you a notification of preregistration, which will include a preregistration number and date. This is the only notice you will receive that preregistration has been made. The Copyright Office does not issue a paper certificate of preregistration.

Copyright Registration

As we explained earlier in this chapter, copyright registration is not necessary to protect your songs—but it can help. There are three strong arguments in favor of copyright registration:

- The registration creates a presumption of ownership and validity. That is, if you register the song within five years of releasing it to the public, it is presumed that you are the owner of the song and that copyright is valid.
- If a work has been registered prior to an infringement or within three months of publication, the copyright owner may be entitled to special payments known as "statutory damages" in the case of a successful lawsuit against an infringer. You may also be entitled to receive your attorney fees from the person you sued.
- A registration is required to file a copyright infringement lawsuit. That is, if you sue someone over infringement of your song, you will have to register before filing your lawsuit. If you wish to accomplish registration within a week, there is a method for expediting it. For a special handling fee of $800 (plus the $35 to $85 filing fee), the Copyright Office will process an application within five working days. However, this service is not for convenience; it is allowed only in urgent cases. The Copyright Office has prepared a form for *Request for Special Handling* (see Circular 10 at www.copyright.gov).

Completing a copyright application is not difficult. If you need help, the Copyright Office provides guides for filling out the application.

Preparing a Copyright Application for a Song

Once you have decided you want to register, your next decision is whether to register electronically or to file a paper application. Electronic is cheaper, results in faster turnaround, allows you to track the application, permits you to pay using secure credit or debit card payments or via ACH bank account withdrawal, and lets you, in some cases, upload deposit materials.

Note copyright fees change often (on average at least every three to four years) so you should check at the Copyright Office website for the current fees schedule before filing. The Fees Schedule is located at copyright.gov/docs/fees.html. At the time this edition was published, the fee to register was $35 if you file electronically and provided you're registering one song written by one songwriter who also owns the copyright. All other electronic application filings were $55. Paper application filings were $85.

In order to complete the application, you'll need the names of the songwriters as well as their citizenship and their contributions—for example, music or lyrics. And of course, you'll also need the song titles. You may also include any main or primary title for a collection of songs. If you are not claiming copyright in some portion of a song—for example, you didn't write the lyrics but instead took them from the Gettysburg Address—you'll need that information, too in order to exclude that portion and limit your claim to specifically what you created and are claiming. You'll also need to categorize whether the songs are published or unpublished.

Besides this information, you'll need a digital or hard copy of your song. The type of format and the number of copies depend on a few factors discussed later in this chapter.

The Copyright Office provides extensive help for the application process. There are downloadable circulars that explain registration procedures for every type of work—for example, the Copyright Office provides advice on registering comic books, software, songs, websites, and much more. The eCO electronic system is also heavily documented with online guidance. For example, the Copyright Office website offers a PowerPoint presentation,

FAQs, and more. All of this can be found at www.copyright.gov. Click "Circulars and Brochures" for advice on filing. Click "Forms" to access copyright application forms. An explanation for each of the three primary methods of filings is provided below.

Registering Multiple Songs on One Application

The Copyright Office allows you to save money by registering a group of songs on one application. To do so, you must meet a few requirements. First you'll need to determine whether your songs were published. As a general rule, a song is published if physical or digital copies change hands—that is, they are distributed or sold to the public.

If your songs were *not* published, you can register an unlimited group of them on one application provided the collection bears a single identifying title (you may also identify each song title on the application), and that the person or persons claiming copyright is the same for all of the songs. In addition, there's one more qualification: if the songs were written by more than one writer, one of the writers must have written or cowritten all of the songs.

> EXAMPLE: Your band has ten unpublished songs. Jill and Ted wrote nine, and Jill wrote one. You can register all ten songs on one application.

> EXAMPLE: Your band has ten unpublished songs. Jill and Ted wrote seven, two were written by Jill, and one was written by Bud. You can register the nine songs on which Jill is a songwriter on one application. A separate application will have to be used for Bud's song.

If the songs were published, you can register several songs on one application provided your songs were all first published together on the same date (in what the Copyright Office refers to as a "unit of publication"). In other words, if you release an album, EP, or a digital collection of songs published together (all on the same date), you can register those songs on one application, provided of course that the same person or persons owns the copyright for all the songs. Unlike unpublished songs, one writer does not have to contribute to all of the songs.

If you plan on registering a group of songs, here's one tip: Be sure to list the titles for all of the songs. Don't simply list a title such as "The Collected Songs of The Smokers, June 2018."

Using One Application to Register Songs and Sound Recording

Although they are separate works, a musical composition and a sound recording may be registered together on a single application if ownership of the copyrights in both is exactly the same. To register a single claim in both works, give information about the author(s) of both the musical composition and the sound recording. For more information, see Chapter 11, or consult Copyright Circular 56a.

Registering a Song Using the eCO Copyright Application

The electronic copyright (eCO) application process has three parts. The applicant:

- completes the online interview
- pays the fee (payment can be made by credit/debit card, ACH, or by setting up a deposit account), and
- uploads or mails copies of the work. Unpublished songs and songs published only electronically (downloads or streaming only) can be uploaded. The Copyright Office accepts most common formats—for example, AIF, MP3, WAV, and WMA format files—but there is a 30-minute upload limit. All other works must be sent by U.S. Postal Service (USPS). You will be instructed to print out a shipping slip to be attached to the work for delivery by the USPS.

Need help? The Copyright Office has done a nice job of explaining the process and making it user friendly. There is a good tutorial and set of FAQs to walk you through the electronic filing process. In addition, the eCO process is peppered with helpful drop-down menus, as well as hypertext links that provide pop-up explanations for each aspect of the application process. The explanations for paper forms provided earlier in this section should aid you answering the online interview—for example, how to respond to questions regarding the nature of work, title, date of publication, etc.

You will need to create a user account and password. The eCO system includes a special "Save for Later" feature that will preserve your work in the event you sign off and then sign on at a later time.

Below are some the steps for filing online with eCO (along with explanations and some screenshots).

Step 1: Sign In

Go to the Copyright Office website (www.copyright.gov) and click "register a Copyright." Then click "Log in to the Electronic Copyright Office (eCO) Registration System." If you are already a registered user, then log in. If not, click to register and get your ID and password. Choose "Register a Work: Standard Application," then "Start Registration."

Step 2: Choose the Work

Using the drop-down menu, choose the type of work. For songs, choose "Work of the Performing Arts."

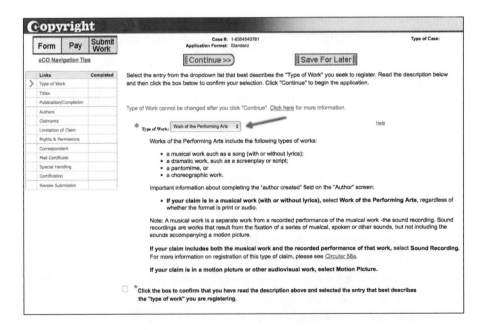

Step 3: Titles

If you are registering only one song, click "New." From the Title Type drop-down menu, choose "Title of work being registered" and then enter the title in the box marked "Title of this work." Then click "Save."

If you are registering several songs (see the section "Registering Multiple Songs on One Application," above) you would first click "New," then choose "Title of work being registered" from the Title Type drop-down menu. If the songs were published as a unit, give the title of the project. If the songs were unpublished, name the collection.

Then click "New" and this time choose "Contents Title" from the Title Type drop-down and then enter the first song title in the box marked "Title of this work." Then click "Save" and repeat the procedure for each song in the project.

You'll notice that a spreadsheet is created that includes each title and also provides the ability to edit or delete the title. Wherever you are in the application, you can return to this section by simply clicking the "Titles" link on the left sidebar.

When you're satisfied with the entries, click "Continue."

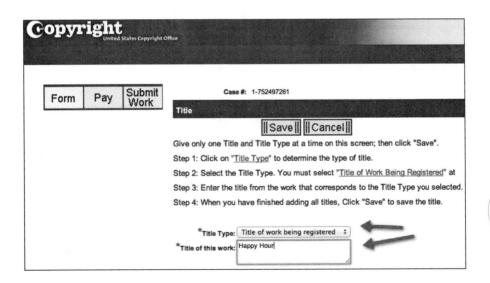

Step 4: Publication/Completion

When completing the copyright application, you will note that the Copyright Office distinguishes between published and unpublished songs. A song is published when it is first made available to the public on an unrestricted basis. For example, if you permit downloads, play the song at your website, or distribute CDs on an unrestricted basis, the song has been published. If your song has *not* been published, choose "No" from the drop-down menu. If you choose "No," you will only be required to provide the year of completion (below). If you choose "Yes," you will be required to complete the screen shown below.

Year of completion. Give the year in which creation of the song was completed—the date you stood back and said, "I'm done." If the song has been published, the year of completion cannot be later than the year of first publication.

Date of publication. Give the complete date, in mm/dd/yyyy format, on which the song was first published. If you're unsure, get as close as reasonably possible. Do not give a date that is in the future. Leave this line blank if the song is unpublished.

International Standard Number. You can leave this blank.

Nation of publication. Give the nation where the song was first published. If the song was first published simultaneously in the United States and another country; you can list the United States. Leave this line blank if the song is unpublished.

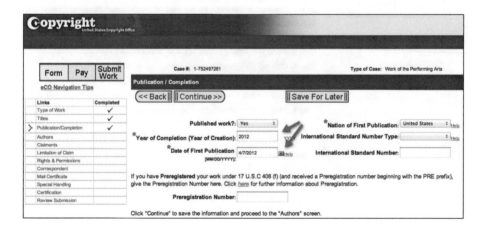

Step 5: Authors

Next you are going to enter information about the songwriters (or "authors" as the Copyright Office refers to them). If you're not sure who qualifies as a songwriter, you can sort that out by reviewing the previous information about cowriters in this chapter.

You will see a button entitled "Add Me." Assuming you're a songwriter, click the Add Me button and your name will populate the next screen. You are also offered a chance to name an organization as an author. That would be the case only if your song is considered a work made for hire. If you are unsure whether the song is a work for hire—for example, a company paid you to write the song—review the earlier segment on who owns a song or review Copyright Circular 9.

If it is not a work made for hire—which is most likely the case—answer "No" to the question, "Is this author's contribution a work made for hire?"

If all the members of a band wrote a song, don't list the band as the author (in the Organization box). Instead list each band member separately.

Choose your "Nation of Citizenship" or the nation in which you are domiciled (where you make your permanent home).

If for some reason you wish to remain anonymous check the "Anonymous" box and you may remove your name as an individual author. Keep in mind, you can only claim "anonymous" if your name is not credited on copies of the song that are distributed to the public.

A songwriter is "pseudonymous" if the songwriter's real name is not used on copies of the song, but instead the songwriter is identified under a fictitious name. If so, check the Pseudonymous box and enter the pseudonym. You may either reveal the pseudonymous songwriter's identity in the application (which is not uncommon—for example, "Robert Zimmerman, whose pseudonym is Bob Dylan") or leave the author fields blank. In any case, you must enter the pseudonym that is used.

Give the year the songwriter was born (and deceased, if applicable). The year of birth is optional. If you provide it, the birth year will be made part of the online public Copyright Office records and cannot be removed later. However, it is sometimes useful as a form of author identification when there are several songwriters with the same name.

On the next screen, indicate the author's contribution. To aid your decision, keep in mind that this information only provides a broad statement about what the person has contributed. Completing this section becomes more complicated if you want to divide up contributions per song when registering a group.

You can also use the "Other" box to more specifically describe the contribution, for example "melody," or if you wanted to claim all writing on a song, you could write "song: Happenstance" in the Other box. The Copyright Office recommends against designating contributions as an "idea," "concept," "title," or "name." Also, don't refer to instrumentation generally—for example don't write "trumpet" for the contribution. Instead write, "trumpet melody" or "music for trumpet." Finally, don't simply characterize a contribution as "rap," or "beats"—instead use a term such as "lyrics" or "musical beat."

Click "Save" and then click "New" if you are entering the names of cowriters. Repeat this procedure for all cowriters.

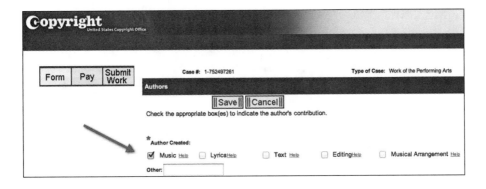

Step 6: Claimants

Here you are listing the person or entity that owns the copyright—either the author/songwriter or the person or organization to which the copyright has been transferred by an author or other authorized copyright owner. Choose "new" to enter the first claimant. You can also use the "Add Me" button to enter your registered name and contact information directly.

If you are registering a group of published or unpublished songs, the owner(s) must be the same for all of the compositions being registered (see "Registering Multiple Songs on One Application," above).

Keep in mind that the claimant postal address will be made part of the online public Copyright records and cannot be removed later. However, the email address and phone number will not appear in the public record unless it is also included in the section for Rights and Permissions Contact, below.

If the claimant (the person claiming copyright ownership) is the author of the song, skip the section about transfer information. Transfer information is required if the claimant is not an author but has obtained ownership of the copyright from the author or another owner. In that case, check the appropriate box to indicate how ownership was acquired. When you check "Written agreement" that includes a transfer by assignment or by contract. "Will or inheritance" applies only if the person from whom copyright was transferred is deceased. If necessary, check "Other" and give a brief statement indicating how copyright was transferred.

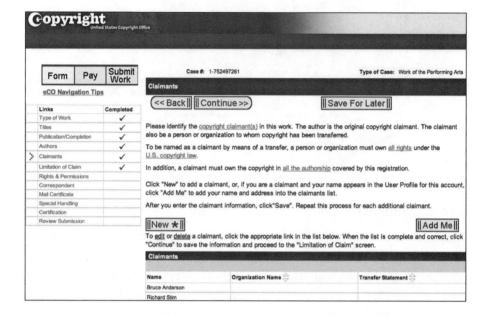

Step 7: Limitation of Claim

You do not need to complete this section unless the work contains or is based on previously registered or previously published material, material in the public domain, or material not owned by this copyright claimant. The purpose of this section is to exclude such material from the claim and identify the new material upon which the present claim is based.

Material excluded. Check the appropriate box or boxes to exclude any previously registered or previously published material, material in the public domain, or material not owned by this claimant. For example, if you were registering the music for a song but not the lyrics, you would check the "Lyrics" box to indicate you were excluding the lyrics.

Previous registration. If the song for which you are now seeking registration, or an earlier version of it, has been registered, give the registration number and the year of registration. If there have been multiple registrations, you may give information regarding the last two. If you are registering the first published version of a song that is identical to a previously registered unpublished version (contains no new material not already registered), check the "other" box and state "First publication of work registered as unpublished."

New material. Check the appropriate box or boxes to identify the new material you are claiming in this registration. Give a brief statement on the line after "other" only if it is necessary to give a more specific description of the new material included in this claim or if none of the check boxes applies.

For example, if you are providing a new arrangement of a public domain song, you would check the "text" and "music" boxes and state "new arrangement" on the "Other" line.

Step 8: Rights and Permissions

The eCO application asks for a listing of the person to contact for permission to use the material. If you are the person, you can simply click the "Add Me" button and the information will be generated to complete this section. Again, all the information given in this section, including name, postal address, email address, and phone number, will be made part of the online records produced by the Copyright Office and cannot be removed later from those public records. So, for example, you may wish to avoid posting your email or your personal phone number or home address.

Step 9: Correspondent

This is the person in your band that the Copyright Office should contact with any questions about this application. If this is the same as the first copyright claimant or the rights and permissions contact, simply check the appropriate box. (Information given only in this space will not appear in the online public record.)

Step 10: Mail Certificate

In this section, list the person in your band to whom the registration certificate should be mailed. If this is the same as the first copyright claimant, the rights and permissions contact, or the correspondence contact, simply check the appropriate box. (Information given only in this space will not appear in the online public record.)

Step 11: Special Handling

Special handling refers to an expedited registration. Most likely you will not be using this (it costs hundreds of dollars more) unless you are preparing to sue someone.

Step 12: Certification

Here is where you certify that all of the information in the application is true. It is a crime to provide false information and may result in invalidation of your application as well as a fine.

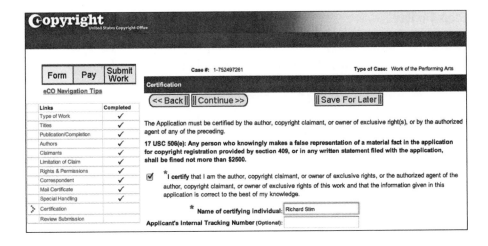

Step 13: Review

Here you will be provided with a chance to review all of the information you submitted in your application. If that is suitable, click the "Checkout" button.

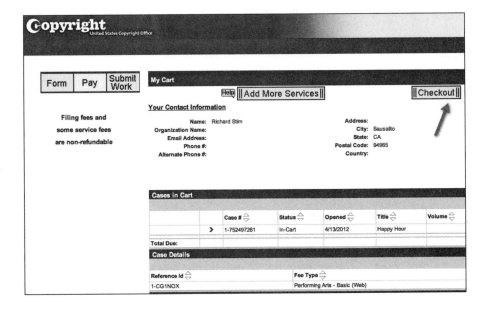

Step 14: Pay

In order to pay, you temporarily leave the Copyright Office website and pay at separate site, after which you will be directed back to a final screen.

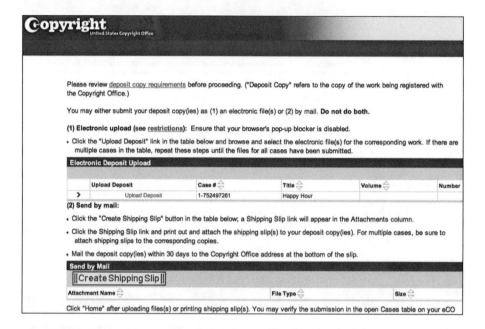

Step 15: Deposit

Your copyright application is not considered complete until the Copyright Office receives deposit materials—a copy (or copies) of your music. After paying for your application you will be directed to a page to assist with deposits. You will have two choices: Electronic Deposit Upload or Send By Mail. Here's how it works.

Unpublished songs. If your songs are unpublished, you can upload one complete copy (everything covered in the registration). The Copyright Office accepts common sound-file formats but there is a 30-minute per track upload limit. (Please note: The system has a 60-minute upload time out. This means if any one upload session takes longer than 60 minutes to complete, the system will time out, and you will have to break up that file into two or more smaller files in order to upload.) Alternatively, you can send in a CD or sheet music. The Copyright Office will provide you with a cover sheet to print out when mailing hard copies (Note: this is referred to as a "Shipping Slip/Receipt"; it is not a mailing label). The title of the collection should be legible on the CD.

Published songs. If your songs are published only in digital format—that is you never offered hard copies such as CDs—you can upload a complete copy. Otherwise, you'll need to use the mail. If the songs were only published on disks, tapes, or other hard-copy formats, send in one copy. However, if they were offered in digital and hard copy, or in a notated copy, or if your registration includes a sound recording copyright claim (see Chapter 11), you must send in two copies.

If you'll be uploading your deposit, click the "Upload Deposit" button and follow the instructions. If you'll be mailing your deposit, click the "Create a Shipping Slip" button. A form entitled "U.S. Copyright Office Receipt" will appear. A few of the fields will self-populate—Case, Case Date, and Title. Under "Materials Submitted," type in the number of copies you are sending, one or two, and the format, most likely compact disc.

Print it out, attach it to your copies, and mail it to the address provided on the bottom of the form. Once you've uploaded or mailed your deposit materials, you've completed the application process.

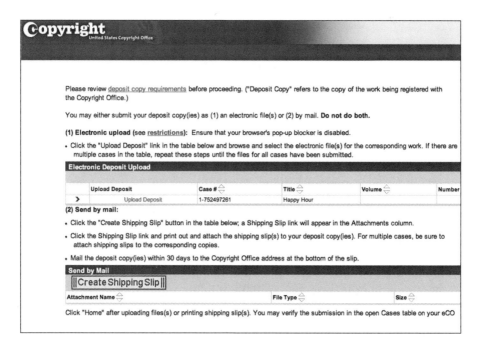

If you need to check the status of your application, sign back in to eCO and you can review its status or obtain a copy of the application (an example is shown below).

-APPLICATION-

Title ———————————————————————————————————————

Title of Work:	Happy Hour
	Calcutta Cutaway
	Smoky
	The Unsuspected
	Major Pipe
	The Bridge
	Paper Hat
	HoDaddy Humanoid
	Tall Boy
	Bar Stool Walker

Completion/Publication ———————————————————————

Year of Completion:	2012		
Date of 1st Publication:	April 7, 2012	**Nation of 1st Publication:**	United States

Author ———————————————————————————————————————

■ **Author:**	Richard Stim
Author Created:	music
Work made for hire:	No
Citizen of:	United States
Year Born:	1949
■ **Author:**	Bruce Anderson
Author Created:	music
Work made for hire:	No
Citizen of:	United States
Year Born:	1949

Registering a Song Using Form PA

Although used by less than 10% of current applicants, Form PA (available on the Copyright Office website) will soon be the only other alternative for filing for song copyright at the Copyright Office. To discourage its use, the Copyright office charges an $85 fee to file a Form PA (versus $35–$55 for electronic filings)

Below, we will walk you through the Form PA by referencing each of the numbered spaces on the form. You should be aware that some of the numbered spaces require more than one piece of information. Special instructions are included for registering collections of songs.

Space 1

Title and Nature of the Work. Every song must have a title in order to be registered. The title is used to index the work in Copyright Office records. If your title is in a foreign language, do not use a foreign alphabet to write it; use the Roman alphabet. (For information on registering multiple songs, see "Step 3: Titles," in the electronic filing section, above.)

Previous or Alternate Title. The alternate or previous title is any additional title under which someone searching for the song might look. For example, the song, "Everybody's Talkin'" is also known by an alternate title, "Theme From Midnight Cowboy."

Nature of Work. Space 1 of Form PA also requires information about the "nature of the work." You should state "words and music" unless there are no lyrics, in which case simply write "music."

Space 2

The Author. In this space, you must identify all songwriters and their contributions. For example: "Gary Wilson, words and music." If songwriters in your band are known by a nickname such as Slash or Flea, you may use the nickname, although when it comes to matters of song ownership and payments it's usually wiser to use your legal name. Among other things, there will be fewer hassles when cashing royalty checks at the bank. If a songwriter wants to be listed by a pseudonym, give the pseudonym and identify it as such (for example, "Flea, pseudonym"); or reveal the author's name, making it clear that it is a pseudonym (for example, "Robert Zimmerman, whose pseudonym is Bob Dylan"). You should also note that, in certain cases, using a pseudonym may shorten the period of copyright protection.

Works Made for Hire. A work made for hire is a song prepared by an employee hired to write songs or a song that is commissioned and meets certain legal requirements. Most likely, your song is not a work made for hire and you should check the "No" box. If your band hired people to write songs (for example, if the bandleader employed a songwriter), check the "Yes" box. If in doubt, refer to Copyright Circular 9.

Nature of Authorship. Provide a short statement of the nature of each writer's contribution. For example, if Bob wrote the words and music to a song, the nature of authorship would be "words and music." If Bob wrote the music and Sally wrote the words, the nature of Bob's authorship would be "music" and the nature of Sally's authorship would be "words" or "lyrics."

If Registering a Collection of Songs. For a collection of songs, see the requirements.

Dates of Birth and Death. The date of birth of each author should be provided. If one of the songwriters has died, the year of death should be provided.

Nationality. State each author's nationality.

Space 3

Creation and Publication. Creation and publication have two very different meanings under copyright law. A work is created when a final version of it is fixed (see "How Do You Obtain a Copyright?" above) for the first time in sheet music or on a recording. So as a general rule, the date of creation is when the work is completed and recorded or put into sheet music. For example, if you've been working on a song for months but finally finish it and record it in December 2018, then that is the date of creation.

A work is published if it is distributed to the public—for example, offered for sale or given away at shows. If you've made some demo recordings and sent them to music publishers or record companies, that is not considered a publication of the work; it hasn't been distributed to the public.

Date and Nation of First Publication. If you have not published your song (that is, pressed it on recordings and distributed it to the public), leave this section blank. If you have published the song, give the full date (that is, month, day, and year) when the work was published. If you're unsure, it is okay to state "approximately" (that is, "approximately June 4, 2018"). If the work was first published in the United States, the initials, "U.S.A." may be used. If the work was simultaneously published (within 30 days) in two countries, for example, the U.S. and Canada, it is acceptable to state, "U.S.A." If the work was first published in a foreign country, the foreign edition constitutes the first publication.

Space 4

The Copyright Claimant. The copyright "claimant" is either the author of the work, or a person or company to whom the song has been sold or transferred. For example, if all the songwriters transferred their rights to a band publishing company, the name (and address) of the band publishing company would be listed here. If the song hasn't been transferred, list the names of the writers. You can list each of their addresses or one address for all of them. If the song is a work made for hire, the claimant is the person who hired or employed the songwriter.

If Registering a Collection of Songs. You should not register a collection of songs if some of the songs have been transferred and others have not. All of the songs should have the same claimants.

Transfer. If the claimant is not the same as the person in Space 2 (the "Author"), you must provide a brief statement of how the claimant acquired copyright. For example, if you sold your song rights to a music publisher or transferred them to a band publishing company, you can insert the statement "by written contract." Do not attach the contract to the application.

Space 5

Previous Registration. You should check the "No" box unless you have earlier filed a registration for the song.

Space 6

Derivative Work or Compilation. This section deals with songs that are derived from other sources. For example, if you used several lyric lines from the Bible (such as the song "Turn, Turn, Turn"), you would complete Section 6 as follows:
- 6a (preexisting material): selected lyrics from the Bible.
- 6b (material added): additional original lyrics and original music.

If you revised a melody from the old folk song "Froggy Went a' Courtin'" and wrote new lyrics, complete Section 6 as follows:
- 6a (preexisting material): music from folk song "Froggy Went a' Courtin'."
- 6b (material added): original words and revision of music.

If you revised your own song, complete Section 6 as follows:
- 6a (preexisting material): music and lyrics from song "The Rat #1."
- 6b (material added): new words and revision of music.

Space 7

Deposit Accounts and Correspondence. The Copyright Office maintains deposit accounts for applicants who register works on a regular basis. If the applicant maintains a deposit account, the registration fee can be charged against the balance. Information about establishing a deposit account is provided in Copyright Circular 5. Space 7 also requires the name, address, area code, and telephone number of the person to be contacted if there is a question about the application.

Space 8

Certification. The person preparing the application must check one of the four boxes in Space 8 as either the author, other copyright claimant, owner of exclusive rights, or authorized agent. If you are one of the songwriters, check the box marked "Author." If you are filling out the application on behalf of the songwriters, check the box marked "Authorized Agent" and insert the names of the songwriters.

After checking the appropriate box, you should type or print your name and date and sign it where marked. You are certifying to the Copyright Office that the information contained in the application is correct to the best of your knowledge.

Space 9

Mailing Information. Space 9 becomes the mailing label when the certified registration is mailed back to the applicant. That is, after the application has been processed, it will be mailed back in a window envelope, and Space 9 (Mailing Information) is the mailing address.

Copyright Office fees are subject to change.
For current fees, check the Copyright Office
website at *www.copyright.gov*, write the Copyright Office, or call (202) 707-3000.

Privacy Act Notice: Sections 408–410 of title 17 of the *United States Code* authorize the Copyright Office to collect the personally identifying information requested on this form in order to process the application for copyright registration. By providing this information you are agreeing to routine uses of the information that include publication to give legal notice of your copyright claim as required by 17 U.S.C. §705. It will appear in the Office's online catalog. If you do not provide the information requested, registration may be refused or delayed, and you may not be entitled to certain relief, remedies, and benefits under the copyright law.

Form PA
For a Work of Performing Arts
UNITED STATES COPYRIGHT OFFICE

REGISTRATION NUMBER

PA   PAU

EFFECTIVE DATE OF REGISTRATION

Month   Day   Year

DO NOT WRITE ABOVE THIS LINE. IF YOU NEED MORE SPACE, USE A SEPARATE CONTINUATION SHEET.

1

TITLE OF THIS WORK ▼

PREVIOUS OR ALTERNATIVE TITLES ▼

NATURE OF THIS WORK ▼ See instructions

2 **a**

NAME OF AUTHOR ▼

DATES OF BIRTH AND DEATH
Year Born ▼   Year Died ▼

Was this contribution to the work a "work made for hire"?
❏ Yes
❏ No

AUTHOR'S NATIONALITY OR DOMICILE
Name of Country
OR { Citizen of _____
Domiciled in _____

WAS THIS AUTHOR'S CONTRIBUTION TO THE WORK
Anonymous?   ❏ Yes ❏ No
Pseudonymous? ❏ Yes ❏ No

If the answer to either of these questions is "Yes," see detailed instructions.

NATURE OF AUTHORSHIP Briefly describe nature of material created by this author in which copyright is claimed. ▼

NOTE
Under the law, the "author" of a "work made for hire" is generally the employer, not the employee (see instructions). For any part of this work that was "made for hire" check "Yes" in the space provided, give the employer (or other person for whom the work was prepared) as "Author" of that part, and leave the space for dates of birth and death blank.

b

NAME OF AUTHOR ▼

DATES OF BIRTH AND DEATH
Year Born ▼   Year Died ▼

Was this contribution to the work a "work made for hire"?
❏ Yes
❏ No

AUTHOR'S NATIONALITY OR DOMICILE
Name of Country
OR { Citizen of _____
Domiciled in _____

WAS THIS AUTHOR'S CONTRIBUTION TO THE WORK
Anonymous?   ❏ Yes ❏ No
Pseudonymous? ❏ Yes ❏ No

If the answer to either of these questions is "Yes," see detailed instructions.

NATURE OF AUTHORSHIP Briefly describe nature of material created by this author in which copyright is claimed. ▼

c

NAME OF AUTHOR ▼

DATES OF BIRTH AND DEATH
Year Born ▼   Year Died ▼

Was this contribution to the work a "work made for hire"?
❏ Yes
❏ No

AUTHOR'S NATIONALITY OR DOMICILE
Name of Country
OR { Citizen of _____
Domiciled in _____

WAS THIS AUTHOR'S CONTRIBUTION TO THE WORK
Anonymous?   ❏ Yes ❏ No
Pseudonymous? ❏ Yes ❏ No

If the answer to either of these questions is "Yes," see detailed instructions.

NATURE OF AUTHORSHIP Briefly describe nature of material created by this author in which copyright is claimed. ▼

3 **a**

YEAR IN WHICH CREATION OF THIS WORK WAS COMPLETED This information must be given in all cases.
Year

b DATE AND NATION OF FIRST PUBLICATION OF THIS PARTICULAR WORK
Complete this information ONLY if this work has been published.
Month _____ Day _____ Year _____
Nation

4

See instructions before completing this space.

COPYRIGHT CLAIMANT(S) Name and address must be given even if the claimant is the same as the author given in space 2. ▼

TRANSFER If the claimant(s) named here in space 4 is (are) different from the author(s) named in space 2, give a brief statement of how the claimant(s) obtained ownership of the copyright. ▼

DO NOT WRITE HERE
OFFICE USE ONLY

APPLICATION RECEIVED

ONE DEPOSIT RECEIVED

TWO DEPOSITS RECEIVED

FUNDS RECEIVED

MORE ON BACK ▶ · Complete all applicable spaces (numbers 5-9) on the reverse side of this page.
· See detailed instructions.   · Sign the form at line 8.

DO NOT WRITE HERE
Page 1 of _____ pages

EXAMINED BY

CHECKED BY

☐ CORRESPONDENCE
Yes

FORM PA

FOR
COPYRIGHT
OFFICE
USE
ONLY

DO NOT WRITE ABOVE THIS LINE. IF YOU NEED MORE SPACE, USE A SEPARATE CONTINUATION SHEET.

PREVIOUS REGISTRATION Has registration for this work, or for an earlier version of this work, already been made in the Copyright Office?

☐ Yes ☐ No If your answer is "Yes," why is another registration being sought? (Check appropriate box.) ▼ If your answer is No, do **not** check box A, B, or C.

a. ☐ This is the first published edition of a work previously registered in unpublished form.

b. ☐ This is the first application submitted by this author as copyright claimant.

c. ☐ This is a changed version of the work, as shown by space 6 on this application.

If your answer is "Yes," give: **Previous Registration Number** ▼   **Year of Registration** ▼

5

DERIVATIVE WORK OR COMPILATION Complete both space 6a and 6b for a derivative work; complete only 6b for a compilation.

Preexisting Material Identify any preexisting work or works that this work is based on or incorporates. ▼

a **6**

See instructions
before completing
this space.

Material Added to This Work Give a brief, general statement of the material that has been added to this work and in which copyright is claimed. ▼

b

DEPOSIT ACCOUNT If the registration fee is to be charged to a Deposit Account established in the Copyright Office, give name and number of Account.

Name ▼   **Account Number** ▼

a **7**

CORRESPONDENCE Give name and address to which correspondence about this application should be sent. Name / Address / Apt / City / State / Zip ▼

b

Area code and daytime telephone number   (   )   Fax number   (   )

Email

CERTIFICATION* I, the undersigned, hereby certify that I am the

Check only one ▶

☐ author
☐ other copyright claimant
☐ owner of exclusive right(s)
☐ authorized agent of _____

Name of author or other copyright claimant, or owner of exclusive right(s) ▲

of the work identified in this application and that the statements made by me in this application are correct to the best of my knowledge.

8

Typed or printed name and date ▼ If this application gives a date of publication in space 3, do not sign and submit it before that date.

_____   **Date** _____

Handwritten signature (X) ▼

X _____

Certificate will be mailed in window envelope to this address:

Name ▼

Number/Street/Apt ▼

City/State/Zip ▼

YOU MUST:
• Complete all necessary spaces
• Sign your application in space 8
SEND ALL 3 ELEMENTS
IN THE SAME PACKAGE:
1. Application form
2. Nonrefundable filing fee in check or money order payable to Register of Copyrights
3. Deposit material
MAIL TO:
Library of Congress
Copyright Office-PAD
101 Independence Avenue SE
Washington, DC 20559-6230

9

*17 U.S.C. §506(e): Any person who knowingly makes a false representation of a material fact in the application for copyright registration provided for by section 409, or in any written statement filed in connection with the application, shall be fined not more than $2,500.

Form PA—Full Rev: 02/2009 Print: 06/2010 — 50,000 Printed on recycled paper

U.S. Government Printing Office: 2010-357-993/80,085

When Is a Song Published for Copyright Purposes?

When completing the copyright application, you will note that the Copyright Office distinguishes between published and unpublished songs. A song is published when it is first made available to the public on an unrestricted basis. For example, if you permit downloads or distribute CDs on an unrestricted basis, the song has been published.

Dear Rich: How Do I Register Sound Recording and Songwriting Copyright?

Dear Rich, I recently recorded a CD with my fiancée and am trying to figure out how many applications I should submit to the copyright office. Here's a breakdown of contributions for this CD/project: I wrote all ten songs (music and lyrics), except one that was written with my fiancée. I recorded/arranged/mixed most of the music. Vocals and another instrument (performed by my fiancée) were recorded at her father's studio. Her father mixed the tracks (that I had put together) with these additional recordings (vocals, etc.), then he mastered the CD. So, should I submit one application for music and lyrics for songs one through nine (for myself), another application for the tenth song (my fiancée and me), then a third for the sound recording including all three of us?

You need to submit two applications, one for the songwriting (musical composition/performing arts) and the other for the recording (sound recording). You can do this via an online filing using the eCO system at the Copyright Office website. You're allowed to list songs by more than one writer on a single application provided that one writer is the same for all of the songs. Copyright Circular 56 explains the rules. Next, you would use an online application and claim sound recording copyright. Although we don't think it applies in your case, you can use just one application for everything if the same person owns the copyright in the songs and the sound recording. This could happen, for example, if your fiancée and her father assigned you their rights in the sound recording.

Publishing Your Band's Music

Making money from publishing songs is different from earning money from sales of recordings, though the two sources of income are closely related. In this chapter we'll explain the quirky world of music publishing, and show you how to earn money by publishing your band's songs. Basically, your band's songs can be published by an outside music publishing company, or your band can be its own publisher. One reason that bands often act as their own publishers is that it gives them more freedom to divide the income from published songs. When a song is published, the publisher receives royalties whenever the song is played or manufactured into a recording.

In this chapter, we'll explain your options for publishing your music, and the kinds of royalties you can earn. We'll also discuss different ways for your band to divide song income. We'll look at how to work with music publishers—companies that own songs and collect money on behalf of songwriters. And we'll go through the factors you should consider in determining whether you should create your own music publishing company, and explain how to create one.

How Songs Earn Money

Before jumping into music publishing and song revenue, you may find it helpful to look at an example of how a song earns money (and lots of it).

"Have Yourself a Merry Little Christmas": How a Decades-Old Song Earns Over $1 Million a Year

Each year, EMI Publishing, the music publishing company that owns the copyright for the song "Have Yourself a Merry Little Christmas," collects between $1 to $2 million in revenue from the song. Not bad for a tune that was written in 1944! A large source of revenue is performance royalties earned from radio and TV play. When versions of the song are played on the radio, the stations must pay for each play—usually a few cents. In one year for example, the song was played on television shows such as *ABC World News Tonight* and *General Hospital*. A TV station must pay several dollars each time the song is played.

Music Publishing Glossary

Here are some basic terms used in music publishing. These terms are discussed in more depth throughout the chapter.

Interactive webcaster: This refers to an on-demand website or service—such as Spotify, Apple Music, Google Play, or Amazon Unlimited—in which listeners can select the songs they want to hear.

Mechanical royalties: Each time a song is reproduced on a recording, whether on a CD or as a digital download, the song owner is entitled to a payment from the company doing the reproduction—usually the record company. (Digital downloads are officially referred to as digital phonorecord deliveries or DPDs.) This payment is called a mechanical royalty because it's paid each time the song is mechanically reproduced (as opposed to being performed). Federal law has established a uniform mechanical royalty, which is currently 9.1 cents per copy of a song that's five minutes or less (and 1.75 cents per minute, or fraction of a minute, for those over five minutes). Therefore, if 100 copies of a four-minute song are pressed (or downloaded), the song owner is entitled to approximately $9.10. Mechanical royalties are also paid for interactive webcast streams (referred to as "streaming mechanicals") from sources like Spotify and Apple Music. These are paid at a varying rate, but the average streaming mechanical rate is $0.0067. The percentage of revenue to be distributed to songwriters will escalate from 11.4% in 2018 to 15.1% in 2022.

Music publisher: A music publisher is a company that owns song copyrights. A music publisher will control how a song is used and collect money from people who sell, perform, or modify the song. A songwriter either sells the songs to an established music publisher or creates his or her own music publishing company. We will explain the advantages and disadvantages of each system in this chapter.

Music publishing agreement: A music publisher acquires ownership of a song copyright by signing a music publishing agreement with the songwriter. Usually the music publishing agreement provides for the songwriter to continue receiving income as the song earns money. The songwriter's portion usually ranges from 60% to 75% of the total song income.

Noninteractive webcaster: A website or service in which listeners cannot select the songs, such as Pandora or Live365.

Performance royalties: Every time a song is played on the radio, in live concert, on an Internet radio station, in a business establishment, on television, or on a website, the party playing the song must pay for the performance.

> ## Music Publishing Glossary, continued
>
> **Performance rights organization (PRO):** An organization that monitors radio and television stations, nightclubs, websites, and other entities that play music, collects royalties from these places, and pays the royalties to the appropriate music publishers (see further discussion of PROs below).
>
> **Sync licenses:** A song earns money if it is used in a movie or television commercial. The copyright law provides for a special payment when the song is synchronized (or linked) with a moving image. There are no fixed fees for this synchronization right, and usually the music publisher negotiates a fee and signs an agreement known as a "sync license."

The song also earned money from mechanical royalties when recordings were sold. For example, in one year Natalie Cole, Melissa Manchester, Amy Grant, Vince Gill, Shawn Colvin, Dave Koz, and Grover Washington recorded versions of the song. If any version sold a million copies, the music publisher would receive over $75,000 from the record company selling the recording alone.

"Have Yourself a Merry Little Christmas" was also used in many movies, and each of these uses is negotiated between the music publisher and movie company. The movie companies often pay $25,000 or more for the "sync right" (see glossary, above). Additional mechanical royalties are paid by the record company that releases the movie soundtrack. If the movie is shown on TV, the TV station must pay a performance fee when the movie is broadcast or streamed over the Internet. If the song is used in a commercial, the company using the song must pay the music publisher. Finally, the song also earns money if sheet music of the song is sold.

Wow! Seven decades after two songwriters composed "Have Yourself a Merry Little Christmas," it is still generating an amazing annual income. You should be aware, however, that one of the reasons that the song remains a classic and continues to earn money is that the song owner (in this case, the music publisher EMI) aggressively pushes for its use in different ways.

We will see that not all publishers are the same, and that some music publishers work harder than others to make and maintain a hit. Below we will discuss each of the methods by which a song earns money.

Performance Royalties

Radio and television stations must pay for the right to play a song. How much is paid? As a general rule, FM or AM radio performances result in payments between five cents and 15 cents per play per song, depending on the station's signal power (how far it broadcasts), advertising revenues, and audience size. When a song is played on a national television program such as *Saturday Night Live,* a songwriter receives between $5 and $9 per individual television station broadcasting the song (again depending on the broadcast signal and size of the audience).

It is also considered a "performance" when a noninteractive webcaster like Pandora streams a song, or when an interactive webcaster like Spotify plays a track. The music publisher does not collect this money directly. It's collected by the performance rights organizations (PROs), which pass it on to the music publisher and songwriter. For this reason, every music publisher and songwriter must affiliate with a PRO, so that the PRO knows what songs to collect royalties for and who should receive those royalties.

A Download Is Not a Performance; an Interactive Stream Is

Until 2010, performance rights societies sought payments for digital downloads of songs—for example, a purchase at the iTunes Store. In 2010, a federal court in New York ruled that a download was not a performance, and therefore organizations such as ASCAP and BMI could not collect when songs were sold online. The songwriter is still entitled to payment for mechanical rights (see below) for downloads. A streaming song on an interactive service such as Spotify or Apple Music results in a mechanical royalty (sometimes called a "streaming mechanical") and a performance royalty.

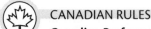

CANADIAN RULES

Canadian Performance Royalties. Most of the rules discussed in this chapter apply for Canadian bands. Canadian copyright law, like the U.S. law, establishes various sources of song revenue, including payments for performance and for mechanical reproductions on records. Canadian performance royalties are collected by a collective known as SOCAN, whose rates are regulated indirectly by the Canadian Copyright Board. There is no fee for a songwriter to apply to SOCAN online. However, the writer must either have a song published by a music publisher or have a song recorded by a record company or performed on the radio. Like its American equivalents, SOCAN does not monitor every radio broadcast, but instead uses a survey system. SOCAN is affiliated internationally and can collect for performances of Canadian music in other countries. SOCAN refers to its clearance form as a "Work Registration Form," and each new song created by your Canadian band should be registered with the collective. For more information, contact SOCAN (www.socan.ca).

Performance Rights Organizations

In order to collect performance royalties, songwriters and music publishers must register (or "affiliate") with a performance rights organization (PRO, also known as a performing rights organization or a performing rights society). PROs collect fees from U.S. radio and TV stations, as well as other establishments where music is played, such as concert halls, clubs, clothing stores, taverns, and restaurants. The money is then distributed to songwriters and music publishers who have registered with these organizations. A songwriter can affiliate with only one of these organizations.

The two major PROs in the U.S. are BMI and ASCAP. (A third company, SESAC, accounts for a small fraction of the performance rights business. SESAC is available only to songwriters—like Bob Dylan and Neil Diamond—who receive an invitation to join.)

One of the many quirky rules of music publishing is that performance royalties are not paid in full to music publishers. BMI and ASCAP each generally divide performance royalties earned by a song in half and pay half to the music publisher and half to the songwriter. This system ensures that songwriters will receive income directly from performances and won't have to wait while it is filtered through the music publisher.

Potential New Law on Music Licensing and Royalties

Federal legislation, called the Music Modernization Act ("MMA"), is likely to become law after the current edition of this book has been printed. The MMA is actually an "omnibus" bill with four distinct legislative items:

- **Music Modernization Act.** This creates a single licensing source (a new organization) for granting songwriting rights to interactive music services such as Spotify or Apple Music, and it creates a songwriting database that identifies who controls those rights.
- **Allocation for Music Producers (AMP).** This creates a system for assigning royalties to producers and engineers when their music is played on digital radio stations.
- **Compensating Legacy Artists for their Songs, Service, and Important Contributions to Society (CLASSICS).** This provides copyright protection for pre-1972 sound recordings and sets a statutory payment schedule for these recordings when they are played on digital radio stations.
- **Songwriter Equity Acts.** This permits the government to set rates for songwriter royalties based on what a buyer and seller negotiate in an open market (what's known as "willing buyer, willing seller").

As this edition went to press, the House of Representatives had unanimously passed the MMA. Check this book's companion webpage (at www.nolo.com/back-of-book/ML.html) for up to date information.

Just Because It's Played Doesn't Mean You Get Paid

Just because your song is played on the radio doesn't mean a check will be issued from a PRO. For example, BMI and ASCAP do not review every hour of traditional radio play. Instead, they periodically survey the stations and base payments on a statistical average. The bottom line is that if your song is played fairly infrequently, these performances may not show up on an ASCAP or BMI survey. The PROs provide more detailed performance reports for noninteractive webcaster sites such as Pandora and Live365, and interactive services such as Spotify.

What If the Song Is Played in a Foreign Country?

BMI and ASCAP are affiliated with foreign performance royalty organizations and will collect fees when your song is played in foreign countries. As a general rule, songs earn more per play when played in foreign countries than when played on stations in the United States. This is because many foreign stations (for example, the BBC in Britain) are national stations and broadcast to the entire populace of the country. For example, one play on the BBC in Britain may result in a payment of several dollars (versus several pennies in the United States). In addition, the surveying techniques on these stations may be more precise.

Doesn't the Performance Royalty System Favor Hit Songs?

Yes! Since radio payments are pennies per play and payments are based on statistical surveys, a songwriter earns substantial payment money only if the song is a hit. A hit song will show up on surveys, and the radio play will quickly add up to thousands (or hundreds of thousands) of dollars. Not only that, BMI rewards frequently played songs with higher payment rates.

Mechanical Royalties

The second way that a song earns money is when it is reproduced on compact discs, digital downloads, or at interactive webcasters such as Spotify.

Pennies From the Record Company

Under federal law, a record company (or any company that is manufacturing CDs or distributing digital downloads) must pay the copyright owner a mechanical royalty—currently 9.1 cents per copy per song—for the right to manufacture or "press" the song. For example, if your band writes and records a song and 1,000 copies of the song are pressed, the record company would owe the copyright owner a mechanical royalty of approximately $91 (1,000 times $.091).

As we indicated in the glossary above, however, few record companies actually pay the full mechanical royalty rate but instead negotiate for a reduced payment, usually 75% of the current rate (sometimes referred to as a "three-quarter" rate). In addition, federal law requires that the mechanical royalty be paid for every copy manufactured. Record companies often negotiate to pay for every copy sold (not manufactured). Why would a songwriter accept less than what the law provides? Because the record company may refuse to make a deal unless the songwriter accepts the lower rate. And of course, if you are distributing your band's MP3s (and not using a record company), then technically, you would owe the band songwriters the mechanical royalties payment (though few bands choose to do this). If your band is releasing CDs or downloads containing songs by songwriters who are not in your band, you would need to obtain a compulsory license as explained in Chapter 12.

Collecting and Determining Mechanical Royalties

Many record labels pay the mechanical royalties for compact discs and "digital phonorecord deliveries" (also known as "permanent digital downloads" or PDDs) directly to the owner of the copyright, usually the music publisher. However, there are organizations, like Easy Song Licensing and the Harry Fox Agency, that will collect mechanical royalties for a song owner. These organizations will also negotiate with record labels that may want to record new versions of the song. In Canada, the Canadian Music Reproduction Rights Agency (CMRRA) performs the same function.

The mechanical royalty rate is set by Congress. The royalty rate for CD and PDD copies is currently 9.1 cents per song or 1.75 cents per minute for songs over five minutes, whichever is larger. To verify the current rate, check the Copyright Office website (www.copyright.gov). Search for "M-200a" ("Mechanical License Royalty Rates").

The "Spotify" Rate Hike: Collecting Mechanical Royalties for Interactive Streams

When a song is streamed by a user of Spotify (or any other interactive choose-the-song service, such as Apple Music or Amazon Unlimited), the song owner is entitled to both performance and mechanical royalties. PROs collect the performance royalties, but it's up to the owner to collect the mechanicals—usually by affiliating with a service such as the Harry Fox Agency or an administrator such as CD Baby Pro (see discussion of "The New Music Publishing Administrators," below). Unlike the regular mechanical royalty rate of 9.1 cents, the rate for interactive streams reflects a formula in which the companies carve out a pool of revenue distributed to song owners. As of 2018, the streaming mechanical rate averaged $0.0067 per play. From 2018 to 2022, the amount paid to songwriters will increase by 44%. (For example, a song owner who receives $5,000 in 2018 will receive $7,200 in 2022.)

Sync Payments From Movies and TV Commercials

Another way that your song can earn money is if it is used in a movie or television commercial. There are no fixed fees for this synchronization right, and usually the music publisher negotiates what is known as a sync license. Sync licenses can range from several thousand dollars for independent films to $25,000 or more for major Hollywood films. Sync license fees for using a song in a national TV commercial can range from $15,000 for spot ads to $75,000 for a six-month advertising campaign; we discuss licensing of music in Chapter 15.

Other Ways Songs Earn Money

Songs also earn money from the sales of sheet music, foreign record sales, or adaptation for use in another format such as a video game.

The Music Publishing System

While publishing your songs may seem simple in theory, in reality it's a strange and rather complicated process. The reason for this is that the music industry has clung to an old music publishing system even though many aspects of it are antiquated and confusing. If you want to publish songs, you'll need to use both an external publisher and a publishing company created by your band. In a nutshell, the publishing system used by the music industry allows only music publishers to collect money for the use of copyrighted songs and requires that a certain share of the money collected goes to the songwriters, while a certain share goes to the publisher. As we'll explain below, for songwriters to collect their full share of royalties, they need to create their own publishing company—even if they already use an external music publisher.

The New Music Publishing Administrators

In recent years, companies like Songtrust, TuneCore, and CD Baby Pro have stepped into the jungle of music publishing by offering simplified management of music publishing duties. They do not replace PROs or international collection services but rather work with them to track down revenue. The strongest appeal of these new music publishing administrators is in the area of international collections. So if your songs are getting a lot of activity outside the U.S., the fees and commissions may be worth it. (For example, Songtrust has a $100 setup fee and a 15% commission.)

Music Publishers

Although organizations like BMI, ASCAP, and Harry Fox collect various forms of song royalties, they do so on behalf of music publishers. A music publisher is a company that owns and profits from song copyrights. Some music publishers are also known as administrators, because they "administer" copyrights. They may not own the copyright, but they earn revenue by handling business tasks for the songwriter. Some bands publish their music under their own music publishing company rather than using an external company. In that case, the songwriters in the band simply transfer their song copyrights to the publishing company, which then publishes the music. Sometimes, a manager or record label will ask you to give up your publishing rights. As explained below, be extra careful in such situations.

Some music publishers are large multinational companies, while others may be nothing more than a name on stationery. The only thing that all music publishers have in common is that they own and/or administer song copyrights.

How the System Works

The music industry has established a system that, although illogical, has become the accepted method of collecting and dividing songwriting income. At its foundation is a basic (though irrational) principle that any income from songs should be divided roughly equally between the publisher and the songwriter. For example, if a song earns $1,000, $500 is supposed to go to the songwriter and $500 to the publisher.

This half-and-half idea was born back when most recording artists weren't writing their own music but were recording tunes that were written by songwriters hired by publishers. In other words, in the old days (pre-Beatles), the real players in music publishing were publishers and songwriters, not bands. It made more sense back then to split the proceeds between the publisher and songwriter, because they often worked as a team.

But in today's world, bands are usually composing their own music. Much more than in the old days, the creators of the music are now also the performers. Since most of today's bands generally both write and perform the music they release, the industry recognizes that the old traditional division of the publishing pie isn't fair anymore. It's now accepted that external music publishers no longer deserve half of the income from publishing a song.

But rather than simply change the allocation of music publishing income to give the publisher less, the industry has adopted a strange system in which the publisher still gets half of the money and the songwriter gets half—but if a band that's already signed with a publisher sets up its own publishing company, then the external publishing company will split its "half" with the band publishing company. The final result of this convoluted system is that the external publishing company gets 25%, the band's publishing company gets 25%, and the band songwriters get the same 50% they've gotten all along.

In other words, the music publishing system slates half for publishers and half for songwriters, even though the publishers know they don't really deserve half. To even things out, they split their publishing half with the band—but since it's a "publisher's" half, the band has to create a publishing company to get it. That's why bands that want to publish music find themselves creating publishing companies, even though they'd just as soon go with an outside company altogether.

Since they have to create a publishing company anyway to get their full share of the publishing income, some bands don't bother working with an external company at all. That way, the band gets all the money: The publishing half goes to the band publishing company, and the other half goes to the band songwriters.

> **EXAMPLE:** Your band signs a publishing deal with Megaglom Publishing, and a song earns $1,000. The writers' share of the payment—$500—goes to the writers. Megaglom would get $250, which is half of the publishing portion of the pie. The other $250 (or remaining half of the publishing portion) goes to the publishing company set up by the band.

Do You Need a Music Publisher?

Your band will need a music publishing company—either internal or external —only if some or all of the band members are writing original songs that you want to publish. If you do want to publish songs, your main decision is whether to go it alone with your band's own publishing company or to go with an external company. You may wonder: "Why should we go with an external company if we have to create our own company anyway to get our full share of song income?" The main reason to sign with an external company is that some of them offer large cash advances and other perks for your band, such as marketing and publicity power. If your band is in doubt about what to do regarding a music publisher, compare your situation with the following scenarios:

- **Your band is unsigned and has no recordings.** If there's no song income to think about—that is, your band is not signed to a record company and your songs are not presently recorded for distribution—then your band does not need to create its own publishing company. However, your band may benefit from an affiliation with an established music publisher that can promote your band.

- **Your band is releasing its own recordings or is signed to an independent label.** If your band is putting out its own recordings or is signed to an independent record label, your band should create its own music publishing company in order to get your full share of song income. An explanation of what this means and how to do so is provided later in this chapter. But whether you need an outside publisher is a trickier question. Generally speaking, it doesn't make much sense to transfer any rights to a music publisher at this point unless that publisher can give you decent advances or can help promote your band's songs in some significant way.

- **Your band is selling a lot of independent records or is signed to a major label.** You will probably be contacted by an established publisher, and your band will need to decide whether to sell music publishing rights to one of these publishers if your band is:

  1. selling a sizable amount of recordings (more than 10,000 units total)
  2. getting substantial radio or webcast play, in heavy rotation on satellite radio stations, or
  3. signed to a major label.

  A publishing deal will usually result in an advance payment of $50,000 or more. The publisher may be able to assist in the promotion of your songs on radio or television or in the movies. Your attorney and manager can help you sort through the decision.

- **Your band is signing a management or record deal, and the manager or record company insists on acquiring your music publishing.** If a manager is pressuring you to give up your publishing rights, review Chapter 3. Be *very* wary of giving up a publishing interest to a manager who does not have a proven track record. If a record label is pressuring you into giving up publishing rights, then review Chapter 14. There may be financial reasons to give up your publishing rights to a record company, and your band will need to review the arrangement with a music business attorney.

What About the Horror Stories?

In the early days of rock and roll, there were many music publisher rip-offs. For example, in 1956, Richard Berry, the composer of the song "Louie, Louie," sold all rights to his song for $750. The song went on to earn millions and was recorded by over 1,200 artists. Unlike modern publishing deals, Berry did not have an agreement that continued to pay him as the song earned money.

Songwriters are better protected today. For example, Sting, not his publisher, receives the lion's share of the song income earned by "Every Breath You Take." Songwriters have become more knowledgeable and are better protected by attorneys and songwriter organizations. Lawyers are also willing to fight on behalf of songwriters, sometimes in return for a cut of the recovery. For example, in 1986, Richard Berry won a court battle over "Louie, Louie" and was awarded over $2 million.

Dividing Up Song Income Within the Band

After the music publisher has taken its cut, the income that goes to the songwriters must be divided up however the band agrees. Dividing song income within a band is often a touchier issue than dividing it with the music publisher. Bands can easily get screwed over song income when band members cannot determine how to divide it up. How songwriting income is allocated in a band can have a huge effect on the members long after the group breaks up.

Credited Songwriters Always Earn More Performance Royalties

If publishing already seems confusing, then be prepared for another wrinkle. Although you can set up a system whereby everyone (songwriters and nonwriters) share equally in song income, it's still possible that a credited songwriter will receive more money from performance royalties. That's because in the case of performance royalties, BMI and ASCAP split the revenue for each song and make separate payments to music publishers and songwriters. In other words, with performance royalties the songwriter's portion is paid *directly* to the songwriter and does not pass through the band's publishing company. Therefore, if a song is a big hit on the radio or in a TV show, a credited songwriter will probably receive more money than a nonsongwriter. It is possible that the agreement among the band or between the band and the publisher could deal with this share, but usually it's not addressed and the writer's portion of performance royalties is paid directly to the credited songwriters.

For example, in 1983, Gordon Sumner (a.k.a. Sting) wrote "Every Breath You Take" and recorded it with his band, The Police. The song was a worldwide hit. Fourteen years later, Sean "Puffy" Combs (a.k.a. Puff Daddy and P. Diddy) rerecorded the song with new lyrics as "I'll Be Missing You," and it was again a worldwide hit. Sting, not the members of The Police, earned between $2 and $5 million for the Combs recording.

There is no standard as to how to divide up song income. In order to avoid getting screwed, your band needs to work out a system for dividing the income. There are two steps:

1. At some point soon after a song is recorded, the band must decide who the songwriter or songwriters are (that is, who should get credit for writing the song) and what their relative contributions are (generally a percentage, such as 30% or 50%). If you are unsure what it means to be a songwriter, review Chapter 7.

2. After you have decided on the songwriters and their contributions, you'll need to decide how to divide the income from the song. Remember, nonwriters can still receive song income if the band agrees on such a division—and many do.

Below we have provided examples of four systems that have been adopted by other bands. In addition, we have provided the language you should add to your band partnership agreement (BPA) if you want to adopt one of the systems. (BPAs are covered generally in Chapter 2.)

System #1: Songwriters Take All

Under this first system, only the songwriters receive song income. That is, the writer gets the songwriting credit, and the writer usually has a separate publishing company. Under a "songwriter takes all" system, there probably is no need for a band to create its own publishing company (unless a record company requires it as part of a record deal). For information on independent record deals, see Chapter 14.

What Type of Band Is System #1 Most Suitable For?

System #1 works best for a band that is centered around a songwriter who is usually the bandleader. It can also work for a band in which two members write most or all of the songs. It should also be considered if the band members (other than the songwriters) are constantly changing.

How Much Does Each Band Member Get?

Unless agreed otherwise, the songwriters take equal shares of the song income after the publishing company (if there is one) has taken its cut. The rest of the band would not receive any publishing proceeds.

> EXAMPLE: The Centipedes are a four-member band, and two members, Phil and Ernie, write all of the songs. A publishing company pays a $50,000 advance for the songs. Phil and Ernie each get $25,000. The other two members do not receive any money.

Language to Use in Your Band Agreement

Under this system, there would not be a band-created music publishing company, and you would not need to add any language to your band agreement.

System #2: Band Splits Songwriting Money Equally

Under this system, all of the song income is divided equally among all band members. To use this system, a band must create its own music publishing company in order to get its cut of the publishing portion.

What Type of Band Is System #2 Most Suitable For?

System #2 would work best for a "jam" band in which songs evolve at performances or at practice. This system might also work for a techno, acid-jazz, or dance band in which the members build songs around grooves. This system could also work for a band that believes in "band democracy" and considers songwriting as just another band task and the members believe all money should be divided equally (for example, Rage Against the Machine). Note: Many bands, such as Nirvana, started with a system like this, only to change later when the key songwriters realize the cash cow they'd given up.

How Much Does Each Band Member Get?

All band members take an equal share of publishing proceeds.

> EXAMPLE: The Fleas are a four-member band, and two members (Lindsay and Avi) write all of the songs. A song they publish through their own company earns $50,000 in royalties. Each band member gets $12,500.

Language to Use in Your Band Agreement

In your BPA, choose the following language in the Division of Publishing Revenue section:

"All music publishing income derived from Recorded Compositions, including both writer's and publisher's shares, will be divided equally among the band members."

System #3: Band Splits "Publishing Income" Equally; Songwriters Split "Songwriter Income" Proportionately

Under this system, the band divides the publishing half equally, and the songwriters divide the songwriting half based upon their contributions.

What Type of Band Is System #3 Most Suitable For?

Many rock and pop groups use this system. It is a compromise approach in which all band members receive some song income, yet the songwriters still receive the bulk of the money. Note, however, if your band later signs with a large publisher, then the publisher will probably take half of the publishing income. As a result, band members no longer share *half* of the song income; they share a *quarter* of it.

How Much Does Each Band Member Get?

Consider the following examples.

> EXAMPLE: The Waterbugs are a four-member band, and two members (George and Tommi) write all of the songs.
>
> **Scenario #1:** The Waterbugs do not use an external publisher. If a song earns $50,000, half ($25,000) is divided equally among the band, giving $6,250 to everybody. The other half would be divided equally between the songwriters, giving George and Tommi an additional $12,500 each.
>
> **Scenario #2:** The Waterbugs use an external publisher, and the song earns $50,000. The external publishing company would keep half of the publishing portion ($12,500) and give the other half to the band's publishing company. The band's publishing company would distribute its half equally among all members, giving each one $3,125. The songwriting half ($25,000) would go to George and Tommi, the songwriters. They would divide it in half for an additional $12,500 each.

Language to Use in Your Band Agreement

In your BPA, choose the following language in the Division of Publishing Revenue section:

"The Band Partners will share equally in the publishing income from all Recorded Compositions. The writers of each Recorded Composition will receive an equal pro rata share of the songwriters' income with respect to each Recorded Composition. By way of example, if two Band Partners write a Recorded Composition, each will share equally in the songwriters' income from that song. The publishing income from that song will be distributed equally to all Band Partners."

System #4: One Credit for Performing on a Song; Two Credits for Writing and Performing on a Song

This is a unique compromise system (and it may give your band ideas for creating other methods of dividing song income). Take a band song. How many people played on it? How many people wrote it? Add up these totals (for example, if there were four players and two writers, that's six). That becomes the denominator (the bottom number of a fraction). If a person is a writer and performer of the song they get two credits, for two-sixths of the song income. If they only perform, they get one credit, for one-sixth of the song income. All of the song income is pooled (regardless of its source), and the money is divided according to these fractions.

What Type of Band Is System #4 Most Suitable For?

This compromise system works well for a band in which songwriting and performing are equally important tasks (for example, a jazz band in which the members improvise on each song).

How Much Does Each Band Member Get?

Consider the following example.

> **EXAMPLE:** The Termites are a four-member band, and two members (Chet and Max) write all of the songs. The Termites use their own publishing company,

and it receives $50,000 in income from the songs. Since four people played on the songs and two wrote them, the denominator in the Termites' formula for dividing song income is six. Chet and Max both wrote and performed on each song, so they each get two credits, giving each of them a third of song income, which totals $16,666.60 for each of them. The other two band members get one credit each for performing on the songs. That gives each of them one-sixth of the song income, or $8,333.33 each.

Language to Use in Your Band Agreement

In your BPA, choose the following language in the Division of Publishing Revenue section:

"All revenue derived from Recorded Compositions will be pooled (whether it is characterized as publishing or songwriter revenue). Each Band Partner will receive one credit for performing on each Recorded Composition. The writers of each Recorded Composition will receive one credit for writing. Each Band Partner's total number of credits equals the numerator (top number of a fraction). The total number of credits equals the denominator or bottom number of a fraction. Each Band Partner then receives this fraction of the song income. By way of example, if four Band Partners perform on a song and one Band Partner has written that song, the songwriter Band Partner would receive two-fifths of the revenue and the other three band members would each receive one-fifth of the revenue."

It's possible that a band member may not perform on a song because of the song's arrangement (for example, a guitar is not needed). This can influence the amount of money earned by a band member. If the band agrees, this can be altered by modifying the second sentence to read: "Each Band Partner who is a member of the Partnership at the time of the recording will receive one credit for each Recorded Composition."

Create Your Own System

You can create any system you want to divide song income. After you have devised your system, write it out and include it in your band agreement. If possible, provide a short, written example of how the system works, as well.

How to Form Your Own Music Publishing Company

Forming your own music publishing company will take a few hours and may cost anywhere between $25 to $100. The major cost is for filing a fictitious business statement at the local county clerk's office.

Don't Bother Creating a Music Publishing Company If ...

Don't bother forming a music publishing company unless a song has been released for sale, or you know a song will be released for sale in the near future. Otherwise, there won't be any song income to be collected or divided up, which eliminates the need for a music publishing company.

Affiliate With Either BMI or ASCAP

The first step in creating a music publishing company is to affiliate with BMI or ASCAP.

- **Songwriter affiliations.** A music publisher represents the interest of its songwriters. Each songwriter usually registers with a performance rights organization (PRO), because the writer is guaranteed to get songwriter payments directly from the organization (BMI or ASCAP). A songwriter can affiliate with only one PRO. It would be helpful if the songwriters in your band all affiliate with the same PRO. Otherwise, it gets confusing when forming a music publishing company.

- **Request the application and contract.** In order to create a music publishing company, contact either BMI or ASCAP online (www.bmi.com or www.ascap.com). You can request that an application for a music publisher be sent to you by mail, or you can apply as a songwriter online (you must download and complete a paper application to become a BMI publisher). To join BMI as a publisher, there is a one-time fee of $250 for a publisher (partnership, LLC, or corporation) or $150 (if individually owned). (Note: You do not need a publishing company to collect your publisher's share of royalties at BMI.) There is a one-time $50 fee to join ASCAP as either a songwriter or music publisher.

- **Pick a name and complete the forms.** You will need to furnish a name for your music publishing company. Since many names are already in use, your band will have to furnish alternate titles with the application. Now that BMI and ASCAP have websites, it is possible to search these sites to find out if a name is already being used. If possible, try to use your band name or band partnership name for your music publishing company, as it may make it easier for you to cash checks (see below).

- **Clearance forms.** Your band registers its songs with BMI and ASCAP by completing a clearance form, which can be done online. If you don't submit a clearance form for each song that is being released, you will not get paid! (Songwriters can complete separate writer's clearance forms.) The publisher's clearance form asks for each writer's "share." As we discussed earlier in the chapter, your band needs to decide on each songwriter's percentage contribution to the song.

- **Writers' shares.** The writers' shares on the clearance form should total 100% (for example, Tom 75% and Nancy 25%). This section is concerned *only* with credited songwriters. It's possible that nonwriting band members will receive song income under your band system as discussed above, but their names should *not* be listed on the clearance form.

- **Publisher shares.** The clearance form also asks for the names of all publishers and their shares. If your music publishing company is the only publisher of the song, indicate 100% for the publisher's share. If you are splitting the song between two publishers, list each and give the appropriate percentage of ownership.

EXAMPLE: Spyder has formed a publishing company called SpyderBiter Music and is registering a song that is written by two of its members, Tom and Nancy. For purposes of the clearance form, Tom and Nancy each have a 50% songwriter share. SpyderBiter Music has a 100% publisher share.

File a DBA/FBN and Set Up a Bank Account

After you have registered as a music publisher with BMI or ASCAP, you need to set up a bank account so that you can deposit and cash checks. For example, if your band Spyder creates a music publishing company called SpyderBiter Music, a bank will not allow you to deposit checks written to SpyderBiter Music into an account with a different name (such as your personal account), or to cash that check without proof that you are in fact an authorized representative of SpyderBiter Music. The only accepted proof is usually a certified fictitious business name statement (FBN), also known as a DBA statement, for "doing business as." The statement basically asks you to give the names and addresses of the people who are doing business under a name different from their legal names. You file this statement with the clerk of the county in which your band resides.

Usually the procedure is as follows: You fill out a form furnished by the county clerk, pay a fee, and then arrange to have the contents of the form published in a local newspaper. (The county clerk will be able to walk you though the procedure.) After publication in the local newspaper, your band will receive a certificate that will enable you to cash checks or to start a bank account. In some places, when you file a DBA, you must also pay a local business tax.

Setting up a business bank account can be an expensive proposition, with monthly fees and check-printing charges, so shop around if you intend to create an account. Some banks may also require a federal tax ID or Social Security number. See Chapter 17 for information about obtaining a federal tax ID. See Chapter 9 for information regarding the relationship between DBAs and protecting your band name.

Take Care of the Administration

A music publisher administers the songs. So as your own music publisher, you need to take care of some paperwork. One of the most important jobs is to register copyrights for the songs (see Chapter 7). In addition, you should file clearance forms for any new songs that will be released. Six to eight weeks after submitting a clearance form, you should also review the BMI or ASCAP website to make sure that the song has been registered properly. If there is an error, contact the indexing department for that performing rights organization. ●

Band Names

This chapter deals with disputes between bands over the right to use a name. Disputes about band names can have disastrous effects. For example, the country band Shenandoah was sued by bands with similar names from Kentucky, Nevada, and Massachusetts. Shenandoah got to keep its name, but the cost of the lawsuits eventually landed the group in bankruptcy court.

In this chapter, we provide some basic information about trademark law—the legal specialty that deals with band names—and explain how to avoid the two common name problems: when your band chooses a name similar to another band or another band chooses a name similar to yours. We also show you some inexpensive ways to research band names and explain how to prepare a federal trademark application. (For information on who owns your band name or who can use the name if the band breaks up, review Chapter 2.)

Trademark Basics for Bands

Your band name is protected under trademark law—an altogether different body of law from the copyright laws that protect your songs and recordings. This section discusses the basic rules of trademark law that your band should know.

It's Easy to Get a Trademark; the Trick Is Protecting It

A common misconception is that owning a trademark allows you to prevent anyone else from using it. Contrary to what many believe, owning a trademark doesn't give the owner a specific set of rights (like copyright or patent), and it doesn't necessarily mean you can prevent another band from using it. A trademark is nothing more than a word, phrase, or other symbol used in commerce to identify your business—in your case, your band. The real question is not whether the trademark is yours, but whether or not you can protect it. In very broad terms, the first user of a band name can prevent another band from using their trademark if it's likely that people would be confused by the use of the name by both bands. The "likelihood of confusion" rule is discussed below.

CANADIAN RULES
Trade-Mark Rules for Canadian Bands. Trademark laws in the United States and Canada are both derived from British trademark laws, and thus are based on the same principles. That is, the first user within a geographic area has superior rights. However, there are some minor differences between the United States and Canada. For example, in Canada it is "Trade-Mark" with a hyphen, not "Trademark." The registration process is also different (see the icon "Canadian Trade-Mark Registration," below).

For more information, go to the Canadian Intellectual Property Office website (http://cipo.gc.ca).

First to Use; Others Lose

It doesn't matter who is the first to create a band name. What matters is which band is the first to use it in public commerce—on posters, in newspaper advertisements, online, or on recordings. As soon as you publicly use the word or symbol—and assuming no one else has already used it for music purposes—it is your trademark. Public use of your name doesn't include using it only among yourselves or on a demo submitted to a club or record company. It must be used in public to identify yourselves to your potential audience who may buy your downloads or tickets to your show.

Likelihood of Confusion

If you are the first to use a name and another band starts using the same or a similar name, you have the legal right to stop them if it's likely that people will be confused by the dual uses of the name. The "likelihood of confusion" rule is the bottom-line question for trademark disputes. That is, is a consumer of music likely to buy the other group's records or attend its shows, thinking it was your band?

In a legal dispute over a band name, a court will look at a number of factors to determine whether customer confusion is likely. Two of the most important factors are:

- how distinctive the name is, and
- to what degree you and the other band are actually competitors in the same geographic area.

If a different band already has the same name that you want to use, don't be tempted to get around trademark law by changing the name slightly. Names that sound alike or have the same meaning—even if they're spelled differently or are in a different language—are often likely to cause customer confusion. The name "Le Band," for instance, might be confused with the trademarked name "The Band," even though part of the name is translated into French. Similarly, the name "Arcade Fear" would likely get confused with "Arcade Fire," even though the names were spelled differently. (See "What If the Band Names Are Not Identical?" below.)

Distinctiveness of Name

A band's name is distinctive if it is unique or if it is so well known that music buyers can distinguish it from other bands. For example, the name "The Beatles" is clever and immediately distinctive. Band names that are not distinctive are referred to as "descriptive." For example, "The Hard-Rocking Salsa Band" is a descriptive name—not distinctive—because it simply describes a hard-rocking salsa band.

A descriptive name can, over time, become a distinctive name. That's because the most important factor affecting distinctiveness is how well-known the name has become. For example, the name "The Band" is a perfect example of a descriptive, undistinctive band name. However, through extensive performing, large record sales, and substantial radio play, the 1960s group The Band has made their name distinctive and protectable. Since distinctiveness is based on how well-known your mark has become, the more you use the name, the stronger your trademark rights. That is, the longer you use the name, the more show posters you paste up, and the more downloads you sell, the greater your legal rights to your band name.

Whether the Bands Actually Compete in the Same Area

Band names (like all trademarks) are limited by geographic areas. That is, the use of a trademark in one country does not automatically mean that the owner can stop the use of a similar mark in another country. For example, a U.S. singer/songwriter had been using the name "Suede" for many years.

When a British band with a similar name began competing in the United States, the singer/songwriter sued and made the band change its name to "London Suede." However, this name change was necessary only in the United States. In the rest of the world, the British band retained its name "Suede." Why? Because the singer/songwriter had not established superior rights to the name outside of the United States.

It takes less time to expand a band's geographic popularity than it used to, thanks to the Internet. For example, if your band maintains or is featured at a website, this could expand your band's usage of the name across the United States, particularly if you have fans in different states. (Many website hosts provide a website owner with demographic breakdowns indicating where fans are from.) It may also demonstrate a non-U.S. fan base. But because of the complexity of foreign trademark laws, unless your band is generating substantial revenue in a foreign country, you are unlikely to acquire superior rights based solely on your website.

Sometimes, a court may also be influenced by the style of music performed. That is, if different bands are marketed to different types of listeners (for example, a barbershop quartet and a hard-core punk band), there is not much likelihood of confusion among their respective fans, and both bands could exist with a similar name. For example, in one case a court reviewed evidence as to whether two genres of music—heavy metal and rap—competed for the same consumers and determined that there was not much overlap. Generally, when measuring confusion, a court will consider not only record buyers but also whether there is confusion among radio stations and record distributors.

Registration Helps

You don't have to register your name with the state or federal government to get trademark protection—but it helps. A trademark is automatically created when you use the name in connection with your shows and records. However, registration will give you additional rights, and we recommend that you register if your band is signing a record deal or if you are earning over $10,000 a year. We explain how to file a federal trademark registration later in this chapter.

Your Logo, Design, and Slogan Can Also Be Protected

Your band's name isn't the only thing protected by trademark: logos, designs, slogans, packaging features, and more can also be protected by trademark. The same principles of trademark protection that protect names apply to these other features.

Give a Hoot—Don't Dilute

Your band can run into hassles if you use a band name based on a famous trademark, even if there is barely any likelihood of customer confusion. That's because federal trademark law allows owners of famous marks to prevent someone from tarnishing or diluting their trademark's distinctive quality. This is based on different principles from ordinary claims of trademark infringement. In most infringement cases, one band sues another because record buyers or concertgoers are confused by similar band names. In a dilution case, the issue is not whether consumers are confused, but whether the famous mark's reputation is being degraded or tarnished. A "famous mark" is determined by various factors, including the distinction the mark has achieved within its channel of trade. Examples of famous marks would be Nike, Intel, McDonald's, or Pepsi-Cola.

> EXAMPLE: Toys "Я" Us is a famous mark because it is well-known as a retail source for toys. A rap group using adult lyrics names itself Boys "Я" Us. The retail store chain sues the band, claiming that the use of the band name tarnishes the toy store's reputation.

Service Marks Versus Trademarks

Throughout this chapter we have referred to band names as trademarks. When registering your band name, however, you will refer to it as a service mark. What's the difference? A trademark is used on goods or products; a service mark is used in connection with services. When your band sells merchandise under the band name, the name is used as a trademark. When your band gives a show, the name is used as a service mark, because you are providing entertainment services. Except for some minor differences, the rules of trademark law are applied the same for both types of marks, and the term "trademark" is used interchangeably for both types of marks.

When applying to register the band name, we recommend that you apply for a service mark. (The application we describe below is for a service mark.) By doing this, you will secure the necessary rights to use your name in performance and stop other bands from using a similar name.

One reason to seek a service mark registration is because it is more difficult to acquire trademark registration for a band name. The Trademark Office traditionally views the name of the record company, not the band, as the appropriate trademark for recordings, and is unlikely to grant a trademark registration to a band name unless certain criteria are met. If your band is achieving widespread success and sales, it may justify your proceeding with filing of trademark applications for recordings and merchandise. Until then, the filing of a service mark application will suffice.

Can You Trademark a Song Title?

You will have a hard time getting a trademark for one of your band's song titles unless you can demonstrate that the song has been a *big* hit. For example, it may be possible to trademark a song such as "Stand by Your Man," which has been publicly performed over two million times. But a court found that a trademark was not available in the case of a country song, "Better Class of Losers," which had been publicly performed 47,000 times at the time.

A song title that achieved trademark protection is "Sing, Sing, Sing" by Benny Goodman, which according to a poll introduced in court, was one of the 100 most important musical works of the 20th century. In summary, it's unlikely that one of your band's songs will have attained the level of popularity required to create trademark rights.

Registering Your Fictitious Business Name Is Not the Same as Trademark Registration

In most places, when you conduct business under a fictitious business name you must register a fictitious business name (FBN) statement (also called a DBA statement for "doing business as") with your local government. This is because the band name that you're doing business under (for example, "Giant Sand" or "Ween") is not the same as your real names (for example, Joe Smith and Joanna Jones). Registering your fictitious business name generally involves filing a form with the name you're using and the names and addresses of all owners of the business. Before registering, you're usually required to check a database of other business names in that area to make sure no one else is doing business under that name.

It's important to understand that the process of registering a fictitious business name does not grant any form of trademark rights. Your local fictitious business name requirements are totally separate from federal and state trademark laws. In other words, you still must follow the trademark rules in this chapter even if you have filed a DBA.

Domain Names Versus Trademarks

Registration of a domain name is not the same thing as registering a trademark, but it is affected by trademark law. If you register a domain name that is similar to a famous registered trademark, you may later discover that you've infringed someone else's trademark (see the discussion of trademark dilution, above). For example, if your band's name was Candyland and you created a website, www.candyland.com, you would likely soon hear from Milton Bradley, the company that owns the children's game Candyland. Keep in mind that trademark disputes can involve complex issues—particularly for conflicts over domain names and other Internet-related claims. (There are dispute resolution procedures for people who claim rights to the same domain name, and we discuss these in Chapter 15.)

If you use a domain that is different from your band's name—for example, one of your band's song titles—that domain name may also function as a trademark. And in that case, the domain name would be subject to the same rules as your band's name trademark. For example, you would want to avoid using a domain name that is similar to another band's name or that dilutes a famous trademark.

Researching Band Names

The best way to deal with trademark disputes is to avoid them in the first place. And the single most effective method of avoiding a dispute is to research your band name before using it. Although there is no foolproof way to determine if another band has a similar name, below are some common methods of checking.

Searching the Internet

Searching the Internet is an inexpensive method of researching band names. There are many search engines and different databases of information that you can research.

In addition to search engines such as Google, you should also try the following online resources:

- **Social Media.** It may be obvious but we'll mention it anyway. Almost every band has a presence on Facebook, Twitter, or Instagram. It's easy to search these sources by band name.
- **Online music stores.** Check online music stores such as CDBaby.com and Bandcamp.com. These stores allow you to search by the name of the recording artist. Type in your band name to see if there are any recordings by artists with a similar name.
- **Domain names.** You should check whether another band is using the same name as its domain name. To check on the availability of a name, go to any approved domain registry and look for the search feature. For an alphabetical list of approved registrars, go to www.icann.org. If you want to learn the name of the individual who owns it, use the Whois tool (www.whois.net). If a band is using your name in its domain name for its website, it should appear in this database.

When searching for certain words or phrases, always consider simple variations on the spelling or pronunciation (for example, Beatles and Beetles). Also, be sure to include music-related search terms such as "band" or "music." For example, if you're searching for another band with the name "The Spyders," you should search for not only the words "spider" and "spyders" but also the word "band" or "music." This will keep your search results in the music world and avoid pulling up websites dealing with arachnids.

Federal Trademark Database on the Internet

Since it's free, start your trademark search by reviewing the database of registered marks in the U.S. Trademark Office (www.uspto.gov).

Using a Trademark Searching Company

When a record label wants to be sure that a name is safe, the label hires a professional searching service to prepare a report. These professional searching companies check band names that are registered with the state and federal government. They also check some unregistered band names. An extensive written report is provided showing any potential conflicts. Type "trademark searching" into your search engine to obtain a list. Since these searches are fairly expensive ($200 to $500), your band probably doesn't need to pay for one unless you are preparing to sign a major label recording deal where you have to make a contractual promise that the name is safe, or if your band has been sued by another band and you need to research the facts.

Dealing With Trademark Disputes

Unfortunately, disputes over band names are fairly common in the music industry. Here are some examples from the past two decades:

- Ratt's lead singer Stephen Pearcy sued members of Ratt over the use of their band name.

- Singer Geoff Tate sued his former band mates in Queensryche over their continued use of the name.
- Craig Chaquico of Jefferson Starship sued former band mates over the right to use "Starship."
- John Fogerty sued ex-members of Creedence Clearwater Revival who used the name Creedence Clearwater Revisited.
- Dave Mustaine, lead singer of Megadeth, sued David Ellefson, the band's former bass player, for allegedly using the name of the group without permission in an ad for musical equipment.
- Tina Weymouth and Chris Frantz were sued by ex-bandmate David Byrne when they used the name Heads as a truncated version of their former band name, the Talking Heads.
- John Densmore, former drummer and cofounder of the Doors, sued to prevent keyboardist Ray Manzarek and guitarist Robby Krieger from performing as the Doors.

In this section we will address three common types of disputes: Your band wants to stop another band with a similar name; another band wants to stop your band; or current and/or former members of your band are battling over which of you are allowed to use the band name.

Your Band Chooses a Name That Is Already Being Used by Another Band

As a general rule, if another band has been using the same name longer than your band, then the other band can stop your band from using the name. Other factors, such as the amount and location of record sales or the geographic area in which the bands perform, may influence the result.

> EXAMPLE: Your band begins to use the name Spyders in 2018 in Kansas. Unknown to you, another band was using the name The Spyders in 2008, toured the West Coast, and released independent albums that were distributed throughout the United States in 2015 and 2017. The other band can stop you from using the name, because they had nationwide use of the name prior to your band's use.

What If the Band Names Are Not Identical?

Can one band stop another from using a similar but not identical name—for example, The Spiders and Spyder? The answer again depends on the likelihood of confusion. Is it likely that music fans or music business people will confuse one band with the other? If people are likely to be confused by the sound or meaning of the two names, then one band will have to stop. For example, a band named Far Side is likely to be confused with the pop band Pharcyde, because both names sound alike even though they are not spelled alike.

If fans and business people are not likely to be confused—that is, it's easy enough to understand these are two different bands—then both bands can continue without a name change. This might be the case if the bands play radically different kinds of music. Because this issue is often difficult to resolve, you should consult with a trademark attorney or review *Trademark: Legal Care for Your Business & Product Name,* by Stephen Fishman (Nolo).

The best way to avoid this type of dispute is to research your band's name before adopting it. If you have already adopted a name and suspect a problem, don't manufacture large quantities of recordings or merchandise. If you have to change your name, try to keep some aspect of your former name in order to retain familiarity with your fans. For example, the other band may agree to let you use Spyders & Snakes or The Kansas City Spiders. If you've adopted a name and received a "cease and desist" letter (a letter telling you to stop using the name), consult a trademark attorney. (Methods for locating legal help are provided in Chapter 4.)

Another Band Chooses the Same Name as Yours

Generally, if you have used a name for a longer period than a new band, your band has the legal right to stop the other band from using the similar name.

For example, say your band has been touring and releasing records in the United States under the name "Crystal" for seven years. You learn that a U.S. record company is releasing a recording by a new band with an identical name. Assuming that you are the first user of the band name, you have superior rights and can stop the other band.

Other Confusing Uses of a Band Name

What happens if someone uses your band name for a purpose other than to name a band? For example, a band called Pump attempted to stop Aerosmith from naming its album *Pump*. A band named Aftermath tried to stop Dr. Dre from naming his new record company Aftermath. In both cases, the bands failed to stop these alternate uses. The courts did not feel that consumers would be confused. For example, the court did not believe that fans of the band Pump would think that the Aerosmith album was made by the group Pump. A similar result was reached in the Aftermath case. Therefore, as a general rule, you will probably be able to stop only similar use of your band name by other bands. If your band becomes very well known and sells a lot of records, the situation may change, and you may be able to stop alternate uses. (We discuss album titles in Chapter 10.)

Remember, however, that even though you have a superior right (that is, you have been using the name longer), it's tough to enforce your rights unless you hire an attorney. Unfortunately, the other band or its record company may not take you seriously unless you file a lawsuit. In reality, *both* bands usually get screwed by a legal dispute over the name. For most bands, the expense (from $10,000 to $100,000 in legal fees) outweighs any benefit.

Before filing, consider whether the other band is really going to cause your group a problem. Is there a chance that fans of your band will be confused? Will your group suffer any real damage? If not, then it may not be worthwhile to pursue the matter. Remember, many bands disappear within a year, and your group may be able to simply outlast your competition.

If you do have to sue the other band, the usual solution is either:

- **The newer group changes its name.** Many bands have modified their names to avoid a lawsuit. For example, Charlatans UK, the English Beat, and Wham UK adopted the "British" references in their name to avoid lawsuits from U.S. bands with similar names.
- **Your band changes its name in return for a money payment.** It may seem odd to take money to change your band's name if it has the superior right. However, some bands don't mind changing their name in return for some cash. Payments are commonly between $1,500 and $5,000.

In some cases, it's possible that you can handle at least some aspects of a name dispute without the aid of an attorney. Consult the self-help guide *Trademark: Legal Care for Your Business & Product Name*, by Stephen Fishman (Nolo).

Registering Your Band Name With the Government

Being the first to use a trademark that no one else is using is enough to establish your rights to the name. Still, registering the name with the federal government will strengthen your rights. This section will discuss why you might want to formally register your name, and how to do so if you choose. (For information about state registration, see "State or Federal Registration?" below.)

CANADIAN RULES

Canadian Trade-Mark Registration. The Canadian Trade-Mark application process is similar to the one in the United States. An application is prepared, filed, and examined, and then, if there is no opposition, it is registered. There are some bureaucratic differences in Canada but for the most part, the procedures are similar. You can obtain all of the necessary information and forms from the Canadian Intellectual Property Office website (http://cipo.ga.ca).

State or Federal Registration?

This book covers only federal registration procedures. For information on state registrations, contact your state's Secretary of State. You should find contact information for your state's Secretary of State office online at the National Association of Secretaries of State (www.nass.org). State registration is usually not worth the effort or expense. Your band should seek state registration only if you perform in one state and have little or no Internet presence.

Dear Rich: Should You Register With Bandname.com?

We have three possible band names that we want to use. We're going to decide when we finish our record next month. We can't afford to file a federal registration for all three so you do you think it's worth it to pay $45 to register the three names at Bandname.com?

We're not positive, but we don't think that Bandname.com would want you to register band names unless you are using them. To "reserve" band names at the directory would defeat one of the purposes of the site, which is to put the world on notice as to which names are currently being used.

Is it worth it to register? According to our research, Bandname.com is an online directory of band names that you can search at least six times without having to pay a fee. After six searches, there is a $15 fee that enables unlimited searching and registration of your band's name. Is it worth it to register? If you're doing a lot of searching for band names, it's probably worth the $15. Bandname.com appears to be a fairly thorough band directory that includes bands that have registered and more importantly, many who have not. We tested two obscure bands that had not registered with the service and they both showed up. At the same time—and as the site points out—just because a band name is in the directory doesn't mean that the name is currently in use.

What does registration of the band name get you? We're not sure what the registration of a band name at Bandname.com gets you. Apparently your band's name is included in the online and print directories, thus serving as notice to others searching the directory that you are claiming rights in the name. It's true—as the website claims—that establishing prior usage is the key to preventing legal challenges. But registering at Bandname.com does not establish prior usage, it merely records your claim. You establish prior usage by selling recordings, playing shows, and by selling music and merchandise on the Internet under the band name. In other words, we don't think that registering with the service will gain any new rights for you.

Should You Register Your Name?

As we have explained, your band has legal rights to its name without registering. That is, even without filing trademark papers with the government, you can still go to court and stop a newer band from using a confusingly similar name. In fact, you can even stop a newer band that has registered its name.

Because federal registration can cost $225 to $400, you may wonder: "Why should we bother to register?" For one thing, regardless of the legal benefits, federal trademark registration often has a deterrent effect on infringing bands and their attorneys, because it lets them know that you are serious about protecting and enforcing your rights. There are other benefits as well:

- **Nationwide rights.** If you register, you can claim trademark rights in all regions of the country, not just where you perform or sell records.
- **Right to use the ® symbol.** As the owner of a federally registered mark, your band may use the symbol ® in conjunction with your shows and records. (Note: If a mark is not federally registered, it is illegal to use the ® symbol or to state that the mark is federally registered.)
- **Advantage in website disputes.** If a dispute arises as to who has the right to use a name for a website, the organization that oversees the award of website names (www.icann.org) has indicated that it will award the name to the owner of a federally registered trademark.

What If You Haven't Begun Using a Name But You Intend To?

If you haven't started using a name but plan to in the near future, you can file a special application with the federal Trademark Office that will in effect reserve the name for you. The form is called an Intent to Use Application, also known as an ITU. In order to file an ITU, your band must have a sincere intention to use the name within six months. That is, you can't reserve the name merely to prevent someone else from using it. The ITU is fairly simple, but it requires the filing of an additional form and an extra $100 payment when the mark is put into use. For more information on this type of filing, consult *Trademark: Legal Care for Your Business & Product Name*, by Stephen Fishman (Nolo).

Filing for Trademark Registration

In this section, we explain how to complete a federal trademark application. Applicants can also obtain help from the instructions provided at the U.S. Patent and Trademark Office (USPTO) website (www.uspto.gov).

The USPTO site assists only in the preparation and processing of electronic applications. The fees reflect this bias. An electronic filing is $225 to $400 per class (depending on which filing option you choose); a paper filing—should you prepare a paper application on your own—is $600.

Your options for electronic filing are:

- **TEAS Plus**—This is the least expensive approach with a filing fee of $225 per class of goods and/or services. The USPTO also considers this the "strictest" application and requires: (1) payment of the filing fee for all classes listed in the application; (2) an identification of goods and/or services taken directly from the USPTO Trademark ID Manual; and (3) authorization to communicate electronically. If you use TEAS Plus, you must pay an additional fee of $125 per class if, at any time during the examination of the application, the USPTO decides you did not meet the requirements set forth.

- **TEAS Reduced Fee** (TEAS RF)—The TEAS RF filing option has a filing fee of $400 per class. The big difference between it and TEAS Plus is that TEAS RF applicants do not need to select an identification of goods and/or services from the Trademark ID Manual (as well as satisfy a few other TEAS Plus requirements at the time of filing). However, like TEAS Plus, an applicant who files a TEAS RF application but does not satisfy the relevant requirements will be required to submit an additional processing fee of $125 per class of goods or services.

- **TEAS Regular**—The TEAS Regular filing option has a filing fee of $400 per class. TEAS Regular applicants have the same requirements as TEAS RF except they don't have to communicate electronically and don't have to pay an additional $125 per class if the application does not satisfy the relevant requirements.

We think most bands should choose TEAS Plus as it is the least expensive option.

Before you begin your federal application, you'll need to figure out what theory it's based on. Most federal trademark applications are based on either "use in commerce" or an applicant's intention to use the trademark (referred to as an "intent-to-use" or ITU application). The process for both "in use" and "intent-to-use" application involves three steps:

- **Preparation and filing of application.** A trademark application consists of a completed application form, a drawing of the mark, the filing fee, and a specimen of the mark. You can either mail the materials to the USPTO or file the application electronically and pay by credit card.

- **Examination by the USPTO.** Upon receipt, the trademark application is given a number and assigned to a USPTO examining attorney. If there is an error or inconsistency in the application, or if the examining attorney believes that registration is inappropriate, the attorney will contact the applicant to discuss the objection. The applicant can respond to the objections or can abandon the application. The examining attorney will either approve the mark for publication or reject it. If it is rejected, the applicant may challenge the rejection.

- **Publication in the *Official Gazette*.** Once the examining attorney approves the mark, it is published in the *Official Gazette*. The public is given 30 days to object to the registration. If no one objects, a trademark registration will be issued (or in the case of an ITU application, the mark is allowed pending use in commerce). If there is an objection from the public, the matter will be resolved through a proceeding at the USPTO.

The total time for an application to be processed may range from a year to several years, depending on the basis for filing and the legal issues that may arise in the course of examining the application. The registration expires ten years from the date of registration. You have certain obligations to maintain your trademark registration—for example, you must file a Section 8 Declaration of Continued Use between the fifth and sixth anniversaries of the registration. Information about these maintenance requirements can be obtained at the USPTO website or by reviewing *Trademark: Legal Care for Your Business & Product Name*, by Stephen Fishman (Nolo).

The Trademark Application: the TEAS System

The preferred method of preparing the federal trademark application is to use the online Trademark Electronic Application System (TEAS), located at the USPTO's website (www.uspto.gov). TEAS is an interactive system in which the user is asked a series of questions. If a question is not answered or an essential element is not completed, the applicant is asked to correct the error. The system is remarkably easy to use, and there's a low probability of error in preparing the form. (In addition to the electronic system, applicants can create their own application forms by typing the necessary information onto a sheet of paper and paying the higher $600 fee.) The information provided below is intended for use on a standard TEAS application.

To get started, go to the website at www.uspto.gov. Click the Trademarks tab and choose "Apply online" (under "Application process" in the dropdown menu). Choose "Initial application forms," then click "File a TEAS Plus Application." You should be able to complete much of the form without assistance, but the following suggestions may help.

Name: If you are applying as partnership, insert the name of the partnership.

Entity Type: Since most bands are partnerships, you will probably click on the partnership box, insert the state where you are organized (usually the state where you reside), and insert each partner's name and citizenship. If only one person in the band owns the name, click on "Individual." If your band is a corporation, click on "Corporation."

As you fill in the rest of this form, make sure that your specimen, mark information, and description of goods and services are all consistent with each other. That is, if your specimen shows a different band name from what you enter in the mark information box (or submit in a GIF or JPEG file), you'll have some explaining to do. Similarly, if your specimen shows a different band name from what you describe in the application, you'll have to submit another specimen or change your product/service description. If you are filing an intent-to-use application, you won't be worried about the specimen requirement at this stage in the process, but you will ultimately have to submit a specimen (once you begin using the mark) to complete your registration.

Mark Information: If your band name consists of unstylized words or numbers (or both), click the circle above the words "Standard Character Format." In the box just below the words "Enter the mark here," enter your band name in capital letters. Pay close attention to the rules regarding what punctuation is allowed. In general, we recommend you register your band name for the first time in a nonstylized format—for example, the word "KISS" instead of registering "KISS" in its stylized lightning bolt design. If you prefer to register the mark in a stylized or design format (such as a logo or trade dress), read the help and attach a GIF or JPEG file showing the mark.

Basis for Filing and Goods or Services Information: The information required here varies depending on whether you are already using your band name in commerce or are filing on an intent-to-use basis. The top part of this box shows you which type of application you are filling out: Section 1(a) Use in Commerce or Section 1(b) Intent-to-Use.

Specimen: If you're using the band name (and not filing an intent-to-use application), you'll need to provide a specimen image file in JPEG format as well as a description of the specimen in the next box. You must scan an advertisement or poster of one of your band's shows or some other evidence that you provide live entertainment services. The specimen must show your band's name in connection with a performance. For example, you can furnish a poster indicating that The Falcons will appear at Lindsay's Castle at 10 p.m. on March 31. However, a business card with name and address of The Falcons would not be suitable, because there is no connection with a specific performance. As we indicated above, for purposes of this application, the Trademark Office is interested only in proof that you provide entertainment services (performances), not that you sell products (records). If you're an intent-to-use applicant, you will not have a specimen information section on your application and should go to the International Class step.

Description of Specimen: The next part of the specimen box asks you to describe the specimen. You will probably insert a statement such as "poster advertising live performance." See the help topic for what is required.

International Class: Enter Class 041 for entertainment services. Or, if you prefer, you can send in your application without specifying a class and let the trademark examiner help you.

Listing of Goods or Services: Here is where you describe the goods or services to which your mark is (or will be) attached. We recommend that you state "musical entertainment services." A trademark examiner who doesn't approve of your description, or is confused by it, will let you know and work with you to come up with an appropriate description.

If you are filing an intent-to-use application, the following two items about use will not appear. Skip to "Final Instructions for All Applicants."

Date of First Use of Mark Anywhere: Here you are asked to provide the date your band first started using the name in the marketplace. Insert the date you first used the name in an advertisement or poster. It's usually the date of your first show. If you're not sure of the exact date, estimate as accurately as possible. If necessary, use imprecise dates, such as "before March 25, 2010," "on or about January 16, 2007," "in 2004," or "in February 2015." Use the earliest possible date that you can reasonably assert as correct.

Date of First Use of the Mark in Commerce: Insert the date when your band first advertised its services in more than one state—for example, the date a newspaper or website ad about your performance reached concertgoers in Kansas and Missouri or the date when you did a show in a neighboring state. This date is often the same date as "Date of First Use of Mark Anywhere." Keep in mind, you should not use references to sales of recordings; use dates for performances and related advertising only. Again, if you're not sure of the exact date, estimate as accurately as possible.

Fee Information: There are three ways to pay the fees for your trademark application: credit card, automatic payment account, and electronic funds transfer. Read the descriptions of these options by clicking the appropriate links.

Declaration: The declaration is a statement that the facts in the trademark application are true. Read it carefully. If there are statements in the declaration that raise serious doubts or questions in your mind, do not file the application until you see a trademark lawyer.

Signature: The information box right above the signature section provides the surprising information that your electronic "signature" can be any combination of letters, numbers, or other characters. Each signature must begin and end with a forward slash (/). For example, /pat smith/, /ps/, and /268-3421/ are all acceptable signatures. There's no trick here. Entering your own name is the simplest option. Click the signature link just below the information box for the USPTO's own words on this subject.

Validate: This process checks your application and alerts you if you forgot to include any information. If the missing information is mandatory, you can go back and fill it in.

Disclaimers: Many trademarks include words or phrases that, by themselves, cannot be protected under trademark law. For example, no band can claim an exclusive right to the word "blues" or "mambo." To allow one person an exclusive right to use such terms would decimate the English language. Therefore, the Trademark Office usually requires a disclaimer as to certain portions of trademarks. For example, if a band wanted to register the mark, Philly Dog Blues Band, the applicant would likely be required to disclaim "blues band." This means that apart from the use as a part of the trademark, the applicant claims no exclusive right to use the word "blues band."

Completing the Process

You complete the process by paying the fees, authorizing your electronic signature, and validating the application. After you click "Pay/Submit" and your transaction is successful, you will receive a confirmation.

Later, you will receive email acknowledging the submission of your application. Hold on to that email, because it is the only proof you'll have that the USPTO has your application. It is also proof of your filing date and contains the serial number assigned to your application.

After Filing

The USPTO filing receipt explains that you should not expect to hear anything about your application for approximately three months. If you have not heard anything in three and a half months, it is wise to call and inquire as to the status of your application. The easiest way to do this is through Trademark Status and Document Retrieval (TSDR), which you can access at the main USPTO site (www.uspto.gov) under "Checking application status and viewing documents" in the dropdown menu under the Trademarks tab. TSDR allows you to get information about pending trademarks obtained from the USPTO's internal database by entering a valid trademark serial number.

You will likely receive some communication from the USPTO within three to six months. If there is a problem with your application, you will receive what's called an "action letter." This is a letter from your examiner explaining what the problems are. Most problems can be resolved with a phone call to the examiner.

When the examiner approves your application for publication, you will receive a Notice of Publication in the mail. Your mark will then be published online in the *Official Gazette*. For 30 days following publication, anyone may oppose your registration. Only 3% of all published marks are opposed, so it is very unlikely you will run into trouble.

Once your mark has made it through the 30-day publication period, and you are filing on an actual use basis, you will receive a Certificate of Registration. It may take a year or more to process your application.

If you filed on an intent-to-use basis, your mark will not be placed on the trademark register until you file an additional document with the USPTO when you put it into actual use. You can find this form, called "Statement of Use/Amendment to Allege Use for Intent-to-Use Application," at the USPTO site when you click "Intent-to-use (ITU) forms" under "Apply online." It tells the USPTO the date you started using the mark and completes the registration process. You must also provide a specimen at that time, showing how you are using the mark.

The U.S. Supreme Court Rules on Objectionable Band Names

Prior to 2017, the USPTO had the ability to reject objectionable trademarks such as "BULLSHIT" under a provision of the trademark law known as the "disparagement" clause. An Asian-American band's application for the name SLANTS was rejected because the USPTO considered it was disparaging to persons of Asian descent. The band appealed the decision all the way to the Supreme Court. In 2017, the High Court unanimously ruled in favor of the band and held that the "disparagement" clause violated the First Amendment's free speech clause. Acknowledging that speech that demeans on the basis of race is hateful, Justice Alito wrote that "the proudest boast of our free speech jurisprudence is that we protect the freedom to express 'the thought that we hate.'"

Communicating With the USPTO

The chances are good that you will be communicating with the USPTO after you have filed your application. Few applications sail through completely unscathed.

You are required to be diligent in pursuing your application. If you are expecting some action from the USPTO (the ball is in their court) and more than six months have elapsed without your hearing from them, immediately check the TSDR system. If you discover a problem, bring it to the USPTO's attention. If you fail to respond promptly to a request from a USPTO examining attorney, your application may be considered abandoned. If that happens, you may petition the Commissioner for Trademarks within 60 days to reactivate your application.

Celebrity Names as Band Names

The Trademark Office will not permit registration of a band name that consists of a living celebrity's name (such as "the Tori Spellings") without the consent of the celebrity. In addition, the use of a celebrity's name could trigger a lawsuit based on a claim known as a "right of publicity." This is different from trademark law, and is based on the principle that each person has a right to control the commercial use of his or her name. For these reasons, your band name should steer clear of the use of celebrity names unless one of you is already a celebrity.

If the examiner wants you to change your application, such as claiming a different description of services or goods, there is usually some room for negotiation.

An examiner with a brief question might call you and then issue and mail you an examiner's amendment. This is a form on which the examiner records in handwriting a phone conversation or meeting with the applicant. Read the amendment carefully to make sure it matches your understanding of the conversation. If you disagree or don't understand the amendment, first call the examiner and then, if necessary, write the examiner a letter with your concerns, explaining your point of view on the communication.

Artwork

n this chapter, we'll walk you through the issues related to artwork used in connection with the sale or performance of your music. For example, we'll advise when you need to obtain permission to use a photograph, or to obtain a release from a model. We discuss the information that is legally required on physical products (such as copyright and trademark notices) and suggest where it should be placed. We also provide sample agreements for acquiring rights to use artwork and for permitting your band to use a person's image in the connection with the sale of your music.

Copyright and Trademark Issues With Artwork

A good deal of the information we discuss in this chapter has to do with avoiding copyright and trademark trouble with your album artwork. For more detailed information about these areas of intellectual property law, see Chapter 7 on copyright issues and Chapter 9 on trademark.

Legal Issues With Artwork

Creating artwork can be fun, but you also have to take care of business. This section covers some legal issues related to preparing your artwork for albums and merchandise.

Album Titles

The trademark laws that we discussed in the previous chapter apply not only to your band's name, but also to the names of your albums. If you aren't careful when titling your albums, you could find yourself in serious hot water. Consider the following example.

In 1991, the group Negativland released an album entitled *U2/Negativland* which poked fun at the famous Irish rock band U2. U2's record label sued Negativland and its record label, SST. One of the major issues was the use of U2's name on the cover. As part of the settlement, SST agreed to stop using the name "U2" on the Negativland album cover, to destroy all existing copies, and to pay the attorneys' fees for U2's record company. Then, SST sued Negativland for over $90,000 to cover its costs from the lawsuit.

Was the use of "U2" in the Negativland title worth all that hassle? Perhaps it was for Negativland, which prided itself on rock and roll performance art. Most bands, however, don't want to be dragged into court over the use of an album title. Here are a couple of suggestions for choosing a title:

- **Don't Infringe.** You can use any phrase or wording for your title provided that it doesn't confuse consumers into thinking they're buying another group's music. For example, you probably should not title your album *Miley*, as fans of Miley Cyrus may be confused.

- **As a general rule, you may use the title of any book or a famous phrase.** The band Oasis, for example, released an album called *Be Here Now*, which is the title of a spiritual book from the 1960s. Titles of movies are also not protected by copyright and trademark law and may be used as album titles. For example, the Ramones album title *It's Alive* is borrowed from the name of a horror movie. If you do use a title, however, avoid using books or movies that have become series (for example, *Hunger Games*), blockbuster best-sellers (*50 Shades of Grey*), or classics (*Star Wars,* or *Gone With the Wind*). Under trademark law, the owners of these works may have a right to prevent your title use. The reason for this is that if the title of the work or series is extremely well known, then consumers can be expected to associate this title with one particular source. Therefore, your band's use could be confusing to consumers. Avoid using a film title if the film has a well-known soundtrack, for the same reasons.

- **Don't Dilute.** You should avoid using corporate names or well-known trademarks such as Holiday Inn or Mickey Mouse. Trademark law permits the owners of famous marks to prevent these marks from being "diluted." That means you can be sued if you somehow diminish the way people perceive these marks, such as by using the McDonald's trademark "You Deserve a Break Today" for the title of a thrash recording with explicit lyrics. Regardless of your legal rights in these cases, your band probably can't afford the hassles.

Images in Artwork

An artist should be able to use whatever is necessary to make great artwork, right? Not exactly. Your artwork cannot use another artist's copyrighted work unless you have permission. You cannot use a person's image (a picture of the person) on your artwork unless you have permission. We'll explain some of these principles below.

Avoiding Copyright Infringement

If you don't have the legal right to use something in your artwork, your band runs the risk of a lawsuit. If your band, for instance, uses a copyrighted picture from a newspaper without permission, your band might have to stop using the photo or even have to pay a financial settlement. Recalling compact discs, destroying artwork, and supplying new artwork is an expensive and time-consuming proposition.

How can you tell if artwork is protected by copyright? Unless it was published before 1923, you should assume the artwork is protected and the owner of the artwork controls the right to use it. For example, a graphic artist owns his or her images; a photographer owns the rights to his or her photos. These people can decide who may use the work. Also, don't assume that because artwork is included on a computer program or is included in a "stock" photography catalog, that it is free for use. For computer programs, check the accompanying "Read Me" files to determine if there is a licensing fee.

It is a violation of copyright law to use a work without permission from the owner. The reality is that you probably won't get sued unless the copyright owner is aware of your cover art—for example, by seeing it at iTunes. Even then, if your band has no money, the copyright owner probably wouldn't bother to sue you. But if sales increase or if the record is featured in the press or distributed by a record label, or if a band member inherits a family fortune, the chances for a lawsuit increase. That's why major labels and large independent labels insist on obtaining rights for all artwork on an album. A simple way to avoid artwork copyright problems is to obtain the rights for all artwork before using it. Model agreements are provided later in this chapter.

Obtaining Permissions From Models

Imagine this scenario: The guitarist in your band takes a "personal" photo of his girlfriend clad in lingerie. The band (being all-male) determines it is the perfect cover photo. After the guitarist breaks up with his girlfriend, the album is released. The ex-girlfriend, who never consented to the use, sues the band. She wins the lawsuit, and all copies of the artwork must be removed from Pandora, Spotify, iTunes, etc. Oops! In the previous section we indicated that you needed the photographer's permission to use a photograph. When a photo includes a person, your band must *also* obtain a release from the model (that is, the person in the photo). That's because under most state laws, a person can prevent the use of his or her image when it is used for commercial purposes. This is known as the "right of publicity." There are some exceptions: For example, you can usually use photos of people in large public gatherings, such as the crowd at an outdoor show. As with artwork copyright problems, the best solution to this problem is to avoid it in the first place: Obtain the permission of the model with a model release agreement. A sample agreement is provided in this chapter.

Objectionable Titles and Artwork

Some bands may want the controversy surrounding an indecent title or artwork; that's what makes rock and roll rebellious. John Lennon, Guns 'N' Roses, and Jane's Addiction all dealt with public outcry over album artwork. In the case of these well-known artists, such controversies may actually help to sell records.

However, objectionable artwork or titles can often cause problems and delays for bands. In the pre-Internet days, those concerns were occasionally about obscene or offensive artwork. For example, albums by the Dead Kennedys were seized as obscene in California, even though the offensive artwork was not even visible from the outside. The band's record label eventually prevailed in court, but only after years of legal hassles.

Nowadays, your band's decisions about artwork are geared more toward concerns that your cover will be rejected as offensive by an online distributor such as iTunes. (See the discussion below.) In other words, your decision about artwork should be balanced by aesthetic and business realities. Offensive artwork or titles may keep your band's record from being distributed.

Meeting Digital Artwork Standards

The artwork you furnish to online distributors such as CD Baby or TuneCore must be:

- square (that is, the width and height are the same)
- at least 1,600 x 1,600 pixels (iTunes prefers 3,000 x 3,000 pixels), and
- best quality RGB Color Mode (this includes black and white images).

Artwork for iTunes must not:

- be blurry, pixelated, mismatched, misaligned, rotated, incorrect, or have other quality issues
- contain website addresses for websites that sell music downloads or compete with iTunes
- contain the words "iTunes" or "Apple Inc.," the Apple logo, or the term "Exclusive" without prior authorization from Apple
- include references to the physical packaging (for example, CD or cassette) or any other retailers
- include references to it being a digital product
- include references to pricing, including "Reduced Price," "Low Price," "Available for $9.99," or "For Promo Use"; or
- contain pornography or a URL for a website that contains or has links to pornography.

Your Band's Website

Because a website is primarily artwork and graphics, we have included a few suggestions and tips in this chapter. The good news is that many bands get by without a website by taking advantage of social media (Facebook, Instagram), media upload sites (YouTube and Soundcloud), blogs and podcasting sites (Blogger, iTunes), and music ecommerce sites (Bandcamp and CD Baby). At the same time, creating a band website keeps getting easier. You can accomplish this task using off-the-shelf website-creation software, online software, or customized musician/band templates. To get an idea of your choices, just type "Create a band website" into your search engine. Many sites such as BandZoogle (www.bandzoogle.com) help you set up a site with an online retail feature. Whether you create the site yourself or use a developer, you must have some notion of what you'd like your website to do and what it should look like. If you have to have only four things on your website, we recommend a well-written bio, several free rotating songs on MP3, a tour itinerary, and merchandise and band downloads and CDs for sale. As for your graphic style, sometimes the easiest approach is to use the graphic and stylistic preferences seen in your logo, album artwork, and show posters, and adapt them for your website. This provides continuity and uniformity for your band's public image.

The Website Development Contract

If you're paying someone to perform website development, try to get the agreement in writing. There are too many legal issues involved to leave it to a handshake. Chances are that the developer will provide you with his or her company's standard written contract. Below are some key issues that should be included:

- **Specifications and timelines.** You'll need to reach an agreement with the developer as to the details of the website and dates when work should be completed.
- **Warranties and indemnity.** You should seek a promise that no copyrights or trademarks were infringed and that no one was libeled by any content created by the developer.
- **Ownership of the site.** You should obtain an assurance that your band claims copyright ownership of the site's design and appearance.
- **Contract assignability.** If you don't want the developer farming out the work to someone else, you'll need a clause that prevents assignment of the agreement.
- **Objections and approvals.** You'll want a simple system for approving or objecting to the developer's work—for example, an approval system that has several stages.
- **Termination.** You'll want an escape hatch in case things go sour during the development process—for example, a right to terminate the agreement, provided you pay for work completed.

Getting Permission to Use Content

Your band site will likely use lots of text, photos, and similar subject matter to attract and maintain fans. This content may be protected under copyright or trademark law. If you don't have the right to use it, you're courting trouble. The owner can sue to stop your use. You may have to remove the content from your site and pay damages for your wrongful use. To avoid problems, you can either buy the rights or ask the copyright owner for permission to use the work.

Here are five tips for staying out of trouble:

- **Get it in writing.** When dealing with artists, models, photographers, independent contractors, and other outside sources who prepare content for your site, get your agreement in writing. Later in this chapter, we provide releases for models and agreements for acquiring rights in artwork.
- **Assume it's protected.** Just because an article or photograph doesn't carry a copyright notice doesn't mean it's safe to use it without permission. Find out who owns the copyright and get permission in writing before using it on your website.
- **Don't rely on fair use exceptions.** Some website owners using works without permission rely on a legal defense known as fair use (see Chapter 7). This is a risky strategy, and we advise you to either get permission or create your own content.
- **Take infringement claims seriously.** If you receive a letter from someone who claims you are infringing a copyright, don't ignore it. Stop using it, temporarily at least, while you look into the facts and try to resolve the matter. If you leave the material on your website and a judge later finds you've infringed, the money damages you'll have to pay may be higher than if you had taken it down right away.
- **Be careful with links.** We recommend that you avoid linking to sites that you know contain infringing material.

Information to Include in Your Artwork

The following guidance is aimed at bands that will distribute CDs or vinyl LPs. In the case of these physical products, certain legal information, such as copyright and trademark notices, should be included on all physical versions of the music, usually on the back cover. To the extent that it's possible, you should include these notices in connection with digital reproductions such as website uses, or if possible embedded in digital downloads (though not on digital artwork if it conflicts with the digital standards discussed above).

Other information, though it does not have a legal significance, should be included for business purposes. This section discusses what information your artwork should include and where it should appear.

Legal Information

To enhance your legal protection under copyright and trademark laws, your band should include certain copyright and trademark notices on the artwork. This information places the world on notice that your band (or record label) owns the exclusive rights to the recordings, titles, and band names.

Copyright Notices

Copyright notice is not required, but it is strongly recommended. There are a number of different notices that you should use, including a copyright notice for the recording, for the songs, and for the artwork.

- **Recording copyright notice.** Your band should include a copyright notice for the recording. This notice has three parts: the symbol ℗ followed by the year of first publication of the recording and the owner of the record (probably your band or record label). The year of first publication is usually the year when the first copies were made. If last year your band made 20 to 30 copies of the same recording and distributed them to friends or radio stations, that is not considered a "publication." Note: It's difficult to find the symbol ℗ on most computer programs. (Sometimes it can be found in Hebrew lettering sets as the symbol for Kosher foods.)

- **Artwork copyright notice.** Your band should also include a notice such as "© 2018 Spyders." Usually this notice is joined with the recording copyright notice—for example, "℗ and © 2018 Spyders." This notice protects the artwork and text on the cover, booklet, or label. This notice has three parts: the "C" in a circle followed by the year of first publication of the recording and the owner of the artwork rights (probably your band; see the artwork agreement at the end of this chapter). The year of first publication is the year when this artwork is first distributed to the public (usually the year when the manufacturer first makes copies).

- **Song lyric copyright notice.** If you have included song lyrics, you should include a separate copyright notice, such as "© 2018 SpyderBiter Music," with the year of the song's first publication and the name of the song owner (usually the music publisher; see Chapter 8). The year of first publication is when the lyrics or sheet music were first distributed to the public, which is probably the year of the recording's manufacture.

Song Copyrights and Recording Copyrights

You may wonder why there is a copyright notice for the songs and another notice for the recording. That's because there are two types of music copyrights: song copyrights (as discussed in Chapter 7) and recording copyrights, which protect the manner in which music is arranged and recorded (that is, the way the music is fixed on the recording). Usually the song copyright is owned by a music publisher and the sound recording copyright is owned by a record company. In Chapter 7 we explain how to register a song copyright with the Copyright Office. In Chapter 11 we explain how to register a recording copyright.

Trademark Notices

If you have received a federal registration for your band name, you should include the symbol ® near your name—for example Spyders®. *Do not* use the ® symbol if you have not received a federal trademark registration. You can, if you wish, use the symbols ™ or SM (trademark or service mark) by your name, but we do not recommend it as they do not guarantee trademark protection.

What About the Parental Advisory?

According to the Recording Industry Association of America (RIAA) website (www.riaa.com), the Parental Advisory Label (PAL) is a notice to consumers that recordings identified by this mark may contain strong language or depictions of violence, sex, or substance abuse, and that parental discretion is advised. You can view the guidelines, as well as information on how to get permission to use the PAL Mark, at the RIAA website. (The RIAA owns the rights to the PAL.)

Suggested Information to Include

The following information is not required under law but is usually included on most artwork.

Basic Information

Album title; band name; song titles; song lengths (in minutes and seconds); total playing time; songwriters and music publisher (for example SpyderBiter Music); BMI or ASCAP; name, logo, and address of the record label; mail-order information; website and email address; and credits for producers, engineers, musicians, art direction, photographers, recording studio, mastering, and manufacturer.

Catalog Number

Catalog numbers are composed of six to eight letters or digits and are used to keep track of inventory. The first three or four digits indicate the record company or format, and the last three to four digits indicate the company's catalog number. If you're signed to a label, the label will furnish you with a catalog number, such as ARCD001 for compact discs. AR stands for the record company, CD stands for compact disc, and 001 indicates that it is that label's first release. Record labels assign consecutive numbers to the records they release. If your band is acting as its own label, you will need to create a catalog number. Follow the formula above: initials for the label and configuration, and number for the release.

Bar Codes

The Universal Product Code (UPC), also called a bar code, is a series of black lines that usually appears on the back of the compact disc. Distributors and retail stores use the bar code to keep track of inventory, and it is also used to monitor nationwide record sales. You probably don't need a bar code if you're planning to sell recordings only at concerts and local stores. However, if you are signed to a label or plan on selling your recordings through nationwide distributors or chain stores or at Amazon, or you want to offer your music through download services such as iTunes, you'll probably need the UPC code. Some manufacturers, distributors, or online stores (for example, Disc Makers and CD Baby) will assist you in obtaining the bar code. For more information about UPC bar codes, contact the Uniform Code Council (www.uc-council.org).

Record Speed and Noise Reduction

If you're releasing a 7-inch or 12-inch vinyl recording, make sure to indicate the speed (33 or 45 rpm).

Tagging MP3s

If you're distributing digital downloads either via your own website or through a download service, you will want to provide much of the same information on your CD but encoded within your MP3. This is done through "tagging." Most music encoding programs can tag—usually via pop-up window or dialog box—the title, album, and cover art so that it is available to those who download the MP3. Tagging can also be done when submitting metadata to a distributor such as TuneCore or CD Baby.

Getting the Artwork Done

As a general rule, your band will have an easier time if you entrust the job of artwork to an experienced graphic artist who can provide appealing and professional imagery. However, many bands cannot afford a graphic artist and instead rely on assistance from friends or the manufacturer. (When we refer to manufacturers, we're talking about the companies that duplicate compact discs and vinyl records.)

Regardless of who prepares the imagery and layout, your band will share the responsibility of providing the basic information required for the artwork. That is, your band will have the responsibility to guarantee titles are spelled correctly, credits are accurate, and legal notices are proper. Below, we discuss the artwork process and your band's responsibilities.

Learn the Lingo

Graphic artists and manufacturers use special terms when dealing with album artwork. If you're not familiar with the terminology, here are some of the basics. A *template* is a pattern or outline for each piece of artwork, including the measurements and specifications. For example, a CD manufacturer will provide you with templates showing the dimensions of each piece of artwork (booklet, tray card, and so on). Each template usually includes extra space on all four sides of the artwork known as *bleed*. Your photos or artwork should "bleed" into these blank spaces so that when the artwork is finally cut, the artwork and any background color or images reach all the way to the edge.

If you are preparing artwork on a computer or if it will be converted into computer format, your photographs and artwork will have to be scanned to convert the two-dimensional image into a digital image. The typestyles used are called *fonts*. A full-color design is referred to as a *four-color* design, because it includes the three primary colors and black. When the artwork is completed, it is *camera-ready*. That is, your band's artwork needs no further modification and can be reproduced "as is" by the manufacturer.

Working With a Professional Artist

You can follow many of the same rules for hiring an artist as you would for hiring any professional. That is, rely on referrals from others, ask to see examples of the work, and obtain a written estimate for the work.

Be sure to discuss ownership of the artwork and to make clear your band's intended purposes for it. Under copyright law, a freelance artist retains copyright ownership of the artwork. Generally, if you hire someone to create art for a purpose, you as the hiring party have an implied license to use the art for that purpose. For instance, if you hired a photographer to take a picture for an album, you can use the picture on your album without having to obtain a written license from the artist. But remember, that's *all* you can use it for, and the photographer retains ownership of the picture and could even sell it to another band for use on their cover.

Since these ownership issues can be complicated, we recommend that you obtain written permission to use the work or that the artist assign *all* ownership to your band. The artwork agreement, below, covers these ownership issues.

What to Do If the Artwork Is Wrong

Most artwork problems result from not reviewing credits and test prints carefully. To avoid errors, check and double-check the credits before submitting them. When you get the test prints of the artwork, check again.

If the error is your fault (that is, you submitted incorrect information or failed to spot errors in test prints), then you'll have a hard time getting the printer or manufacturer to redo the work for free. Your best hope is to have the artwork done at a reduced rate. Larger manufacturers, because of the large volume of business they do, are often better suited to make this type of arrangement.

Artwork Is Always Late

Don't bother booking the date for your record release party until the artwork is completed. Generally, the artwork is the item that holds up the manufacturing, either because it's late or must be corrected. If you are doing the artwork yourself, be prepared for it to take several weeks. Also, friends may be helpful in offering graphic services, but as a general rule, you're more likely to get what you want on time if you're paying for services or doing it yourself.

Abbreviated Artwork Agreement

If your band wants a simple artwork agreement that transfers all rights in the artwork to the band for one payment, then use this abbreviated artwork agreement. We'll walk you through the simple task of putting this agreement together. A sample appears below. If your band needs a more detailed agreement for an artist who is not willing to transfer all rights, use the agreement that follows this one.

FORMS
You can download this form (and all other forms in this book) from Nolo.com; for details, see "Get Forms, Updates, and More at This Book's Companion Page," in the appendix.

In the introductory section, insert the name of your band partnership if it owns your recordings. If you created a separate company for the release of your recordings (such as "Our Band's Records"), list that name. If the name doesn't make it clear what kind of business form it is (for example, "The Spyder Partnership"), indicate the business form (for example, "Centipede, a general partnership"). The artist can be a photographer, illustrator, or any type of graphic artist.

Services

Indicate the specific services. For example, "design camera-ready artwork and text for a four-panel booklet, tray card, and compact disc label and furnish that artwork in a digital format" or "photography services to create a suitable band photo for use in album artwork." You should also insert the date when the artwork or photography will be completed. If the artwork has already been completed, simply state "Completed."

Payment

Insert the total amount of the payment and the method for payment (for example, "Half at time of commencement of work and half on acceptance by Band").

Rights

Under this agreement, your band owns the artwork and can do whatever you wish without any further reimbursement (other than provided in the Payment section) to the artist.

Expenses

In this section your band agrees to pay for the artist's expenses incurred in the course of completing the artwork. It establishes that expenses must be itemized to be paid, and that your approval is necessary for expenses over $50.

Credit

Indicate the type of credit the artist will get in your album information. For example, "Graphic Design and Cover Artwork by Joan Smith."

Artist Warranties

Warranties are contractual promises. If the artist breaks this promise (for example, the artist infringes someone's photo), the band can seek money damages from the artist.

Mediation; Arbitration

This provision provides a less-expensive method of resolving disputes than filing a lawsuit. (See Chapter 2 for an explanation of mediation and arbitration.)

We suggest that you choose the county, province, or city in which the band resides for arbitration. If all the members do not reside within one area, choose a place that is convenient. Enter your location of choice in the blank.

In several states, there are organizations that specialize in arbitration for people in the arts, such as California Lawyers for the Arts (www. calawyersforthearts.org) and Volunteer Lawyers for the Arts (in New York at www.vlany.org, as well as in other cities and states). You can substitute the rules for one of these organizations in your agreement for those of the American Arbitration Association. If your band is based in Canada, you can still use the AAA's rules, as they perform arbitration in all major Canadian cities. Check one of the choices or delete the unwanted alternative.

Signatures

Only one member of your band needs to sign the agreement, though, of course, it's best to make sure that everybody agrees about hiring the artist. Enter the business name of the band, the name of which band member is signing, and the band member's title (usually "Partner"). That band member should sign and date the form. Have the artist enter his or her address, and sign and date the form.

[Abbreviated] Artwork Agreement

This Artwork Agreement (the "Agreement") is made between _____
_____ ("Band") and
_____ ("Artist").

Services

Artist agrees to perform the following services and create the following artwork (the "Art"): _____
_____
_____
_____

    The Art will be completed by the following date: _____ .

    During the process, Artist will keep the Band informed of work in progress and will furnish test prints of the Art prior to completion.

Payment

Band agrees to pay Artist $_____ as follows: _____
_____
_____
_____

for performance of the art services and acquisition of the rights provided below.

Rights

Artist assigns to the Band all copyright to the Art and agrees to cooperate in the preparation of any documents necessary to demonstrate this assignment of rights. Artist retains the right to display the work as part of Artist's portfolio and to reproduce the Art in connection with the promotion of Artist's services.

Expenses

Band agrees to reimburse Artist for all reasonable production expenses including halftones, stats, photography, disks, illustrations, or related costs. These expenses will be itemized on invoices, and in no event will any expense exceed $50 without approval from the Band.

Credit

Credit for Artist will be included on reproductions of the Art as follows: _____
_____ .

Artist Warranties

Artist warrants that the Art will not infringe any intellectual property rights or violate
any laws.

Mediation; Arbitration

If a dispute arises under this Agreement, the parties agree to first try to resolve the
dispute with the help of a mutually agreed-on mediator in _____ .
Any costs and fees other than attorney fees will be shared equally by the parties. If it
is impossible to arrive at a mutually satisfactory solution within a reasonable time, the
parties agree to submit the dispute to binding arbitration in the same city or region,
conducted on a confidential basis pursuant to the Commercial Arbitration Rules of the
American Arbitration Association, or the rules of _____ .

Band Partnership Name _____

Band Partner Name and Title _____

Band Partner Signature _____

Address _____

_____

Date _____

Artist Name _____

Artist Signature _____

Address _____

_____

Date _____

Full-Length Artwork Agreement

If your band wants a full-length artwork agreement that offers more choices regarding ownership rights and more detailed protection for your band, then use this Full-Length Artwork Agreement. This section explains how to fill out this agreement. A sample appears below.

 FORMS
You can download this form (and all other forms in this book) from Nolo.com; for details, see "Get Forms, Updates, and More at This Book's Companion Page," in the appendix..

In the introductory section, put the name of your band partnership if it owns your recordings. If you created a separate company for the release of your recordings (such as "Our Band's Records"), list that name. If the name doesn't make it clear what kind of business form it is (for example, "The Spyder Partnership"), then indicate the business form (for example, "Centipede, a general partnership"). The artist can be a photographer, illustrator, or any type of graphic artist.

Services

Indicate the specific services. For example, "design camera-ready artwork and text for a four-panel booklet, tray card, and compact disc label and furnish that artwork in a digital format" or "photography services to create a suitable band photo for use in album artwork." You should also insert the date when the artwork or photography will be completed. If the artwork has already been completed, simply state "Completed."

Payment

Insert the total amount of the payment and the method for payment (for example, "Half at time of commencement of work and half on acceptance by Band").

Rights (Includes Optional Provisions)

We have provided five different rights provisions to deal with five common situations. Check one of the provisions, or delete the unwanted provisions entirely.

Option #1: Under the first choice, your band owns the artwork and can do whatever you wish with it without any further reimbursement (other than the Payment section) to the artist. This is the provision that is preferable if you intend to furnish this artwork to a major record label, because major music companies prefer to own all rights.

Option #2: If the artist is willing to sell (assign) to your band all rights to the artwork but wants to be paid for merchandise sales, then use this selection. Merchandise sales include products other than recordings, such as T-shirts, stickers, hats, and so on. Check one of the two different ways to pay for merchandise. You can select a royalty payment for the artist (usually ranging from 2% to 10%), or you can make a lump sum payment per every 1,000 T-shirts or items sold.

Under all of the remaining choices, the artist retains copyright ownership and your band gets permission to use the artwork for different purposes. Think of it as a "rental" of the artwork rights. The primary difference is that under these choices, the artist retains all rights to the artwork that are not granted to the band. Therefore, for example, the artist could permit the use of the artwork on postcards.

You may find that some artists bristle at the thought of allowing modification of the artwork. You should explain that modification is often necessary for formatting and advertising purposes. If the artist is adamant about not permitting modification, strike the word "modify." (In the United States, you do not need to seek permission for modification if you have used one of the first two choices. However, in Canada, you may have to obtain permission under a principle known as "moral rights." (See Chapter 7.))

Option #3: Under the third choice, your band can use the artwork solely for use in connection with recordings, but not merchandise. That is, you can use the art on recordings and materials promoting those recordings such as your website, but if you want to sell merchandise such as T-shirts with the artwork, you'll need to go back to the artist and get permission.

Option #4: Under the fourth choice, your band can use the artwork in connection with recordings and merchandise without any further reimbursement (other than the Payment section) to the artist. That is, you have the right to use the art on recordings, ads, and promos at your website, and you can sell merchandise with the artwork. Most savvy artists do not grant such rights without further reimbursement for the merchandise. In this case, you would use the last choice, described below.

Option #5: This final choice is the same as the previous one, except your band pays for merchandise rights as the money comes in from those sales. The theory behind these payments is that the artist's work, as well as the band's popularity, is triggering merchandise sales, and, therefore, the artist should receive a royalty. Check one of the two different ways to pay for merchandise. You can select a royalty payment for the artist (usually ranging from 2% to 10%), or you can make a lump sum payment per every 1,000 T-shirts or items sold.

Expenses

In this section your band agrees to pay for the artist's expenses incurred in the course of completing the artwork. It establishes that expenses must be itemized to be paid, and that your approval is necessary for expenses over $50.

Credit

Indicate the type of credit the artist will get in the album information. For example, "Graphic Design and Cover Artwork by Joan Smith."

Artist Warranties and Indemnification

Warranties and representations are contractual promises. If the artist breaks one of these promises (for example, the artist infringes someone's photo), the band can seek money damages from the artist. By "indemnifying" your band the artist agrees to pay for your damages that are caused by the artist. For example, if your band is sued because the art includes unauthorized images, the artist would have to pay for your band's legal expenses.

Assignment

This allows the band to grant its rights to another company. For example, if a label wanted to release your recording, your band could assign the rights to the artwork to the label.

Mediation; Arbitration

This provision provides a less-expensive method of resolving disputes than filing a lawsuit. (See Chapter 2 for an explanation of mediation and arbitration.)

We suggest that you choose the county, province, or city in which the band resides for arbitration. If all the members do not live in one area, choose a place that is convenient. Enter your location of choice in the blank.

In several states, there are organizations that specialize in arbitration for people in the arts, such as California Lawyers for the Arts (www.calawyersforthearts.org) and Volunteer Lawyers for the Arts (in New York at www.vlany.org, as well as in other cities and states). You can substitute the rules of one of these organizations in your agreement for those of the American Arbitration Association. If your band is based in Canada, you can still use the AAA's rules, as they perform arbitration in all major Canadian cities. Check one of the choices, or delete the unwanted alternative.

General

The following provisions are standard contract provisions referred to as boilerplate. Boilerplate provisions are explained in Chapter 2.

In the blank space, insert the state (or province, in the case of Canadian bands) of residence for the band partners. In the event of a dispute, this determines which state law will govern the arbitration or lawsuit. This provision also provides that the winner in any lawsuit between the band and the artist will receive attorneys' fees.

Signatures

Only one member of your band needs to sign the agreement, though you should make sure that everybody agrees about hiring the artist. Enter the business name of the band, the name of the band member who is signing, and the band member's title (usually "Partner"). That band member should sign and date the form. Have the artist enter his or her address, and sign and date the form.

Artwork Agreement

This Artwork Agreement (the "Agreement") is made between _____
_____ ("Band") and
_____ ("Artist").
The Band wants Artist to create artwork to be used in conjunction with their musical recordings. The parties agree as follows:

Services

In consideration of the payments provided in this Agreement, Artist agrees to perform the following services and create the following artwork (the "Art"): _____
_____

    The Art will be completed by the following date: _____ .

    During the process, Artist will keep the Band informed of work in progress and will furnish test prints of the Art prior to completion.

Payment

Band agrees to pay Artist $_____ as follows: _____
for performance of the art services and acquisition of the rights provided below.

Rights

The rights to the artwork will be as follows: (*choose one*)

    ☐ Artist assigns to the Band all copyright to the Art and agrees to cooperate in the preparation of any documents necessary to demonstrate this assignment of rights. Artist retains the right to display the work as part of Artist's portfolio and to reproduce the Art in connection with the promotion of Artist's services.

    ☐ Artist assigns to the Band all copyright to the Art and agrees to cooperate in the preparation of any documents necessary to demonstrate this assignment of rights. Artist retains the right to display the work as part of Artist's portfolio and to reproduce the Art in connection with the promotion of Artist's services. In addition to any other payments provided under this agreement, if the Art is used on merchandise authorized by the Band that is sold to the public, Artist is entitled to the following payments, which will be paid twice a year at the end of June and December:

(*Choose one and fill in the blank*)	Amount
☐ Royalty on net profits from sale of merchandise	_____%
☐ Lump sum payments for every 1,000 _____ sold	$_____

(Net profits are all revenues received minus the costs of production, shipping, and any discounts or fees paid to distributors or retailers.)

☐ Artist grants to the Band for the length of copyright the exclusive worldwide right to use, sell, modify, and distribute the Art in connection with the sale of the Band's musical recordings and for purposes of advertising and promotion of the Band's musical recordings. All other rights are reserved to Artist.

☐ Artist grants to the Band for the length of copyright the exclusive worldwide right to use, sell, modify, and distribute the Art in connection with the sale of the Band's musical recordings and for purposes of advertising and promotion of the Band's musical recordings and in connection with Band merchandise including upper-body apparel, hats, and other items. All other rights are reserved to Artist.

☐ Artist grants to the Band for the length of copyright the exclusive worldwide right to use, sell, modify, and distribute the Art in connection with the sale of the Band's musical recordings and for purposes of advertising and promotion of the Band's musical recordings and in connection with Band merchandise including upper-body apparel, hats, and other items. All other rights are reserved to Artist. In addition to any other payments provided under this agreement, if the Art is used on merchandise authorized by the Band that is sold to the public, Artist is entitled to the following payments, which will be paid twice a year, at the end of June and December:

(*Choose one and fill in the blank*)	Amount
☐ Royalty on net profits from sale of merchandise	_____%
☐ Lump sum payments for every 1,000 _____ sold	$_____

(Net profits are all revenues received minus the costs of production, shipping, and any discounts or fees paid to distributors or retailers.)

Expenses

Band agrees to reimburse Artist for all reasonable production expenses including halftones, stats, photography, disks, illustrations, or related costs. These expenses will be itemized on invoices, and in no event will any expense exceed $50 without approval from the Band.

Credit

Credit for Artist will be included on reproductions of the Art as follows: _____

_____

_____

Artist Warranties and Indemnification

Artist warrants to Band that: (a) Artist has the power and authority to enter into this Agreement; (b) the Art will not infringe any intellectual property rights or violate any laws; and (c) Artist has or will obtain all necessary rights or licenses associated with any artwork, photos, or illustrations incorporated into the Art. Artist indemnifies Band and undertakes to defend Band against and hold Band harmless (including, without limitation, attorney fees and costs) from any claims and damage arising out of any breach of Artist's warranties, above.

Assignment

The Band has the right to assign its rights under this Agreement.

Mediation; Arbitration

If a dispute arises under this Agreement, the parties agree to first try to resolve the dispute with the help of a mutually agreed-on mediator in _____ .
Any costs and fees other than attorney fees will be shared equally by the parties. If it is impossible to arrive at a mutually satisfactory solution within a reasonable time, the parties agree to submit the dispute to binding arbitration in the same city or region, conducted on a confidential basis pursuant to:

☐ the Commercial Arbitration Rules of the American Arbitration Association, or

☐ the rules of _____ .

Any decision or award as a result of any such arbitration proceeding will include the assessment of costs, expenses, and reasonable attorneys' fees and include a written determination of the arbitrators. Absent an agreement to the contrary, any such arbitration will be conducted by an arbitrator experienced in music industry law. An award of arbitration is final and binding on the Band Partners and may be confirmed in a court of competent jurisdiction. The prevailing party has the right to collect from the other party its reasonable costs and attorney fees incurred in enforcing this agreement.

General

Nothing contained in this Agreement constitutes either Band or Artist a partner or employee of the other party. This Agreement expresses the complete understanding of the parties and may not be amended except in a writing signed by both parties. If a court finds any provision of this Agreement invalid or unenforceable, the remainder of this Agreement will be interpreted so as best to effect the intent of the parties. This Agreement is governed by and interpreted in accordance with the laws of _____ _____ . Notices required under this agreement can be sent to parties at the addresses provided below.

Band Partnership Name _____

Band Partner Name and Title _____

Band Partner Signature _____

Address _____

_____

Date _____

Artist Name _____

Artist Signature _____

Address _____

_____

Date _____

Model Release Agreement

The Model Release Agreement is a simple agreement that allows your band to use a person's image on your artwork, such as a photograph of a friend or a professional model. Band members who may appear on album artwork would not need to sign this release. Although the term "model" is used, we're not necessarily talking about professional models. The term applies to any person whose image is used. Below is an explanation of how to put together this agreement. A sample appears below.

 FORMS
You can download this form (and all other forms in this book) from Nolo.com; for details, see "Get Forms, Updates, and More at This Book's Companion Page," in the appendix.

In the introductory section, insert the name of your band partnership if it owns your recordings. If you created a separate company for the release of your recordings (such as "Our Band's Records"), list that name. If the name doesn't make it clear what kind of business form it is (for example, "The Spyder Partnership"), then indicate the business form (for example, "Centipede, a general partnership"). Insert the name of the model.

Rights

Describe the imagery your band is using for the artwork. For example, "outdoor photos of Model taken at Ocean Beach in May 2018." If possible, attach a photocopy of the image. Under this provision, your band gets the exclusive right to use the model's image for any purpose related to your music, such as recordings or merchandise. If the model does not want to give up the merchandise rights, or if the model wants to be paid an additional fee for merchandise rights, you will need to negotiate a merchandise royalty fee. We do not recommend paying royalties to models, especially if you are also paying royalties to the artwork artists.

Payment

Insert the amount of the payment. Even if the model is a friend, your band should make a nominal payment, such as $1. This payment will cover all of your uses. However, if the model insists on royalties or additional payments for use of the model image on merchandise, you will need to add an additional page (or exhibit) detailing this arrangement. Both parties should sign this exhibit.

Credit

Models often do not receive credit on artwork, and, for that reason, this provision is optional. If the model will receive credit, indicate the type of credit that will appear. For example, "Man on Back Cover: M. Polazzo."

Mediation; Arbitration

This provision provides a less expensive method of resolving disputes than filing a lawsuit. (See Chapter 2 for an explanation of mediation and arbitration.)

We suggest that you choose the county, province, or city in which the band resides for arbitration. If all the members do not reside in one area, choose a place that is convenient. Enter your location of choice in the blank.

In some states there are organizations that specialize in arbitration for people in the arts, such as California Lawyers for the Arts (www.calawyers forthearts.org) and Volunteer Lawyers for the Arts (in New York at www. vlany.org, as well as in other cities and states). You can substitute the rules of such an organization in your agreement for those of the American Arbitration Association. If your band is based in Canada, you can still use the AAA's rules, as they perform arbitration in all major Canadian cities. Check one of the choices or delete the unwanted alternative.

General

The following provisions are standard contractual provisions referred to as boilerplate. Boilerplate provisions are explained in Chapter 2.

In the blank space, insert the state (or province, in the case of Canadian bands) of residence for the band partners. In the event of a dispute, this determines which state law will govern the arbitration or lawsuit.

Signatures

Only one member of your band needs to sign the agreement, though you should make sure that everybody agrees about hiring the model. Enter the business name of the band, the name of the band member who is signing, and the band member's title (usually "Partner"). That band member should sign and date the form. Have the model enter his or her address, and sign and date the form.

Model Release Agreement

This Model Release Agreement (the "Agreement") is made between _____
_____ ("Band") and
_____ ("Model").

Rights

The Band is using Model's image in conjunction with the artwork for their musical recordings. In consideration of the payments provided in this Agreement, Model grants to the Band and its assigns or licensees the right to use Model's picture as embodied on in all forms and media and (including composite or modified representations) for use in connection with the sale of the Band's musical recordings, for purposes of advertising and promotion of the Band's musical recordings, and in connection with Band-related merchandise.

Payment

Band will pay Model as follows: $_____ .

Credit

(*Check and fill in blank if applicable*)

☐ Model is entitled to the following credit: _____

Mediation; Arbitration

If a dispute arises under this Agreement, the parties agree to first try to resolve the dispute with the help of a mutually agreed-on mediator in _____.
Any costs and fees other than attorney fees will be shared equally by the parties. If it proves impossible to arrive at a mutually satisfactory solution within a reasonable time, the parties agree to submit the dispute to binding arbitration in the same city or region, conducted on a confidential basis pursuant to:

☐ the Commercial Arbitration Rules of the American Arbitration Association, or

☐ the rules of _____ .

Any decision or award as a result of any such arbitration proceeding will include the assessment of costs, expenses, and reasonable attorneys' fees and a written determination of the arbitrators. Absent an agreement to the contrary, any such arbitration will be conducted by an arbitrator experienced in music industry law. An award of arbitration is final and binding on the Band Partners and may be confirmed in a court of competent jurisdiction. The prevailing party has the right to collect from the other party its reasonable costs and attorney fees incurred in enforcing this Agreement.

General

Nothing contained in this Agreement is deemed to constitute either Band or Model a partner or employee of the other party. This Agreement expresses the complete understanding of the parties and may not be amended except in a writing signed by both parties. If a court finds any provision of this Agreement invalid or unenforceable, the remainder of this Agreement will be interpreted so as best to carry out the intent of the parties. This Agreement is governed by and interpreted in accordance with the laws of _____ .

Band Partnership Name _____

Band Partner Name and Title _____

Band Partner Signature _____

Address _____

_____

Date _____

Model Name _____

Model Signature _____

Address _____

_____

Date _____

Recording

A recording studio is like a magnifying glass. Your band's music is placed under laboratory-like scrutiny. Suddenly, mistakes that may have been acceptable on stage are no longer tolerable when heard through studio monitors. In the same way, the recording studio places your band's business under scrutiny. Your band must produce a desired result within an expected time period and within a budget. Can you do it? How do you juggle financial limits with your artistic intentions?

This chapter deals with issues that tend to arise in the course of recording music. We will help you prepare a recording budget, and we will advise you on legal issues such as obtaining releases from musicians who perform on your recording or for using a digital sample of someone else's music. We will also offer advice on choosing a studio and how to save money while recording. At the end of the chapter we provide information about registering your copyright in the recording.

Legal Issues in the Recording Studio

When we discuss legal issues in the recording studio, we are concerned primarily with whether you are giving up (or risking) your rights in the recordings. That is, by using an outside musician or by sampling a recording, have you in any way diluted your ownership of the recordings? Or, looking at it from a more practical perspective, are you risking a lawsuit over the rights to your music?

Recording Studios

Your relationship with a recording studio is a straightforward "service" arrangement. You either pay in advance for a block of time or you pay an hourly rate after each session. The studio, by recording your music, obtains no legal rights to the music. That is, the studio cannot claim an ownership in your music simply because the recording was made there. Beware, however, that this may not be true in two situations: (a) Studio employees arrange your music or perform on your recordings; or (b) the studio does the recording on "spec" in return for a percentage of any income.

Studio Employees

In cases of performing studio employees, the situation is the same as if any nonband musicians played on your recording. Those musicians may have coauthorship claims to the song or to the recording copyright based on their contributions. The claim may or may not be validated by a court—that depends on the quality of the contribution and other factors. However, any claim is enough to temporarily cloud your ownership.

You probably do not need to be concerned about such issues with studio employees, because studios usually do not want to claim rights in songs or recordings (it's bad for business). However, if you are signed to a record label, you can guarantee your rights are protected by having all musicians who assist in the making of the recording sign a musician's release.

Recording on Spec

If a studio does your recording on spec, that means the studio will allow you to record for free or at a reduced rate because the studio is speculating that your recording will be a success. If the record is a success, you will be required to repay the recording costs—and more. A studio may request a percentage of the record company advance or future royalty income. You should be cautious entering into spec deals, as the payout may far exceed the value of the recording services. If you enter into a spec arrangement, get it in writing and avoid transferring any ownership interest of the copyright in the songs or the recording.

Producers

If you are signed to a major label, you will have to use a producer—a professional who directs the recording and mixing sessions. Most producers are paid a fee for their work and receive a percentage of the income from the recording. Unlike an engineer, a producer will provide an impartial criticism of your performance, as well as an objective analysis of your songs. If you are signed to an independent label, the company may suggest (but not demand) that you work with a producer.

Usually a producer (or the producer's agent or attorney) provides a written agreement or deal memo establishing the producer's fee. These agreements also establish the record company's rights to the recording, thereby avoiding any potential claims of copyright ownership by the producer.

Some unsigned bands work with producers, often under an arrangement known as a producer-demo deal. In this arrangement, a recording is made at the producer's expense, often at the producer's studio. The producer then shops the band to a record label. Demo deals vary, and in some cases the producer is entitled to a cut of any money received from a band record deal regardless of whether the demo was responsible. The demo deal may also grant publishing rights to the producer.

Generally, bands have little negotiating ability in producer-demo deals. That is, you're usually told to take it or leave it. Since such deals are often extremely one-sided, you should review them carefully and research the producer to determine if he or she is trustworthy and well connected. Since these deals have some of the features of management agreements, you should compare the provisions of any demo deal you're considering to those in the management agreement in Chapter 3. You can also compare it to the label-shopping agreement in Chapter 4. Finally, you might want to have the demo deal reviewed by an attorney.

Dear Rich: Where Do I Get a Music Producer Agreement?

I have your Music Law *book, but it doesn't contain an agreement that can be used with a music producer. I am an artist and need a producer agreement.*

There are a few music producer agreements floating around the Internet. But before you start downloading, keep in mind that these agreements come in three major flavors:

- **Record company/producer agreement.** In this arrangement, a record company hires a producer to produce a song or an album. Even though the record company hires the producer, the payment typically comes from the artist. That is, the record company pays the producer and then later deducts that cost from the artist royalties. The royalties that are paid to the producer, often in addition to the producing fee, are also usually deducted from the artist royalty. So, for example, if the artist is getting a 15% royalty, the artist may have to pay 3% or 4% of that to the producer. This type of production agreement usually includes a few major components including: the producer assigns copyright to the label, the producer takes on some specific administrative tasks (such as hiring the studio or paying musicians), and the producer performs certain production tasks in terms of delivering acceptable master recordings.

- **Artist/producer agreement.** In this case, the artist, not a record company, hires the producer. This is a common course of action for an indie artist who wants to release music directly or wants a suitable master to shop to a record company. In this case, there may be a flat fee (say $500 per song) and no royalty payments. This type of agreement would include an assignment of all copyright to the artist, as well as a detailed listing of the producer's obligations. Typically, in this situation, the artist pays for the studio and any extra costs.

- **Spec agreement—production company/artist.** In this situation, a production company or producer agrees to produce a song or an album, often on spec (that is, without an up-front payment), and in return, the production company usually helps to shop the final product and obtains various future rights. These may include future royalties, part ownership in songwriting, a percentage of any record company advances, or even more, such as dibs on merchandise.

Putting together an agreement? We're going to assume you don't need the first or the third agreements, mentioned above. Both of those are fairly complex and are usually prepared by lawyers. You might be able to prepare an informal, enforceable version of the second type of agreement—an agreement between an artist and a producer—by yourself, particularly if you already know and get along with the producer. A bare-bones version would contain the following provisions: (a) an assignment of all copyright for work created, performed, or produced by the producer, (b) a schedule for payment and delivery, (c) a division of labor (who does what and pays for what), and (d) a system for resolving disputes. Payment should be fixed (per track) and you may want to set it up to make the payment in stages based upon delivery of the tracks. You might also want to include an approval process, although such provisions are tough to create and difficult to enforce.

Engineers

Generally, an unsigned band does not use a producer but instead relies on an experienced engineer to guide the band through the recording. Some engineers, eager for producing experience, may waive a portion of their hourly fee in return for a coproduction credit and a payment if the recording is released by a label.

Musician Releases

In the studio, your band may use other musicians, such as a cello player used on one song. Copyright law requires that your band obtain permission to use the performance on your recording. We have provided a sample release agreement, below. We advise getting a signed release, but, practically, if you're only making a demo or releasing your own record, your band can probably get by without it. However, all major labels and some independents will require a release.

If a musician is under an exclusive recording agreement with a record company, you will need to find out if the musician is permitted to perform on "outside" recordings. If so, there may be a special credit required in your album information (for example, "Lindsay Hutton appears courtesy of NBT Records"). If a musician on your recording is a member of the American Federation of Musicians union, then the musician must be paid according to union rates. The musician will furnish your band with the AFM forms for each recording session. Every recording made for a major label must use union musicians.

Sampling

It's possible that you turned directly to this section because your band is planning to use a sample on your recording and you want to know your rights. Can you use the sample for free? If you have to pay, whom do you ask about it? Unfortunately, there are no one-size-fits-all solutions. We'll walk you through the legal side and then offer you some practical suggestions.

As you are probably aware, sampling is the process of copying a piece of recorded music—usually on a computer or sampler—and then reproducing it on your recording. Sometimes the sample is repeated to create a drum pattern or a chorus; sometimes the sample is used only once. If you sample your band's own musical recordings, that's never a problem (assuming you haven't sold the rights to the recording to a record company). But if you sample another recording, that raises legal issues.

(Note: There is another quite different legal definition of sampling. In the *Napster (A&M v. Napster)* case, the court defined the practice of making temporary copies of a recording before purchasing as "sampling." That definition is not applicable to our discussion here.)

Sampling is a violation of copyright law if it's done without the permission of the owner of the recording (usually the record company) and the owner of the song (usually the music publisher). There are some exceptions to this rule, discussed below.

Dear Rich: Are Music Loops and Samples Copyrighted?

Can I ask you why music sample CDs include a clause that their material is copyrighted when you've made it clear that you can't copyright short music samples and vocal samples?

As we've mentioned before, samples (or "loops," as they are sometimes called) are short sound snippets—perhaps two measures of drums, or a vocal phrase ("ice, ice, baby"), or a bass riff—that can be inserted as a "standalone" audio file or repeated ("looped") to create a song. Yes, you can copyright loops and samples. First, you can get a compilation copyright on your unique collection of loops. Second, individual loops of music may be protected under sound recording copyrights. Third it's possible that a loop that is long enough and that demonstrates sufficient originality may be the subject of a music composition copyright. Our previous explanations regarding loops and copyrights had to do with whether someone using someone else's loops—a customer or purchaser of a loop collection—could claim copyright in the loop. In that situation, the user is similar to that of a user of a clip art collection. They are prevented from claiming copyright in the loop or art, by itself, because (1) they are subject to a license agreement, (2) they are not the authors of the loop (and didn't create it), or (3) the individual loop can't be subject to a music composition copyright.

Precleared Samples

Some samples have been "precleared." That means that it's okay with the owner for others to sample the recording. For example, if you use the ACID-brand or Garage Band loops in your band's compositions, you don't need to get permission to do so. This is also sometimes the case with other companies "DJ" recordings that include precleared drum beats and musical riffs, and it also may be true for digital sounds included on a computer disk. Consider these sampled sounds like audio clip art—free to use. But before freely using the sample, check the notice on the recording or disk package to make sure that the material is available for your use.

To Sample or Not to Sample?

For musicians and songwriters there are many dangers involved in unauthorized sampling … but don't tell that to Brian Burton aka DJ Danger Mouse, whose career as a music producer was launched through illegal use of samples. In 2004 Burton created *The Grey Album*, a mash up of the Beatles *White Album* and Jay-Z's *Black Album*. He pressed 3,000 copies of *The Grey Album* and distributed them to indie music sources.

EMI, the owner of rights to the Beatles album, learned of the project and quickly squelched it by sending a cease and desist letter. "EMI is absolutely in favor of music sampling," an EMI spokesperson told the press. "There's a very well established way to get sampling and [Burton] did not participate."

Burton complied with the EMI order and stopped distribution of the recording. But fans uploaded the album to the Internet where it became a worldwide sensation. Since EMI never pursued Burton after he agreed to stop, he suffered no serious legal consequences. And *The Grey Album* led to a slew of producing opportunities as well as recognition in *Rolling Stone* and the *New York Times*.

Sampling, however, has not been as kind to other artists. Consider the makers of the film *I Got the Hook-Up*, who were sued because a two-second sample (a three-note riff) from George Clinton's "Get Off Your Ass and

Jam" (sampled by N.W.A. in their song "100 Miles and Runnin'") appeared in the film. Although many listeners could not even discern the sample in the mix, a federal court ruled that any sampling from a recording amounts to copyright infringement and found the filmmakers liable for infringement and financial penalties. Ouch!

So should you make use of samples from someone else's copyrighted music? How does the average working musician decide what to do?

In a nutshell, you should always seek clearance for use of a recognizable sample when you are signed to a recording contract or when preparing music for a commercial client—for example, for a video game, advertisement, commercially released film, or the like. If you don't get permission under these circumstances, you could get sued, your record label or client could get sued, and you might be prevented from distributing your music to the public at all.

As a practical matter, if you're selling recordings only at shows and don't expect to press more than 1,000 copies of a record, you run less risk for uncleared samples, because it's unlikely that the owner of the source recording will ever learn of your samples—and if they do learn of it, they may not be inclined to pursue you unless they sense you have deep pockets (legal slang for people with substantial assets).

However, always keep in mind that if your recording becomes popular and becomes a staple of clubs, a radio hit, or a major download sensation, you'll likely have to deal with the issue of clearance. And unfortunately, using uncleared samples can be dangerous to your financial health. Artists have been forced to pay sums in the range of $100,000 as settlement for the uncleared use of samples (and often must give up substantial music publishing royalties).

You're also probably familiar with the Catch-22 of sample clearance: In order to get a signed sample clearance agreement, you'll have to provide the owners of the sample (a music publisher and record company) with a recording that shows how much of the source you intend to use, and how you intend to use it. So you'll likely be doing your recording first, with no permission. If you then find that you can't get permission, a lot of hard work will have gone to waste.

CAUTION
If you intend to proceed without clearance, you should be familiar with some legal principles that we'll explain a little later.

So what should you know about getting permission to use samples? The process of getting permission from the owners of the sampled music is referred to as "sample clearance." When you sample music from a pop recording, you'll need two clearances: one from the copyright owner of the song, who is usually a music publisher, and the other from the copyright owner of the master tapes, which is usually a record company. In general, clearance is required only if you're planning to make copies of your music and distribute the copies to the public, not for sampling at home. If you're using samples only in your live performance, you probably don't need to bother with clearance unless your act is drawing the type of attention that would awaken a copyright owner as to your use. (In any case, most venues have blanket licenses with performing rights organizations such as ASCAP and BMI, and these licenses may cover the sampled music as well.)

The costs for clearance are negotiable, and there are no standard fees. However, as a general rule the music publisher usually wants an up-front "advance" payment (which, unfortunately, could be anywhere between $5,000 and $10,000) plus a percentage of the song income (anywhere between 15% and 50%). The owner of the master recording will also want an up-front payment (usually at least $1,000) plus a "rollover." A rollover is a payment made when a certain number of copies have been sold. Sometimes, instead of a rollover, the owner of the master may want a portion of future record royalties (although sampling consultants advise against this practice).

Sample rates have become so steep that it's often difficult for small independent labels to acquire clearance. An independent artist with a recording budget of $20,000 may, for example, have to pay $10,000 on up-front payments for two or three samples.

In some ways sample clearance has become easier than it was ten years ago, and in some ways it has become more difficult. Some labels and publishers have begun to make it easier for artists to acquire rights by providing online sample clearance procedures and by permitting the emailing of the proposed use. But a bigger issue—mergers and acquisitions within the music industry—has slowed down the licensing process.

Find the Copyright Owners

The first step in obtaining permission is to locate the copyright owner(s) of both the song and the master recording. The song and the master recording will often be owned by different entities, and you need permission from both of them. Since it's always easier to find the music publisher, you should start there. The best way to locate a publisher is through performance rights organizations (PROs) such as BMI, ASCAP, and SESAC. These groups collect money on behalf of songwriters for radio, TV, and other public performances of songs. (In Canada, the PRO is SOCAN.) You may also be able to obtain similar information from the Harry Fox Agency and Easy Song Licensing.

You can locate the key information on the Internet by visiting the performing rights society websites and determining which organization controls rights for the source song. That will lead you to the music publisher.

Some detective work may be required. BMI's searchable database includes more than 20 entries, for instance, for songs titled "Yesterday." If you can't locate the song you're looking for online, try phoning the PROs and ask for the song indexing department. Once you have the publisher's name and address, phone or write the publisher to determine if they will grant clearance for the source music. Many publishers, unfortunately, have a policy not to grant permission for sampling.

If the publisher can't lead you to the owner of the master recording, you can check online music retailers to find the record company that is currently releasing the source music. Major labels have special departments to handle sample clearance. Locating master owners may prove troublesome—record companies may fold or sell their copyrights to other companies. In addition, rights in masters may revert to the original artists after a number of years. In that case, you may have to use the assistance of a sampling consultant. Here are a few tips if you plan to sample:

- **Use a clearance expert.** For an hourly fee, sampling consultants can guide you through the clearance process (search online for "sample clearance service"). Consultants are familiar with the procedures, costs, and key people who license rights at the major music publishing and record companies.

- **Plan ahead.** "The biggest mistakes [in sampling clearance] are not planning far enough ahead and not having enough alternatives if a sample is rejected," says a representative of EMI Music. "Sometimes it can take months to get all of the approvals." Remember, some copyright owners have a no-sampling policy. If the sample request isn't approved, be prepared to replace the sample with something else.

- **Recreate the sample.** Some artists have avoided paying part of the sampling clearance fee by rerecording the sampled section. How does this work? Let's say you want to use a six-second sample from "Green Onions." Instead of sampling the original recording, you play the parts yourself and rerecord the music to sound exactly like the original. In that case you have not infringed the master recording. (Due to a quirk in copyright law, you can infringe a master recording only if you actually copy it—not if you imitate it.) You will not need to seek permission from the master owner, and need pay no fees. You will, however, still need to seek permission from the music publisher of "Green Onions."

- **Show them the money.** If you're an independent or unsigned artist, you may be able to overcome the "never heard of you" syndrome by offering to make the payment up front. If you show them that you can write the check to pay the advance, they'll be more inclined to deal with clearance.

- **Find sample-friendly copyright owners.** Some copyright owners are willing to clear samples—so much so that they encourage the process. Copyright owners of songs by the Average White Band and the Gap Band have in the past proactively sought to promote their music for sampling.

- **Contact the artist or songwriter directly.** If you run into problems with a music publisher or owner of a master, you may have better luck contacting the artist directly. This works if the artist still has some say or control in what gets cleared. For example, Shirley Manson of Garbage wanted to use the line, "You're the talk of the town," at the end of a song. Lawyers for the band ordered her to drop it, but Shirley called up Chrissie Hynde, who sent the following letter to Garbage's attorneys: "I, Chrissie Hynde, hereby allow the rock band Garbage to sample my songs, my words, and indeed my very ass." (Of course, this works only if the musician or songwriter controls the copyrights—not a third-party music publisher or label.)

- **Try the creative commons license.** A newer, more enlightened method of obtaining sampling clearance is available through the Creative Commons, an organization that proposes an alternative to traditional copyright thinking. Musicians can post their music under a Creative Commons license and permit others to take and transform pieces of the music for sampling purposes (but not for advertising). Check out their website (www.creativecommons.org) for more details.

Operating Without Clearance

If you are using an uncleared sample, you can lower your risks by making it unrecognizable, by not using the sample as the groove or hook, and by burying it in the mix. And of course, don't use the title of the source music in the title of your song. Under the copyright law, you may be in the clear in the following situations:

- **If your use of the sample doesn't infringe or is considered inconsequential.** Unfortunately the current state of sampling law is not so clear that we can chart a noninfringing course for you. As noted earlier, a federal court ruled that the use of any sampled recording—even as little as two seconds—was an infringement. Although many legal experts think the ruling went too far and was improper under copyright law (including the Recording Industry Association of America (RIAA), which stated in legal papers that the decision is "unprecedented and unsustainable"), this ruling is law … at least in Michigan, Tennessee, Ohio, and Kentucky where this court has jurisdiction. (In other states, it's not clear if this "zero-tolerance" policy applies.)

  Certainly if the master recording clearance is not an issue, you may be permitted to use only certain elements of a song without permission. For example, when the Beastie Boys recorded the song "Pass the Mic," they repeated a six-second sample from a song entitled "Choir," from an album by the award-winning flautist James Newton, Jr. The sample consisted of a three-note pattern, C, D-flat, C. Newton simultaneously sang and played these notes, a method known as vocalization. The

Beastie Boys obtained permission to use the sample from ECM, the label that owned the sound recording copyright, but they did not get permission from Newton, the owner of the musical composition copyright. Newton sued and in 2002, a federal judge ruled that the three-note pattern from "Choir" was not, by itself, a protectable composition and that permission from Newton was not necessary. In other words, the three-note pattern, even though it included Newton's rare vocalization skills, was not original enough to merit a payment and it was labeled "de minimis" (too small to matter).

- **If your use of the sample qualifies as a fair use.** Fair use is the right to copy a portion of a copyrighted work without permission because your use is for a limited purpose, such as for educational use in a classroom or to comment upon, criticize, or parody the work being sampled. For example, the Supreme Court determined it was a fair use when rap group 2 Live Crew reproduced the musical tag and the opening lyric line from Roy Orbison's "Oh Pretty Woman." In that case, the Court established that the most important factor (of several factors) when determining fair use is whether the new use transforms the original. Keep in mind that 2 Live Crew used the riff only once and it was for purposes of parody. 2 Live Crew did not include a sample from the Orbison master recording.

Two decades later, the transformative standard arose again when musician Drake sampled a 1982 jazz recording on which Jimmy Smith stated, "Jazz is the only real music that's gonna last/All that other bullshit is here today and gone tomorrow. But jazz was, is and always will be." Drake edited the sample so that on his recording, it states," "Only real music's gonna last. All that other bullshit is here today and gone tomorrow." Drake obtained permission to use the master recording but not the composition. However a court excused his use of the sample on his recording, "Pound Cake." The court concluded that in Smith's recording, his words spoke of the supremacy of jazz; Drake converted their meaning for a broader class of "real music." The court held that the use was transformative and permitted as a fair use.

There's a widespread myth in the sampling community that "less than two seconds is fair use." Don't believe it. What a judge and jury will feel is fair use depends on a number of factors other than the length of the sample. Generally, when reviewing fair use questions, courts are looking for three things:

1. you did not take a substantial amount of the original work
2. you transformed the material in some way, and
3. you did not cause significant financial harm to the copyright owner.

What kind of financial harm might sampling cause? It could cause the loss of income from other artists who might want to use the sample but were discouraged because you sampled it first. Or what you consider a "parody" might be so close to the original that substantial numbers of music lovers buy it *instead* of the original.

In principle, it's good to know these defenses, but the obvious difficulty with all of them is that they are *defenses*. The time you'll use them is when someone is coming after you. There is no predictable way to guarantee that you'll win your court case based on these defenses (assuming you can even afford to hire attorneys to fight the case). Of course, in some cases, this fact can give rise to a form of legal blackmail: The fear of a lawsuit may outweigh any benefits of winning the legal battle, so you may prefer not to use a sample even if the usage would have been ruled permissible.

You'll find yourself on safer legal ground if you seek permission. This is especially true if you're signed to a record label and your record contract puts the burden of sample clearance on your shoulders. Your contract probably contains an indemnity clause, which means that if you and the record company are sued, you must pay the record company's legal costs. Ouch!

Using Samples With Commercial Clients

There's an extra wrinkle if you use a sample for purposes of selling or endorsing a product (for example, in a Volkswagen ad) and the sampled artist is identifiable. In cases like this, your band will need to get the source artist's consent. That's because the ad creates the impression of an endorsement. Without the consent, the source artist could sue for what is known as the violation of the "right of publicity." (The same would be true if you imitated the source artist's voice without sampling it.) So when you use a sample for an advertising agency or other commercial client, be aware that a third type of clearance or "release" may be necessary.

Recording a Nonband Member's Songs

If your band is recording a song that is written by a nonband member (in other words, a cover—such as a new version of Michael Jackson's "Thriller"), the law requires that your band, or the company releasing your record, obtain what's known as a compulsory license. Under copyright law, you do not have to "ask" for a compulsory license to cover a song. Instead, you can obtain one simply by following certain procedures established in the Copyright Act. These procedures are discussed in detail in Chapter 12. If, on the other hand, the song you are covering has never been released (for example, it was written by a friend), there is a different licensing procedure. This is also discussed in Chapter 12.

Precleared samples. What about sample CDs and downloads—recordings that contain sounds and riffs specifically sold to be used in samplers? Most sample collections are "precleared," which means that by buying the sample or collections of samples, you're automatically granted permission for music usage without the payment of any further fees. (Note: The permitted use of precleared samples may vary from one company to another. Don't assume you can use the sample in whatever way you like: Review the documentation that comes with the sample for any license information.)

Most companies that sell sample collections grant the user a "nonexclusive license" to use the samples. A "license" is a grant of permission to do something (for example, use the sample in your composition). "Nonexclusive" means that you're not the only person who can use the samples. Also, you're not buying the right to sell or share the samples by themselves, only the right to use them in musical works.

The fact that the license is nonexclusive can make a difference if you're composing music on behalf of a client—for example, creating music for commercials. The issue is "ownability," says Rick Lyon of New York's Lyon Music, who has scored spots and TV themes for the likes of ABC, MCI, Volvo, and ESPN. "'Ownability' is the holy grail of advertising," says Lyon. "It helps ensure uniqueness in the marketplace. That's why brands work so hard to control the creative elements of their identities. Clients want to be sure that a riff featured in their new campaign isn't going to appear in another spot for someone else. We're talking about the sanctity of brand image, with millions of dollars at stake." Since the composer doesn't own exclusive rights to the precleared sample, he or she will probably be unable to sell the requested rights to the client.

Even with these legal issues aside, the greater concern is whether you're going to aggravate a client. So beware of using a precleared sample as an important element of an ad campaign. Anyone who buys the same sample collection has the potential to dilute your campaign and may raise legal and business risks for you.

Musician Release Agreement

In this section we'll explain how to put together a musician release agreement. A sample appears below. This is a simple release that permits you to use a nonband musician's performance on your recording. Band members would not need to sign this release.

 FORMS
You can download this form (and all other forms in this book) from Nolo.com; for details, see "Get Forms, Updates, and More at This Book's Companion Page," in the appendix.

Below, we explain the provisions in the musician release agreement.

Introduction

In the introductory section, put the name of your band partnership if it owns your recordings. If you created a separate company for the release of your recordings (such as "Our Band's Records"), list that name. If the name doesn't make it clear what kind of business form it is (for example, "The Spyder Partnership"), then indicate the business form (for example, "Centipede, a general partnership"). Insert the name of the musician.

Rights

List the songs on which the musician played on your recording.

Payment

Insert the amount of the payment. If there is no payment, indicate $1.

Credit

Indicate the type of credit the musician will get on the album information. For example, "Saxophone: S. Murphy." If the musician is under an exclusive recording agreement with a record company, you will need to find out if the musician is permitted to perform on other people's recordings. If so, there may be a special credit required, such as "S. Murphy appears courtesy of Pretend Records."

Mediation; Arbitration

Under this clause, if a dispute arises the parties agree to try to resolve it through mediation or, if that fails, binding arbitration, rather than immediately going to court. Enter the location where you agree to mediate and arbitrate (most likely the city where you all live).

In several states, there are organizations that specialize in arbitration for people in the arts, such as California Lawyers for the Arts (www.calawyersforthearts.org) and Volunteer Lawyers for the Arts (in New York at www.vlany.org, as well as in other cities and states). You can substitute the rules for one of these organizations in your agreement for those of the American Arbitration Association. If you band is based in Canada, you can still use the AAA's rules, as they perform arbitration in all major Canadian cities. Check one of the choices or delete the unwanted alternative.

General

Most of the following provisions are standard contractual provisions referred to as boilerplate. In the blank space, insert the state (or province, in the case of Canadian bands) of residence for the band partners. In the event of a dispute, this determines which state law will govern the arbitration or lawsuit.

Musician Release Agreement

This Musician Release Agreement (the "Agreement") is made between _____
_____ ("Band") and
_____ ("Musician").

Rights

The Band has recorded Musician's performance in conjunction with a Band recording
under the titles _____
_____ . In consideration of the payments provided in this Agreement,
Musician assigns all rights in the performance to the Band and its assigns or licensees.

Payment

Band will pay Musician $_____ .

Credit (*Check if applicable and fill in blank*)

☐   Musician is entitled to the following credit: _____
_____ .

Mediation; Arbitration

If a dispute arises under this Agreement, the parties agree first to try to resolve the
dispute with the help of a mutually agreed-on mediator in _____ . Any
costs and fees other than attorney fees will be shared equally by the parties. If it proves
impossible to arrive at a mutually satisfactory solution within a reasonable time, the
parties agree to submit the dispute to binding arbitration in the same city or region,
conducted on a confidential basis pursuant to the Commercial Arbitration Rules of
the American Arbitration Association or the rules of _____ .

General

Nothing contained in this Agreement is deemed to constitute either Band or Musician
a partner or employee of the other party. This Agreement is governed by and
interpreted in accordance with the laws of _____ .

Band Partnership Name _____

Band Partner Name and Title _____

Band Partner Signature _____

Address _____

_____

Date _____

Musician Name _____

Musician Signature _____

Address _____

_____

Date _____

Signatures

Only one member of your band needs to sign the agreement. Enter the band business name, the name of which band member is signing, and the band member's title (usually "Partner"). That band member should sign and date the form. Have the musician enter his or her address, and sign and date the form.

License for Use of Sampled Music From Record Company

As we explained above, the use of a recognizable digital sample can create legal problems for a band and its record company. Although the law is still evolving on this issue, you should presume that when you use a portion of someone's music without authorization, you have violated copyright law and may be subject to a lawsuit. For that reason, many bands and record companies have samples "cleared" by obtaining permission from the owners of the sample. This clearance is usually referred to as a license. The person who owns the rights is the licensor, and the person seeking to use the sample is the licensee.

We've provided two clearance agreements: one to give to the owner of the recorded music (the record company), and the other to give to the owner of the song (the music publisher). Sometimes the record company controls the publishing rights and you can clear everything with only one agreement. Below we provide an explanation of the various provisions of the agreement, titled "Agreement With Record Company for Use of Master Recording Sample." A sample appears below.

 FORMS
You can download this form (and all other forms in this book) from Nolo.com; for details, see "Get Forms, Updates, and More at This Book's Companion Page," in the appendix.

Introduction

This section defines the parties. Insert the name of your band partnership, your record company, or whoever is responsible for paying for the sample usage. In the second blank, insert the name of the record company that owns the sample.

Master Recording and New Recording

These sections establish the parties' respective rights to the original recording and the new recording. Insert the name of the song or track that has been sampled in the first blank. In the next blank, insert the name of the artist who originally performed the version of the song that you want to sample. In the "New Recordings" section, insert the name of your band's song that uses the sample, and in the second blank insert the name of your band.

Approved Usage

This establishes that your band cannot create another version that uses more of the original sample than in the version you first furnished to the owner of the sample.

Grant of Rights

This provision is what allows you to use the sample on recordings and for promotional videos. The statement, "This grant is binding on Licensee's assigns and sublicensees" means that if your band gets a record deal, you can still use the sample, but the record company will be bound to the terms of the license.

Territory

Insert the World, United States, or Canada, or whatever region you have agreed on. It would be best for your band to obtain worldwide rights. However, if the company you are dealing with only has rights in certain countries, then your agreement will be limited to that "territory," and if you intend to sell in other territories you will have to acquire rights there as well.

Agreement With Record Company for Use of Master Recording Sample

Introduction

This Agreement is between _____
("Licensee") and _____
("Licensor").

Master Recording

Licensor owns all rights in a recording entitled _____
(the "Master Recording") as performed by _____ .

New Recording

Licensee intends to use a portion of the Master Recording (the "Sample") in a recorded
composition entitled _____ (the "New Recording"),
as performed by _____ .

Approved Usage

Licensee agrees that the amount of the Sample usage will not exceed that in the copy
of the New Recording furnished to Licensor ("the Approved Usage").

Grant of Rights

Licensor grants to Licensee the nonexclusive right to use, reproduce, and sell the
Sample as included in the New Recording. Licensee may remix, edit, or create new
derivative versions of the New Recording, but in no event will Licensee's usage exceed
the Approved Usage. This grant of rights is for the full length of copyright of the
New Recording. Licensor also grants to Licensee and its assigns the right to include
and exploit the Sample in the Approved Usage for digital Internet usage, video clips,
and audiovisual uses, all solely for advertising and promoting the sale of the New
Recording. This grant is binding on Licensee's assigns and sublicensees. Licensor retains
all rights other than those granted in this Agreement.

Territory

The rights granted in this Agreement are for use in _____
_____ (the "Territory").

Other Uses

In the event that the Licensee intends to use the Sample for any purposes other than those stated in this Agreement, Licensor agrees to negotiate those licenses in good faith.

Payments

Licensee will pay Licensor as follows. Payments based on unit sales shall be due regardless of the configuration of the New Recording or whether released by Licensee or Licensee's affiliates or sublicensees. Any payments provided in this Agreement are contingent on the embodiment of the Original Recording within the New Recording. That is, if the Original Recording is not included, no payment is due to Licensor.

(Choose one and fill in the blank)

☐ **Flat Fee.** Licensee will pay Licensor a flat fee of $_____ on execution of this Agreement as full payment for all rights granted.

☐ **Flat Rate.** Licensee will pay Licensor a flat rate of $_____ per 100,000 units of the New Recording manufactured and distributed. Licensee agrees to pay Licensor a recoupable advance of $_____ for the first 100,000 units on execution of this Agreement.

☐ **Royalties and Advance.** Licensee agrees to pay Licensor a royalty rate of $_____ per each copy of the New Recording manufactured and distributed. Licensee agrees to pay Licensor a recoupable mechanical royalty advance of $_____ on execution of this Agreement.

Licensee will pay Licensor within 30 days after the end of each quarter. Licensee will also furnish an accurate statement of sales of Records during that quarter. Licensor will have the right to inspect Licensee's books on reasonable notice.

Copyright Registration

If the New Recording is registered for a sound recording copyright, the Master Recording will be identified in space six of the Form SR as a preexisting work, and a copy of the application will be sent to Licensor.

Credit

(Check if applicable and fill in blanks)

☐ All releases of the Recording must contain the following statement: "Contains portions of _____ used by permission of _____ . All rights reserved."

Warranties

Licensor warrants that it has the power to enter into and grant the rights in this Agreement.

Commercial Release

Licensee will furnish Licensor with two copies of any compact disc, single, or any other configuration of the New Recording within two weeks of its commercial release.

Mediation; Arbitration

If a dispute arises under this Agreement, the parties agree to first try to resolve the dispute with the help of a mutually agreed-on mediator in _____ _____ . Any costs and fees other than attorney fees will be shared equally by the parties. If it is impossible to arrive at a mutually satisfactory solution within a reasonable time, the parties agree to submit the dispute to binding arbitration in the same city or region, conducted on a confidential basis under:

☐ the Commercial Arbitration Rules of the American Arbitration Association, or

☐ the rules of _____ .

Any decision or award as a result of arbitration will include the assessment of costs, expenses, and reasonable attorneys' fees and a written determination by the arbitrators. Absent an agreement to the contrary, arbitration will be conducted by an arbitrator experienced in music industry law. An award of arbitration is final and binding on the Band Partners and may be confirmed in a court of competent jurisdiction. The prevailing party has the right to collect from the other party its reasonable costs and attorney fees incurred in enforcing this agreement.

General

Nothing contained in this Agreement makes either Licensee or Licensor a partner or employee of the other party. This Agreement expresses the complete understanding of the parties and may not be amended except in a writing signed by both parties. If a court finds any provision of this Agreement invalid or unenforceable, the remainder of this Agreement will be interpreted to carry out the intent of the parties. This Agreement is governed by and interpreted in accordance with the laws of _____ .
Notices required under this Agreement can be sent to Band at the address provided below.

Licensee

Name of Licensee _____

Licensee Representative Signature _____

Licensee Representative Name and Title _____

Address _____

_____

Date _____

Licensor

Name of Licensor _____

Licensor Representative Signature _____

Licensor Representative Name and Title _____

Address _____

_____

Date _____

Payments

In the early days of sampling, many companies obtained worldwide rights for a flat fee. Today, payments for use of rights may range from $500 to $5,000 per 100,000 copies of your recording. These amounts often depend on the amount of the sample and its relative importance in your band's song.

Copyright Registration

This provision is optional, although many sample owners insist on it. It is not a burdensome request. When applying for copyright for your recording, you must indicate that you are using a sample.

Credit

This provision is optional, and not all companies insist on receiving a credit.

Warranties

This is simply a legal promise that the person you are dealing with owns the recording.

Commercial Release

Usually the record company wants a copy of your recording to verify the sample usage.

Mediation; Arbitration

This provision provides a less expensive method of resolving disputes than filing a lawsuit. (See Chapter 2 for an explanation of mediation and arbitration.)

We suggest that you choose the county, province, or city in which the band resides for arbitration. If all the members do not reside in one area, choose a place that is convenient. Enter your location of choice in the blank.

In some states there are organizations that specialize in arbitration for people in the arts, such as California Lawyers for the Arts (www.calawyers forthearts.org) and Volunteer Lawyers for the Arts (in New York at www.vlany.org, as well as in other cities and states). You can substitute the rules of such an organization for those of the American Arbitration Association in your agreement. If your band is based in Canada, you can still use the AAA's rules, as they perform arbitration in all major Canadian cities. Check one of the choices or delete the unwanted alternative.

General

The following provisions are standard contractual provisions referred to as boilerplate. Boilerplate provisions are explained in Chapter 2.

In the blank space, insert the state (or province, in the case of Canadian bands) of residence for the band partners. In the event of a dispute, this determines which state law will govern the arbitration or lawsuit.

Signatures

Only one member of your band needs to sign the agreement. Enter the band business name, the name of the band member who is signing, and the band member's title (usually "Partner"). That band member should sign and date the form. The record company representative should do the same.

License for Use of Sampled Music From Music Publisher

As we explained above, if your band uses a sample, you must obtain the permission of the record company and the music publisher that owns the song. Below is an explanation for the provisions of an agreement with the music publisher. A sample appears below.

FORMS
You can download this form (and all other forms in this book) from Nolo.com; for details, see "Get Forms, Updates, and More at This Book's Companion Page," in the appendix.

Introduction

This section defines the parties. Insert the name of your band partnership, your record company, or whoever is responsible for paying for the sample usage. In the second blank, insert name of the music publisher that owns the sample.

Original Composition and New Composition

These sections establish the parties' respective rights to the original recording and the new recording. Insert the name of the song that has been sampled in the first blank. In the next blank, insert the name of the artist who originally performed the song being sampled. In the "New Composition" section, insert the name of your band's song that uses the sample and, in the second blank, insert the name of your band.

Approved Usage

This establishes that your band cannot create another version that uses more of the original sample than in the version you first furnished to the owner of the sample.

Grant of Rights

This provision is what allows you to use the sample on recordings and for promotional videos. The statement "This grant is binding on Licensee's assigns and sublicensees" means that if your band gets a record deal, you can still use the sample, but the record company will be bound to the terms of the license.

Territory

Insert the territory (for example, "the world"). It would be best for your band to obtain worldwide rights. However, if the publishing company you are dealing with has rights only in certain countries, then your agreement will be limited to that "territory," and if you intend to sell in other territories you will have to acquire publishing rights there, as well.

Mechanical Income

If you are unfamiliar with mechanical royalty payments, review Chapter 8. It is often preferable to acquire all rights for a flat fee, because there are no further payments to make. However, it may be a good thing to base the payments on a royalty, because that way you may have to pay more than the advance only if the song is a hit. Music publishers often seek anywhere from 15% to 50% of the music publishing income. That is, the owner of the sampled song receives 15% to 50% of all the money earned by the song. It is reported, for example, that Sting received at least half the royalties for the use of his sample at the end of the Dire Straits song "Money for Nothing," and the same percentage or more for the Puff Daddy song "I'll Be Missing You."

Performance Income

If you are unfamiliar with performance royalty payments, review Chapter 8. The percentage payments for performance royalties are always the same as for the mechanical income (above). That is, if the owner of the sampled song is getting 33% of the mechanical income, then the owner would get the same percentage of the publishing and writing income from the performance royalties.

> **EXAMPLE:** Happy Publishing owns "You Conquered My World," written by Sasha and Andrea Rose. The publisher has negotiated for 25% of the mechanical income. The publisher has negotiated for the same performance royalty, and each writer would get 12.5% of the writer's share of the performance royalties.

Credit

This provision is optional, and not all companies insist on receiving a credit.

Copyright Registration

This provision is optional, although many sample owners insist on it. It is not a burdensome request. When applying for copyright for your song, you must indicate that you are using a sample.

Warranties

This is simply a legal promise that the person you are dealing with owns the recording.

Commercial Release

Usually the music publisher wants a copy of your recording to verify the sample usage.

Mediation; Arbitration

This provision provides an alternative method of resolving disputes than filing a lawsuit. (See Chapter 2 for an explanation of mediation.)

We suggest that you choose the county, province, or city in which the band resides for arbitration. If all the members do not reside in one area, choose a place that is convenient. Enter your location of choice in the blank.

In some states there are organizations that specialize in arbitration for people in the arts, such as California Lawyers for the Arts (www. calawyersforthearts.org) and Volunteer Lawyers for the Arts (in New York at www.vlany.org, as well as in other cities and states). You can substitute the rules of such an organization for those of the American Arbitration Association in your Agreement. If your band is based in Canada, you can still use the AAA's rules, as they perform arbitration in all major Canadian cities. Check one of the choices, or delete the unwanted alternative.

General

The following provisions are standard contractual provisions referred to as boilerplate. Boilerplate provisions are explained in Chapter 2.

In the blank space, insert the state (or province, in the case of Canadian bands) of residence for the band partners. In the event of a dispute, this determines which state law will govern the arbitration or lawsuit.

Signatures

Only one member of your band needs to sign the agreement. Enter the band business name, the name of the band member who is signing, and the band member's title (usually "Partner"). That band member should sign and date the form. The music publishing company representative should do the same.

Agreement With Music Publisher for Use of Song Sample

Introduction

This Agreement is between _____

("Licensee") and _____

("Licensor").

Original Composition

Licensor is the owner of an original composition _____

_____ (the "Original Composition").

New Composition

Licensee intends to use a portion of the Original Composition in a new composition
entitled _____ (the "New Composition"),
as performed by _____ (the "Artist").
The New Composition will appear on Artist's recording (the "Recording").

Approved Usage

Licensee agrees that the amount of the Original Composition usage will not exceed
that in the copy of the New Composition furnished to Licensor ("Approved Usage").

Grant of Rights

Licensor grants to Licensee the nonexclusive right to use, reproduce, and sell the
Original Composition as included within the New Composition. Licensee may remix,
edit, or create new derivative versions of the New Composition, but Licensee's usage
cannot exceed the Approved Usage. This grant of rights lasts for the full length of
copyright of the New Composition. Licensor also grants to Licensee and its assigns
the right to include and exploit the Original Composition in the Approved Usage
for Internet usage, video clips, and audiovisual uses, all solely for advertising and
promoting the sale of the New Composition. This grant is binding on Licensee's assigns
and sublicensees. Licensor retains all rights other than those granted in this Agreement.

Territory

The rights granted under this Agreement cover _____

_____ (the "Territory").

Other Uses

In the event that the Licensee intends to use portions of the Original Composition for any other purposes (other than those stated in this Agreement), Licensor agrees to negotiate those licenses in good faith.

Mechanical Income

Licensee will pay Licensor as follows. Payments based on unit sales will be due regardless of the configuration of the Recording or whether released by Licensee or Licensee's affiliates or sublicensees. Any payments provided in this Agreement are contingent on the embodiment of the Original Composition within the New Composition. That is, if the Original Composition is not included within the Recording, no payment is due to Licensor. Licensee will pay Licensor as follows:

(Check and fill in blanks)

☐ **Flat Fee.** Licensee will pay Licensor a flat fee of $_____ on execution of this Agreement as full payment for all rights granted.

☐ **Royalties and Advance.** Licensee agrees to pay Licensor a reduced mechanical royalty rate of _____% of the statutory rate. Licensee agrees to pay Licensor a recoupable mechanical royalty advance of $_____ on execution of this Agreement.

Licensee will pay Licensor within 30 days after the end of each quarter. Licensee will also furnish an accurate statement of sales of Records during that quarter. Licensor has the right to inspect Licensee's books on reasonable notice.

Performance Income

(Check and fill in blanks, if applicable)

☐ The Recording must be cleared with the appropriate performance society (that is, BMI, ASCAP, SOCAN, and so on), and the clearances must state that the Recording includes the Original Composition. Licensor will be credited with _____% of the Licensor Income, and the writers of the Original Composition _____

_____

will be credited with a total of _____% of the Writer's Income.

Credit

(Check and fill in blanks, if applicable)

☐ All releases of the Recording will contain the following statement: "Contains
portions of _____
used by permission of _____ .
All rights reserved."

Copyright Registration

In the event that the New Composition is registered for copyright, the Original
Composition must be identified in space six of the Form PA as a preexisting work,
and a copy of the application must be sent to Licensor.

Warranties

Licensor warrants that it has the power to enter into and grant the rights in this
Agreement.

Commercial Release

Licensee will furnish Licensor with two copies of any compact disc, single, or any
other configuration of the Recording within two weeks of its commercial release.

Mediation; Arbitration

If a dispute arises under this Agreement, the parties agree to first try to resolve the
dispute with the help of a mutually agreed-on mediator in _____
_____. Any costs and fees other than attorney
fees will be shared equally by the parties. If it is impossible to arrive at a mutually
satisfactory solution within a reasonable time, the parties agree to submit the
dispute to binding arbitration in the same city or region, conducted on a confidential
basis under:

☐ the Commercial Arbitration Rules of the American Arbitration Association,
or

☐ the rules of _____ .

   Any decision or award as a result of arbitration will include the assessment of
costs, expenses, and reasonable attorneys' fees and a written determination of the
arbitrators. Absent an agreement to the contrary, arbitration will be conducted
by an arbitrator experienced in music industry law. An award of arbitration is final

and binding on the Band Partners and may be confirmed in a court of competent jurisdiction. The prevailing party has the right to collect from the other party its reasonable costs and attorney fees incurred in enforcing this Agreement.

General

Nothing contained in this Agreement makes either Licensee or Licensor a partner, joint venturer, or employee of the other party for any purpose. This Agreement may not be amended except in a writing signed by both parties. No waiver by either party of any right can be construed as a waiver of any other right. If a court finds any provision of this Agreement invalid or unenforceable as applied to any circumstance, the remainder of this Agreement will be interpreted to carry out the intent of the parties. This Agreement is governed by and interpreted under the laws of the State of _____ . This Agreement expresses the complete understanding of the parties and supersedes all prior proposals, agreements, representations, and understandings. Notices required under this Agreement can be sent to the parties at the addresses provided below. In the event of any dispute arising from or related to this Agreement, the prevailing party is entitled to attorneys' fees.

Licensee

Licensee Name _____

Licensee Representative Name and Title _____

Licensee Representative Signature _____

Address _____

_____

Date _____

Licensor

Name of Licensor _____

Licensor Representative Name and Title _____

Licensor Representative Signature _____

Address _____

_____

Date _____

Budgeting for Recording

Bands run into problems in the recording studio because they do not budget realistically. Suddenly the money's run out, and the recording or mixing is incomplete. To avoid this "recording interruptus" syndrome, you need to prepare a budget (see below) and to follow some of the tips provided below.

To avoid financial problems in the studio, your band needs three things: a realistic budget, a person to watch the clock so that the budget is enforced, and techniques to get the most of each dollar spent in the studio.

- **Budget realistically.** If you're making a live recording with little or no overdubs, expect to spend two to three hours for setup and at least an hour per song for recording. Expect to spend at least an hour or more mixing each live song. If you're making a multitracked recording with overdubbing, expect to spend three to five hours per song and the same amount of time for mixing. As a general rule, recording and mixing always take longer than expected. As a buffer, many bands add an hour or two when budgeting. Automated mixing saves time, money, and aggravation. Apply these estimates to your budget.

- **Get a good rate.** Shop around for studios and recording deals. Ask other bands for recommendations. If you're doing multitracking and overdubbing, consider using different studios for different tasks: for example, one for recording and another for mixing. Ask about block rates (a reduced rate when you buy a chunk of hours up front) and after-hours rates. Find out if the studio charges for setup time or charges for the use of pianos or other studio equipment.

- **Be prepared.** Make demos before your recording session and play them for the engineer. Know your tracks! Decide on the system for recording before your first session (for example, start with drums and bass). Try to do all of the recording of one instrument or all of the vocals at one session (it saves setup time). If you're using a click track (a metronome heard in headphones), have the drummer practice with a metronome ahead of time. Bring in printed lyric sheets, and write out each line of the chorus (don't simply state "chorus"). The engineer will use these in conjunction with the track sheets, so the clearer the sheets, the easier the recording and mixing. Pay attention to playback tracking numbers. That way, when you have a question, the engineer can quickly find the trouble spot instead of searching.

Sample Recording Budget

The recording budget will vary from project to project, but the experience of sitting down and estimating the costs is always the same. As realistically as possible, you need to determine how many hours your band will spend recording and mixing, and then you need to estimate all of the related costs (tape, other musician fees, and so on). This process prepares you for working with independent and major label record companies, who always establish financial limits on spending.

Below is a budget for a four-song demo done at a small production studio. In our sample budget, there will be no producer fee (the band is producing the recording with the help of the engineer). In addition, the band is bringing in a saxophone player (Musician #1) to overdub some parts. Below are explanations for each item. We have also included a blank form.

Preproduction/Rehearsal

Some studios have preproduction or rehearsal facilities. This budget includes ten hours of preproduction to prepare drum and sound samples that will be added into the mixes.

Recording

The band plans to spend 2.5 hours recording each song. Most of the recording will be live (that is, the band members will play at the same time). The band expects to overdub the vocals and some instruments.

Mixing

Most songs require as much time to mix as to record, and this band has budgeted accordingly.

Budget for Recording Costs

Hourly Costs	Hours	Rate	Amount
Preproduction/Rehearsal	10	$ 15	$ 150.00
Recording	10	35	350.00
Mixing	10	35	350.00
Engineer	20	10	200.00
Producer			
Musician #1	2	25	50.00
Musician #2			
Equipment/Inst. Rental #1	8	10	80.00
Equipment/Inst. Rental #2			
		Total Hourly Costs:	$ 1,180.00

Tape Costs	Units	Unit Cost	Amount
External Hard Drive	1	110	110.00
Media Mix (Flashdrive)	4	28	112.00
		Total Tape Costs:	$ 222.00

Travel, Lodging, & Food Costs

Gas		$	$
Hotels			
Food	4	20	80.00

Total Travel, Lodging, & Food Costs:	$ 80.00
Subtotal	1,397.00
10% Overrun	139.70
Estimated TOTAL	1,536.70

Engineer

Many studios include the engineer's time within the studio rate. However, this studio bills the engineer separately.

Producer

There is no producer on this recording.

Musician

An outside musician (at $25 an hour) will add saxophone, flute, and clarinet.

Equipment Rental

A Leslie organ was rented for eight hours.

External Hard Drive

Nowadays, recording studios accomplish all of their recording using computer software such as *ProTools* or *Digital Performer*. You may have to provide an external hard drive to store your recording at the studio. Expect to pay $100 to $200 depending on the size of the drive.

Mix Media

Band members will want mixes. The studio may email MP3s, burn tracks to CD-Rs, or provide the mixes on flash drives. The costs for these media range from $15 to $50 for a multigig flashdrive.

Gas

If the drive to the studio is more than an hour, you should consider budgeting gas money.

Hotels

Some budgets include hotel rooms for session musicians or producers.

Food

This budget won't include all of the food for three days of recording, but it does include four take-out meals (sandwiches and soda) at $20 apiece. Most bands don't serve food, but if you can afford it, providing a small spread has a positive effect on the band and engineer.

10% Overrun

No matter how accurately your band estimates its costs, the total often turns out to be higher than expected. The purpose of the "overrun" (usually 10% of the total) is to cover these additional costs.

Estimated Total

This is the final estimate. Now is a good time to also estimate additional costs such as duplication and mechanical royalty payments (see Chapter 12).

FORMS
You can download this form (and all other forms in this book) from Nolo.com; for details, see "Get Forms, Updates, and More at This Book's Companion Page on Nolo.com," in the appendix.

Choosing a Recording Studio

If your band has not had much experience with recording, then you should review some of the following suggestions for choosing a studio and for saving time and money in the session.

Types of Studios

Below are some of the common types of recording studios:

- Project studios that are used primarily for preproduction (preparing drum and sequenced tracks) and for mixing electronic and sampled music. These studios usually do not have a recording room, just a control room. Expect to pay $25 to $100 an hour.
- Midsized studios that are suitable for bands that want more multitracking and overdubbing capability. Expect to pay $25 to $50 an hour.
- 24- to 64-track studios that feature extensive sound processing and editing gear. Expect to pay $75 to $200 an hour.
- "Mobile Direct to two-track" studios that will record your band in performance and simultaneously mix down to a master recording. Expect to pay $25 to $100 an hour.

What's Important When Choosing a Studio?

Here are some tips:

- **The "feel" of the studio.** According to Craig Leon (producer for the Ramones, Blondie, and Front 242), the most important factor is the feel of the studio. "Is the studio too sterile? Too posh? You have to make sure the rooms feel comfortable. This is where you'll be living while you make your music, whether it's for three hours or three months. If you are a loud band, there has to be enough space to carry the power and energy of your performance. If you work with a lot of samplers and sound modules, the control room has to be large enough for your equipment."
- **Choice of engineer.** An engineer manages the technical details of the recording such as mike placement, track sheets, and the mixing board. "A great engineer can get a good sound out of almost any equipment," says Leon. The studio manager can help your band choose an engineer best suited for your style and studio experience.

- **Lounge or kitchen.** A studio with a lounge or kitchen area is a priority, because it can relieve tension and boredom. "It's not important for everyone to be in the control room all the time," says Leon, "and you'd be surprised how fresh something sounds if you step away from it for a few minutes." A kitchen can also save money on food if the band doesn't have to go out for lunch and dinner.

When Band Arguments Disrupt the Recording Session

If band members are arguing, the final recording will often reflect an "uptight" session. To avoid this problem, consider the following suggestions:

- **Avoid disputes while the meter is running.** If the band is having an argument, move to another song and resolve the dispute when you're not on studio time.
- **Fix it: Don't argue about it.** If one band member wants to rerecord something and another doesn't, it's usually faster to fix it than to discuss fixing it.
- **See the big picture, not just individual parts.** According to producer Craig Leon, one of the major sources of arguments is that band members are more concerned with their individual part or performance than with working together as a whole for the entire sound and feel of the record. Somehow, you need to focus the band into the same team mentality that is exhibited on stage.
- **Don't bring friends into the studio.** Besides getting bored quickly, friends distract from the work and often lead to arguments.
- **Don't burn out.** Don't book an eight-hour session unless you're sure your ears can concentrate. If you do have long sessions, make sure you eat a decent meal. Overwork, hunger, and lack of concentration are leading causes of arguments. Book your sessions so that there is ample time in between for the band to listen to rough mixes. Avoid listening to playbacks at high volume; it will tire your ears and reduce concentration.

- **Quality of microphones.** A microphone is to recording like a camera is to filmmaking—the better the quality, the better the result. "Within the budget," says Leon, "the band should go to the studio that has the best mikes available."

- **Familiarity with software applications.** All studios use some combination of software and hard-disk editing. Generally, transferring or converting audio files from the studio to your home recording situation is easy. However, there may be some instances—for example, when plug-ins work only with certain programs—that you may want to match the studio's software with software that your band uses.

- **Outboard gear.** Outboard gear is used to process the recording, adding effects such as reverb, delay, or equalization. It's usually not that important for bands that make live or "organic" recordings. "The important thing, especially on a demo," says Leon, "is to get the feel and sound of the song and the band across. Usually, the more gloss on the recording, the more distracting."

- **Number of tracks.** Don't choose a studio solely based on the number of tracks. If your band is recording live, you can make a great demo using eight tracks. Multitracking and overdubbing can create great demos with 16 tracks.

What About DIY (Do It Yourself) Recording?

The process has become so inexpensive that it's led to the demise of many small studios across the country. A typical setup might include several computers, digital editing software, a digital-to-analog converter, a 16- or 24-track mixer, and microphones. Some DIY bands split the recording and mixing duties between home studio and professional studio, by recording tracks at home and mixing at a studio or vice versa. For more on home recording, check out publications such as *Electronic Musician* or *Mix Magazine*.

The Sound Recording Copyright

In Chapter 7, we discussed filing online or using paper copyright application (known as Form PA) to protect your songs. In this section, we discuss copyright protection for your sound recordings, which is different from your song copyrights. The primary purpose of a sound recording copyright is to protect against bootlegging (the unauthorized copying of your recording) and unauthorized sampling (using a portion of your recording). Generally, only record companies register sound recording copyrights, because they are concerned with bootlegging and sampling. If your band is selling only 1,000 to 2,000 copies, you probably don't need to bother.

Sound recording copyright applications can be made by using the Copyright Office's electronic filing system (eCO), or by using the Form SR. You can download Form SR from the Copyright Office website (www.copyright.gov). In addition to completing the application, you must furnish the Copyright Office with two copies of your recording. The Copyright Office requests the best version available. At the time this edition was printed, the fee to register a Sound Recording copyright is $35 if you file electronically and you're registering one sound recording created by one musician who also owns the copyright (referred to as a Single application). If the recording was created by several musicians (most likely the case with a band recording) then you would file a regular electronic application for $55. All paper application filings are $85.

If your band partnership owns the copyrights to all of the songs (see Chapter 7) and if the band partnership also owns the sound recording, there is a method to register both song copyrights and sound recording copyright at one time. When the form asks for nature of authorship, check music, lyrics, and sound recording/performance. Special instructions for this type of application are also available in Circulars 56 ("Copyright Registration of Sound Recordings") and 56a ("Musical Compositions and Sound Recordings"), which are available from the Copyright Office website. For more information about completing copyright applications, see Chapter 7.

Ownership of a sound recording copyright provides some rights. For information about the ways that sound recording owners earn money, check out Chapter 13. As a general rule, sound recording owners do not receive any income from over-the-air radio play—that is, when the recording is played by an AM or FM station. However, a sound recording owner is entitled to payments from play via digital transmissions from SoundExchange. (See below, "What Is SoundExchange and How Does It Work?")

What Is SoundExchange and How Does It Work?

Copyright law requires that companies that provide music to the public via digital broadcast transmission pay a set royalty to the owner of the recording. SoundExchange (www.soundexchange.com) is the company designated to collect these payments from cable and satellite subscription services (DMX, Music Choice, and Muzak), noninteractive "webcasters" (including stations such as Pandora and Live365, and original programmers and retransmissions of FCC-licensed radio stations by aggregators), and satellite radio services (XM and SIRIUS). SoundExchange then pays the copyright owner of the recording, usually the band or record company. (Note: this is a different royalty than that paid to songwriters for the right to broadcast a song over these stations; that payment is made by ASCAP or BMI as described in Chapter 8.)

Before your band fills out the SoundExchange paperwork, you may want to find out whether SoundExchange has logged any action for your band's recordings. You can check by looking at the list of unregistered artists. To do that click the tab for "artist & copyright owner" and then choose "does soundexchange have royalties for you?" to search for the artists who are currently owed money but who have not yet claimed it. Or you can create a username and password at SoundExchange and use the site to see whether your band has logged any action. If your band does not appear, there is no immediate rush to register (as no money is currently waiting for you).

 CANADIAN RULES

Registration of Musical Contrivances. The principles of U.S. copyright law are very similar to Canadian copyright law. For example, you do not need to register your sound recording to obtain copyright protection in Canada: It is granted on creation of the work. As a general rule, you can apply most of the principles in this chapter to recordings by Canadian citizens. One difference is in the terminology, however. In Canada, sound recordings are referred to as "musical contrivances."

In many ways, the Canadian copyright application process is easier than the U.S. system. For one thing, the Canadian Application for Registration of Copyright is simpler and shorter. It's so simple that you may not even need any instructions. If you do need assistance, you can obtain instructions from the Canadian Copyright Office.

The CIPO website (http://cipo.gc.ca) is also extremely helpful, because you can download circulars about various copyright subjects as well as copyright applications and forms. Circular 2, *Musical Works and Mechanical Contrivances*, is particularly helpful.

Dear Rich: Does a Music Producer Own the Copyright in a Band's Sound Recording?

Help us out here. My band wants to register the copyright in our recording but we're not sure whom to list as owner. Is it the producer, or the band, or do we split it?

There's no definite answer for your band because determining the ownership of a sound recording copyright (as with a songwriting copyright) depends on the contributions made by each person. Usually, yes, a producer is coauthor of the recording because the producer performs a wide range of tasks including performing, arranging, and mixing. (That's why they get paid the not-so-big bucks.) On the other hand, as happened in a case involving the White Stripes, a coproducer who set up mics and chose reverb settings did not have a claim to copyright because his contributions were not considered sufficiently creative. And of course, just because you produced or played on the recording, doesn't mean you own copyright—for example, record companies routinely require producers and musicians to assign all their rights back to the company. This guarantees that the record company can claim sound recording copyright.

Duplication

I n the previous chapter, we provided information about recording your band's music. We're devoting a separate chapter to duplication and manufacturing because this process has its own legal and practical implications. For example, when you make copies of your recording (such as CDs or digital downloads), you must pay a mechanical royalty to the owner of every song on the recording. Obviously, this won't be an issue if your band owns all the rights to the songs. But if you are covering another artist's material, you must obtain a compulsory license and pay the appropriate royalties. This chapter explains how to use a compulsory license and what royalties will be due. It also reviews practical issues in the duplication process, such as how to deal with manufacturing problems and defective products.

Paying for the Right to Duplicate Songs

Under copyright law, when you duplicate recordings (that is, make compact discs, vinyl records, or digital downloads), you are making "copies" of the songs on those recordings. Unless you have permission of the owners of the song and you pay mechanical royalties, your duplication is illegal. (For general information on copyright issues, including compulsory licenses and mechanical royalties, see Chapter 7.)

Compulsory Licenses

By law, a publisher *must* permit you to record any song that has previously been recorded and released to the public. In fact, there is a simple legal procedure for obtaining a license for this purpose—called a compulsory license—that doesn't even involve direct contact with the publisher. In other words, you do not need to ask for permission for a compulsory license. It's quite easy to acquire this mechanical license online using the services of SongFile (www.songfile.com), a division of the Harry Fox agency. Or if you wish to avoid the hefty fees charged by these organizations, you can do it yourself by sending a Notice of Intention to Obtain Compulsory License to the copyright owner (usually the music publisher) at least 30 days prior to distributing the recordings, and then pay mechanical royalties to the publisher. A sample compulsory license notice appears below.

Compulsory licenses apply only to songs that have already been released to the public on a sound recording such as a digital download, a CD, or record. You cannot use a compulsory license if your recording will be the first one to be sold to the public. In other words, if the songwriters never recorded their song, or if it was played on TV or in a movie but never released on a sound recording, you cannot use the compulsory license. Instead you'll have to seek authorization from the song owners. We provide a form for obtaining authorization for a first-time use.

Finally, your band cannot use a compulsory license if you change the basic melody or fundamental character of the song. For example, your singer cannot alter a song's lyrics without permission.

Mechanical Royalties

Mechanical royalties are payments to a song owner for the right to make copies of a song. These payments are made by your record company or, if you have no record company, by your band. The mechanical royalty rate is set by the government (which is why it is also called the "statutory rate"), and it rises every few years. At the time of printing of this book (Fall 2018), the statutory rate is 91 cents per song. So if your band recorded a version of Alanis Morisette's "Ironic" and pressed 1,000 vinyl singles, you would have to pay the owner of the song (the music publisher) $91 for the 1,000 copies. The same rules would apply if your band provided digital downloads of a cover song via iTunes, Rhapsody, or any of the other download services.

Mechanical royalties are due only when songs are reproduced on digital downloads, compact discs, and records (collectively called "phonorecords" or "sound recordings" under copyright law).

Many bands are surprised to learn that most large record companies do not pay the statutory rate of 91 cents per song. These companies negotiate a lower rate—usually three-quarters of the statutory rate—with the music publisher. It is not a violation of the law to negotiate a rate lower than that provided in the Copyright Act. If both parties consent to the lower rate, it is legal and enforceable. If you are recording a cover song, you can attempt to negotiate a lower rate on behalf of your band, although for small pressings many music publishers may not reduce the rate.

Video, Film, and Internet Licenses

Compulsory licenses and mechanical royalty rates apply only when reproducing songs on vinyl records, as permanent digital downloads (PDDs), or compact discs (sound recordings). These rates do not apply if you are streaming music on a website or syncing it to a video. In one case, a court ruled that the compulsory license did not apply for a song used on a sing-along laser disc recording in which lyrics were reproduced on a TV screen. Therefore, if you are reproducing a song for video, Internet, laser disc, movies, or any use that is not purely audio, then you must contact the music publisher or an agent for the publisher, such as Easy Song Licensing or the Harry Fox Agency (www.harryfox.com), and negotiate a separate license for each use. There are no fixed statutory rates for such uses.

How Songs Are Used

Below are some scenarios regarding the use of songs on your recording.

> **CAUTION**
> **Covering someone else's song is not the same thing as sampling.** Although the two situations have some copyright principles in common, there are important legal and practical differences between them. See the previous chapter for information on sampling and how to get permission to use a sample of someone else's recording.

Previously Released Songs

Say, for instance, your band records a version of "Smells Like Teen Spirit" by Nirvana. Since that song has already been released to the public, you can use a compulsory license to include your version of it on your recording. As long as you follow the compulsory license rules—sending a Notice of Intention to Obtain Compulsory License and paying the statutory mechanical royalty rate per copy—the owner of "Smells Like Teen Spirit" must allow you to record and distribute the song via CD, vinyl LP, or digital download. Most song owners are music publishing companies that have bought the rights from the songwriters. You can locate the music publisher by using the Internet and visiting the BMI and ASCAP websites. See Chapter 8 for information about searching for music publishers.

Unreleased Songs Written by Nonband Members

If a friend of the band or some other nonband member has written a song and your band is the first to record it, then you cannot use a compulsory license, because the song has not been previously released. In that case, you must have an authorization from the song owners to record the song for the first time and to duplicate the song. (A sample authorization is provided below.) In addition, your band would be required to pay mechanical royalties.

Sometimes, if you personally know the songwriter, you can ask to forgo the mechanical royalties on the first 1,000 or 2,000 copies. If there is grumbling about this, you can agree to pay the mechanical royalties at a later date, such as after the band has met its breakeven point.

Songs Written by Your Band's Members

If the songs on your recording are all written by band members, you don't need to obtain permission to duplicate them. You do, however, still have to pay mechanical royalties to the owners of the song—either the songwriters or a music publisher. When the owners of the song are band members, some bands request that the songwriters forgo mechanical royalties, at least for the first few thousand copies. Otherwise the band will have to pay the songwriters approximately $91 per song per 1,000 copies—for ten songs, that equals $910. If the songwriters aren't willing to agree to this, the band can agree to pay the mechanical royalties at a later date—for example, if the band acquires a recording or publishing deal.

What If You Don't Play by the Rules?

Many bands don't bother with obtaining compulsory licenses or paying mechanical royalties. They record songs and press them without asking permission or paying the publisher, because they don't believe they will get caught. For small pressings and limited digital downloads, this illegal activity often goes undetected, but if the copyright owner learns of the unauthorized use, the band may be forced to pay past-due mechanical royalties, sometimes plus interest, or the band may be required to stop distributing the recording entirely. If the music publisher brings a lawsuit, there may be additional costs including attorneys' fees.

Notice of Intention to Obtain Compulsory License

If your band is doing covers—songs that have already appeared on records—the Notice of Intention to Obtain Compulsory License should be sent to the copyright owner of the song. A sample appears below. We will walk you through the procedure for completing the notice.

 FORMS
You can download this form (and all other forms in this book) from Nolo.com; for details, see "Get Forms, Updates, and More at This Book's Companion Page," in the appendix.

Introductory Paragraphs

In the first blank of the first paragraph, insert the name of the song owner (usually the music publisher of the song). In the next blank insert the name of the song and, in the final blank, the name or names of the songwriters, for example, "John Lennon and Paul McCartney."

In the second paragraph, you must again insert the name of the song.

Legal Name of Entity Seeking the Compulsory License

Insert the name of the company that owns your recording. If your band or band partnership owns the recording, insert that name.

Fictitious or Assumed Names

If your band is acting as its own label and has made up a name for the company releasing the recording, enter the name of the releasing company. For example, if your band Spyder calls its record company SpyderBite Records, insert "SpyderBite Records" in this space.

Address

Insert your band's mailing address.

Business Form

Check the appropriate choice: sole proprietor, partnership, limited liability company (LLC), or corporation. Your band is probably a partnership. If you're uncertain, review Chapter 2.

Names of Individuals Who Own 25% or More of the Band

If your band (rather than a separate record company) is releasing the record, insert the name of anyone who owns 25% or more of the band, or 25% or more of the shares if your band is a corporation. For example, if your band partnership owns the recording and has four partners who share equally in the band, list the names of the partners. If no one band member owns at least 25% of the band, leave this blank.

Names of Corporate Officers and Directors

If your band is a corporation, list the officers and directors. If your band is not a corporation, leave this blank.

Configuration(s) to Be Made Under the Compulsory License

Check all the configurations (types of technology) of the recording that you expect to release.

Catalog Number

List the catalog number for the recording. (If you don't know the catalog number, see Chapter 10 on album information.)

Label Name

Insert the name of your record label. If your band is putting out the record, the label name is probably the same as the name entered under "Fictitious or Assumed Names," above.

Principal Recording Artists

Insert your band's name.

Anticipated Date of Initial Release

Insert the expected release date.

Final Paragraph

The final paragraph establishes that the statutory rate will be paid for the compulsory license.

Signature

This compulsory license is signed by your band (or your record label, if you have one). It does not need to be signed by the music publisher. That's because you do not need to obtain consent from the music publisher. You only need to notify the publisher and follow the payment rules. Whoever signs the agreement should sign in the space next to the word "By" and, below that, indicate that person's name, title, and company. The company will be either the record company or your band. For example, if Paul Dodd, a member of the band The Margaret Explosion, signs, the space by "Name and Title" would read: "Paul Dodd, a general partner in The Margaret Explosion Partnership." Enter the date the agreement was signed.

Dear Rich: How Do We Account for Compulsory Licenses?

We decided to take the compulsory license route for seven songs on our fourth album. We were comfortable with the idea of paying monthly royalties to seven music publishers, because we only made 150 CDs and we thought the monthly task probably wouldn't last too long. We also thought it would minimize some of our initial costs in making and releasing a new album. However one music publisher sent us a letter stating that since we chose the compulsory license route, we must furnish an annual statement certified by a CPA; otherwise, we "would be in default with respect to the Compulsory License guidelines." I knew that an annual statement needed to be furnished, but I didn't know it had to be certified by a CPA. We phoned and emailed the other six music corporations and asked if they wanted an annual statement certified by a CPA, and all six were very nice and told us they didn't want the CPA certification and that the monthly statements were enough. We started conversations with the CPA who does my business partner's taxes, but he didn't want to take any risk of signing his name on a piece of paper that confirmed the number of CDs we sold in 2011 matched the amount of royalties we paid to Bourne. I spent about ten hours preparing clear instructions and documentation (receipts, evidence, etc.) that prove we only made 150 CDs in 2011, sold 71 in 2011, and have 79 remaining, but the CPA was only willing to sign his name if the language on the annual statement said he can't provide any assurance or guarantee that our payments and inventory are correct. To us, this seemed ridiculous, especially since we agreed to sign a waiver of liability. Do you happen to know of a CPA who speaks our language and who can probably certify our simple annual statement? Sorry about the "ag" (as the young people say). Considering that the total sum at issue appears to be $6.46 (9.1 cents per song per pressing x 71 copies = $6.46), we think there's got to be a simple solution.

What happens if you don't include a CPA statement? Congress (in 17 U.S.C. § 115) empowered the Register of Copyrights to create CPA regulations (found at 37 CFR § 201.19) for compulsory licensing accounting. (And yes, Annual Accountings under compulsory licenses must be accompanied by the CPA's statement.) Section 115 (6) provides:

"If the copyright owner does not receive the monthly payment and the monthly and annual statements of account when due, the owner may give written notice to the licensee that, unless the default is remedied within thirty days from the date of the notice, the compulsory license will be automatically terminated. Such termination renders either the making or the distribution, or both, of all phonorecords for which the royalty has not been paid, actionable as acts of infringement ... "

So, if we assume that failing to include a CPA notice places you in default, you would only be liable for any future sales (after receiving a notice of default). So perhaps an easy solution would be to pay off the remaining 79 CDs ($7.19). Once the publisher cashes that check (and assuming you don't press any more CDs), it appears that the CPA issue would be moot. Alternatively, if you don't want to pay it off and you want to continue pressing and selling the cover song, you could send a letter to the publisher explaining the situation and furnishing all of the documentation asking them to please release you from the onerous CPA requirement.

What's up with your CPA? We can relate to the CYA mentality exhibited by the CPA. Standard accounting practices for small labels are fairly simple and easy to review and confirm. If you used a duplication service that can confirm 150 pressed CDs, and that 79 CDs remain in inventory, it should be relatively easy for the CPA to confirm your accounting and to fulfill the requirements established in the statement, below.

CPA statement that must be included. If you do manage to obtain a CPA's cooperation, the CPA must furnish the following statement:

"We have examined the attached 'Annual Statement of Account Under Compulsory License for Making and Distributing Phonorecords' for the fiscal year ended (date) of (name of the compulsory licensee) applicable to phonorecords embodying (title or titles of nondramatic musical works embodied in phonorecords made under the compulsory license) made under the provisions of section 115 of title 17 of the United States Code, as amended by Pub. L. 94-553, and applicable regulations of the United States Copyright Office. Our examination was made in accordance with generally accepted auditing standards and accordingly, included tests of the accounting records and such other auditing procedures as we considered necessary in the circumstances."

Notice of Intention to Obtain Compulsory License for Making and Distributing Sound Recordings

To _____ ,

the copyright owner of _____ ,

written by _____ .

    Pursuant to the compulsory license provisions of the U.S. Copyright Act (17 U.S.C. § 1115), we apply for a license to make and distribute sound recordings of _____ _____ and provide the following information:

Legal name of entity seeking the compulsory license: _____

Fictitious or assumed names used for making and distributing sound recordings:

_____

Address: _____

_____

Business form (*check one*):   ☐ sole proprietor   ☐ partnership

                                    ☐ corporation   ☐ limited liability company (LLC)

Names of individuals who own a beneficial interest of 25% or more in the entity:

_____

_____

_____

If a corporation, names of the officers and directors:

_____

_____

_____

Configuration(s) to be made under the compulsory license (*check all that apply*):

   ☐ 7- or 12-inch vinyl single   ☐ 12-inch long-playing vinyl record   ☐ compact disc

Catalog number(s): _____

Label name(s): _____

Principal recording artists: _____

_____

Anticipated date of initial release: _____

We agree to pay the copyright owner royalties at the statutory rate provided by the Copyright Act.

By: _____

Name and Title: _____

Date: _____

Mechanical License and Authorization for First-Time Recording of Song

If your band is pressing a song by a nonband member that has never been released to the public, you must obtain a special license from each song owner (usually, but not always, the songwriter) in order to record and release it for the first time. This license is called a "Mechanical License and Authorization for First-Time Recording of Song." Unlike a compulsory license, this must be signed by both the band (or its record label) and the song owners. In other words, permission to do a first-time recording of a song by a nonband songwriter is not automatic; the song owner must agree to the recording. This section provides a sample agreement and explains how to fill it out.

 FORMS
You can download this form (and all other forms in this book) from Nolo.com; for details, see "Get Forms, Updates, and More at This Book's Companion Page," in the appendix.

Introductory Paragraph

In the first blank of the first paragraph, insert the name of the song owner (usually the songwriter, but sometimes the music publisher of the song). In the next blank insert the name of the song, and in the third blank enter the names of the songwriters, for example, "John Lennon and Paul McCartney." In the next blank after the word "authorizes," insert the name of the company that owns your recording. If your band or band partnership owns the recording, insert that name. Finally, in the last blank, again insert the name of the song.

Catalog Number

List the catalog number for the recording. (If you don't know the catalog number, see Chapter 10 on album information.)

Label Name

Insert the name of your record label. If your band is putting out the record, the label name is probably the same as the name entered in the first paragraph after "authorizes."

Principal Recording Artists

Insert your band's name.

Anticipated Date of Initial Release

Insert the expected release date.

Final Paragraph

In the first blank, insert the name of the company that owns your recording. If your band or band partnership owns the recording, insert that name. In the second blank, insert the mechanical royalty rate. Remember that a reduced royalty rate is possible if the songwriter agrees to it. Of course, you should not pay more than the statutory rate, which is 91 cents per song pressed.

Signatures

This agreement should be signed by a representative of your band (or your record label, if you have one) and should be signed by all of the song owners. Everyone who signs should indicate the name, title, and company, for example, "Ricky Gebow, a general partner in the I Love Jenny Partnership." All who sign should also enter a mailing address.

Mechanical License and Authorization for First-Time Recording of Song

_____ ,
the copyright owner of _____ ,
written by _____ ,
authorizes _____
to record and distribute _____ .

Catalog number(s): _____

Label name(s): _____

Principal recording artists: _____

Anticipated date of initial release: _____

_____ agrees
to pay the mechanical royalty rate of $_____ and issue statements and pay royalties
on a quarterly basis. The song owners acknowledge that they are the sole song owners
and that they have the right to authorize this first recording. The song owners do not
require that a notice of intention to obtain a compulsory license be served or filed.
We acknowledge receipt of this agreement and agree to its terms. We have been
advised to seek legal review of this agreement.

Band or Record Company

Name of Company That Owns Recording: _____

Representative Name and Title: _____

Representative Signature: _____

Address: _____

_____

Date: _____

Song Owners

Name of Company That Owns Song: _____

Song Owner Name and Title: _____

_____

Song Owner Signature: _____

Address: _____

_____

Date: _____

Song Owner Name and Title: _____

_____

Song Owner Signature: _____

Address: _____

_____

Date: _____

Song Owner Name and Title: _____

_____

Song Owner Signature: _____

Address: _____

_____

Date: _____

Song Owner Name and Title: _____

_____

Song Owner Signature: _____

Address: _____

_____

Date: _____

CANADIAN RULES

Canadian Mechanical Rights. Although Canada has a system for mechanical licenses, it is not exactly the same as the U.S. system. Canadian musicians deal directly with a collective that administers mechanical rights known as the Canadian Music Reproduction Rights Agency (CMRRA). The CMRRA provides sample Mechanical and Synchronization Licenses, a sample single-song publishing contract, and a sample subpublishing agreement checklist. The French Canadian equivalent is La Société des Droits de Reproduction Mechanique Canada (SDRM), based in Montreal, which administers French music catalogs. For more information on CMRRA, contact www.cmrra.ca and click Mechanical Licensing. The procedure appears to involve the printing out and mailing in of forms. There doesn't seem to be any process like Limelight (in the U.S.) where you can complete the process without paper. In addition, it doesn't appear as if you can obtain a mechanical license for digital downloads in Canada. Apparently that must be negotiated separately.

How Many CD Copies Should Your Band Order?

You don't need a *Billboard* chart to know that CD sales are down … way down. Most stores have stopped carrying them. (Best Buy stopped stocking CDs in 2018.) Older acts and country acts still manage solid CD sales, but any other musical genre, particularly if it appeals to a youthful demographic, is seeing their numbers drop dramatically, replaced by downloads. For that reason we encourage you to be cautious when pressing CDs. Unless you're certain you can sell them at shows or via Amazon or CDBaby.com, you may want to manage a limited CD-R run of 100 to 300 copies.

How to Avoid Getting Screwed During the Duplication Process

What if your compact discs arrive from the manufacturer and they have a defect? In order to deal with this situation, your band must analyze the defects in the recordings and determine who is at fault. In some cases, you may be surprised to find that your band—not the manufacturer—is at fault. (Artwork errors are discussed in Chapter 10.)

The Disc Makers–CDBaby Connection

In 2008, Disc Makers, the leading CD duplicator, acquired CDBaby, the leading online seller of independent music. However, it wasn't until recently that some of the synergy resulting from this acquisition took effect. Most noticeably, if you do regular or short-run CD duplication at Disc Makers, you're now offered the option of seamlessly porting the project to CDBaby. That is, Disc Makers transfers the artwork and even ships the initial batch of five CDs to CDBaby. Once in CDBaby, the project can then be offered online for digital distributors. There's a fee for the service (but it's fairly close to the fee paid if you were to set up at CDBaby on your own). We've tried the system ourselves; in general, it's a major time saver, especially if you running a series of projects.

Generally there are two categories of problems:
- The band failed to review the mastering properly and the music doesn't sound right.
- The manufacturer made an error during duplication.

Situation #1:
The copies don't sound right because the band failed to review the mastering.

If the overall sound of the copies doesn't seem right (for example, band members want more high end), then you're probably dealing with an error that occurred during mastering. During the mastering, the recording is prepared for duplication. Track numbers are digitally inserted, and all of the tracks are made to conform to certain volume and equalization levels. If your band doesn't review the mastering, the resulting copies may not reflect your sound. Some duplicators, such as Disc Makers (www. discmakers.com), offer mastering services for a per-song fee.

How to avoid getting screwed:

The easiest way to avoid mastering errors is for the band to master the recording before shipping it to the manufacturer. Your studio engineer can recommend someone who can master. (It is also possible to perform mastering tasks using home studio software.) If your band does not master the recording, then the manufacturer will handle this task. Be sure it furnishes you with a copy of the master to listen to before duplication, and listen to it carefully.

The mastering process for vinyl recordings is more complex and results in an acetate (a fragile copy made from the master) and a test pressing, which is an initial copy from the press run. The run is halted until you approve. Every vinyl manufacturer will furnish an acetate for approval, but not every company will also furnish a test pressing, because it means holding up the production line. Before ordering, ask the manufacturer whether vinyl test pressings will be furnished.

It's best for your band to listen to each master recording with your recording engineer. If that is not possible, be sure to at least listen to the test on high-quality audio equipment.

Situation #2:
The recordings contain mechanical defects due to a manufacturing error.

An example of a manufacturing error would be a compact disc that won't play. Copies that sound distinctively different from the master also may be the result of a manufacturing error.

How to avoid getting screwed:

A reliable manufacturer will correct this kind of error at no additional charge. Usually, the issue isn't *whether* the manufacturer will correct the defect, but *when*. Your band is in a better position with a large, established manufacturer with direct ties to pressing plants. Otherwise, a "correction pressing" may take a month or two if your manufacturer/broker is waiting for space at a pressing plant.

Before you complain about a defect, review any written contract you have with the manufacturer and determine if there is a method for resolving disputes. You will have to abide by the requirements of the contract. There may be a section such as "arbitration," "dispute resolution," or "error correction" that outlines the procedure for resolving the dispute. For example, if the manufacturer has 30 days to correct an error, then you will have to allow 30 days for correction.

When you contact the manufacturer, detail the problems, indicate the dates of activities (when you ordered, when the copies arrived, and so on), and suggest a course of action. Keep copies of your correspondence. If you return recordings to the manufacturer, do it by a traceable system such as UPS or FedEx. If you paid for the duplication with a credit card, you may be in a better bargaining position. For example, if your dispute is for more than $50 and the manufacturer is within your state (or within 100 miles of your home), your credit card company will not deduct the amount from your account until the dispute is resolved. This is often far easier than dealing with small claims court. Ask your credit card carrier about its dispute resolution rules. ●

Earning Money From Recordings

n this chapter, we discuss three ways that an unsigned band can make money from its recordings: the sale of digital downloads, the streaming of recordings, and the sale of physical products like CDs and vinyl. Your band may be able to accomplish some transactions directly with fans, but to generate the maximum income, you'll need the help of a distribution service, known as a music aggregator. We'll discuss how each of these methods generate revenue, the steps required to make your recordings available to the public, and your choices as to an aggregator.

Other Ways Music Makes Money

There are other ways your band's music can generate revenue, including songwriting (see Chapter 8, Publishing Your Band's Music) and licensing (see Chapter 15, Licensing Your Band's Music for Films, TV, and Advertising).

When We Say "Recordings" ...

The terms "recordings" and "records" are still used within the retail industry as a generic term for prerecorded packaged music. Unless otherwise specified (for example, as vinyl records or MP3s), assume that the terms "records" and "recordings" refers to all forms of prerecorded packaged music offered for sale.

Streaming Revenue

"Streaming" music refers to a method of playing digital tracks without having to download them. Some streaming music services like Spotify and Amazon Unlimited let you choose from a massive cloud-stored jukebox. These services are considered as "on-demand" or "interactive" because the listener chooses what is played. Other services, like Pandora, iHeartRadio, and Live365, are more like traditional radio stations. They're considered noninteractive because the listener can't choose a particular song, album, or the playing order (though they may allow skipping a fixed number of songs).

TIP

To get your music on a streaming service. You need a music aggregator to place your band's music on a streaming service (see discussion of aggregators later in this chapter).

Streaming music, particularly in its interactive format, has rescued the music industry from near-extinction. Just five years after Spotify debuted in the U.S. in 2011 with its massive song catalog, streaming music services became the largest source of income for the music industry, accounting for 51% of music industry revenue. At the same time, streaming eliminated a substantial amount of music piracy because it made the process of downloading and storing music less appealing. It's no wonder that Amazon and Apple (as well as smaller companies such as Napster and Deezer) jumped into the streaming business.

Unfortunately, due to agreements between labels and streaming services, most of the royalty revenue generated by interactive streaming revenue goes directly to the labels while the artist royalties are often infinitesimal. Complaints by musicians seemed to have some effect, because the pool from which musician royalties are paid will increase slightly beginning in 2018. Still, the chances of earning a minimum wage from streaming services is limited to superstars. Below are the estimates of what streaming services paid in 2018 and how many streams (individual plays of a song) were required to earn $100. These figures don't include what streaming services pay to songwriters (see Chapter 8).

Streaming Service	Estimated Payment per Stream*	Number of Plays Needed to Earn $100
Spotify (interactive)	$0.00397	25,188
Apple Music (interactive)	$0.00783	12,771
Google Play (interactive)	$0.00611	16,366
Pandora (noninteractive)	$0.00134	74,626
Amazon Unlimited (interactive)	$0.0074	13,513

*As of 2018, these were estimated rates.

Download Revenue

A digital download refers to the transfer of an audio file into a device such as a cell phone that can "read" and play the audio. Digital downloads, popularized by iTunes (which still accounts for 70% of download revenue) have also been a victim of streaming's success. During the five years that Spotify and other streaming services rose as a dominant revenue source, revenue from digital downloads declined 50%. In 2017 alone, download revenue dropped 24%. As of 2018, downloads accounted for less than 20% of music industry revenue. The declining popularity of downloads is unfortunate for unsigned bands because downloads can be sold directly from a band's website or from a download site such as Bandcamp. In those cases, the band retains most or all of the income. Even at commercial download sites such iTunes, the artist keeps about two-thirds of the revenue. Getting your downloads placed at sites such as iTunes and Amazon requires the assistance of an aggregator, discussed below.

Offering Downloads

To provide downloads (officially known as digital phonorecord delivery, or DPDs) at your site, you'll need to obtain permission from the owner of the song (the music publisher) and the owner of the sound recording (the record company). If you are signed to a record label or are releasing a cover version of a song, you must get permission to permit downloads. (If your band has self-produced the recording and owns the song, there's no problem and no permission needed.)

Before offering a cover song for downloading at your website, you'll need permission from the music publisher, which can be obtained from the Harry Fox Agency or Easy Song Licensing.

Music Aggregators

If you're an unsigned band you can't simply upload your music to iTunes or Spotify or most other digital music platforms. (You may still submit directly to Pandora at submit.pandora.com.) You'll need a middleman. The good news is that's not hard to get placed at these online services using the aggregators listed below.

- **CD Baby.** CD Baby (www.cdbaby.com) caters to the needs of independent or unsigned bands. The company delivers your music to all of the major digital music services, collects revenue, and pays participants after deducting 9% as a fee. There are also one-time processing fees for singles and albums but no recurring fees. CD Baby is owned by Disc Makers, which can coordinate CD (or vinyl) replication, as well as sell and ship the products to customers and retailers. The company will also handle synchronization licensing services (see Chapter 15).

- **TuneCore.** TuneCore (www.tunecore.com) distributes your band's music to all the major and minor digital services. (The site does not sell or distribute physical CDs.) Like CD Baby, there is a per-album and per-single fee. Although TuneCore doesn't take a cut of digital sales, it does require that each album and single be renewed annually. Through its MerchLink program, TuneCore also offers merchandise production services.

Besides these two companies, there is an ever-changing collection of aggregators, including:

- **Ditto Music.** Ditto (www.dittomusic.com) is an easy-to-implement online distributor. Your band pays an annual subscription fee and receives 100% of royalties.

- **MondoTunes.** MondoTunes (www.mondotunes.com) is another online distributor that operates on an annual subscription fee permitting unlimited uploads and paying 100% of royalties.

- **ReverbNation.** ReverbNation (www.reverbnation.com), like Bandcamp, is geared toward bands and promotion. Digital distribution is included in the premium membership, which requires a monthly subscription fee.

- **DistroKid.** DistroKid (www.distrokid.com) also operates on a subscription fee basis. It pays 100% of royalties and offers the ability to route payments for different tracks to different band members.

- **Bandcamp.** Bandcamp (www.bandcamp.com) isn't a true aggregator; it's geared much more to bands and promotion. However, it does offer one of the least expensive, easy-to-use platforms for distributing digital downloads and embedding those downloads at your own site.

> ## What About Crowdfunding?
>
> These days, it's not uncommon for a musician to seek outside funding from crowdfunding sites such as Kickstarter, GoFundMe, Indiegogo, and Rockethub. If you're unaware, crowdfunding is the system used when one raises money from a wide variety of contributors via the Internet. Contributors are usually promised unique goods or services based on the size of their contribution. Crowdfunding has been especially popular among musicians, and many sites have been created that cater specifically to musicians, such as PledgeMusic, ArtisteConnect, and Feed the Muse. Crowdfunding has been used to pay for recordings, touring, videos, and band merchandise. Not all crowdfunding sites operate in the same way. Some are hands-on and will work with you to set a realistic goal. Most sites refund the money to contributors if you don't reach your goal; a few have a more nuanced plan based on levels of contribution. Some, like PledgeMusic, will report your sales to SoundScan. Every site we've checked takes a cut of the crowdfunding revenue—anywhere from 5% to 15%. We suggest researching the music-oriented crowdfunding sites, as they can often assist with manufacturing, merchandise, and publicity. An important thing to keep in mind is that crowdfunding is not a gift—that is, you must declare it as income, as discussed in Chapter 17.

Getting Non-Music Data Online

Ever wonder how iTunes recognizes a CD you insert, or Spotify matches the artist bio with the streaming version of the song? This data is pulled from several online sources, as well as information that you supply to an aggregator. Here are three major sources:

- **Metadata.** When an MP3 is created, the file contains encoded metadata, text, and graphics information that is not visible unless decoded by a software program. This metadata is important because it controls how the artist's name and song title appear and is used when fans search for your music at places like iTunes and GooglePlay. If an aggregator controls the creation of your MP3s, the metadata will be collected from you and inserted. If not, you'll have to do it yourself using a program such as iTunes. There are many fields of metadata, but the key fields are artist name, song name, album title, UPC or barcode (normally supplied by the aggregator), artwork (a square thumbnail image of the album cover), composer, publisher, and the URL for the band website.

- **Gracenote.** Gracenote is the company providing data to CD players and CD-playing programs. If you're an unsigned artist, it's up to you to supply the information to Gracenote. The easiest way to do it is by using iTunes. Insert your CD, but don't import it. Instead, click on the first track name and choose "Get Info." Using iTunes, place a CD in the drive and click "No" when asked to import. Then, click on the track name and select "Get Info." Type in the info for that track and do the same for the rest of the tracks. Then click "Advanced" and "Submit Tracks." In two or three days, the information should appear when you insert the CD.

- **AllMusic Guide.** Information from the AllMusic Guide appears at numerous music sites. Because the site must provide bios for every major label artist and every major label release, don't expect the company to discover your band on their own. You can encourage coverage by submitting materials according to the company's instructions (www.allmusic.com/product-submissions). (You may be surprised to learn that all of AMG's bios are written by a staff of writers employed by TiVo.)

Distributing Physical CDs

First, the bad news: Compact discs, once the music industry's major bread-winner, now accounts for about one-fifth of music industry revenue. The major record chains have folded, and except for some used stores such as Amoeba in California, little remains of the retail brick and mortar world of CD sales. Walmart has cut its floorspace for CDs in half and Best Buy has given up entirely. The idea of consigning CDs or entering into independent distribution deals for CDs—so popular just a decade ago—now almost seems archaic.

But there is some good news. Although marked for extinction, the CD continues to hang in there. Fans of some music—particularly Christian, hard rock, and country—are still happy with the format (or unhappy with the digital alternatives). For some bands, sales of CDs at shows are still worthwhile, because many music fans want to collect an artifact. In addition, many reviewers and writers, including bloggers and podcasters, still request CDs. If the CD does survive for another five to ten years, sales will probably be made exclusively online. The primary online retailers for CDs from unsigned bands are Amazon and CD Baby.

Note: Because CD sales outlets have disappeared, we no longer include examples of the Independent Distributor Agreement or the Consignment Agreement in this book, although you can still get copies of these forms (and all other forms in this book) from Nolo.com; for details, see "Get Forms, Updates, and More at This Book's Companion Page," in the appendix.

Direct Sales

Establishing a band website that sells CDs or digital downloads directly to consumers takes some time and expense, because you need to build a back end for processing credit card or other payments. This back-end creation (which includes a "shopping cart" procedure) has been made much easier in recent years by companies like PayPal (www.paypal.com) that provide simple arrangements to link to your site (particularly if you are handling fewer than 100 transactions a month), but generally it still involves some tech skills. Direct sales may also depend on your website hosting agreement and how your site is constructed. For example, monthly costs for maintaining a site with shopping carts and credit card processing can run from $50 to $200 a month. These fees can seriously cut into your profit margin. Because purchasing CDs and downloads can be tricky, many businesses have sprung up to assist, as we'll describe below.

Now That You're in the Mail Order Business...

Once your band starts selling directly to consumers, you're in the mail order business, so you should be familiar with mail order rules regarding shipping, taxes, and refunds. First, you do not have to provide a shipment date to your website customers. If you do give the consumer a shipping date, you must state it clearly and prominently and have a good reason to believe you can meet that deadline. And if you don't state a shipping date, you still must have a reasonable expectation that you can ship any product you advertise within 30 days of taking the order. If you can't ship within the time promised on your website or within 30 days, you must notify the customer of the delay, provide a revised shipment date, and explain that the order can be canceled for a full and prompt refund.

You always have the right to cancel an order that you can't fill on time. If you decide to cancel, you must promptly notify the customer and refund the payment. Once a sale is complete, you are not required to give refunds. This is based on traditional contract law, which treats a sale as a completed contract. If you do decide to offer refunds, post your rules conspicuously at your site.

State sales taxes apply to online sales if the customer is a resident of the state where your band is based. In other words, you must follow your state's sales tax rules in any transactions with in-state customers.

Independent Record Agreements

Musician Magazine once ran an article entitled "Getting Signed: The Day After." The story featured musicians who had signed recording agreements only to discover that once signed, they were faced with insurmountable problems and no money. "The worst part was definitely after we got signed," said the guitarist from one top-ten band that has since broken up.

A lot has changed in the years since that article appeared. At the time there were six major labels; there are now three. Dozens of indie labels have disappeared (or simply gone digital with their back catalog). And the deals being offered by major or indie labels bear little resemblance to the deal-making in those golden pre-Napster days.

If you are approached by Warners, Universal, or Sony—the three remaining majors—you will need the aid of a seasoned music business attorney to negotiate the onerous one-hundred-page deal. If a smaller indie label makes you an offer, this chapter can help. Note that although we focus on independent record company agreements, many of the contract principles apply to major label agreements as well.

We concentrate on some of the problem issues that arise when entering into a record deal—for example, the infamous "controlled composition" clause and the money-losing principle known as "cross-collateralization." At the end of the chapter we provide some examples of record agreements, and we also walk you through an interpretation of a typical royalty statement.

No Deal May Be Better Than an Awful Deal

According to legend, a record company executive was once negotiating a recording contract with a famous artist. The two men could not agree on the royalty rate—whether to pay the artist 4% to 6%. After an hour of angry arguing the executive shouted, "Okay, I'll put six in the contract, but I'm only going to pay you four." The moral: It doesn't matter what it says in your contract if you can't trust the record company. Review the company as well as the contract. If the owners and executives at the label are untrustworthy or incompetent, then your band will be in for a lot of headaches. It may be better to pass on the deal and wait for something else. Not all recording agreements are worth signing.

Record Agreements: Key Elements

Record companies, like most businesses, are guided by two principles: Reduce the company's risk and maximize the company's profits. These two principles are evident when you examine record agreements. In most deals, the band, not the record company, is actually taking the biggest risk with the smallest potential return. This isn't to say that your band can't earn a profit under a recording agreement. It's just that the record companies often make it as hard as possible to do so.

Record companies commonly enter into two types of "record contracts" with bands: record agreements, where a band agrees to make one or more recordings exclusively for a company; and licensing deals, where a label acquires the rights to release something that a band has already recorded. There are a lot of similarities between the two types of record deals, and samples of both types are at the end of this chapter.

A record agreement commonly has several key elements. These are:
- the length of time for the agreement (called the "term")
- the number of recordings you must deliver
- the amount of advance for each recording
- the amount of royalty paid for each recording
- the deductions from your income
- related rights such as merchandising and videos
- whether all band members are locked into the agreement even if the band breaks up
- the presence or absence of a controlled composition clause, and
- whether the band must sign a copublishing deal.

Options and Term

A record company usually wants to sign a band for as long as possible and to make as many recordings as possible. Assume, for example, that the company wants to sign your band to make six albums. Each album will typically be referred to in the recording agreement as an "option," because it will be at the record company's option whether you will make each recording. If the company wants to drop you after one album, that's it. But if they want to keep you for all six, you're locked into the arrangement. By doing this, the record company lowers its already low risk and increases its chances of profits. Independent record companies usually seek options to make one to three albums; majors typically seek four to seven. A band is screwed if it is forced to stay with a company it hates.

Should Your Band Start a Record Label?

If your band is considering creating its own record label, the first question to ask is "Why?" One reason bands create labels is that they feel it gives some legitimacy to their release, as if to say to the world, "See, somebody has signed us." If that's your prime motivator, don't bother. Your fans won't care and anyone in the music industry will be able to discern that you've just created a fictitious label for your release. However, if you're serious about building a small business around a series of releases (including other artists), then it might make sense to create a label.

The second question to ask is how you will handle the money. Who will pay for the pressings and artwork? How will you finance promotion? Are you borrowing money to start up? Or are you seeking investments? Will you pay for recording costs? Can you afford to keep going when times are tough?

All of these things are worth considering before your band launches its music mini-empire. If you're still eager to move forward, you'll need a name for your label and you'll want to make sure no other music or entertainment services are using a similar name. Next, if you're not familiar with basic business start-up information, you might want to get a primer. That's because you may need to figure out your business form—partnership, LLC, corporation—and file a fictitious business name with your county clerk. You'll need to open a bank account and use an accounting system (see Chapter 16). And you may want to affiliate with an independent music distributor, which may prove challenging unless you have an artist on your label who is already selling well.

Remember, it may be tempting to sign a deal providing for several albums, even if they are only options. However, you must remember that because they are options, the band is not guaranteed anything. In other words, the promise of future recordings is truly an illusion.

Therefore, as a general rule, it benefits your band to keep all time periods as short as possible. We recommend that you limit the agreement to two recordings and learn as much as you can about the record company before signing the agreement. Talk to other bands signed to the record company, search for online information, or review trade publications.

Advances

When your band is signed to a record deal, you receive an advance to pay for the recording. In other words, the company is lending you money to make your recording. The advance is eventually deducted from money that is earned by the band. In other words, if you had a $10,000 advance and earned $10,000 in royalties, your band would not receive any money after the advance. So, is it better for the band to seek a low advance in order to earn royalties sooner? Conventional wisdom says no. The more popular approach is that the band should get as much money as possible in advance because the band may never see any more checks from the company.

Of course, the good news is that the band does not have to pay the advance back if the album doesn't sell. The label can only recoup the advance in the manner described in the agreement, typically from incoming revenue. It's sometimes recouped specifically from the album for which the advance was used, but in most agreements, it may come from any recording made under the agreement. Some labels deduct a recording advance from nonrecording revenue—for example, from merchandise or music publishing revenue. The process of recouping from a source other than the album for which the money was used is sometimes known as cross-collateralization (or cross-recoupment).

If possible, it's in a band's best interest to avoid cross-collateralization—that is, it's always better for an artist to keep each recording discrete and tie the recoupment only to the recording for which the advance was made.

Royalties

When recordings are sold, your band receives a percentage of the sales, known as a royalty. A royalty is based on a rate of payment (a percentage). There are four common royalty rate arrangements:

- a percentage of the suggested retail list price (or SRLP; see "What Is the Suggested Retail List Price?" below)
- a percentage of the wholesale price
- a fixed amount (for example, 20 cents per download), or
- a fixed royalty based on net revenue (all income is pooled and royalty is applied to that sum).

The royalty rate is negotiated and included in the payment portion of your contract. For example, your band may negotiate a royalty rate of 12% of the SRLP. This royalty rate is multiplied against the SRLP, and that determines your actual royalty. For example, say the SRLP for a compact disc is $16 and your royalty rate is 12%. Your royalty would be $1.92 per CD. In other words, your band earns $1.92 every time a CD is sold.

Nowadays, many independents don't bother with the SRLP. They just pay a fixed sum per recording sold, whether digital or physical. For example, the contract may simply provide for a fixed royalty of $1.80 per album, whether downloaded or as a CD or vinyl. Alternatively, all revenue is tossed together as net revenue, and the band receives a percentage of that. Below is an example of how a royalty rate and an advance affect the amount paid to, and owed by to a band.

> **EXAMPLE: The Gordos Earn $800**
>
> The Gordos receive an advance payment of $10,000, and their contract provides for a royalty of 12% of all net revenue. The sale of Gordos recordings (digital and CD) earns $90,000; 12% of $90,000 is $10,800.

What Is the Suggested Retail List Price?

The suggested retail list price (SRLP) is an ancient soon-to-disappear concept. It refers to the record company's suggested price for the recording. It is not related to the actual price paid by the consumer, and it is not tied to the wholesale price paid by distributors. It's a fictitious number dreamed up by the record companies for accounting purposes. The compact disc SRLP hovers at $16. Most consumers don't pay the SRLP; instead they pay the lowest price advertised.

Deductions: Less Is More

Deductions are categories of expenses and payments that the record company can subtract from your income. For example, one band was surprised to find that the beer and chips that a label executive supplied at a recording session were deducted from their record royalties. As a general rule, when it comes to deductions in your recording contract, less is more. That is, the less the record company deducts, the more the band earns.

It may be difficult to avoid deductions. Major labels and some independents are often unwilling to make changes. Fortunately, some indies don't bother with many of these deductions. Below are some of the common ones:

- **Packaging deductions.** Some record companies still deduct 15% to 25% of the suggested retail price for "packaging" costs. In other words, they sometimes take one-quarter of a band's potential royalty base to pay for the artwork and CD packaging costs. If your band has any bargaining power in the record contract dealings, attempt to negotiate it to 15% or lower.

EXAMPLE: **The Grenadiers Lose $3,800 in Packaging Deductions**
The Grenadiers sell 10,000 units at $16. Their contract provides for a 20% packaging deduction. They received a $10,000 advance, and the Grenadiers royalty rate is 12%.

Compact disc (suggested price)	$	16.00
Minus packaging costs (20%)	–	3.20
Retail net of packaging costs		12.80
Royalty rate	x	12%
Royalty per unit	$	1.54
Units sold		10,000
Royalty per unit	x	1.54
Total royalty earned		$ 15,400
Minus advance		– $ 10,000
TOTAL		$ 5,400

If there were no packaging deduction, the Grenadiers would have earned $9,200. Therefore, the packaging deduction cost the band $3,800.

- **90% of net sales.** Fortunately, most independents don't bother with this concept. If it is in your agreement and you have some bargaining power, negotiate to strike it. Under this so-called "Rule 90," a record company pays royalties on only 90% of the units sold because the remaining 10% is supposed to cover "breakage" (a remnant of the 1940s, when shellac recordings often cracked).

- **Returns and reserves.** Hopefully, this provision is not in your agreement. It's a remnant of the old days. Under the "reserves" principle if a store returns your records, the record company deducts the returns from your next invoice. Obviously, there are no returns with digital downloads, and most record stores have disappeared. With the expected disappearance of the CD, this clause should also soon be MIA.

- **Real free goods and promos.** It is acceptable for a record company to exclude promotional copies from your total units sold. "Promos" are free copies distributed to radio stations and reviewers. "Real free goods" is a term used to describe copies that are "given" to distributors and stores as promotion. (This is a concept that is usually seen in major label agreements, but it can also be found in some indie deals.)

- **Manufacturing, shipping, promotional, and marketing costs.** Some record companies deduct manufacturing, artwork design, shipping, independent promotion, or marketing costs from money that is earned by the band. If a record company is deducting items such as manufacturing costs from your royalties, you may want to think twice about entering into the recording agreement. Why? *The record company is charging you for the cost of manufacturing the recordings!* It's bad enough you were charged for recording it; you should not have to pay for the company's overhead expenses.

Merchandising and Video Rights

Perhaps you're hoping that your band can make a video. Often, videos cost as much (or more) than the making of an entire album. This cost is usually shared by the band and the label. For instance, If a video costs $100,000, your band is supposed to pay $50,000. Of course, your band doesn't have $50,000, so the record company lends you the money as part of your advance. Since videos rarely earn money (they're almost solely used for promotional purposes), that means you have to pay back the advance from record sales. In the event that the video is sold directly to consumers, your band will probably receive a reduced royalty (that is, a royalty lower than your record royalty) for video sales.

Many labels also seek a percentage of merchandise sales. Merchandise sales refers to sales of band T-shirts and paraphernalia. Usually this is a new band's only source of income, because they're so heavily in debt to the record company already. If you give up part of your merchandise sales to the label, then you further reduce the chances of your band having enough money to stay on the road and promote the record. If your band has the bargaining power, we recommend holding on to your merchandising rights.

Leaving Members

A "leaving member" provision often requires that if a band member leaves, the record company can pick up the member for future recording under the same terms as the original deal. This rule can apply if the band breaks up as well. The label can choose who it will keep under contract. Worse, the members that must stay with the record company are sometimes saddled with the debts of the group. In other words, if the band breaks up and the label requires that you, the lead singer, must keep recording for them, it's possible that your solo career income will be held by the label until all of your band debts are paid off. Ouch!

Controlled Composition

A controlled composition is any song written by your band or any song in which your band has an ownership interest (for example, your band cowrote it with an outside songwriter). As we explained in Chapter 8, the record company must pay a special songwriting royalty known as mechanical royalty each time a song is duplicated (or pressed) on a recording. This is a separate payment from your record royalties. The "controlled composition clause" limits how much mechanical royalties the record company will pay for your songs.

Most record companies pay 75% of the statutory mechanical royalty rate (sometimes referred to as the three-quarter rate) for controlled compositions. In addition, it is not uncommon for a record company to limit the total payment to ten songs. In other words, the record company will pay only ten times 75% of the statutory rate per album (approximately 50 cents per album). Even if you include 12 songs, the record company will pay you for only ten. Many record companies set this limit for *all* songs on your album, even if they are not all controlled compositions (that is, some were written by nonband members). Bands are screwed, because they do not receive a full mechanical rate and do not get paid for more than ten songs. In some cases, the band may record a song written by another songwriter. If the band cannot obtain a 75% rate from the other songwriter, the difference (the remaining 25%) is deducted from the band's mechanical royalty income.

If you can negotiate at all, try either of the following:

- If there is a limit to the number of original songs you can include on your recording, attempt to increase the number of songs (to 11 or 12). This is especially important for compact discs, which often feature bonus tracks.

- Attempt to strike any deductions for noncontrolled compositions (written by nonband members). If you don't, your band will have to pay the difference. How does this work? Let's say you agreed that the label will have to pay only a 6.8 cent mechanical royalty (instead of 9.1 cents) for every song. Your band has recorded a song by a nonband songwriter who demands the full 9.1-cent rate from the label. Since you agreed on 6.8 cents, your band must pay the difference of 2.3 cents per record. These pennies can add up quickly as your band sells records.

What About Creative Control?

Some bands want a provision in their recording agreements allowing them creative control over the album's content and its artwork. Rarely does a record company permit this provision. Usually, record companies want to have control over the albums and artwork for consistency and marketing purposes. The clause is not of much value anyway, because the only way to enforce it is to sue the record company. Such lawsuits are expensive to initiate and difficult to win. If you are concerned about creative control, talk to other bands signed by the record company and find out how the company treats them. In addition, take the initiative to control as much as you can. For example, oversee any mastering and furnish camera-ready artwork if possible.

Copublishing

A copublishing provision requires that the band enter into a separate agreement with the label's publishing company; as result, the label's publishing company will then keep 15% to 25% of the songwriting income. That is, it's not enough that the label has sunk its fangs into your recordings and merchandise. Now they want income from your songs. For example, if you copublish with your label, and a famous singer such as Taylor Swift covers your song, you and the label will share the income from the cover. Some record companies may seek copublishing deals. Depending on the copublishing agreement, the band may find itself losing control of songs to an ineffective copublisher.

If you have the bargaining power, avoid copublishing with an independent label. If you cannot strike the copublishing deal, consider the following suggestions:

- Limit the arrangement to the songs *released* by the record company. That is, if the record company hasn't released the song, it cannot claim copublishing rights.
- Limit the copublisher's song royalties to your band's versions of the songs—not someone else's cover of the song.
- Get an advance for publishing.
- Avoid reducing the mechanical royalty rate for controlled compositions.
- Don't allow the record company to establish a long-term publishing deal separate from the recording deal. The two must be tied together.
- Don't allow the record company to cross-collateralize publishing and record royalties. (Cross-collateralization is covered below.)

Reversionary Rights: Reclaiming Rights to Recordings

Some record companies want ownership rights forever ("in perpetuity"); other companies return the rights ("reversion") after a period of years (usually five to ten).

Always attempt to get a reversion of rights. Insist on it if the record company has not paid you any advances and you have self-financed your recording. If you have the bargaining power, make the reversion period as short as possible—five years is reasonable. Bands have benefited by their ability to later license the selections for compilations or reissues.

Perpetuity and Beyond

If the record company wants to own *all* rights in your work forever (or in perpetuity), that's referred to as an assignment. We recommend against making an assignment of your recording unless you believe in the record company, and the terms of the agreement, such as royalties and advances, are very good. (Compare the terms to the suggested royalties in the sample agreement in this chapter.) Although it's possible under copyright law to reclaim rights in an assignment after 35 years, you should view an assignment as if you are saying goodbye to the recording forever.

A Record Company Can Turn a Profit on a Recording Even Though the Band Is Still Owed Money

When negotiating a record company agreement, there are two points of profitability: the point when the record company profits, and the point when the band profits (or recoups). The record company generally earns a profit much earlier than the band. For example, if a record company advanced your band $5,000 to make a recording that subsequently sold 3,000 copies, chances are good that the record company has turned a profit of $3,000 or more. However, even with a 12% royalty, your band is still probably in debt. This explains how many record companies can afford to release recordings by bands that do not recoup their advances.

Cross-Collateralization

Cross-collateralization is a process by which a record company uses band income from one source to pay off a band debt from another source. For example, let's say the record company controls the band's merchandising. The record company may withhold the merchandise royalties until the record royalties are paid off.

EXAMPLE: Snappy's first album is in the red for $5,000. (The album cost $10,000 to make and earned only $5,000 in royalties.) Snappy has assigned some merchandising rights to its record company, and, under that arrangement, Snappy has earned $15,000 in merchandise royalties. The record company will cross-collateralize the debt for the first album with the income from the merchandise. As a result, Snappy will not receive all of its merchandising income and will get a payment of only $10,000.

360 Deals?

Beginning in 2002, major labels tried out a new type of all-encompassing record deal: a contract in which the label agreed to make firm marketing commitments in return for a percentage of some combination of the artist's income, including endorsements, acting, book sales, publishing, merchandise, ringtones, and touring. In these "360 deals," (or "multiple rights" deals), the record label functions like a manager, albeit a manager with a big bankroll, cross-collateralizing all these sources of income and generally taking a cut before any deductions. In some 360 deals, the artists may even retain all rights and—in a reversal of the typical deal—pay the label its share, instead of vice-versa. The elements that are most often in play during 360 deal negotiations are publishing, merchandise, and touring income.

A 360 arrangement works fine when it propels the artist into branded superstardom, as it did in the case of Lady Gaga. But for every Gaga there are dozens of artists whose 360 deals ended in a sea of red ink. 360 arrangements appear to be confined to major labels with financial clout. But in coming years, it is likely that independents—particularly those in the rap/hip-hop genre—will seek similar deals. Such arrangements involve risks because the odds are stacked heavily against the artist. Consider merchandise revenue while on tour, an important source of artist income. With a 360 deal, 60%–70% of merchandise income goes to the label, the venue, and the manager.

Although it will rarely be in an artist's best interest to sign away so much to a record label, many new artists, intent on doing whatever it takes to make it, will probably continue to accept these 360 deals.

It is standard for record companies to cross-collateralize debts and income from subsequent albums. However, some record companies cross-collateralize merchandise and mechanical royalty income against record royalties. That is, the record company does not have to pay mechanical royalties or merchandise income until all album debts are recouped. This is particularly unfair when the album may have already achieved profitability for the record company. Your band should make it a priority to attempt to negotiate out any attempts at cross-collateralization for songwriting payments (mechanical royalties) or merchandising. Why? Because otherwise, your band will receive little or no songwriting or T-shirt income—money that many bands rely on for living expenses.

Independent Record and License Agreements

This section deals with recording and license agreements: how to analyze them and how to modify them. If you have turned directly to this section without reviewing any other material in this book, you may have some difficulty deciphering the contracts. In order to evaluate an agreement, you will need some familiarity with the principles discussed in this book, particularly the information earlier in this chapter and the information regarding publishing in Chapter 8. We suggest you review that before you begin.

It's very unlikely that your band will draft or furnish the recording or licensing agreement. Instead, you will be handed an agreement and asked to sign it. That's because every record company uses its own agreement, usually prepared by the company's lawyer. The sample agreements below are provided to give you an idea of what to expect in recording agreements and to give you a chance to learn what typical provisions mean. You can use the samples below to compare to any agreements you're given by your record company.

In order to analyze an agreement, we suggest the following strategies:

- *Don't freak out!* Be prepared to spend several hours making your analysis.
- Make a photocopy of the agreement.
- Locate the major provisions (as discussed below) and label them in the margin.

- Compare each provision with the language in the sample agreements in this chapter.
- Underline everything you don't like or don't understand.
- List the number of the provision and write down your concerns about that section.
- Review the list with your band and decide which changes are the most important. List your changes in order of importance.
- Don't expect that the company will agree to every change you request. Most of your changes will not be granted. Instead, focus on those changes that are most important to your band.

Below, we explain the typical provisions of recording and license agreements. The explanation for each provision applies whether the provision appears in a recording agreement or a licensing agreement. We explain each provision only once, because the provisions are essentially the same between the two agreements. But keep in mind that the two agreements are not the same. Recording agreements are used when a record company wants to buy the rights to a new recording of your band. License agreements, on the other hand, are used when a record company wants to acquire rights to an album your band has already cut. For example, say you recorded 12 songs, and an indie label heard them and wants to release them as an album. A license agreement would be used for this purpose, not a recording agreement.

Ready to begin? You'll need a clean (unmarked) photocopy of the agreement, and a pen and a ruler for underlining. Read the explanations for the provisions, and then review the provisions in the agreement furnished by your record company. Unfortunately, there are no rules for the ordering and placement of provisions in recording and license agreements. Many agreements seem haphazardly organized. We've included keywords to help you identify specific provisions in your agreement.

Do You Need an Attorney?

Can your band negotiate the agreement without an attorney? If it is an independent label agreement, you can probably do it yourself. If it's a major label agreement, you'll need an attorney's or manager's assistance. See Chapters 3 and 4 on managers and attorneys.

FORMS

You can download the following agreements (and all other forms in this book) from Nolo.com; for details, see "Get Forms, Updates, and More at This Book's Companion Page," in the appendix.

Introduction

Keywords: Whereas, Introduction

The introduction usually takes up the first few paragraphs of the agreement and often includes the term "Whereas" (as in, "Whereas the parties agree to enter into a recording agreement"). The introduction generally sets out the names of the record company, the band, and the band's individual members. Note that the phrase "collectively and individually" means that each individual member is individually liable under the agreement.

Exclusive Recording Services

Keyword: Exclusive

An exclusive recording services clause establishes that the recording agreement is exclusive and that you can record only for the record company, not for another company. Sometimes this exclusivity requirement is placed in another section of the agreement, such as in the Grant of Rights section, below.

Master Recordings

Keywords: Masters, Recordings, Commercially Satisfactory, Technically Satisfactory

This section defines "Master Recordings" and the standards under which the label must accept the recordings. One standard used is "technically satisfactory," which means that the recording must be accepted as long as it is professionally made and meets traditional recording standards. Some record companies prefer a different standard called "commercially satisfactory." In that case, the company won't release the recording unless the company thinks it is marketable. Labels generally want studio albums, not live albums, and, in that case, the label may insert a statement to that effect. Sometimes the "master recordings" definition is included in a special section titled "Definitions."

Term

Keywords: Term, Length

After you submit a master recording to the record company, you may still be prohibited from recording for any other company. Most recording agreements require that a band grant what are known as "options" to the record company, which allow the company to take some time to decide whether it wants another recording from you. The maximum number of records your band will have to cut (besides the first one) is known as the number of options you grant the company. After you submit a recording, the company will decide whether or not to exercise its option to have you cut another record. While you wait for the company's decision, you are not allowed to record for anyone else, since you're still under the exclusive recording contract. If the label does not exercise its option to make another recording during this period, then your agreement is over and you may record for another company.

This period of time, after you submit your first master recording, during which the label can decide whether to keep you or drop you, is called the term. We recommend a nine-month term. The term will be extended by a specified period if the label exercises an option, called the option term. For option terms, we also recommend nine months. As for the number of options, try to keep them down to one or two if possible, though some labels may insist on more.

In some agreements, this provision is buried at the end near the termination section.

This provision *does not* affect how long the record company can sell the recordings. That is controlled by the section entitled "Ownership of Recordings."

Grant of Rights

Keywords: Rights, Copyright, Ownership

This provision lists the rights that the label is acquiring from your band. In our sample agreement, the first part of the provision determines how long the label owns your band's recording, or what we refer to as the Ownership Period. You have two choices: a fixed period of years, or "in perpetuity" (forever).

What If the Record Company Doesn't Release Your Band's Album?

Most record companies will agree to release a recording within six months of receipt of the masters. When an album isn't released, the band loses momentum and money. There are usually two reasons why a record company won't release a recording: financial problems or marketing problems. For example, the record company might have run out of cash and can't afford to release your album for 12 months, or it may refuse to release your recording because it contains obscene language or uncleared samples.

Here are some suggestions for avoiding these problems:

- **Delays caused by record company problems.** Your band should try for a "guaranteed release" provision requiring the record company to release your album within a period of three to six months of receipt of the master recording. If the label does not meet this deadline, your band can furnish a notice to the record company that they have an additional 30 days to release the album, after which time the agreement is terminated and you can sign with a different record company. If your band paid for the recording, then all rights should revert to your band so you can release the album elsewhere. If the record company paid for the recording, you are usually permitted to buy back the recording at the record company's cost.

- **Delays caused by content of your album.** Every record agreement requires that your band deliver an album that is lawsuit-free. Your band's recording cannot infringe rights or defame someone. Otherwise, the record company has a right to withhold release. Your band can either remove the offensive material or, in the case of samples or other copyrights, seek permission to use it. Your band may have to pay for sample clearances. (For more information on sampling, see Chapter 11.)

Some record agreements contain a requirement that the recording be "commercially satisfactory." Commercially satisfactory means that the record company concludes that your recording is marketable. Most independents don't require "commercially satisfactory" recordings. If that provision is included, attempt to change it to "technically satisfactory," which means only that the recording is professionally made.

We recommend a fixed period of years (commonly between three and ten). The shorter the better, because your band will reacquire rights sooner. *We recommend against granting rights in perpetuity,* especially if you have self-financed your recording (paid for it yourselves without an advance).

If you give up rights in perpetuity, then you will not be able to release the recording with another company later. *The company will always own the rights, or at least own them for 35 years!*

Right to Use Artist's Name and Likeness

Keywords: Artist's Name, Likeness, Image

Under this provision, the company acquires the right to use your band's name and image as necessary to set up promotional photo shoots and interviews. This is common, and every label must acquire these rights.

Side-Artist Recording

Keywords: Side-Artist, Outside Recording

Since you have signed an exclusive recording agreement, then technically you cannot record in any capacity for any other record company or even a friend's recording. This provision gets around this by allowing individual band members to perform on other recordings. If the company requires you to obtain permission before doing a side recording, you would use a provision similar to the first choice in the sample agreement.

Professional Name

Keywords: Professional Name, Band Name, Service Mark, Trademark

Unless the band breaks up or members leave (as described in the section entitled "Leaving Members"), the company wants you to perform under your band name.

Trademark Search

Keywords: Search, Trademark, Service Mark

This section, often omitted from independent deals, protects the label against claims of trademark infringement if another band has a similar name. See Chapter 9 for information on band names.

Production of Master Recordings

Keywords: Recording, Advance

Under this provision, you are responsible for the cost of recording the record. Generally, this is okay, because the label is lending you money (the advance), and your band is responsible for using that to pay recording costs. In some deals, the label may pay the recording costs directly to the recording studio. Even if the label directly pays for the recording, the amount is still deducted against your band's future royalties. Often this provision is included within the Payment provision.

Subsequent Recording of Compositions

Keywords: Subsequent, Compositions, Songs

This is the period of time during which your band is restricted from recording any of the band songs released by the label. We recommend two to three years, although most labels insist on five years.

Advances and Recoupable Costs

Keywords: Advances, Recoupable

This provision is usually part of the "Payment" section of the agreement. It provides the amount of your advance and establishes when you receive it. Independent record companies usually pay advances of $3,000 to $10,000. Some labels do not pay any advances. Some recording contracts are actually just glorified license agreements. The band pays for the recording out of its own pocket, and the label releases the recording. The advantage is that there is no advance to deduct against future royalties. The obvious disadvantage is that your band has to finance the recording. If you self-finance your recording, you will not need this provision. However, if you are self-financing and don't receive an advance payment, you should be sure to avoid giving up rights in perpetuity (see Grant of Rights section, above).

If you are getting an advance, we recommend getting it when you sign the contract (insert the words "execution of this agreement" where it asks for the date). Some labels pay an advance on delivery of the album. In that case, insert the words "delivery of the Master Recording."

Advance for Option Term

Keywords: Advances, Recoupable

This optional provision is the advance for the subsequent recordings. You should use this if you have included option periods. That is, if the label can require additional recordings, you should establish the amount of each advance for those future recordings. (See the Term section of your agreement.) Generally, the advances increase for each subsequent album.

Royalties

Keywords: Royalties, Percentage, Wholesale, SRLP

The royalty section describes how much your band is paid, and it usually permits the company to make certain deductions. The provision in the sample agreement uses the most common royalty system: The band earns a percentage of the suggested retail list price (SRLP). Independent labels usually pay 9% to 13%; majors pay 10% to 15%. Instead of using an SRLP, some independents pay 20% to 30% of the wholesale price, or they pay the band 25% to 50% of the net revenues or total sales income. A deal may also include sliding (or "escalating") royalties. That is, your royalty rate increases as you sell more albums (9% to 13% for independents, 10% to 20% for majors). If the label is still using an SRLP system for paying for CDs, we recommend a royalty of 12% or more of SRLP. If the label is paying a royalty on wholesale (what the label actually receives), we recommend a royalty of 25% or more.

The most common deduction is packaging costs. We recommend that you fight for the minimum possible packaging cost—15% or lower.

Downloads; Electronic Transmissions

Keywords: Downloads, Electronic, New Media, MP3

When a label receives income from streaming services or downloads, we recommend splitting all revenues equally. That is, your band gets 50% (or more if you can negotiate it) of all income from these digital payments.

Foreign Licenses

Keywords: License, Sublicense, Foreign

Usually, the label sublicenses the rights to a foreign label and pays the band a percentage (we recommend 50%).

Reserves

Keyword: Reserves

Under this optional provision, the record company, anticipating returns, holds a percentage of your payment (usually 25% to 35% of the money you are supposed to receive) until the company is convinced there are no returns from stores. The percentage that is not paid to your band is called a "reserve." Attempt to cap the reserves at 25% or less. Some labels hold the reserves for years. We recommend that you ask the label to hold the reserve for two accounting periods or less.

Compilations

Keywords: Compilation, Numerator, Denominator

This is a standard system for dividing up the royalties in case a track from your recording is used on a company compilation. Sometimes, the agreement refers to this calculation as a fraction and uses the terms "numerator" and "denominator."

Flat Fee

Keywords: License, Flat Fee

If part or all of your recording is licensed (that is, rented by your record company to some other company), your band is paid a percentage of a flat fee license; 50% is common. An example of this would be if a cosmetic company wanted to include your song in a radio commercial. (Note: The cosmetic company would also need to obtain permission from your song publisher, as well.)

Nickels for Downloads?

Beware of record company deals in which the label attempts to apply the 9% to 13% CD royalty rate when paying your band for download and streaming income. Under these arrangements, the label often reduces the royalty (sometimes by one-half) and applies packaging deductions (usually 15%) even though there is no packaging for MP3s. Under that arrangement, if the label received $1 per downloaded song, and the artist's royalty was 6%, the artist would receive approximately six cents per download. Under the arrangement provided for in our agreement, the band gets half the income from the download or streaming source.

Promotional Recordings and Cutouts

Keywords: Promotional, Free, Cutouts

Record companies do not pay royalties on copies of the recordings that are distributed for free or for promotional purposes or that are scrapped (that is, where the record is thrown out).

Statements; Audit

Keywords: Audit, Statement

This provision details the company's obligations to pay you; it also explains your rights in the event of an audit. These sections often differ drastically from agreement to agreement. Generally, you want to get paid as soon as possible. We recommend that the company pay within 30 days at the end of the accounting period, although many labels prefer 90 days. Although we endorse the terms of our audit provision, as a general rule, if you have a right to audit, don't get hung up on negotiating the related details such as how often or the amount of the underpayment.

Video

Keywords: Video, Audiovisual, Synchronization

This optional provision permits the company to create a video to promote your recording. If you have a record contract in which the company owns the recordings for a limited number of years (not forever), then this section should have the same length of time as in the "Grant of Rights" section. If the grant is forever (in perpetuity), then insert "in perpetuity." We recommend a video royalty of 50% or more.

Commercial Release of Records

Keywords: Release, Guaranteed Release Date

A guaranteed release date protects your band. We recommend six months from the date you submit the master recording. The first provision in our sample agreement allows the band to acquire rights to the recording if the album is not released in a timely manner. Many labels will want to have any advances returned before allowing the band to reacquire ownership. If that's what you agree on with the record company, you would use something similar to the second choice in the sample agreement.

Artist Promotional Records

Keywords: Promos, Free Copies

Labels commonly provide at least five promotional copies per band member. Make sure this provision is in your agreement; otherwise, you will have to pay for copies of your own recording.

Album Artwork

Keywords: Artwork, Specifications

This provision in the model agreement establishes the band's right to prepare its own artwork at its own expense. You may be able to obtain an artwork advance from an independent label (usually between $300 and $500). Not all agreements will include such a provision.

Artist Warranties

Keywords: Indemnification, Warrant, Covenant, Represent

Warranties are contractual promises. If your band breaks one of these promises, the label can seek money damages from your band. If your agreement contains warranties, compare them to the ones in the model agreement. To protect yourself with regard to warranties, you should have a written agreement with all of the performers and artists who contributed to the recordings. For example, you would need a release (see Chapter 11) from a hired musician or from a photographer who took the album cover photo.

When you provide indemnity (that is, "indemnify" someone), you agree to pay for their damages that you caused. In other words, if the record company is sued because of your album art, you would have to pay for the label's legal expenses.

If your agreement doesn't contain any warranties or indemnification provisions, that's fine. Don't bring it up.

Controlled Compositions License

Keywords: Controlled Compositions, Songs, Copyright, Mechanical License

Controlled compositions are songs written or owned by your band. We discussed controlled compositions earlier in this chapter.

Mechanical Royalties

Keywords: (same as above)

The principles of mechanical royalties are explained in detail in Chapter 8. This provision permits the label to pay full rate (100%) or to pay less than the statutory rate. Seventy-five percent is standard for mechanical royalties, but try for a higher percentage if possible. The second option is provided in the event that the company insists on restricting the total number of songs on which they must pay mechanical royalties. In that case, we recommend at least 12 compositions, although some labels insist on ten compositions.

Leaving Members

Keywords: Leaving Member, Departing Member

This provision allows the label to obtain recording contracts with any band members who leave the group during the term of the recording agreement. Some labels may modify this provision in order to recoup what the band owes from the leaving member. Under that modification, the leaving member who is engaged by the label is stuck with the band's debts. We recommend against that arrangement.

Termination

Keywords: Termination, Breach, End

This provides the basis for either party to terminate. Under the provision in the sample agreement, if the company fails to pay royalties and does not correct it within 30 days of your notification, you can terminate the agreement and reacquire rights to your recordings. If possible, see if you can get this language into your recording agreement.

Termination in the Event of Leaving Member

Keywords: Leaving Members, Departing Members

This provision is related to the other Leaving Member provision, above. This allows the label to terminate the agreement if a key band member leaves the group. That is, the company has the option to terminate the agreement as to the whole band.

Mediation; Arbitration

Keywords: Mediation, Arbitration, Dispute Resolution

This provision provides an alternative method of resolving disputes (that is, other than filing a lawsuit). (See Chapter 2 for an explanation of mediation and arbitration.)

General

Keywords: Miscellaneous, Govern, State, Controlling Law

The following provisions are standard contract provisions referred to as boilerplate. Boilerplate provisions are also explained in Chapter 2.

Signatures

Each party must sign the agreement in relation to the business that is represented, and each party must have the authority to sign the agreement. Use the following rules when determining who should sign:

- **Sole Proprietorship:** If the band or the record company is a sole proprietorship, the sole proprietor can simply sign his or her own name.
- **Partnership:** If the band or record company is a general or limited partnership, then the only person authorized to sign the agreement is a general partner or someone who has written authority (usually in the form a partnership resolution) from a general partner.
- **Corporation or LLC:** If the company is a corporation or limited liability company (LLC), then only a person authorized by the corporation can sign the agreement. The president or chief executive officer (CEO) usually has such power, but not every officer of a corporation has the authority to bind (or legally obligate) the corporation. If in doubt, ask for written proof of the authority. This proof is usually in the form of a corporate resolution. The name of the corporation should be mentioned above the signature line; otherwise, the corporation isn't bound by the agreement—only the person that signed it.

If you have doubts about the person's authority, don't proceed until you are satisfied that the person has full authority to represent the company.

Independent Label Recording Agreement

Introduction

This agreement (the "Agreement") is entered into between _____
_____ ("Company") and
_____ , known collectively as
_____ and performing under the name
_____ (referred to as "Artist").
All references to "Artist" include all members of the group collectively and individually
unless otherwise specified.

    The parties agree as follows:

Exclusive Recording Services

During the Term (as described below), Artist will render recording services only for
the Company and will not, unless otherwise permitted under this Agreement, render
recording services for any other party.

Master Recordings

Artist will deliver to Company technically satisfactory recordings containing not
less than forty (40) minutes of playing time (the "Master Recording"). Company will
release commercial products including physical products [Compact Discs] and digital
products [Downloads] embodying the material contained on the Master Recordings
(collectively, the "Records").

Term

The Artist's obligation to perform exclusive recording services begins on the latest
signature date of this Agreement (the "Effective Date") and continues for _____
months after delivery of the first Master Recording (the "Term"). If Artist grants one
or more options to Company as part of this Agreement, any time prior to the end of
the Term, the Company may extend the Term by exercising its option. If an option is
exercised, the term will continue for_____months after the delivery of the previous
Master Recording ("Option Term"). If Company ever chooses not to exercise an option,
the agreement will terminate regardless of how many options remain.

    Artist grants to Company (*check if applicable*):

☐ one option ☐ two options ☐ three options ☐ four options ☐ _____ options

Grant of Rights

(Check one and fill in appropriate blanks)

☐ Beginning on the date when a Master Recording is delivered to Company, Company will be the exclusive owner of rights to all Master Recordings for the period of time: _____ (the "Ownership Period").

☐ Artist assigns to Company all rights to the Master Recording in perpetuity.

After the Ownership Period, all rights in the Master Recordings revert to Artist. During the Ownership Period, Artist grants to Company all right, title, and interest in the sound recording copyright (as provided under the U.S. Copyright Act of 1976 and international copyright treaties) to the Master Recordings, including:

- the exclusive right to manufacture copies of all or any portion of the Master Recordings
- the exclusive right to import, export, sell, transfer, release, license, publicly perform, rent, and otherwise exploit or dispose of the Master Recordings, and
- the exclusive right to edit, adapt, or conform the Master Recordings to technological or commercial requirements in various formats now known or later developed.

Territory

The rights granted to Company are limited to _____ _____ (the "Territory").

Right to Use Artist's Name and Likeness

Company has the right to reproduce or distribute, in any medium, Artist's names, portraits, pictures, and likeness for purposes of advertising, promotion, or trade in connection with Artist or the exploitation of the Master Recordings. Artist will be available from time to time to appear for photography, video performance, or the like, under the reasonable direction of Company. Artist is not entitled to any compensation for such services except for reimbursement of travel expenses.

Side-Artist Recording

(Check one)

☐ During the Term, Artist may perform as part of another artist's recording project (a "side-artist" performance) provided that: (a) the side-artist recording does not interfere with obligations under this Agreement; (b) only one member of Artist performs on the side-artist project; and (c) the following credit is included on the side-artist recording: "[*Name of Artist*] appears courtesy of [*Company Name*]."

☐ Artist may perform as part of another artist's recording project (a "side-artist" performance) provided that Company has furnished written consent for such performance. Consent must not be unreasonably withheld. In the event of such performance, the following credit is included on the side-artist recording: "[*Name of Artist*] appears courtesy of [*Company Name*]."

Professional Name

With the exception of the Leaving Member sections of this Agreement, Artist will perform and record under the professional name _____ .
Artist will not use a different name in connection with the Master Recordings unless Artist and Company mutually agree in writing.

Trademark Search *(Check if applicable)*

☐ Company, at its discretion, may institute a search to determine whether there are any third-party uses for Artist's name. If the search indicates that the name cannot be used, Company and Artist will mutually agree on a substitute name. Any amounts up to but not exceeding six hundred dollars ($600.00) may be expended for the purposes of the trademark search and will be considered as a recoupable advance.

Production of Master Recordings

Artist is responsible for payment of all expenses incurred in the production of the Master Recordings and will obtain the appropriate permission, clearance, or release from any person or union who renders services in the production of the Master Recordings.

Subsequent Recording of Compositions

Artist represents and warrants that Artist will not record any composition contained on a Master Recording for a period of_____years from the date of first release of a Company recording containing such composition.

Advances and Recoupable Costs

All money paid by Company to Artist, other than royalties paid under this Agreement, will be considered an advance against royalties ("Advances"). All Advances will be set off against future royalties. In connection with the initial Master Recording delivered, Company will pay Artist an Advance of _____ on the date of ____ .

Advance for Option Term (*Check and fill in blank if applicable.*)

☐ In connection with the Master Recording delivered under the Option Terms, Company will pay Artist an Advance of _____ .

Royalties

Company will pay Artist a percentage (the "Royalty") of the Company's sales for all Records as set forth:

Compact Discs. For Compact Discs sold, less the actual container costs (not to exceed _____% of SRLP), plus excise, sales, and similar taxes,

Company will pay Artist _____% of (*choose one*):

☐ suggested retail list price (SRLP) or ☐ wholesale price.

Downloads and Streaming Revenue. For Downloads and Streaming Revenue, Company will pay Artist _____% of net receipts paid to Company regardless of the electronic mechanism for delivery.

Foreign Licenses

Company will pay Artist _____% of the net receipts paid to Company under any foreign license.

Compilations

If a composition from the Master Recording is used on a compilation or recording in which other artists are included, the Artist's royalty will be prorated. For example, if a composition from the Master Recording is included on a compilation containing nine selections from other artists, Artist shall be entitled to one-tenth (1/10th) of the royalty rate.

Flat Fee

Company will pay Artist _____% of the net receipts paid to Company under any flat fee license of the Master Recordings or any portion of the Master Recordings.

Promotional Recordings and Cutouts

No royalties will be due on Records furnished on a promotional basis. Nor will any royalty be due for Records sold by Company as cutouts or for scrap or otherwise on deletion from Company's catalog.

Statements; Audit

Company will pay Artist the Artist's Royalties within _____ days after
the end of each quarter. Company will also furnish an accurate statement of sales
of Records during that month. Company will pay interest on any late payment from
the due date until paid. The acceptance by Artist of any statement or payment
does not prevent Artist's later questioning its accuracy. Company will keep accurate
books of account covering all transactions relating to this Agreement. Artist or its
representatives have the right on reasonable written notice to audit Company's books
relating to the Records. If the audit indicates an underpayment greater than $500 for
any six-month period, Company will pay for the audit.

Video *(Check if applicable and fill in blanks)*

☐ If Company decides during the term of this Agreement to produce one or more
recordings combining the audio performance of Artist with a visual image (the
"Video"), Company and Artist will mutually agree on the budget and production
costs (the "Production Budget") for such Video or Videos. All sums paid by
Company as part of the Production Budget will be considered as an Advance
against royalties. Company is the sole owner of all worldwide rights to each
Video, including the worldwide copyrights. Company has the right to use and
allow others to use each Video for advertising and promotional purposes with
no payment to Artist. "Advertising and promotional purposes" means all uses
for which Company receives no money in excess of incidental fees such as tape
stock and duplication and shipping. Artist is entitled to a royalty as established in
the Royalty Section for all revenue derived from commercial exploitation of the
Videos. Artist will issue a worldwide synchronization license for any Controlled
Compositions embodied on a Video. For a period of _____ years from the
date of first release of any Video, Company has the right to allow others to use
that Video for commercial purposes. If Company licenses or commercially exploits
the Video(s), Company will pay, after deducting all costs advanced for production,
a royalty of _____ % of the net revenues from any license or sale of that Video.
Artist grants to Company the right to synchronize the Master Recordings with
visual images to create Videos.

Commercial Release of Records

☐ Company will release the Records within _____ months of delivery of the Master Recordings (the "Guaranteed Release Date"). Artist will provide written notice if Company fails to release the recording by the Guaranteed Release Date. If, after 30 days from notification, Company has not released the recording, Artist may terminate this agreement. All rights in the Master Recordings will revert to Artist, and Company will have no further rights to the recording, or

☐ Company will release the Records within _____ months of delivery of the Master Recordings (the "Guaranteed Release Date"). Artist will provide written notice if Company fails to release the recording by the Guaranteed Release Date. If, after 30 days from notification, Company has not released the recording, Artist may terminate this agreement and Artist may acquire the unreleased Master Recording and all related rights by paying to Company the sum of any advance for such Master Recording.

Artist Promotional Records

Company will furnish to Artist a total of _____ promotional Records at no charge. Artist may obtain further Records from Company at Company's then-wholesale cost.

Album Artwork *(Check if applicable and fill in blank.)*

☐ Artist, at its own expense, may furnish camera-ready artwork for the Records at the time of delivery of the Master Recording. Such artwork may be delivered in electronic format. Company has the right to modify or conform the artwork to meet Company specifications and standards. However, Company will consult with Artist before making any modification. If Artist elects not to furnish artwork, Company will prepare the artwork and consult with Artist regarding the design. Company will advance the sum of $_____ for artwork preparation. This payment is an advance against future royalties.

Artist Warranties

Artist warrants to Company that Artist has the power and authority to enter into this Agreement, is the Artist and copyright holder of the Master Recordings, or has or will obtain all necessary and appropriate rights and licenses to grant the license in this Agreement with respect to the Master Recordings. Artist warrants that the Master Recordings are original to Artist except for material in the public domain and such excerpts from other works that may be included with the written permission of the copyright owners, and that proper clearances or permission have been obtained from the artists of any copyrighted material, including but not limited to any digitally reprocessed samples of material incorporated in the Master Recordings. Artist warrants that Artist's use of any name or moniker will not infringe on the rights of others and that Artist's use of any musical composition or arrangement will not infringe on the rights of others.

(*Check if applicable*)

☐ Artist further warrants that the Master Recordings do not:
- contain any libelous material
- infringe any trade name, trademark, trade secret, or copyright, or
- invade or violate any right of privacy, personal or proprietary right, or other common law or statutory right.

(*Check if applicable*)

☐ Artist hereby indemnifies Company and undertakes to defend Company against and hold Company harmless (including, without limitation, attorney fees and costs) from any claims and damage arising out of a breach of Artist's Warranties as provided above. Artist agrees to reimburse Company for any payment made by Company with respect to this Section, provided that the claim has been settled or has resulted in a final judgment against Company or its licensees. Artist will notify Company in writing of any infringements or imitations by others of the Master Recording that may come to Artist's attention.

Controlled Compositions License

Artist grants to Company an irrevocable worldwide license to reproduce all compositions wholly or partly written, owned, or controlled by Artist (the "Controlled Compositions"). Artist grants to Company a first mechanical license for all Controlled Compositions.

Mechanical Royalties

Artist acknowledges and agrees that Company will pay a royalty for the mechanical license on all Records manufactured for sale or commercial distribution at _____% of the minimum compulsory license rate (the "Company Mechanical Rate") applicable in the country of manufacture. The applicable minimum statutory rate will be determined as of the date of the commencement of the recording of the applicable Master Recording. Mechanical Royalties are not payable for musical compositions of one minute or less in duration.

(*Check if applicable*)

☐ For each Master Recording, Company will pay only a sum equivalent to the Company Mechanical Royalty Rate multiplied by _____ .

Leaving Members (*Check if applicable*)

☐ If any member of Artist ceases to perform as a member of the group ("Leaving Member"), Artist will promptly give Company written notice. If the group disbands, each member of the group is considered to be a Leaving Member. Artist grants to Company an irrevocable option to engage the exclusive services of any Leaving Member as a recording artist. In the event of Company's exercise of this option, the Leaving Member will be considered to have entered into an agreement with Company on all the terms and conditions of this Agreement, including the initial term, the first option term, payments, royalties, and all other applicable terms. The Leaving Member will not, however, be responsible for any outstanding Artist debts, including unrecouped advances.

Termination

Company may terminate this Agreement within thirty (30) days of the expiration of the Term or any Option Period. Artist can terminate this Agreement if Company fails to pay Artist's Royalties when due or to accurately report Net Sales, if the failure is not corrected within 30 days after notice from Artist. If this Agreement is breached because of a failure to pay or accurately report royalties, all rights granted under this agreement revert to Artist, and Company will have no further rights regarding Artist or the Master Recordings.

If this Agreement is terminated for a reason other than Company's failure to pay or accurately report Artist's Royalties, the termination will not terminate the underlying license and copyrights granted to Company by Artist, nor Company's obligations to pay Royalties under this Agreement.

Termination in the Event of Leaving Member

Within ninety (90) days of receipt of notice of any Leaving Member, as defined in the Leaving Members section, Company will have the right to terminate the Agreement as to the remaining members of Artist. If that happens, all members of Artist will be deemed to be Leaving Members.

Mediation; Arbitration

If a dispute arises under this Agreement, the parties agree to first try to resolve the dispute with the help of a mutually agreed-on mediator in _____ . Any costs and fees other than attorney fees will be shared equally by the parties. If it is impossible to arrive at a mutually satisfactory solution within a reasonable time, the parties agree to submit the dispute to binding arbitration in the same city or region, conducted on a confidential basis under:

☐ the Commercial Arbitration Rules of the American Arbitration Association, or

☐ the rules of _____ .

Any decision or award as a result of arbitration will include the assessment of costs, expenses, and reasonable attorneys' fees and a written determination of the arbitrators. Absent an agreement to the contrary, arbitration will be conducted by an arbitrator experienced in music industry law. An award of arbitration is final and binding on the Artist and may be confirmed in a court of competent jurisdiction. The prevailing party has the right to collect from the other party its reasonable costs and attorney fees incurred in enforcing this agreement.

General

Nothing contained in this Agreement makes either Company or Artist a partner, joint venturer, or employee of the other party for any purpose. This Agreement may not be amended except in a writing signed by both parties. No waiver by either party of any right is a waiver of any other right. If a court finds any provision of this Agreement invalid or unenforceable as applied to any circumstance, the remainder of this Agreement will be interpreted to carry out the intent of the parties. This Agreement is governed by and interpreted in accordance with the laws of the State of _____ .

This Agreement expresses the complete understanding of the parties on the subject matter and supersedes all prior proposals, agreements, representations, and understandings. Notices required under this Agreement can be sent to the parties at the addresses provided below. In the event of any dispute arising from or related to this Agreement, the prevailing party is entitled to attorneys' fees.

Artist Business Name _____

Artist Representative Name and Title _____

Artist Representative Signature _____

Artist Address _____

Date _____

Company Name _____

Company Representative Name and Title _____

Company Representative Signature _____

Company Address _____

Date _____

Independent Label License Agreement

Introduction

This agreement (the "Agreement") is entered into between _____ ("Company") and _____ , known collectively as and performing under the name _____ (referred to as "Artist"). All references to "Artist" include all members of the group collectively and individually unless otherwise specified. The parties agree as follows:

Recordings and Records

Company wants to license rights to a sound recording entitled _____ (the "Master Recording") consisting of the following songs:

_____

_____

_____

_____

_____

Company will release a commercial product embodying the material contained on the Master Recordings (the "Records").

Grant of Rights

Company will be the exclusive licensee of all rights to the Master Recording for _____ years from the date of receipt of each Master Recording (the "Ownership Period"). After the Ownership Period, all rights granted under this Agreement will revert to Artist. Artist grants to Company the following rights to the Master Recording:

- the exclusive right to manufacture copies of all or any portion of the Master Recording whether in digital or physical media
- the exclusive right to sell, transfer, release, license, publicly perform, rent, and otherwise exploit or dispose of the Master Recording, and
- the exclusive right to edit, adapt, or conform the Master Recording to technological or commercial requirements in various formats now known or later developed.

Territory

The rights granted to Company are limited to _____ (the "Territory").

Right to Use Artist's Name and Likeness

Company has the right to reproduce or distribute, in any medium, Artist's names, portraits, pictures, and likeness for purposes of advertising, promotion, or trade in connection with Artist or the exploitation of the Master Recording. Artist will be available from time to time to appear for photography, video performance, or the like, under the reasonable direction of Company. Artist is not entitled to any compensation for these services except for reimbursement of travel expenses.

Delivery of Master Recording

Within _____ months of the Effective Date, Artist will deliver to Company the Master Recording.

Production of Master Recording

Artist will be responsible for payment of all expenses incurred in the production of the Master Recording and will get the appropriate permission, clearance, or release from any person or union who renders services in the production of the Master Recording.

Advances (*Check if applicable and fill in blanks*)

☐ All monies paid by Company to Artist, other than royalties paid pursuant to this Agreement, will be considered an advance against royalties ("Advances"). All Advances will be set off against future royalties. In connection with the initial Recording delivered, Company will pay Artist an Advance of $_____ on the date of _____ .

Royalties

Company will pay Artist a percentage (the "Royalty") of the Company's sales for all Records as set forth:

Compact Discs. For Compact Discs sold, less the actual container costs (not to exceed _____ % of SRLP), plus excise, sales, and similar taxes,

Company will pay Artist _____% of (*choose one*):

☐ suggested retail list price (SRLP) or ☐ wholesale price.

Downloads and Streaming

For Downloads and Streaming Income, Company will pay Artist% of net receipts paid to Company regardless of the electronic mechanism for delivery.

Compilations

If a composition from the Master Recording is used on a compilation or recording in which other artists are included, the Artist's royalty will be prorated. For example, if a composition from the Master Recording is included on a compilation containing nine selections from other artists, Artist will be entitled to one-tenth (1/10th) of the royalty rate.

Promotional Recordings and Cutouts

No royalties will be due on Records furnished on a promotional basis. No royalty will be due for Records sold by Company as cutouts or for scrap or otherwise upon deletion from Company's catalog.

Statements; Audit

Company will pay Artist the Artist's Royalties within _____ days after the end of each quarter. Company will furnish an accurate statement of sales of Records during that month. If late in any payment, Company will pay interest from the due date until paid. The acceptance by Artist of any statement or payment does not prevent Artist later questioning its accuracy. Company will keep accurate books of account covering all transactions relating to this Agreement. Artist or its representatives have the right on reasonable written notice to audit Company's books relating to the Records. If the audit indicates an underpayment greater than $500 for any six-month period, Company will pay for the audit.

Video (*Check and fill in blanks if applicable*)

☐ If Company decides, during the term of this Agreement, to produce a recording combining the audio performance of Artist with a visual image (the "Video"), Company and Artist will mutually agree on the budget and production costs (the "Production Budget") for such Video. All sums paid by Company as part of the Production Budget will be considered as an Advance against royalties. Company will be the sole owner of all worldwide rights to each Video, including the worldwide copyrights. Company will have the right to use and allow others to use each Video for advertising and promotional purposes with no payment to

Artist. "Advertising and promotional purposes" means all uses for which Company receives no money in excess of incidental fees such as tape stock and duplication and shipping. Artist is entitled to a royalty as established in the Royalty Section for all revenue derived from commercial exploitation of the Videos. Artist will issue a worldwide synchronization license for any Controlled Compositions embodied on a Video. For a period of _____ years from the date of release of any Video, Company will have the right to allow others to use the Videos for commercial purposes. If Company licenses or commercially exploits the Videos, Company will pay, after deducting all costs advanced for production, a royalty of _____% of the net revenues from any license or sale of the Video. Artist grants to Company the right to synchronize the Master Recordings with visual images to create Videos.

Commercial Release of Records (*Check one and fill in blanks*)

☐ Company will release the Records within _____ months of delivery of the Master Recordings (the "Guaranteed Release Date"). Artist will give written notice if Company fails to release the recording by the Guaranteed Release Date, and if, after thirty (30) days from notification, the Company has not released the recording, Artist may terminate this agreement, and all rights in the Master Recordings will revert to Artist and Company will have no further rights to the recording.

☐ Company will release the Records within _____ months of delivery of the Master Recordings (the "Guaranteed Release Date"). Artist will give written notice if Company fails to release the recording by the Guaranteed Release Date, and if, after thirty (30) days from notification, the Company has not released the recording, Artist may terminate this agreement and acquire the unreleased Master Recording and all related rights by paying to Company the sum of any advance for the Master Recording.

Artist Promotional Records

Company will furnish to Artist a total of_____promotional Records at no charge. Artist may obtain further Records from Company at Company's then-wholesale cost.

Album Artwork (*Check if applicable and fill in blank*)

☐ Artist, at its own expense, may furnish camera-ready artwork for the Records at the time of delivery of the Master Recording. Such artwork may be delivered in electronic format. Company has the right to modify or conform the artwork to meet Company specifications and standards. However, Company will consult with Artist before making any modification. If Artist elects not to furnish artwork, Company will prepare the artwork and consult with Artist regarding the design. Company will advance the sum of $_____ for artwork preparation. This payment is an advance against future royalties.

Artist Warranties

Artist warrants to Company that Artist has the power and authority to enter into this Agreement, is the Artist and copyright holder of the Master Recordings, or has or will obtain all necessary and appropriate rights and licenses to grant the license in this Agreement with respect to the Master Recordings. Artist represents and warrants that the Master Recordings are original to Artist except for material in the public domain and such excerpts from other works as may be included with the written permission of the copyright owners and that proper clearances or permission have been obtained from the Artists of any copyrighted material, including but not limited to any digitally reprocessed samples of material incorporated in the Master Recordings. Artist warrants that Artist's use of any name or moniker will not infringe on the rights of others and that Artist's use of any musical composition or arrangement will not infringe on the rights of others.

Artist further warrants that the Master Recordings do not:
- contain any libelous material
- infringe any trade name, trademark, trade secret, or copyright, or
- invade or violate any right of privacy, personal or proprietary right, or other common law or statutory right.

Artist indemnifies Company and will defend Company against and hold Company harmless (including, without limitation, attorney fees and costs) from any claims and damage arising out of a breach of Artist's Warranties as provided above. Artist agrees to reimburse Company for any payment made by Company with respect to this Section, provided that the claim has been settled or has resulted in a final judgment against Company or its licensees. Artist will notify Company in writing of any infringements or imitations by others of the Master Recording that may come to Artist's attention.

Controlled Compositions License

Artist grants to Company an irrevocable worldwide license to reproduce all compositions wholly or partly written, owned, or controlled by Artist (the "Controlled

Compositions"). Artist grants to Company a first mechanical license with respect to all Controlled Compositions.

Mechanical Royalties

Artist acknowledges and agrees that Company will pay a royalty for the mechanical license on all Records manufactured for sale or commercial distribution at _____% of the minimum compulsory license rate (the "Company Mechanical Rate") applicable in the country of manufacture. The applicable minimum statutory rate will be determined as of the date of the commencement of the recording of the applicable Master Recording. Mechanical Royalties are not payable with respect to musical compositions of one minute or less in duration.

Termination

Artist can terminate this Agreement if Company fails to pay Artist's Royalties when due or to accurately report Net Sales and the failure is not corrected within 30 days after written notice from Artist. If this Agreement is terminated because of a failure to pay or accurately report royalties, all rights granted under this agreement will revert to Artist and Company will have no further rights regarding Artist or the Master Recording.

If this Agreement is terminated for a reason other than Company's failure to pay or accurately report Artist's Royalties, the termination will not terminate the underlying license and copyrights granted to Company by Artist or Company's obligations to pay Royalties under this Agreement.

Mediation; Arbitration

If a dispute arises under this Agreement, the parties agree to first try to resolve the dispute with the help of a mutually agreed-on mediator in _____ .

Any costs and fees other than attorney fees will be shared equally by the parties. If it is impossible to arrive at a mutually satisfactory solution within a reasonable time, the parties agree to submit the dispute to binding arbitration in the same city or region, conducted on a confidential basis under:

    ☐ the Commercial Arbitration Rules of the American Arbitration Association, or

    ☐ the rules of _____ .

Any decision or award as a result of any such arbitration proceeding will include the assessment of costs, expenses, and reasonable attorneys' fees and a written determination of the arbitrators. Absent an agreement to the contrary, arbitration will be conducted by an arbitrator experienced in music industry law. An award of arbitration is final and binding on the Artist and may be confirmed in a court of competent jurisdiction. The prevailing party has the right to collect from the other party its reasonable costs and attorney fees incurred in enforcing this agreement.

General

Nothing contained in this Agreement makes either Company or Artist a partner, joint venturer, or employee of the other party for any purpose. This Agreement may not be amended except in a writing signed by both parties. No waiver by either party of any right shall be construed as a waiver of any other right. If a court finds any provision of this Agreement invalid or unenforceable as applied to any circumstance, the remainder of this Agreement will be interpreted to carry out the intent of the parties. This Agreement is governed by and interpreted in accordance with the laws of the State of _____ . This Agreement expresses the complete understanding of the parties with respect to the subject matter and supersedes all prior proposals, agreements, representations, and understandings. Notices required under this agreement can be sent to the parties at the addresses provided below. In the event of any dispute arising from or related to this Agreement, the prevailing party is entitled to attorneys' fees.

Artist Business Name _____

Artist Representative Name and Title _____

Artist Representative Signature _____

Artist Address _____

_____

Date _____

Company Name _____

Company Representative Name and Title _____

Company Representative Signature _____

Company Address _____

_____

Date _____

Reviewing Royalty Statements

The record company's royalty statement may be confusing. To simplify your review of the statement, we have provided an example of an independent label royalty statement. In the statement below for the group the Bird Feeders, signed with Figment Records, the band has sold about 2,000 copies of its debut CD and has generated $12,000 in digital download sales in the first six months. The group's deductions are fairly small because they recorded at their home studio and did not take an advance payment from the label. Fortunately, the Bird Feeder's contract did not provide for deductions such as packaging, breakage, and manufacturing.

The statement shows the total units shipped, followed by the units returned by two distributors. (The parentheses in financial reports indicate negative figures or numbers being subtracted.) The returned units are deducted from the shipped units. The result is the Total Units Sold. This amount is then multiplied by the band's royalty rate. When you review your band's statement, make sure that the royalty rate is accurate. Following this, sales of downloads are provided.

In the next section, the label lists deductions. You will see that the label and the band split the costs for a cooperative advertisement in a newspaper. In addition, the label fronted the band some CDs for sale at a show. These expenses are all included in the deductions. When you review your band's statement, make sure that the label has the right to make all of the deductions. That is, check the list of deductions against those permitted under the agreement.

The total deductions are subtracted from the royalties to arrive at the Total Due. This is the amount to be paid to the band, and it should be enclosed with the statement to the band. Not all statements will resemble this form, but the contents should be similar: a statement of sales, royalty rates, deductions, and earnings (or losses).

Figment Records—Sample Royalty Statement

Artist: The Bird Feeders
Title: Feeding Red-Beaked Seagulls
Cat# FG67CD
UPC# 7-35286-19672

Format CD

Units shipped	2,448	
Units returned	(448)	
Units sold	2,000	
Royalty per compact disc (12% x $15.98 = $1.92) x $	1.92	
Total CD Royalty Amount		$ 3,840

Format: Downloads

Total Revenue	$12,000	
Royalty for downloads	25%	
Total Download Royalty Amount	3,000	
Total Royalty Amount		$ 6,840

Deductions

Mastering	$ (310.00)	
FedEx costs	(51.00)	
Co-op ad for show (50-50 split)	(150.00)	
Artwork design proofs	(170.00)	
Inventory for show	(93.15)	
Total Deductions		(774.15)
Total Due (Royalty – Deductions)		$6,065.85

Licensing Your Band's Music for Film, TV, and Advertising

Way back in 1955, Bill Haley and the Comets licensed "Rock Around the Clock" for use in the movie *Blackboard Jungle* and a new market exploded for bands. Combining pop music and visuals has become an obsession for film and TV producers and particularly for advertisers. From U2's *Special Edition* iPod to Lady Gaga's pitch for Google's computers, musicians have licensed their music ad infinitum (and some would say ad nauseam). What's new in the past decade is that the music business—sinking into the doldrums from years of dwindling sales revenue—has taken a new look at licensing as a means of generating revenue and kick-starting and reinvigorating careers.

Licensing pop music with film, TV, and ads, is accomplished primarily by synchronization licenses (also known as a "sync license"). In this chapter we'll discuss the business of sync licensing and how it may fit into your band's business.

What Is Music Licensing?

There's no mystery to licensing your music; you simply give someone else permission to use your copyrights. As you are aware from previous chapters, every musical recording includes two copyrights: one for the song itself and another for the particular recording of the song. Licensing music often requires granting the permission of both of these copyright owners (if they happen to be two separate entities—for example, songwriters own the song but a record company owns the sound recording).

As you may be aware from previous chapters, the music industry is built around licensing these two copyrights. Below are some examples:

- **Radio play.** Radio stations acquire a license to broadcast ("perform") songs from the songwriters via performance rights organizations (PROs), which in turn have licensed these rights from the songwriters or music publishers.
- **Performances at stores and bars.** Public performance of music at retail establishments—whether the music is played live or via recording—

requires a performance license from the owners of the songwriting copyright owner (the music publisher). No permission is required from the owner of the sound recording copyright (record label).

- **Digital downloads.** Consumers at iTunes and Amazon who purchase downloads don't actually buy music; they license it. The MP3 retailers have licenses to sell the music from the copyright owners (record companies and music publishers).

- **Streaming musical services.** Interactive streaming companies like Spotify and Apple Music license sound recordings from record companies, and they license songwriting copyrights from music publishers. Unsigned bands accomplish these licenses using aggregators.

- **Ringtones.** Companies that sell ringtones license those rights from record labels that own sound recording copyrights and music publishers that own songwriting copyrights.

- **Webcasting.** Noninteractive webcasters such as Pandora and Live365 license the right to "perform" the songs from PROs and from SoundExchange, which in turn have licensed the rights from the respective copyright owners.

- **Mechanical and compulsory licenses.** When CDs or downloads are sold, the record company that is selling the copies is required to pay the songwriters a fixed amount (currently 9.1 cents) per song. This is a license payment to mechanically reproduce the song (known as a "mechanical license"). (Under U.S. law, a songwriter who has released a version of the song has to permit others to perform that song if they pay this mechanical license fee—a process known as a "compulsory license").

- **Sampling.** When using a sample, musicians and record companies license rights from record labels that own sound recording copyrights and from music publishers that own songwriting copyrights.

RESOURCE

More information on licensing. This chapter provides a cursory look at licensing music. If you want more in-depth information, check out *The Musician's Guide to Licensing Music,* by Darren Wilsey with Daylle Deanna Schwartz (Billboard Books).

Dear Rich: What's the "Right" Way to Post Cover Songs on YouTube?

My band had a nice show at a local venue and we'd like to post some YouTube video, but all but one of our tunes is a cover song. What's the current custom on that score on YouTube? I've peeked at some stuff on the Web about this, but am not getting very clear answers. The whole YouTube ethic seems to be post and ask forgiveness later, but I'd like to just do it right, if there is a "right" way.

The short answer is to give up on doing it the "right" way. The proper way to post a video of a cover tune is to obtain a "sync license" from the owner of the song—usually a music publisher that owns songwriting rights. The chances of you, as an unsigned artist, accomplishing that task are very slim. It's for that reason everyone including an aspiring Justin Bieber apparently posts covers without permission. We're talking only about covers, here. YouTube does have a means of locating videos that use major label recordings—for example if you use a Prince song as a soundtrack for your child's dance routine. YouTube seems to possess digital fingerprints for prerecorded pop tunes, because when we posted a video of our commute to work and included a track by everybody's favorite '80s one-hit wonder, Rockwell, we received a notice within hours of posting. YouTube had found unauthorized material on our video (and as punishment was going to run ads over our video). YouTube reserves the right to take down our video, but as an alternative, the company apparently divides the advertising revenue with the rights holders—music publishers and record companies. We're pretty sure YouTube doesn't have a similar method for detecting cover versions—that is, when someone else performs a Prince song. Of course, these unauthorized uses could still be located via old-fashioned text searches or spot scanning of videos. And songwriters who discover covers of their material can still issue a DMCA (Digital Millennium Copyright Act) notice to YouTube (although you don't hear much about that practice these days). So, in summary, the "post now, deal with it later" approach is the default mechanism for covers.

What about Harry Fox? Harry Fox provides a means of obtaining a compulsory license—the right to release CDs and MP3s of cover songs. These licenses do not apply to audiovisual works. Harry Fox's eSynch system can provide some sync licensing if you are distributing a video for noncommercial use. However, this system is not intended for commercial use. In that case, you must contact the publisher directly.

Music Licensing Terminology

The sync licensing business has some distinct terminology. Here is a glossary of some of the more common terms.

- **Blanket agreement.** This arrangement is typically made between a company that wants to use music for film, TV, video, etc. (the "licensee") and a production music library (PML; see below) in which the licensee obtains unlimited use of all PML music on a compact disc or disc library for a specified period of time, such as two years. If continued use is required, the license must be renewed. Blanket licenses may range from several hundred dollars to four or five thousand dollars per year.

- **Buyout agreements.** This is similar to the blanket license (above) except the licensee acquires exclusive or unlimited rights from the production music library.

- **Cue Sheet.** A form that lists all of the music used in a film or TV show. It's most commonly furnished to performance rights organizations so that they can determine who gets paid.

- **Master Use License.** A company that wants to use a specific recording of a song in a movie, TV, or film needs a master use license from the record company, or whoever is the owner of the sound recording copyright. (The term "master use" means the company is obtaining permission to use the master recording of the song.) Of course in order to use a particular recording of a song in a movie, television program, or ad, the company will also need a synchronization license (usually from the music publisher).

- **Music supervisor.** This extremely influential person facilitates licensing by acting as the middleperson, choosing and acquiring the music for films, TV, and ads, and making sure that all legal rights have been granted (or "cleared"). The supervisor may act independently or be employed by the film, TV, or advertising company seeking the music. The supervisor is typically given a budget for a production and doles out payments based on length of use, placement in the project, and prominence (or importance) of the music.

- **Needledrop.** This is a reference to the days of vinyl recordings when a radio or film producer paid each time the needle was dropped onto a piece of music. It now means a per-use agreement in which the film or TV company makes payments when it uses music compositions in a production. Per-use fees depend on the length and type of use and can range from $50 for a five-minute use in a local television show to $500 for the same music in a feature film.

- **Production Music Library (PML).** PMLs are companies that acquire licensing rights from copyright owners, group compositions into libraries, and offer them to companies on a nonexclusive basis, often as digital downloads, or on CDs or DVDs. A typical PML package may contain 10 to 15 original compositions, including a full-length version of each composition as well as shorter "tag" or "cue" version. Because the PML owns both the music publishing and sound recording rights, obtaining permission to use PML recordings is simple. PML music, which is primarily instrumental, is used for films, websites, slide shows, radio and television programming, commercials, software, and multimedia, training videos, in-flight services, and similar applications. Like stock photography, PML music is categorized by genre or mood (for example, old-time rock and roll or outer space music). A PML license does not permit use of the music in audio recordings sold to the public. For example, while PML music may be used in a film, it cannot be included on a commercial soundtrack album sold to consumers without special permission from the PML.

- **Sync License.** In order to use a song in a movie, TV show, or advertisement, you'll need permission from the owner of the songwriting copyright (typically the music publisher). An exception to this is if the song is in the public domain. In that case, the company would only need the master use license from the owner of the sound recording being used—the protected specific version of the underlying song that is now in the public domain.

- **Videogram License.** This is a specific type of synchronization license which gives the production company the right to include the music on physical copies of the film, video, or TV show (typically sold as DVD or Blu-Ray discs). Typically the videogram license is included as part of a sync or master use license.

How Do You Get a Licensing Deal?

This is the big question … and perhaps the reason you opened this chapter. Unfortunately the people who make film, TV, and advertising licensing decisions are rarely open to unsolicited material. (Welcome to the music business!) Music supervisors—like major labels, booking agents, and music managers—usually don't want to hear your music if they don't know you. So, like everything else in the music business, it comes down to contacts, tenacity, luck, and oh yeah … talent. You may have some luck with one of these strategies:

- **Seek out a music publisher with a successful track record.** A quality music publisher—one that's been around for more than a decade and has a solid licensing track record—will pitch your music for films, TV, and ads. These music publishers are aggressive and have contacts, and as we discuss in Chapter 8, they also take a healthy chunk of your revenues. The challenge (as always) comes down to convincing the publisher to listen to your music and sign you.

- **Seek out a rep/agent.** Enterprising companies and individuals—often with previous experience from the film, TV, or music industries—represent many bands and musicians as licensing agents. (You can find them using an Internet search engine.) Because these individuals can tie you and your music up to exclusive deals, do some research if one them expresses an interest in repping your band.

- **Music licensing services.** A host of online services seek to connect your music with licensing opportunities. Perhaps most well known is Taxi.com, which comes a with a hefty sign-up fee (and per song submission fee). Similar or related services include Sonicbids.com, Broadjam.com, Rumblefish.com, Pumpaudio.com, Musicsupervisor.com, Musicgorilla.com, and Songcatalog.com. Most require payment of fees.

- **Make your music known to music supervisors.** This can be done by generating buzz as a performing band, having a viral video on YouTube, or sometimes by having success with production music library (PML) collections. The latter occurs when a PML enters into an exclusive deal to represent certain of your tracks, and in return you get a cut if a music supervisor selects one of those tracks to use. You can find contact information for PMLs by searching online or through intermediary services such as Taxi.com.

- **Work for free (or at low rates).** Sad to say, sometimes the only way to get your music out there is to offer it for free or at discount. For example, working with student filmmakers, using Creative Commons licensing, or doing anything that gets attention (and has some viral potential) will get your music and name out in front of music supervisors. When working below scale, always insist on prominent credits.

Commissioned vs. Licensed?

In a typical license, the music already exists. For example, you've recorded and distributed a track, a music supervisor heard it, and she now wants to acquire rights for a reality TV show. Another way that music is acquired is when it is commissioned specifically for a project—for example, a computer game operator pays for a new work. When music is created specifically for a project, the rights are acquired one of two ways:

- an assignment, or
- a work-for-hire agreement.

An assignment is a transfer of ownership of the copyright in the music. Assignments are discussed in Chapter 7, and an example of an artwork assignment is provided (as part of the full-length agreement) in Chapter 10. A work-for-hire arrangement occurs when the hiring party acquires ownership of the music through an employer-employee relationship or an independent contractor agreement. To learn more about works made for hire visit the Copyright Office website (www.copyright.gov) and use the search tool on the site to find and download Circular 30, *Works Made for Hire*.

Sync Fees for a Film, Television Show, or Video

One of the most common music licensing myths is that one sync deal—for example, getting one song on a TV show or commercial—can bring in bundles of money. That's usually not the case. Revenues for sync fees are typically under $20,000 per deal. And that's before you deduct the cut for the licensing agent or publisher who got you the deal. There's also an even more disturbing trend—some film or TV companies pay less and rationalize it by telling the band it will get them exposure. That said, a band that becomes a reliable source for licensable source music on film, TV, or in ads, can earn a reasonable chunk of revenue, particularly if the licensed music is played in reruns or syndicated.

Fees for using a song in a film depend on the nature of the film (documentary or theatrical; independent or major studio release) and the use in the film—whether the song is used in the background, foreground, or in some special manner (such as when a character sings the song). Fees for using a composition as a film's theme song range from $50,000 to $75,000. The fee for use of a song in the background of an independent documentary may start at $500. Fees for nontheatrical corporate video synchronization licenses may range from $500 to $1,500. Fees for using a song in an independent theatrical release may range from $5,000 to $15,000. Fees for use in a major motion picture are generally between $10,000 and $25,000. These synchronization fees do not include separate fees and royalties for videogram licenses, described above. If the production company plans to make the production available for sale on DVD or the like, they will also have to pay videogram fees as well.

Simple Master/Sync License

Although we provide examples of Master and Sync Licenses below, your band may want a very simple license that includes both master use and sync rights. For example, you may want a simple license so that someone can use your band's music in a student film, a webcast, or a local TV show. The agreement below should be suitable provided that one entity (the band, an individual, or a company) owns both the compositions and recordings. It would not be suitable, for example, if one party (a record company) owns the recordings and another party (a music publisher or a songwriter) owns the songs.

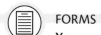 **FORMS**
You can download this form (and all other forms in this book) from Nolo.com; for details, see "Get Forms, Updates, and More at This Book's Companion Page," in the appendix.

Master Use and Sync License (Short Form)

This Master Use and Sync License Agreement (the "Agreement") is made between: _____ ("Licensor") and _____ ("Producer").

Licensor is the owner of rights for the master recordings:

Masters: _____

Licensor is the owner of rights for the compositions:

Compositions: _____

Performance Rights Organization:

_____

Producer is interested in licensing the Masters and Compositions for the following:

Production: _____

Territory: _____

Term: _____

Licensor grants to Producer and Producer's successors and assigns the nonexclusive right to use and reproduce the Masters and Compositions solely in synchronization with the Production within the Territory and during the Term. Licensor grants to Producer the right to publicly perform the Masters and Compositions solely in synchronization to the Production.

☐ Payment. Producer shall pay Licensor _____
for the rights granted in this Agreement. Payment shall be made _____ .

Warranty

Licensor warrants that it has the power and authority to grant the rights in this Agreement and that the Masters and Compositions do not infringe any third-party rights. In no event shall Licensor's liability for a breach of this warranty exceed the amount of payments received under this Agreement.

Credits

Licensor shall receive credit in the following form: _____

_____

Cue Sheets

Producer agrees to furnish Licensor a cue sheet of the Motion Picture within thirty (30) days after the first public exhibition of the Motion Picture.

Miscellaneous

This Agreement may not be amended except in a writing signed by both parties. If a court finds any provision of this Agreement invalid or unenforceable, the remainder of this Agreement shall be interpreted so as best to effect the intent of the parties. This Agreement shall be governed by and interpreted in accordance with the laws of the State of _____ . This Agreement expresses the complete understanding of the parties with respect to the subject matter and supersedes all prior representations and understandings. Any controversy or claim arising out of or relating to this Agreement shall be settled by binding arbitration in accordance with the rules of the American Arbitration Association, and judgment upon the award rendered by the arbitrator(s) may be entered in any court having jurisdiction. All notices provided for under this Agreement must be in writing and mailed to the addresses provided in the signature portion of this Agreement.

_____

LICENSOR

_____

ADDRESS

_____

PRODUCER

_____

ADDRESS

Explanation for Master Use and Sync License

- The introductory paragraph identifies the parties entering into the agreement. Insert the name of owner of the recordings and songs ("Licensor") and producer ("Producer") of the film or video.
- Fill in the subsequent blanks and list the film or video production (Production), the names of the albums or song titles (Masters), the song titles (Compositions), the performance rights organization (PRO), and the Territory (typically worldwide). The Term is the length of time of the grant, typically, the length of copyright.
- The Grant provisions establish the rights under copyright law (the licenses) that the licensor is granting to the producer.
- Include any payment information in the Payment section and indicate the timing of the payment (for example, "upon execution"). You can see examples of payment provisions in the Master Use and Sync Agreements later in this chapter.
- The Warranty is a contractual promise that the Licensor is legally capable to grant the rights in this agreement. The last sentence in the Warranty section limits the amount of damages the Licensor must pay if it breaches the warranty.
- In the Credits section, the Licensor will establish the type and size of credit the producer should use. A failure to properly credit the composition may result in a loss of licensing rights.
- A Cue Sheet lists each separate musical use in a film or video.
- For an explanation of the Miscellaneous sections, see Chapter 2.
- The agreement must be signed by individuals with the authority to represent the Licensor and the Producer. For information about determining who has authority to sign (also known as "signing capacity"), see the Signatures section in Chapter 2.

Sync License

Below is an agreement that provides for synchronization and videogram rights from a music publisher. It can be used for film, TV, or any audio-visual work that will be released in theaters or on video (simply substitute the medium and type of production). This agreement can be used for purposes of comparison, since a music publisher will likely provide its own license agreement.

If the work will only be released on video and not theatrically, you can remove the synchronization language, as described in the explanation following the agreement. Although this agreement is for films and videos, much of the language and principles apply to other audiovisual uses as well.

Explanation for Sync License

- The introductory paragraph identifies the companies entering into the agreement (the "parties"). Insert the name of the music publisher ("Publisher") and producer ("Producer") of the film or video. Sometimes, a synchronization license may substitute the terms "Licensee" for Producer and "Licensor" for Publisher. The terms "Television Show" or "Audiovisual Work," if applicable, can be substituted for the term "Motion Picture." In this event, change all references throughout the agreement.
- The Grant provisions establish the rights under copyright law (the licenses) that the music publisher is granting to the film producer. The Grant of Audiovisual License establishes the right to synchronize—or use—the music in conjunction with public presentations of the film or video—for example, in theaters or on a television broadcast. The Grant of Videogram License establishes the right to synchronize—or use—the music with the video version of the motion picture, as well as to make copies for sale for home use. If the licensee is going "direct to video" and the film will not be shown in theaters, he or she does not need the Grant of Videogram License, so do not check the box. If no video rights are sought and the film will only be shown in theaters, the licensee does not need the Grant of Videogram License, so do not check that box. The Use in Trailers section permits the use of the Composition in trailers advertising the film.
- The Reservation of Rights section establishes that any rights not covered in this agreement are held by the music publisher.
- The Modifications to Composition section provides that the producer must acquire written permission from the music publisher to make modifications to the song. Failure to obtain permission may endanger the rights to use the music.

Music Synchronization and Videogram License Agreement

Music Synchronization and Videogram License Agreement (the "Agreement") is made between _____ ("Publisher") and _____ ("Producer"). Publisher is the owner of rights for the compositions listed below:

_____

_____

(the "Compositions").

Producer is the owner of rights for the Motion Picture tentatively entitled _____ _____ (the "Motion Picture"). Producer desires to license the Compositions for use in the Motion Picture and in audiovisual devices for home use such as videotapes and DVDs ("Videograms"). The parties agree as follows:

Grant
(Select one or more Grant provisions)

☐ **Grant of Audiovisual License.** Publisher grants to Producer and Producer's successors and assigns the nonexclusive right to record the Compositions solely in synchronization with the Motion Picture (in any medium, now known or later created) within the Territory. Publisher grants to Producer the right to publicly perform the Compositions solely in synchronization with the Motion Picture within the Territory. These public performance rights include public exhibitions of the Motion Picture in theaters and other public places where motion pictures are customarily exhibited, provided that performances outside the United States are cleared by performing rights organizations in accordance with customary practice and customary fees. The public performance rights also include television exhibition of the Motion Picture within the Territory, including all methods of television reproduction and transmissions, provided that the entities broadcasting those performances have licenses from the appropriate performing rights organizations. Any television performance not licensed by performing rights organizations must be cleared directly by the Publisher.

☐ **Grant of Videogram License.** Publisher grants to Producer and his successors and assigns the nonexclusive right to record, copy, and synchronize the Composition, solely as part of the Motion Picture, on audiovisual devices including, but not limited to DVDs and similar compact audiovisual devices that reproduce the entire Motion Picture in substantially its original form ("Videogram"). This Videogram license is solely for the distribution of Videograms intended primarily for home use in the Territory.

☐ **Use in Trailers.** Publisher grants to Producer and his successors and assigns the nonexclusive right to record, copy, synchronize, and perform the Composition in connection with trailers used for the advertising and exploitation of the Motion Picture.

Reservation of Rights

Publisher reserves all rights not granted in this Agreement.

Modifications to Composition

Producer shall not make any change in the original lyrics, if any, or in the fundamental character of the music of the Composition or use the title or any portion of the lyrics of the Composition as the title or subtitle of the Motion Picture without written prior authorization from Publisher.

Territory

The rights granted in this Agreement are for the following: _____ _____ (the "Territory").

Audiovisual License Payments

As payment for the rights granted for the Audiovisual License, Producer shall pay Publisher as follows:

(Select payment option and fill in blanks)

☐ **One-Time Payment.** Producer shall pay Publisher a one-time payment of $ _____ upon first public performance of the Motion Picture or within nine (9) months of signing this agreement, whichever is earlier.

☐ **Advance and Royalties.** Producer shall pay Publisher a nonrefundable advance ("Motion Picture Advance") in the sum of $ _____ recoupable against royalties derived from the Audiovisual License ("Audiovisual Royalties"). Producer shall pay Publisher Audiovisual Royalties of _____ % of net profits from the public exhibition and public performance of the Motion Picture.

☐ **Royalties.** Producer shall pay Publisher ___ % of the net profits from the public exhibition and public performance of the Motion Picture.

Videogram License Payments

As payment for the rights granted for the Videogram License, Producer shall pay Publisher as follows: (*Select payment option and fill in blanks*)

☐ **One-Time Payment.** Producer shall pay Publisher a one-time payment of $_____ within nine (9) months of signing this agreement.

☐ **Advance and Royalties.** Producer shall pay Publisher a nonrefundable advance ("Videogram Advance") in the sum of $ _____ recoupable against royalties derived from the Videogram License ("Videogram Royalties"). Videogram Royalties for Videogram copies of the Motion Picture shall be paid as follows:

☐ **Net Profits.** Producer shall pay Publisher _____ % of the Producer's net profits for all Videogram revenues, including all sales, licenses, or other sources of revenue for Videogram distribution (not including shipping charges or taxes).

☐ **Pro Rata Option.** Producer shall pay Publisher ___ % ("Publisher's Pro Rata Portion") of ___ % of the net revenue for all Videogram income including all sales, licenses, or other sources of revenue for Videogram distribution. Publisher's Pro Rata Portion represents the proportion the Composition bears to the total number of Royalty-bearing compositions contained in the Motion Picture.

Payments & Statements

Within forty-five (45) days after the end of each calendar quarter (the "Royalty Period"), Producer shall furnish an accurate statement of net revenues derived from the licenses granted in this agreement along with any royalty payments. Producer may withhold a reasonable reserve for anticipated returns, refunds, and exchanges of Videograms, and this reserve shall be liquidated no later than twelve (12) months after the respective accounting statement.

Favorable Rates

If a higher royalty rate than set forth in this Agreement becomes payable by operation of law with respect to Videograms sold in a particular country within the Territory, Producer shall either pay the higher royalty to Publisher with respect to that country or delete the Compositions from the Motion Picture with respect to this country. In the event that a musical composition is licensed for a substantially similar use in connection with the Videogram exploitation of the Motion Picture on a more favorable rate, Producer agrees that such favorable rate shall also be granted to Publisher for the licensing of the Composition.

Audit

Producer shall keep accurate books of account and records covering all transactions relating to the licenses granted in this Agreement, and Publisher or its duly authorized representatives shall have the right upon five (5) days prior written notice, and during normal business hours, to inspect and audit these accounts and records.

Warranty

Publisher warrants that it has the power and authority to grant the rights in this Agreement and that the Compositions do not infringe any third-party rights. In no event shall Publisher's liability for a breach of this Warranty exceed the amount of payments received under this Agreement.

Credits

Publisher shall receive credit in the following form: _____ .

This credit shall be provided as follows:

(Select all that apply)

- ☐ similar to all other musical compositions used in the Motion Picture.
- ☐ a single card in the main titles on all prints of the Motion Picture and Videograms.
- ☐ in all paid advertising similar to all other musical compositions used in the Motion Picture.

Samples

Producer shall promptly furnish Publisher with _____ copies of each format of Videogram release.

Cue Sheets

Producer agrees to furnish Publisher a cue sheet of the Motion Picture within thirty (30) days after the first public exhibition of the Motion Picture.

Term

The term of this Agreement is for the term of United States copyright in the Composition including renewal terms, if any.

Termination & Breach

In the event that Producer (or Producer's assigns or licensees) breaches this Agreement and fails to cure such breach within thirty (30) days after notice by Publisher to Producer, this license will automatically terminate and all rights granted under this Agreement shall revert to Publisher. Failure to make timely payments or to provide credit as provided in this Agreement shall be considered a material breach of this Agreement.

Miscellaneous

This Agreement may not be amended except in a writing signed by both parties. If a court finds any provision of this Agreement invalid or unenforceable, the remainder of this Agreement shall be interpreted so as best to effect the intent of the parties. This Agreement shall be governed by and interpreted in accordance with the laws of the State of _____ . This Agreement expresses the complete understanding of the parties with respect to the subject matter and supersedes all prior representations and understandings. Any controversy or claim arising out of or relating to this Agreement shall be settled by binding arbitration in accordance with the rules of the American Arbitration Association, or the rules of _____ , and judgment upon the award rendered by the arbitrator(s) may be entered in any court having jurisdiction. All notices provided for under this Agreement must be in writing and mailed to the addresses provided in the signature portion of this Agreement.

_____

PUBLISHER

_____

ADDRESS

_____

PRODUCER

_____

ADDRESS

- As for the Territory, worldwide rights are preferred if the producer intends to show or distribute the film outside the U.S. If the publisher cannot grant worldwide rights, permission will be required from the holder of rights (usually a foreign music publisher) in each country in which the film will be distributed.

- There are separate payment sections for the audiovisual and the videogram licenses. For each one, choose the payment method that reflects the agreement with the publisher. For the Audiovisual License Payments, you can choose either a one-time payment, an advance against royalties, or royalties with no advance. For the Videogram License Payments, you can choose a one-time payment or an advance against royalties. You also can choose which type of royalties you will be paid—royalties based on net profits or prorated royalties. The pro rata choice provides that you are paid a portion of income based on the total number of songs being used in the video. For example, if ten songs are used on a video, you would receive 1/10 of the music royalty. If you choose this option, enter the composition's proportional share of the whole video in the first blank and the overall royalty rate in the second blank. If there is no videogram license, do not check any options in the Videogram License Payments section.

- The provision entitled Favorable Rates is sometimes referred to as a "Most Favored Nation" clause. It provides that if a country establishes a higher rate of payment for any of the uses described in this agreement, the producer must pay the higher rate. Some film producers may not want to include this provision.

- The Warranty is a contractual promise that the publisher is legally capable of granting the rights in this agreement. The last sentence in the Warranty section limits the amount of damages the publisher must pay if it breaches the warranty.

- In the Credits section, the publisher will establish the type and size of credit the producer should use. A failure to properly credit the composition may result in a loss of licensing rights. The term "single card" refers to a separate credit on a screen with no other credits.

- If the publisher wants the producer to provide samples, indicate the number agreed upon in the Samples section.

- A Cue Sheet lists each separate musical use in a film or video.

- For an explanation of Term, Termination, and Miscellaneous sections, see Chapter 2.
- The agreement must be signed by individuals with the authority to represent the music publisher and the film production company. For information about determining who has authority to sign (also known as "signing capacity"), see the Signatures section in Chapter 2.

Master Use License

In order to use a particular recording on a motion picture or TV sound track, the record company that owns the recording (or your band, if you own rights) must grant a master use license. For instance, if a filmmaker wants to use a recording—not a remake—of Johnny Cash's "Ring of Fire" in a film, the filmmaker will need to obtain a master use license from the record company that owns the recording. The license permits the filmmaker to duplicate the recording on the film sound track. The cost of the master use license depends on the size and type of production and the prominence of the song use within the film (for example, in the foreground or in the background). The cost may range from a few hundred dollars for a student film to thousands of dollars for a feature film.

If a sound track album is released, the record company that owns the original recording will seek a percentage, or "royalty," based upon the sound track album's sales. In some cases, a band (or its record company) may seek an advance payment plus a "rollover"—a payment made when a certain number of video or soundtrack copies have been sold. Costs are also affected by extra payments (known as "reuse fees") that the record company must make to union and guild members who worked on the recording.

Videogram Licenses

If the program will be released on video, DVD, or offered for sale as a download, you must also obtain a videogram license from the record company. In other words, the record company's permission to use the recording in a movie or other program does not authorize the use of the recording on video or DVD releases of the same program. If your program will be available for sale to the public on video (as opposed to only being shown but not sold), you'll need a videogram license regardless of the original format of the program.

Master Use and Videogram License

This Master Use and Videogram License Agreement (the "Agreement") is made between:

_____ ("Owner") and _____ ("Producer").

Owner is the owner of rights for the master recordings:

_____

_____

_____

(the "Masters").

Producer is the owner of rights for the Motion Picture tentatively entitled _____ (the "Motion Picture").

Producer desires to license the Masters for use in the Motion Picture and in audiovisual devices for home use such as videotapes and DVDs ("Videograms"). The parties agree as follows:

Grant

(Select one or more Grant provisions if applicable)

☐ **Grant of Audiovisual License.** Owner grants to Producer and Producer's successors and assigns the nonexclusive right to use and reproduce the Masters solely in synchronization with the Motion Picture in any medium, now known or later created within the Territory. Owner grants to Producer the right to publicly perform the Masters solely in synchronization with the Motion Picture within the Territory. These public performance rights include the public exhibitions of the Motion Picture in theaters and other public places where motion pictures are customarily exhibited and for television exhibition of the Motion Picture including all methods of television reproduction and transmissions within the Territory.

☐ **Grant of Videogram License.** Owner grants to Producer and Producer's successors and assigns the nonexclusive right to record, copy, and synchronize the Masters, solely as part of the Motion Picture, on audiovisual devices including, but not limited to video cassettes, DVDs, and similar compact audiovisual devices that reproduce the entire Motion Picture in substantially its original form ("Videogram"). This Videogram license is solely for the distribution of Videograms intended primarily for home use in the Territory.

☐ **Use in Trailers.** Owner grants to Producer and Producer's successors and assigns, the nonexclusive right to record, copy, synchronize, and perform the Masters in connection with trailers used for the advertising and exploitation of the Motion Picture.

Reservation of Rights

Owner reserves all rights not granted in this Agreement.

Modifications to Masters

Producer shall not make any change in the Masters without written prior authorization from Owner.

Territory

The rights granted in this Agreement are for the following: _____ _____ (the "Territory").

Union Reuse Fees

Owner agrees to provide Producer with all information regarding any reuse fees required by unions or guilds as a result of this license. Producer agrees to pay all such reuse payments including related pension or welfare payments and to indemnify Owner from claims arising from such payments.

Musical Works Synchronization Rights

Producer agrees to obtain all appropriate synchronization, performance, and reproduction rights for the musical compositions embodied on the Masters and to indemnify Owner for any claims arising from such rights.

Audiovisual License Payments

As payment for the rights granted for the Audiovisual License, Producer shall pay Owner as follows:

(Select payment option and fill in blanks)

☐ **One-Time Payment.** Producer shall pay Owner a one-time payment of $ _____ upon first public performance of the Motion Picture or within nine (9) months of signing this agreement, whichever is earlier.

☐ **Advance and Royalties.** Producer shall pay Owner a nonrefundable advance ("Motion Picture Advance") in the sum of $ _____ recoupable against royalties derived from the Audiovisual License ("Audiovisual Royalties"). Producer shall pay Owner Audiovisual Royalties of _____ % of net profits from the public exhibition and public performance of the Motion Picture.

☐ **Royalties.** Producer shall pay Owner _____ % of the net profits from the public exhibition and public performance of the Motion Picture.

Videogram License Payments

As payment for the rights granted for the Videogram License, Producer shall pay Owner as follows:

(Select payment option and fill in blanks)

☐ **One-Time Payment.** Producer shall pay Owner a one-time payment of $ _____ within nine (9) months of signing this agreement.

☐ **Advance and Royalties.** Producer shall pay Owner a nonrefundable advance ("Videogram Advance") in the sum of $ _____ recoupable against royalties derived from the Videogram License ("Videogram Royalties"). Videogram Royalties for Videogram copies of the Motion Picture shall be paid as follows:

    ☐ **Net Profits.** Producer shall pay Owner _____ % of the Producer's net profits for all Videogram revenues including all sales, licenses, or other sources of revenue for Videogram distribution (not including shipping charges or taxes).

    ☐ **Pro Rata Option.** Producer shall pay Owner _____ % ("Owner's Pro Rata Portion") of _____ % of the net revenue for all Videogram income including all sales, licenses, or other sources of revenue for Videogram distribution. Owner's Pro Rata Portion represents the proportion the Composition bears to the total number of Royalty-bearing compositions contained in the Motion Picture.

Payments & Statements

Within forty-five (45) days after the end of each calendar quarter (the "Royalty Period"), Producer shall furnish an accurate statement of net revenues derived from the licenses granted in this agreement along with any royalty payments. Producer may withhold a reasonable reserve for anticipated returns, refunds, and exchanges of Videograms, and this reserve shall be liquidated no later than twelve (12) months after the respective accounting statement.

Audit

Producer shall keep accurate books of account and records covering all transactions relating to the licenses granted in this Agreement, and Owner or its duly authorized representatives shall have the right upon five (5) days prior written notice, and during normal business hours, to inspect and audit these accounts and records.

Warranty

Owner warrants that it has the power and authority to grant the rights in this Agreement and that the Masters do not infringe any third-party rights. In no event shall Owner's liability for a breach of this warranty exceed the amount of payments received under this Agreement.

Credits

Owner shall receive credit in the following form:

_____

This credit shall be provided as follows:

(Select one or more if appropriate)

- ☐ similar to all other Masters used in the Motion Picture.
- ☐ in all paid advertising similar to all other musical Masters used in the Motion Picture.

Samples

Producer shall promptly furnish Owner with ___ copies of each format of Videogram release.

Cue Sheets

Producer agrees to furnish Owner a cue sheet of the Motion Picture within thirty (30) days after the first public exhibition of the Motion Picture.

Term

The term of this Agreement is for the term of United States copyright in the Masters including renewal terms, if any.

Termination & Breach

In the event that Producer (or Producer's assigns or licensees) breaches this Agreement and fails to cure such breach within thirty (30) days after notice by Owner to Producer, this license will automatically terminate and all rights granted under this Agreement shall revert to Owner. Failure to make timely payments or to provide credit as provided in this Agreement shall be considered a material breach of this Agreement.

Miscellaneous

This Agreement may not be amended except in a writing signed by both parties. If a court finds any provision of this Agreement invalid or unenforceable, the remainder of this Agreement shall be interpreted so as best to effect the intent of the parties. This Agreement shall be governed by and interpreted in accordance with the laws of the State of _____ . This Agreement expresses the complete understanding of the parties with respect to the subject matter and supersedes all prior representations and understandings. Any controversy or claim arising out of or relating to this Agreement shall be settled by binding arbitration in accordance with the rules of the American Arbitration Association or the rules of _____, and judgment upon the award rendered by the arbitrator(s) may be entered in any court having jurisdiction. All notices provided for under this Agreement must be in writing and mailed to the addresses provided in the signature portion of this Agreement.

_____

OWNER

_____

ADDRESS

_____

PRODUCER

_____

ADDRESS

Master Use License

Above is an agreement that provides for both master use and videogram rights from the owner of a sound recording (a record company). It can be used for any film, TV show, or video that will be released in theaters or on video. Although this agreement is for films and videos, much of the language and principles applies to other audiovisual uses as well.

Explanation for Master Use License

- The introductory paragraph identifies the companies entering into the agreement (the "parties"). In the Owner blank, insert the name of the owner of the masters (usually the record company), and in the Producer blank enter the name of the producer of the film or video. Sometimes, a synchronization license may substitute the terms "Licensee" for Producer and "Licensor" for Owner. The terms "Television Show" or "Audiovisual Work," if applicable, can be substituted for the term "Motion Picture." In this event, change all references throughout the agreement.

- For explanations regarding the Grant, Reservation of Rights, Modifications to Masters, Territory, License Payments, Payments & Statements, Audit, Warranty, Credits, Samples, and Cue Sheet provisions, see the explanation provided to the Music Synchronization and Videogram License Agreement above. For an explanation of the Term, Termination, and Miscellaneous sections, see Chapter 2.

- The Union Reuse Fees and Musical Works Synchronization Rights sections refer to obligations of the producer. Reuse fees are payments that must be made to the union musicians and engineers who created the masters whenever the masters are used for additional purposes. Musical works synchronization rights are rights that must be obtained from the music publisher to use the song composition. Synchronization rights are acquired from the music publisher by using the Music Synchronization and Videogram License. ●

Keeping Track of Your Band's Money

I n this chapter, we'll look at the various ways that musicians earn and track their money. We'll try to keep the record-keeping instructions brief—this isn't a primer on accounting—and we advise you to implement some simple system to record the money that comes in and goes out of your band. We'll also summarize the revenue sources for bands, most of which are covered in more detail in other chapters.

Tracking Band Finances

When you work a nine-to-five job, one paycheck covers all of your work. But when you're in a band, there are various "paychecks"—for example, streaming income, CD sales, downloads, merchandise, songwriting, and live performance. Tracking and dividing up the money can sometimes be confusing (especially if some band members should receive more than others). In order to sort out payments (and to prepare for your annual tax filing), you'll need to maintain a system for accounting. This doesn't have to be especially formal—a notebook or simple spreadsheet will do—but it should track the money coming in and going out.

For example, if your total band earnings are less than $10,000 a year and you're dealing with common sources of band income like live performing and CD sales, you can probably avoid serious number crunching. A notebook, spreadsheet, or popular software programs—for example, *Quicken*—will be all you need to manage inventory, income, expenses, and taxes. We recommend a spreadsheet or software solution (properly backed up, of course) over a notebook, which could get lost on the tour bus.

If your band business is more complex (for example, you're grossing over $10,000 and you've formed an LLC), you may want to hire a bookkeeper or an accountant, or try a software accounting solution such as *QuickBooks* or a free online accounting service such as Mint.com (see below). By the way, accounting costs are tax deductible.

You can also get some old-fashioned bookkeeping assistance from the IRS by reviewing IRS Publication 583, *Starting a Business and Keeping Records*, free at www.irs.gov.

What Financial Records Should You Keep?

To run an efficient, profitable band business, you will need to track the following:

Income. Income is the money you get from band sales.

- **How to record income.** Separate income into categories such as performance, CD sales, etc.
- **How income affects taxes.** If you get audited by the IRS, unreported income is often the first thing the auditors look for. They will be very suspicious if you have significant bank deposits beyond the income you claimed on your return, even if those deposits are to your personal (not band) account. (If you have significant nontaxable income—an uncle gives you $1,000 as a gift to buy some equipment—make sure to keep the records you'll need to prove where it came from.)

Expenses. Expenses are for band business, such as transportation, salaries, studio rent, telephone, insurance, hotels, and office equipment.

- **How to record expenses.** Download this information to a financial software program or spreadsheet and, as with income, break expenses into discrete categories.
- **How expenses affect taxes.** Don't expect the IRS to allow your tax deductions if you don't keep records to back them up. If you have no records at all, your deductions will be disallowed in an audit, and you might face penalties as well.

Sales tax. You may have a responsibility for assessing and paying sales taxes (see Chapter 17). If sales tax is an issue for you, use a tool that can calculate your sales tax correctly (sometimes, it can vary from county to county) and provide sales tax reports. Programs such as *QuickBooks* provide reports of taxable and nontaxable sales.

Payroll. If your band has one or two employees, you may be able to calculate, track, and record payroll taxes (and the resulting deductions). If you don't want the hassle, consider an online payroll service such as *Paychex Payroll Solutions* or *QuickBooks With Payroll.*

Money owed to your band. Known as "accounts receivable," this is money that others owe to your band business. For bands, accounts receivable are the money owed by a distributor or a record company. You may not need to track this as a separate category if you are maintaining a simple accounting system; simply enter it when you get paid. If you are tracking things more completely, you can enter when the payments are due, then enter when the payment is received and officially becomes income.

Money you owe to others. Known as "accounts payable," this is money that you owe—for example, fees, loans, studio rent, or uncompleted payments for inventory. Once paid, these amounts become part of your business expenses. If you're maintaining a simple bookkeeping system, you don't need to track this; more advanced band bookkeeping systems require that you enter this information.

Income taxes. Accurate accounting of inventory, income, and expenses is essential for preparing your taxes. Most band business owners use tax preparation software that integrates with their accounting software.

Sales and inventory. Your band's inventory consists of the physical items you sell—for example merchandise, vinyl recordings, CDs, DVDs, etc. Inventory is treated differently from other expenses for tax purposes (see Chapter 17), so accurate inventory reporting is essential on April 15. Again, with simple bookkeeping, you can track this with a spreadsheet. More complex inventory management requires software such as *QuickBooks*. Programs such as *TurboTax* can incorporate your inventory information to determine your tax bill.

What About Mint.com for Band Finances?

Mint.com is a free online service that compiles and categorizes all of your accounts —checking, savings, credit cards, and cash—into one Web page. Although designed for personal, not business use, Mint.com is actually more than suitable for most band finance management. What's nice about it is that it doesn't provide access to your online accounts; it merely collects data from these accounts. So, you can provide the username and password to other band members who want to monitor accounting and perhaps help with the categorization of expenses. The program will take a little tweaking for your band's business, but it should work if you devote a little time to it. And you can't beat the price.

Choose an Accounting Method

There are two basic ways to account for a band's income and expenses: the cash method and the accrual method. Most band businesses use the simpler cash method.

The cash method. With this method, you count band income when your band actually receives it and expenses when your band actually pays them. For example, if you perform a show on December 30 but don't get paid until January 5, you record the income in January. Similarly, if you buy a video camera for your band business on credit, you record the expense not when you charge the camera and take it home, but when you pay the bill. (The IRS won't let you manipulate your income by, for example, not depositing a club's check until the next year; you must report income when it becomes available to you, not when you actually decide to deal with it.)

The accrual method. Under the accrual method, you record income as you earn it and expenses as you incur them. For example, if you perform a show in December, that's when you record the income you expect to receive from it, no matter when the club actually gets around to paying you. (If the club never pays, you can eventually deduct the money as a bad debt.) And if you charge some band equipment, you record the expense on the day of purchase, not when you pay the bill.

As you can see, the cash method is much easier to use; most of us deal with our personal finances this way, so it's a system we're familiar with. It also gives you a clear picture of your actual cash on hand at any point in time.

As long as your band business makes less than $1 million a year, you may choose whichever method seems right for your business. If your band business made more than $1 million in any of the last three years, you might have to use the accrual method. (Of course, if your band is pulling in a million dollars, congratulations; you're probably getting some professional tax and accounting advice.) For more information, check out IRS Publication 334, *Tax Guide for Small Business*, and IRS Publication 538, *Accounting Periods and Methods*.

Keep Your Band Business and Personal Finances Separate

For IRS and general record-keeping purposes, it really helps if you maintain separate accounts for your band business. This is essential if you have created an LLC or corporation for your band as these business forms require that you preserve the band's business identity separate from the personal assets of the members. However, we recognize that for a small band partnership, setting up a band bank account is sometimes easier said than done. One reason is that your bank may require fees and documentation (including an Employee Identification Number; see Chapter 17) as well as information regarding individual members and their status.

There are benefits to keeping separate band business accounts; it should simplify your bookkeeping life. If you cannot manage a separate business checking account, at least consider a credit card dedicated solely to your band business. Many bands do this under a personal card handled by one member (provided that the card-carrying member doesn't get stuck with unpaid monthly statements). With one card dedicated to your band expenses, you'll have less trouble downloading and calculating your annual expenses and interest (if you don't pay off the total each month).

What Is Cash Flow and Why Is It Essential?

You've probably heard people complain about cash flow and maybe wondered what exactly that means. Simply put, the money that comes in and goes out of your band is your cash flow. Band business cash flow is really no different from personal cash flow. For example, when you're in a music equipment store trying to decide whether to spend a portion of your paycheck on a new pedal, that's a cash flow decision. If you use the money on the pedal, you may not have enough to pay for your new hubcaps.

Proper cash flow management is the key to profitability for your band business (and for its survivability). Think of cash flow as your band business's lifeblood. If it is interrupted—and this is true even for highly profitable ventures—it can lead to a band's cardiac arrest.

Four Common Causes of Cash Flow Problems in a Band

Four common reasons that band businesses have cash flow problems are:

Accounts receivables are late. When people are not paying your band in a timely manner, you'll always be short of cash. Are you reluctant to chase local club owners, distributors, a record company, or your manager? We know you didn't join a band to collect money but you'll have to overcome that reluctance and speed up payments. The secret of business collections is to get busy, stay at it, be reasonable and don't give up on getting the money. Also, the earlier you go after a late payment, the better; collections experts report that debts are more difficult to collect as more time passes.

Inventory is turning slowly. Inventory—your merchandise, vinyl/recordings, and CDs—are your band's cash transformed into products. So when you're holding unsold inventory, you're really preventing access to your band's cash. In addition, storing, creating, and maintaining inventory creates a financial burden. That's why some bands offer special "two-fers" or "band bundles" (a shirt, a 45, and a band photo) in order to keep the band inventory moving and generating revenue. Whatever it takes, the key to any successful business is to keep the inventory moving.

Expenses are not controlled. It may be axiomatic, but your failure to control your band's costs can be a major factor in cash flow problems. Always look for ways to lower expenses. You'll be surprised: Even the leanest band can shed a few pounds.

Bills are paid before they're due. When possible, we recommend paying your bills early. Often, however, there are benefits to waiting—say, 30 days— and then paying the bill. In fact, in terms of holding on to your cash, it's even better to get longer terms for paying back other businesses.

Using a Credit Card to Finance Your Band

In the heyday of easy credit—back in 2007—the average band member had access to $12,190 from credit cards. So it's easy to see why so many bands are funded with plastic. We don't need to dwell on the downsides—you're probably already aware that credit card companies charge high interest rates and extraordinary penalties. And if you miss a payment on one card, all of your cards can raise their interest rates. You can easily get in over your head when you take a cash advance—more unbearable fees and often no grace period (which means you pay interest from the day you take the advance, even if you pay off your balance within a month).

We advise using credit cards to make purchases that you are confident you can pay off within a month or two. But in general, we advise against using credit cards to fund your band—that is, to make large long-term purchases or cash advances that you will have difficulty paying off in the near future. The interest rates are just too high.

Of course, our advice ignores the reality of operating a band. Bands, like every other small business, depend on plastic. How else will you rent that van at the airport, or secure that emergency amp in some distant town? So, is there any way to alleviate the negatives? Here are a few suggestions.

When shopping for a card for your band (and we're including those acquired in an individual band member's name), be wary of teaser rates (low introductory rates that jump after a few months) and check the grace period (the number of days you're charged interest on purchases). Many companies have been shortening their grace period for purchases from 30 to 20 days. Shop around for perks—airline miles, travel discounts, or other purchasing credits. Your band will benefit. Always compare the periodic rate that will be used to calculate the finance charge. You can find rates at websites comparing current credit offers (type "credit card compare" into a search engine).

Don't charge band expenses if your credit card balances are greater than 80% of your credit limits; you've already got a credit card problem. One other thought: Bankruptcy laws make it much harder to get rid of credit card debts even if you file for bankruptcy—particularly if your income is greater than the median income for your state.

Categorize Sources of Band Income

By tracking income separately, you can attribute expenses to that particular item—for example, you shouldn't be deducting CD manufacturing costs from performing income. Below are the common sources of income for musicians. It's helpful to look at these from a cash flow perspective. What are the expenses involved in earning this money and how much of this money should be put back in—for example, how much of CD sales should be saved for future replication.

Performance (Live) Income

Live performing income is usually divided equally among band members after deductions. Deductions commonly include a cut for managers, booking agents, tour managers, and for rentals, transportation, and food (discussed in more detail in Chapter 6). When bands are on tour, performance income is often plowed back into the general band fund in order to cover unforeseen expenses. You may want to record this income in one general category (performance income); or break it down based on touring and nontouring income, or even based on various venues in order to determine your booking priorities.

Merchandise Income

Merchandise income is commonly divided equally among band members after deductions to the club, manager, agent, and whoever fronted the costs of the merchandise manufacture or artwork. Some bands put aside a sum to be used to manufacture and ship the next order. You may want to record this income in one general category (merchandise); or break it down based on each merchandise item (or even size). For example, if you are constantly selling out of women's sweetheart-cut T-shirts, then by tracking that item separately, you'll know when it's time to reorder (and that your female fans are solid buyers of merchandise).

Sales of Physical Products (CDs, Vinyl, Flash Drives, DVDs)

Bands without a record company (meaning they pay to manufacture their own recordings) usually divide the money equally after deducting their expenses: manufacturing, recording costs, producer and engineer costs, artwork, and publishing royalties (if you must pay them). Some bands put aside a portion of this income to be used to manufacture and ship the next group of CDs or vinyl recordings. You may want to record this income in one general category (CD sales), but it's wiser to break it down based on each individual title. If you participate in a sales program such as CD Baby, you can import sales by title into your spreadsheet program.

If your disc was released by a record company, then your band should periodically receive a check. Review the accompanying statement and deductions to be sure it coincides with your contract (see Chapter 14 for the lengthy list of potential deductions). Bands usually divide record company income equally unless a manager or lawyer also gets a cut.

Digital Downloads and Streaming Income

Payments for sales of digital downloads and from webcaster streaming services should be treated in the same manner as sales of band CDs. The payments may be made directly to your PayPal account (for example, if you are using an aggregator such as CD Baby or TuneCore) or may come in the form a check from your record company (assuming you have granted them the digital rights). As with CD sales, a separate payment may be made to songwriters (see Chapter 8). You may find it beneficial to track the sales by download title, as this will provide you with information about your downloaders.

Crowdfunding

Crowdfunding—when a band raises money from a wide variety of contributors via the Internet—has been used to pay for band recordings, touring, videos, and band merchandise. Contributors are usually promised unique goods or services (autographed CDs, signed set lists) based on the size of their contribution. Crowdfunding has been especially popular among musicians via sites such as PledgeMusic, ArtisteConnect, and Feed the Muse (as well as traditional crowdfunding sites such as Kickstarter, GoFundMe, Indiegogo, and Rockethub). Money acquired from crowdfunding is income for tax purposes (not a gift).

A Band Song Is Played at an AM or FM (Over-the-Air) Radio Station

The only payments made for over-the-air radio play are payments made to songwriters by performing rights organizations such as ASCAP and BMI. As we discussed in Chapters 2 and 8, your band should reach an agreement amongst its members regarding ownership of band songs and how the income is divided. The songwriters will receive separate payments from BMI and ASCAP (assuming you've signed up and listed your songs with either of these organizations); the band's music publishing entity will also receive a payment, to be divided as established in the band's partnership or LLC agreement.

A Band Song Is Played at a Web or Satellite Station

When Internet-based or satellite radio stations play a song, two payments will be made. One is from the performing rights organizations (see the previous section on over-the-air play) and the other is from SoundExchange (see Chapter 11), which pays the owner of the master recording (your band or your record company). (Your band will need to sign up with SoundExchange to get paid.) The publishing income should be divided according to your band agreement; the SoundExchange payment will probably be divided equally among band members after any deductions.

Use of a Band Song in a Television/Movie Soundtrack

If one of your band's songs is used in a movie or TV soundtrack, payments will be established by the master use license (for the sound recording) and a sync license (for the songwriters). There will be additional payments to the songwriters via ASCAP or BMI when the show is aired, streamed, or displayed. When the show is released on DVD, sold as a download, or a soundtrack is released on CD, there may be additional payments to the songwriters for mechanical licenses for reproduction of the song, and to the band for the right to make copies of these disks. Songwriter money is divided by the terms of the band agreement; other income is usually divided equally.

Endorsements/Corporate Sponsorships

Some bands attract attention from corporate sponsors that pay the band for permitting the use of corporate banners or advertising (or other tie-ins) at live shows. The sponsorship may also extend to special club performances, print ads, etc. (This is different than the endorsements in which individual band members receive merchandise in exchange for plugging musical products.) Because the full band participates in these endorsements, it makes sense that the band should divide this income after deducting money for the usual suspects (manager, attorneys, sponsorship agents, etc.). (Note: This is different than if a corporate sponsor chooses a band's song for placement in an ad, discussed below.)

Use of a Band Song in an Advertisement

If you're lucky enough to have one of your band's songs used in an advertisement, the arrangement usually involves two parts (joined in one agreement). One part is a license for use of the master recording; the other is a license for the right to use the song copyright. (If the song is used in an Internet or TV commercial—that is, with images—it's called a sync license.) The payment for the use of the master recording is usually split among band members (after deductions by managers, agents, etc.), and the payment for the music is usually divided in the same proportion established for music publishing arrangements. The methods of division are discussed in Chapters 2 and 8.

Subscription Sales

Online music subscriptions bring in revenue when fans pay a monthly or annual fee to receive free downloads of new songs. Legally, the songwriters are entitled to mechanical royalties from each download (see Chapter 8); however, the band may agree to forgo this and to split all income equally among the band members after deducting costs and fees.

Use of a Band Song in a Video Game

This is generated and treated in the same way as the use of a band song in a movie or TV show (see above; revenue is earned via a master use license and a sync license).

Use of a Band Song as a Ringtone

Companies that sell ringtones made from your recordings must pay a master use license fee to the owner of the recording (your band or your record company) and a mechanical fee to the music publisher/songwriter. Additional payment is made by ASCAP or BMI to the songwriters (divided according to your band agreement).

Table Summarizing Sources of Band Income

Type of Income	Source
Live Performance	Payment to band from club owner or booking agent.
CD Sales	Payment to band in form of direct payment (if sold from website or at shows), store payment (if consignment), distributor payment (if you have a distribution deal), or record company payment (if you are signed). Payment by record company to music publisher/songwriters for mechanical license fee (per unit).
Merchandise	Payment directly to band, or from online sources (CafePress), or indirectly after deductions made by club owner.
Crowdfunding	Payments directly to band via crowdsourcing sites such as Kickstarter, Rockethub, and Pledgemusic.
Digital Downloads	Payment to band in form of direct payment (if sold from your website) or distributor payment (if you have an aggregator). Payment by record company to music publisher/songwriters for a mechanical license fee per download.
Streaming (Webcasting)	Payment to band or record company for sound recordings rights, distributed to unsigned bands via aggregator. Payment to songwriters for streaming mechanicals via aggregator or HarryFox (HFA); payment to songwriters for performance royalties via aggregator or performing rights organization (PRO).
AM/FM Over-the-Air Radio Play	Payment to music publisher/songwriters from PROs (ASCAP, BMI, SESAC).
Webcast or Satellite Station Play	Payment to music publisher/songwriters from PROs (ASCAP, BMI, SESAC). Payment to band (or sound recording owner if band has record company) from SoundExchange.
Movie/TV Soundtrack	Payment to band from movie/TV production company for master use license; additional payment(s) if sound track recording is released. Payment to music publisher/songwriters from movie/TV production company for sync license. Payment from PROs (ASCAP, BMI, SESAC) to music publisher/songwriters when television show is broadcast or movie is shown; payment to music/publisher/ songwriters if soundtrack sold as a download, DVD or CD soundtrack for mechanical license fee (per unit).
Endorsements/Corporate Sponsorships	Payment (or other compensation) to band from corporate sponsor.

Table Summarizing Sources of Band Income (continued)	
Type of Income	**Source**
Advertisement Featuring Song	Similar to movie/TV payments with additional twists if song is used in nontraditional ways (free downloads, etc.).
Subscription Sales	Direct payment to band or, if managed by third-party distributor, treated like digital downloads.
Video Game Featuring Song	Treated like movie/TV soundtrack payments.
Ringtones	Payment to band/record company by ringtone distributor for master use license fee. Payments to the music publisher/songwriter by ringtone distributor for mechanical royalties (per unit); additional payment made by ASCAP or BMI to the music/publisher songwriters.
AdSense or Affiliate Payment	Payment to band from online company (Google, Amazon, etc.) for ads or links that appear at band-related sites.

AdSense/Affiliate Sales and Related Auxiliary Advertising Income

If your band maintains a blog or website, Adsense and Affiliate marketing can be peripheral sources of income. We use the term "Adsense" to refer to any pay-per-click advertising model. Basically, you set up a blog or website and then enroll in a pay-per-click program such as Google Adsense. Affiliate marketing is similar to Adsense in that you earn money by using your website to sell another company's product or services—for example, people click through your site to buy your album at Amazon. Most bands divide this income equally among band members. ●

Taxes

You may not want to think about taxes, but some of the tips in this chapter could save your band hundreds of dollars (or more) in tax payments. If you're one of the lucky bands that makes a healthy profit, you definitely should learn at least the basics on taxes. And if your band is losing money, you might be surprised to learn that you can use those losses to reduce your tax bill from any day job you might have. In other words, learning how tax laws affect your band and its individual members can save you money, whether or not your band is really making it (yet).

In preparing you for the taxman, this chapter will discuss how your business form can affect your taxes and will describe the types of deductions that can save money. Deductions are an important element in the financial success of every band's business. We'll also help you understand principles of payroll taxes and how to obtain a federal employer identification number (called FEIN or EIN). When you become more successful, you will be glad that you learned these tax basics.

Taxing Situations: Understanding Your Band's Tax Responsibilities

There are three types of taxes that your band or individual band members may be responsible for paying:

- **Income tax.** Each year, your band must declare all band income (minus deductions) to the federal, state, and maybe local tax agency. (See "Local Business Taxes and Sales Taxes," below.) How you do this depends on your business form (partnership, corporation, sole proprietorship, and so on). For example, if your band is a partnership, one of the band partners would prepare a partnership tax form declaring the band's profit or loss, and each member would declare a portion of the profit or loss on his or her individual tax return. If the band is a sole proprietorship and you're the sole proprietor, you simply report the band income or loss on your personal tax return. This chapter discusses only federal taxes, though most state taxes have similar rules. Contact your state tax authority for specific instructions for your state. We provide more details on business forms and deductions below.

- **Self-employment tax.** Band members who operate as sole proprietorships, partnerships, and limited liability companies (LLCs) must all pay self-employment taxes if their net earnings from self-employment for the year are $400 or more. You pay self-employment taxes on your net band income, not your entire income. To determine your net self-employment income, you first figure the net income you've earned from your band. If you're a sole proprietor, use IRS Schedule C, *Profit or Loss From Business*, to determine your net business income. If your band is a partnership, your income will be indicated on your K-1 form. It's easy to compute the amount of your self-employment tax. First, determine your net self-employment income as described above. If it's below the Social Security tax ceiling ($127,200 in 2017) multiply it by 15.3% or 0.153. For example, if your net income from the band was $10,000, you would have to pay approximately $1,530 in self-employment taxes. If you have two jobs—for example, one as an employee of a photocopy shop and the other as self-employed musician—the self-employment tax would apply only to the income from your musician gigs. You pay self-employment taxes directly to the IRS during the year as part of your estimated taxes.

RESOURCE

For additional information on self-employment taxes, see IRS Publication 533, *Self-Employment Tax.* You can obtain this and all other IRS publications by calling the IRS at 800-TAX-FORM, by visiting your local IRS office, or at the IRS website (www.irs.gov).

- **Payroll tax.** Whenever your band hires employees, your band is responsible for paying federal and state payroll taxes. If your band hires an independent contractor instead of an employee, you do not have to make these payments. Below, we discuss the differences between employees and independent contractors, and we provide more details about payroll tax payments.

Local Business Taxes and Sales Taxes

If you are registered to do business in your city or county, your band may have to pay a local business tax—either a fixed fee or a fee based on your annual income. If you sell recordings or merchandise directly to consumers (not to retail outlets or distributors), you may have to pay state or city sales tax. Check with your local sales tax office. (Note: Some states, such as California, have become very aggressive about going after sales tax revenue.)

Income Taxes: Different Rules for Different Businesses

Each business form—sole proprietorship, partnership, corporation, or LLC—has its own tax rules and procedures. As a general rule, taxes are much simpler for unincorporated businesses such as sole proprietorships and partnerships. That's because income from unincorporated businesses is simply treated as personal income to the owners. In other words, the business itself is not taxed. For example, if your four-person band is a partnership, any profits the band makes are divided among the four owners, who report them as personal income much like income from a job or investments. Corporations, on the other hand, are considered to be separate entities from their owners, and they pay their own taxes. This section will explain how taxes apply to each different business form and how to file them. For more information on business forms, see Chapter 2.

Reporting Band Income

The IRS has become sophisticated in sniffing out music income. For example, the IRS guide to auditing musicians advises examiners to contact booking agencies and unions for verification about musician income. Auditors are trained to search out income from record and merchandise sales and may even ask for copies of partnership or individual bank accounts.

It is a crime to deliberately fail to report income or to lie to the IRS. If you underreport your income, you could be subject to additional taxes and serious financial penalties—even jail time. In other words, *report your band income*. When in doubt about whether a payment is considered "income," speak to an accountant or tax expert for advice.

Flow-Through and Entity Taxation, Defined

In this section we use two common tax terms—flow-through (or pass-through) and entity taxation (which is related to double taxation).

Flow-through occurs when your band business profits and losses are reported on your individual tax return—that is, they pass through the business to you. Sole proprietorships, partnerships, and, in most cases, LLCs operate as flow-through businesses.

Entity taxation occurs when the IRS considers your band business as a separate tax-paying creature. (Corporations and some LLCs operate this way.) Under an entity-taxation business form, the corporation or LLC must pay taxes and file a tax return.

Partnership Taxes

Most bands are partnerships, because any business in which two or more persons are the owners is a partnership. A formal agreement is not necessary to create a partnership, although we recommend that your band use a written band partnership agreement to establish the details of how the partnership will operate. (A sample is provided in Chapter 2.)

Technically speaking, a partnership itself does not pay taxes. Instead, any profit or loss of the business is divided among the partners and reported with their personal income tax returns. Since income simply passes through the business to the owners, partnerships are called "pass-through" tax entities. (See "Flow-Through and Entity Taxation, Defined," above.) Though a partnership does not owe taxes, it must complete and file a tax return to report any income or losses. Form 1065, *U.S. Partnership Return of Income*, is used. Since no taxes are ever due with Form 1065, it is called an "informational return."

Whoever files Form 1065 (a partner, an accountant, or a lawyer, for example) must also give each partner a report called Schedule K-1, which contains all the relevant profit or loss information about the partnership. Based on the information in the K-1 form, and based on the partnership agreement regarding each partner's share of profit or loss, each band partner declares a portion of the profit or loss on his or her individual tax returns. Each partner reports his or her share of band income or losses on Schedule E, which is submitted with that person's individual 1040 form. If a band partner has a day job and the band loses money, the partner can deduct his or her share of loss from the other income, which can reduce his or her tax bill.

> **EXAMPLE:** Bob is a member of the El Niños, a band that lost money in 2017. According to Bob's K-1 Form, Bob can deduct a $2,000 band loss from his total income, which includes wages from working at a music equipment store. By deducting the band loss, Bob pays less income tax for 2017.

In addition to income taxes, all band partners must pay self-employment tax on band profits. See the section above on self-employment taxes.

Your band will need a federal employer identification number (FEIN) to file a partnership tax return. Later in this chapter we explain how to get one. The FEIN will help your band to open a bank account and deposit checks under your band name.

In summary, if your band is classified as a partnership by the IRS, here are some rules to remember:

- Partnerships, though not taxed separately, must prepare and file a Form 1065, usually filed on April 15.
- The partnership must issue a K-1 form showing each partner's share of the income or loss. The K-1 is filed with each partner's individual return.
- Each partner must pay a tax based on his or her "distributive share," not on what the partner may have actually received. Unless a partnership agreement says otherwise, all partners are presumed to have an equal distributive share in the partnership.
- Even if the partnership leaves profits in the business, the partners must pay taxes on those profits. (If your partnership is able to retain profits each year, consider forming a corporation.)
- Partners must pay quarterly estimated income taxes, as well as self-employment tax for Social Security and Medicare contributions.

Sole Proprietorships

A sole proprietorship is a business that is run by just one person. Unlike a partnership, which must submit an informational return, sole proprietorships do not have to file any tax returns for the business. Only the owner reports the income with a personal return. Like partnerships, sole proprietorships are pass-through tax entities. Income from the sole proprietorship is reported on Schedule C, which is submitted with the individual 1040 form. If the sole proprietorship loses money, the sole proprietor can deduct that loss from income from other jobs, reducing the tax obligation.

Filing as a sole proprietorship is appropriate if the band is run by one person (the band leader) who hires musicians to perform in the band and pays each musician a fee or a salary. The paid musicians do not have an ownership interest in the band. In that situation, the sole proprietor/band leader may have to file payroll taxes if the other band members were treated like employees. Keep in mind that having employees raises a host of legal issues that you may want to avoid. (See the section below on employees and independent contractors.)

An FEIN is not necessary for a sole proprietor to file taxes, because the personal Social Security number of the owner may be used. However, some tax experts suggest obtaining and using an FEIN for business taxes anyway, in order to keep business and personal tax records separate.

Sole proprietorships must pay self-employment taxes.

In summary, if the band business is owned by you and you haven't formed an LLC or corporation:

- You must report your business income or loss on a Schedule C, filed with your individual or joint tax return.
- You must pay quarterly estimated income taxes, as well as self-employment tax for Social Security and Medicare contributions.
- You are eligible for tax-sheltered retirement plans.

Preparing Taxes

Consider hiring a tax preparation expert or accountant knowledgeable in the music business when preparing your tax return. While you can expect to pay $200 to $1,000 for preparation of tax returns, a savvy tax professional will probably save your band the cost of this fee and more. You may not have to use a professional for each year you file, but it is sometimes helpful to have a professional tax preparer create your returns at least for the first year, so that you can see the form and style that will be suitable. In Chapter 16, we explain how to track your band's income and expenses in preparation for tax preparation.

Corporations

Unlike sole proprietorships and partnerships, corporations are considered to be separate legal entities from their owners (also called shareholders). In other words, when you incorporate your business you create a new legal being that is responsible for taxes and is subject to many state and federal laws. Corporations' profits do not pass through to the corporate owners for tax purposes, but instead are taxed at special corporate rates. Among other things, this means that corporate losses cannot be deducted from the shareholders' income on their individual tax returns. In some cases you can save tax money by operating as a corporation, but the fees and legal costs associated with running one often outweigh any financial benefit. In order to become a corporation (to "incorporate"), a band must file incorporation papers with its state's Secretary of State and pay a number of fees and minimum taxes.

If your band is a corporation, you will need the assistance of an accountant or other professional for tax preparation and planning.

Below we provide a basic summary of corporate tax principles:

- Bands that operate as corporations have more tax reporting responsibilities than any other business form. So get ready for paperwork.
- Since corporations are separate tax entities, the owners must prepare a tax return for the corporation and pay corporate taxes, if any are owed.
- If you're an employee of the corporation or receive income from the corporation, you must report that on your individual tax return.
- Under the Tax Cuts and Job Act ("TCJA," effective 2018) all C corporations are subject to single flat tax at the rate of 21%. This replaces the tax rates ranging from 15% to 35% that C corporations paid under prior law.

> **TIP**
> **You can avoid the burden of double taxation**—for example, by paying higher salaries to shareholders, thereby reducing profits, or by reinvesting profits. An accountant can assist you in legally avoiding corporate income taxes.

Limited Liability Companies (LLCs)

A limited liability company (LLC) is a hybrid between a corporation and a partnership. Like a partnership, profits and losses are passed on to the owners of the LLC (your band), who then report them on individual tax returns. But, like a corporation, an LLC generally offers its owners protection from personal liability for business obligations. An LLC does not itself pay taxes but, like a partnership, it does have to file a tax return reporting income and expenses. LLCs are also subject to state fees that make them more expensive to run than partnerships.

All band owners in an LLC must pay self-employment tax on the band's net taxable income (that is, its profit). Below is a summary of rules regarding LLC taxation:

- The owners of a band LLC can choose either pass-through or entity taxation. (Most choose pass-through.) Your tax advisor can help you make that decision.
- If the owners choose pass-through taxation, the LLC operates like a general partnership and prepares and files a Form 1065. The LLC must also issue its members K-1 forms to be included with their individual returns.
- If the LLC has only one owner (and pass-through taxation has been chosen), the owner operates like a sole proprietorship and files a Schedule C to report the LLC's income.
- Although no federal tax is paid for a pass-through LLC, some states such as California impose taxes on LLCs.

Paying Estimated Tax

Self-employed musicians do not have the luxury of waiting until April 15 to pay all their taxes for the previous year. The IRS wants to get its money a lot faster than that, so the self-employed are required to pay taxes on their estimated annual incomes in four payments spread out over each year. These are called estimated taxes and are used to pay both income taxes and self-employment taxes.

Because of estimated taxes, self-employed musicians need to carefully budget their money. If you fail to set aside enough of your earnings to pay your estimated taxes, you could face a huge tax bill on April 15—and have a tough time coming up with the money to cover it.

Who Must Pay

You must pay estimated taxes if you are a sole proprietor, partner in a partnership, or member of an LLC and you expect to owe at least $1,000 in federal tax for the year. If you've formed a C corporation, it may also have to pay estimated taxes.

However, if you paid no taxes last year—for example, because your business made no profit or you weren't working—you don't have to pay any estimated tax this year no matter what your tax tally for the year. But this is true only if you were a U.S. citizen or resident for the year and your tax return for the previous year covered the whole 12 months.

Most States Have Estimated Taxes, Too

If your state has income taxes, it probably requires the self-employed to pay estimated taxes. The due dates are generally the same as for federal estimated tax. State income tax rates are lower than federal income taxes. The exact rate depends on the state in which you live. Contact your state tax office for information and the required forms.

How Much You Must Pay

You should normally determine how much estimated tax to pay after completing your tax return for the previous year. Most people want to pay as little estimated tax as possible during the year so they can earn interest on their money instead of handing it over to the IRS. However, the IRS imposes penalties if you don't pay enough estimated tax. There's no need to get excessively concerned about these penalties. They aren't terribly large in the first place, and it's easy to avoid having to pay them. All you have to do is pay at least the smaller of:

- 90% of your total tax due for the current year, or
- 100% of the tax you paid the previous year.

You normally make four estimated tax payments each year. There are three different ways you can calculate your payments. You can use any one of the three methods, and you won't have to pay a penalty as long as you pay the minimum total the IRS requires as explained above. One of the methods—basing your payments on last year's tax—is extremely easy to use. The other two are more complex, but might permit you to make smaller payments.

RESOURCE
IRS Form 1040-ES contains a worksheet to use to calculate your estimated tax. You can obtain the form by calling the IRS at 800-TAX-FORM, visiting your local IRS office, or downloading it at www.irs.gov. Or, if you have a tax preparation computer program, it can help you with the calculations. If you have your taxes prepared by an accountant, he or she should determine what estimated tax to pay. If your income changes greatly during the year, ask your accountant to help you prepare a revised estimated tax payment schedule.

RESOURCE
See IRS Publication 505, *Tax Withholding and Estimated Tax,* for a detailed explanation of the annualized income method. You can obtain the form by calling the IRS at 800-TAX-FORM, visiting your local IRS office, or downloading it at www.irs.gov.

When to Pay Estimated Tax

Estimated tax must ordinarily be paid in four installments, with the first one due on April 15. However, you don't have to start making payments until you actually earn income. If you don't receive any income by March 31, you can skip the April 15 payment. In this event, you'd ordinarily make three payments for the year starting on June 15. If you don't receive any income by May 31, you can skip the June 15 payment as well and so on.

The following chart shows the due dates and the periods each installment covers.

Estimated Tax Due	
Income received for the period	**Estimated tax due**
January 1 through March 31	April 15
April 1 through May 31	June 15
June 1 through August 31	September 15
September 1 through December 31	January 15 of next year

Your estimated tax payment must be postmarked by the dates noted below, but the IRS need not actually receive them then. If any of these days falls on a weekend or legal holiday, the due date is the next business day.

How to Pay

The IRS wants to make it easy for you to send in your money, so the mechanics of paying estimated taxes are very simple. If you made estimated tax payments last year, you should receive a copy of the current year's Form 1040-ES in the mail. It will have payment vouchers preprinted with your name, address, and Social Security number.

If you did not pay estimated taxes last year, get a copy of Form 1040-ES from the IRS. Do so by calling the IRS at 800-TAX-FORM, visiting your local IRS office, or downloading it at www.irs.gov. After you make your first payment, the IRS should mail you a Form 1040-ES package with the preprinted vouchers.

Paying the Wrong Amount

The IRS imposes a money penalty if you underpay your estimated taxes. Fortunately, the penalty is not very onerous. You have to pay the taxes due plus a percentage penalty for each day your estimated tax payments were unpaid. The percentage is set by the IRS each year.

The penalty has ranged between 3% and 5% in recent years. This is the mildest of all IRS interest penalties. Even if you paid no estimated tax at all during the year, the underpayment penalty you'd have to pay would be no more than 5% of your total taxes due for the year.

> **RESOURCE**
> **You can find out what the current penalty is** in the most recent version of IRS Publication 505, *Tax Withholding and Estimated Tax*. You can obtain the form by calling the IRS at 800-TAX-FORM, visiting your local IRS office, or downloading it at www.irs.gov.

The penalty is comparable to the interest you'd pay on borrowed money. Many self-employed people decide to pay the penalty at the end of the tax year rather than take money out of their businesses during the year to pay estimated taxes. If you do this, though, make sure you pay all the taxes you owe for the year by April 15 of the following year. If you don't, the IRS will tack on additional interest and penalties. The IRS usually adds a penalty of ½% to 1% per month to a tax bill that's not paid when due.

Tax Deductions: Secrets for Saving on Taxes

One easy way to reduce your tax obligation is for your band to take, or "declare," every permissible deduction. The IRS lets musicians deduct "ordinary and necessary" business expenses, such as practice studio rental, equipment, and touring expenses. Deducting these expenses from taxable income will reduce the net amount that is subject to taxes. Despite this opportunity to save money on taxes, IRS examiners routinely find that musicians fail to claim expenses. In other words, musicians often pay more taxes than necessary because they don't deduct their costs.

A deduction is an expense or the value of an item that you can subtract from your gross income to determine your taxable income—that is, the amount you earn that is subject to taxation. The more deductions you have, the less income tax you pay. Let's say your band earned $10,000 in one year. If your band deducted its expenses of $10,000, that would wipe out all your income, so you would owe no taxes. This simple principle—reducing taxable income through deductions—is a mantra of most businesses, and you should use it in your band's business as well.

If your band loses money—that is, the deductions are more than the income—then you may be able to deduct this loss against your income from another job. That is, you can apply your band's loss against income from your day job, thereby lowering your personal taxes.

Keeping Receipts and Records

The trick to saving money with business deductions is to create a system to keep track of financial information. Save your receipts, canceled checks, and credit card statements. Your system doesn't need to be complex; simply place your receipts in a box and tally them up at the end of each month using a ledger or software program. "It's not just for taxes," says one tax practitioner who specializes in the arts. "If you want something left over at the end, you have to see where the money is going. You have to keep track of finances." When you pay for services such as a hired musician or a roadie, ask for a receipt with the person's Social Security number and address—you may need it at tax time.

New Pass-Through Tax Deduction

The 2018 Tax Cuts and Jobs Act established a new deduction for pass-through businesses (I.R.C. § 199A). The vast majority of self-employed individuals have pass-through businesses—that is, they are sole proprietors, limited liability company owners, partners in partnerships, or S corporation shareholders. Thus, they may be eligible to deduct an amount equal to up to 20% of their net business income. However, if total taxable income exceeds $315,000 for marrieds filing jointly or $157,500 for singles, the deduction is wholly or partly limited to the greater of:

- 50% of the owner's applicable share of the W-2 employee wages paid by the business, or
- 25% of the owner's share of the W-2 wages paid by the business, plus 2.5% of the original purchase price of the long-term property used in the production of income.

The deduction is phased out for pass-through owners who provide various types of personal services. The deduction is completely phased out for married service providers whose taxable income exceeds $415,000, and for singles with income over $207,500.

This is a personal deduction that pass-through owners can take on their returns whether or not they itemize. This deduction is scheduled to end on January 1, 2026.

When to Deduct

Some expenses can be deducted all at once; others have to be deducted over a number of years. It all depends on how long the item you purchase can reasonably be expected to last—what the IRS calls its "useful life."

Current Expenses

The cost of anything your band buys for its business that has a useful life of less than one year must be fully deducted in the year it is purchased. This includes, for example, studio rent, telephone and utility bills, photocopying and promotional costs, and postage and other ordinary business operating costs. Such items are called "current expenses."

Capital Expenses

Certain types of costs are considered to be part of your investment in your business—the major costs of setting it up as opposed to the costs of operating it day to day. These are called "capital expenses." Subject to an important exception for a certain amount of personal property, you cannot deduct the full value of such expenses in the year you incur them. Instead, you must spread the cost over several years and deduct part of it each year.

There are two main categories of capital expenses. They include:

- the cost of any asset you will use in your business that has a useful life of more than one year—for example, sound equipment, vehicles, books, and machinery; and
- business start-up costs such as fees for an attorney and accounting fees paid to set up your business.

If the money you spend on your band business exceeds your band's income for the year, your business incurs a loss. This isn't as bad as it sounds, tax-wise. You can use a business loss to offset other income you may have.

> CAUTION
>
> **If you fall into a pattern of incurring losses year after year,** you risk running afoul of the hobby-loss rule. This is no small risk—it could cost you a small fortune in additional income taxes. (See the discussion later in this chapter on whether your band is a hobby or a business.)

> RESOURCE
>
> **For detailed information on deducting business losses,** see IRS Publication 536, *Net Operating Losses*. You can obtain this and all other IRS publications by calling the IRS at 800-TAX-FORM, visiting your local IRS office, or downloading the publications at www.irs.gov.

Deducting the Cost of Business Assets

You can deduct from your band's income taxes and money you spend for things you use to help produce income.

If you qualify for the Section 179 deduction discussed below, your band can deduct the entire cost of these items in the year you pay for them. Otherwise, you have to deduct the cost over a period of years—a process called depreciation.

The rules for deducting business assets can be complex, but it's worth spending the time to understand them. After all, the U.S. government is in effect offering to help you pay for your equipment and other business assets. All you have to do is take advantage of the offer.

Section 179 Deduction

If you learn only one section number in the tax code, it should be Section 179. It is one of the greatest tax boons for bands (and other small businesses). Section 179 permits the band members to deduct a large amount of your business purchases in the year you make them, rather than having to depreciate them over several years. This is called first-year expensing or Section 179 expensing. It allows you to get a big tax deduction all at once, rather than having to mete it out a little at a time.

> EXAMPLE: The band GingerTea buys a $4,000 sound system. The band can use Section 179 to deduct the entire $4,000 expense from its income for the year.

It's up to you to decide whether to use Section 179. It may not always be in your best interest to do so. If you do use it, you can't change your mind later and decide to use depreciation instead.

Property That Can Be Deducted

You can use Section 179 to deduct the cost of any tangible property you use for your business that the IRS has determined will last more than one year—for example, computers, musical equipment, and studio furniture. Special rules apply to cars. You can't use Section 179 for land, buildings, or intangible property such as patents, copyrights, and trademarks.

If you use property both for business and personal purposes, you may deduct under Section 179 only if you use it for business purposes more than half the time. The amount of your deduction is reduced by the percentage of personal use. You'll need to keep records showing your business use of such property. If you use an item for business less than half the time, you must depreciate it.

Deduction Limit

There is a limit on the total amount of business expenses you can deduct each year using Section 179. The deduction is currently (as of passage in 2018 of the Tax Cuts and Jobs Act) $1,000,000.

If you purchase more than one item of Section 179 property during the year, you can divide the deduction among all the items in any way, as long as the total deduction is not more than the Section 179 limit. It's usually best to apply Section 179 to property that has the longest useful life and therefore the longest depreciation period. This reduces the total time you have to wait to get your deductions.

CAUTION

Limit on Section 179 deduction. You can't use Section 179 to deduct more in one year than your total profit from all of your businesses and your salary if you have a job in addition to your business. That is, you can't use Section 179 to reduce your taxable income below zero.

Depreciation

Because it provides a big tax deduction immediately, most band businesses look first to Section 179 to deduct asset costs.

However, your band must use depreciation instead if you:

- don't qualify to use Section 179—for example, you want to deduct the cost of a copyright—or
- use up your Section 179 deduction for the year.

Depreciation involves deducting the cost of a business asset a little at a time over a period of years. This means it will take you much longer to get your full deduction than under Section 179. Depreciable equipment is deducted on the partnership tax return (Form 4562, *Depreciation and Amortization*). If the band members individually own equipment, it is deducted on Schedule C of the individual 1040 return.

> ⓘ **CAUTION**
> **The amounts that can be depreciated may change if tax laws are overhauled.** Check the IRS website (www.irs.gov) for current limitations on depreciation of business equipment.

What Must Be Depreciated

Depreciation is used to deduct the cost of any new or used asset you buy for your business that has a useful life of more than one year—for example, buildings, equipment, machinery, patents, trademarks, copyrights, and furniture. The IRS, not you, decides the useful life of your assets.

You can also depreciate the cost of major repairs that increase the value or extend the life of an asset—for example, the cost of a major upgrade to make your computer run faster. However, you deduct normal repairs or maintenance in the year they're incurred as a business expense.

For example, your band purchases a vintage drum set that costs $2,800 in the summer of 2018. According to the IRS rules, a drum set (new or vintage) depreciates over seven years, so each year you could deduct $400. Since you bought the set in July, however, you can deduct $200 during the 2018 tax year, because you had it for only half of the year. You continue to deduct a portion in later years until the full cost has been deducted.

Alternatively, the 2018 Tax Cuts and Jobs Act gives you a depreciation option similar to Section 179. Using what is referred to as "bonus depreciation," you can—during the first year of use of the item—depreciate 100% of the cost for items purchased after September 27, 2017.

Mixed-Use Property

If you use property both for band business and personal purposes, you can take depreciation only for the business use of the asset. Unlike for the Section 179 deduction, you don't have to use an item over half the time for business to depreciate it.

EXAMPLE: Carl uses his photocopier 75% of the time for personal reasons and 25% for his band business. He can depreciate 25% of the cost of the copier.

Keep a diary or log with the dates, times, and reason the property was used to distinguish between the two uses.

Depreciation Period

The depreciation period—called the recovery period by the IRS—begins when you start using the asset and lasts for the entire estimated useful life of the asset. The tax code has assigned an estimated useful life for all types of business assets, ranging from three to 39 years. Most of the assets you buy for your business will probably have an estimated useful life of five or seven years. You can't deduct any more depreciation after the property's estimated useful life expires.

Depreciable Periods for Commonly Used Band Business Property	
Type of Property	**Recovery Period**
Computer software (software that comes with your computer is not separately depreciable unless you're separately billed for it)	three years
Computers and peripherals, calculators, copiers, typewriters, and other office-related equipment	five years
Autos and light trucks	five years
Any property—including musical instruments and amplifiers—that does not have an established IRS class life and has not been designated by laws as being in any other class	seven years

RESOURCE

If you need to know the depreciation period for an asset not included in this table, see IRS Publication 534, *Depreciation*, for a complete listing. You can obtain this and all other IRS publications by calling the IRS at 800-TAX-FORM, visiting your local IRS office, or downloading the publications at www.irs.gov.

TIP
Even though your equipment may become more valuable over time (such as a vintage guitar), it still is considered depreciable like any other property in its category.

TIP
If you'd rather be writing songs instead of calculating depreciation, then invest in a tax software program such as *TurboTax* (the Home & Business version). Tax programs can help you calculate the depreciation and offer you tax solutions.

RESOURCE
For more information, see IRS Publication 534, *Depreciation*, and Publication 946, *How to Depreciate Property*. You can obtain these and all other IRS publications by calling the IRS at 800-TAX-FORM, visiting your local IRS office, or downloading the publications at www.irs.gov.

Car Expenses

Most band members use their cars or vans to do some driving related to band business—for example, to performances or trade shows, to pick up or deliver work, or to obtain musical supplies. Of course, driving costs money— and you are allowed to deduct your driving expenses when you use your car, van, pickup, or panel truck for business.

There are two ways to calculate the car expense deduction. You can:
- use the standard mileage rate, which requires relatively little record keeping, or
- deduct your actual expenses, which requires much more record keeping but might give you a larger deduction.

If you own a late model car worth more than $15,000, you'll usually get a larger deduction by using the actual-expense method, because the standard mileage rate doesn't include enough for depreciation of new cars. On the other hand, the standard mileage rate will be better if you have an inexpensive or old car and put in a lot of business mileage.

Cars, Computers, and Cell Phones

There are special rules when claiming deductions for certain items that can be used for personal as well as business purposes. These are called listed property and include:

- cars, boats, airplanes, and other vehicles (see below, for rules on mileage and vehicle expenses)
- computers
- cellular phones, and
- any other property generally used for entertainment, recreation, or amusement—for example, Bluetooth speakers and virtual reality headsets.

The IRS fears that taxpayers might use listed property items such as computers for personal reasons but claim business deductions for them. For this reason, you're required to document your business use of listed property. You can satisfy this requirement by keeping a logbook showing when and how the property is used.

Either way, you'll need to have records showing how many miles you drive your car for business during the year—also called business miles. Keep a mileage logbook for this purpose.

Standard Mileage Rate

The easiest way to deduct car expenses is to take the standard mileage rate. When you use this method, you need to keep track of only how many business miles you drive, not the actual expenses for your car such as gas or repairs.

You can use the standard mileage rate only for a car that you own. You must choose to use it in the first year you start using your car for your business. In later years, you can choose to use the standard mileage rate or actual expenses.

Each year, the IRS sets the standard mileage rate—a specified amount of money you can deduct for each business mile you drive. In 2018, for example, the rate was 54.5 cents per mile. To figure your deduction, multiply your business miles by the standard mileage rate for the year.

> **EXAMPLE:** Ed handles all of the business and promotional work for EdNa, a two-man band. He drove his car 10,000 miles for band business in 2018. To determine the band's car expense deduction, he simply multiplies the total business miles he drove by 54.5 cents. This gives the band a $5,450 deduction (54.5 cents x 10,000 = $5,450).

If you choose to take the standard mileage rate, you cannot deduct actual operating expenses—for example, depreciation or Section 179 deduction, maintenance and repairs, gasoline and its taxes, oil, insurance, and vehicle registration fees. These costs are already factored into the standard mileage rate.

Band members can deduct business-related parking fees and tolls—for example, a parking fee you have to pay when you visit a club promoter. But you cannot deduct fees you pay to park your car at your rehearsal space.

Actual Expenses

Instead of taking the standard mileage rate, you can elect to deduct the actual expenses of using your car for business. To do this, deduct the actual cost of depreciation for your car, interest payments on a car loan, lease fees, rental fees, license fees, garage rent, repairs, gas, oil, tires, and insurance. The total deductible amount is based on the percentage of time you use your car for business. You can also deduct the full amount of business-related parking fees and tolls.

Deducting all these items will take more time and effort than using the standard mileage rate because you'll need to keep records of all your expenses. However, it may provide you with a larger deduction than the standard rate.

Note: When you claim actual expenses and use your car for both business and personal purposes, you must also divide your expenses between business and personal use.

> **EXAMPLE:** In one recent year Laura drove her car 5,000 miles for her band business and 5,000 miles for personal purposes. She can deduct 50% of the actual costs of operating her car.

If you own only one car, you normally can't claim that it's used only for business. An IRS auditor is not likely to believe that you walk or take public transportation everywhere except when you're on business. The only exception might be if you live in a place with developed transportation systems, such as Chicago, New York City, or San Francisco, and drive your car only when you go out of town on band business.

Also, when you deduct actual car expenses, you must keep records of the costs of operating your car. This includes not only the number of business miles and total miles you drive, but also gas, repair, parking, insurance, and similar costs. If this seems to be too much trouble, use the standard mileage rate. That way, you'll have to keep track of only how many business miles you drive, not what you spend for gas and similar expenses.

 RESOURCE
For more information about the rules for claiming car expenses, see IRS Publication 463, *Travel, Entertainment, Gift, and Car Expenses.* You can obtain this and all other IRS publications by calling the IRS at 800-TAX-FORM, visiting your local IRS office, or downloading the publications at www.irs.gov.

Travel and Touring Expenses

If you travel with your band—for example, you tour regularly—you can deduct your airfare, hotel bills, and other expenses. If you plan your trip right, you can even mix business with pleasure and still get a deduction for your airfare. However, IRS auditors closely scrutinize these deductions, because many taxpayers claim them without complying with the rules attached to them. This is why you need to understand the limitations on this deduction and keep proper records.

Travel Within the United States

Some musicians think they have the right to deduct the cost of any band-related trip they take. This is not the case. You can deduct a trip within the United States only if:

- it's primarily for band business
- you travel outside your city limits, and

- you're away at least overnight or long enough to require a stop for sleep or rest.

For your trip to be deductible, you must spend more than half of your time on activities that can reasonably be expected to help advance your band. For most bands on tour this is not a problem, since the band spends the bulk of its time either traveling, sound-checking, or performing.

You don't have to travel any set distance to get a travel expense deduction. However, you can't take this deduction if your band just spends the night in a motel across town. You must travel outside your city limits. If you don't live in a city, you must go outside the general area where your band is located.

Finally, you must stay away overnight or at least long enough to require a stop for sleep or rest. Again, for most touring bands, this is not an issue.

Combining Business With Pleasure

Provided that your trip is primarily for business, you can tack on a vacation at the end, make a side trip purely for fun, or go to the theater and still deduct your entire airfare. What you spend while having fun is not deductible, but you can still deduct your expenses while on business.

> **EXAMPLE:** The Bills fly to Austin for the South by Southwest show. The band performs and meets with record executives for two days and then spends one day in Austin enjoying the sights. Since The Bills spent over half their time on business—two days out of three—the cost of the flight is entirely deductible, as are hotel and meal costs during the first two days. The band may not deduct hotel, meal, or other expenses during the one vacation day.

Foreign Travel

The rules differ if your band travels outside the United States, and they are in some ways more lenient. However, as with all expenses, your band must have a legitimate business reason for the foreign trip.

If your band is away no more than seven days, and you spend the majority of your time related to band business, you can deduct all of your travel costs.

However, even if your trip was primarily a vacation, you can deduct your airfare and other transportation costs as long as at least part of the trip was for business. You can also deduct your expenses while on business.

More stringent rules apply if your band's foreign trip lasts more than one week. To get a full deduction for your expenses, you must spend at least 75% of your trip on band business matters. Again, for most bands touring Europe or some other foreign location, this is not a problem.

However, if you spend less than 75% of your time on band business, you must determine the percentage of your time spent on business by counting the number of business days and the number of personal days. You can deduct only the percentage of your travel costs that relates to business days. A business day is any day you have to be at a particular place on business or in which you spend four or more hours on business matters. Days spent traveling to and from your destination also count as business days.

Deductible Expenses During Foreign or Domestic Travel

You can deduct virtually all of your expenses when you travel on business, including:

- airfare to and from your destination
- hotel or other lodging expenses
- taxi, public transportation, and car rental expenses
- telephone and Internet access expenses
- the cost of shipping your personal luggage or equipment or other things you need for your business
- rental fees for equipment, including computers
- laundry and dry cleaning expenses, and
- tips you pay on any of the other costs.

However, only 50% of the cost of meals is deductible. The IRS imposes this limitation based on the reasoning that you would have eaten had you stayed home.

You must keep good records of your expenses. You cannot deduct expenses for personal sightseeing or recreation.

Food

You can deduct your ordinary, necessary, and reasonable food expenses, or you can use a per diem system in which you utilize the per diem rates established by the federal government. These rates vary from city to city. To view the current rates, go to the U.S. General Services Administration (www.gsa.gov) and click Per Diem Rates.

Home Studio/Home Office

A home office deduction allows you to deduct a portion of rent, mortgage, or utilities for your music business. Unfortunately, the IRS has maintained the traditional position that performers in a band earn their income on stage, and therefore, the "home office" deduction may not apply if you use one room for personal practice. You can deduct expenses for a separate freestanding structure such as a studio, garage, or barn if you use it exclusively and regularly for your band business.

Songwriters who compose and record their songs at home, or musicians who maintain a home office for administrative tasks for the band—for example, a home office for keeping track of finances, booking, or promotion—may be able to claim the deduction. Under a tax law passed in 1999, you can claim the home office deduction as long you can show this is where the business's substantial administrative duties occur.

As a general rule, your band can't take the home office deduction unless you regularly use part of your home exclusively for one of these band purposes. Exclusive use means that you use a portion of your home *only* for business. If you use part of your home as your business office and also use that part for personal purposes, you do not meet the exclusive-use test and cannot take the home office deduction.

Satisfying the requirement of using your home office regularly and exclusively for business is only half the battle. It must also be true that:

- your home office/studio is your band's principal place of business, or
- you use a separate structure on your property exclusively for business purposes.

Here are some ways to help convince the IRS you qualify for the home office deduction:

- Take a picture of your home studio or office, and draw up a diagram showing it as a portion of your home.
- Have all your band business mail sent to your home office.
- Use your home office address on all your band business cards, stationery, and advertising.
- Obtain a separate phone line for your band business, and keep that phone in your home office.
- Keep a log of the time you spend working in your home studio. This doesn't have to be fancy; notes on your calendar will do.

In general, to qualify for the home office deduction, your home office does not need to be the place where you generate most of your band business income. It's sufficient that you regularly use it to administer or manage your business—for example, to keep your books, schedule shows, prepare promotions, and order supplies. As long as you have no other fixed location where you do such things—for example, an outside office—you'll get the deduction.

How much you can claim toward your home office deduction depends on how much (what percentage) of your home you use as a home office or studio. For example, if you use 20% of your home, you can allot 20% of your home office expenses to the home office deduction. The main expenses that qualify are:

- your rent if you rent your home, or
- depreciation, mortgage interest, and property taxes if you own your home.

In addition, owners and renters may deduct this same percentage of other expenses for keeping up and running an entire home. The IRS calls these indirect expenses. They include:

- utility expenses for electricity, gas, heating oil, and trash removal
- homeowner's or renter's insurance
- home maintenance expenses that benefit your entire home including your home office, such as roof and furnace repairs and exterior painting
- condominium association fees
- snow removal expenses

- casualty losses if your home is damaged—for example, in a storm, and
- security system costs.

You may also deduct the entire cost of expenses just for your home office. The IRS calls these direct expenses. They include, for example, painting your home office or studio or paying someone to clean it. If you pay a housekeeper to clean your entire house, you may deduct your business-use percentage of the expense.

Tossing Your Tax Records

Have you been storing your band's canceled checks from 1989 just in case the IRS audits you? Then it's time to climb up the attic stairs and get rid of that financial fire hazard. What tax records do you need to keep? Start with the basic rule that, with rare exceptions, the IRS is prohibited from asking you about returns that are more than three years old—that is, three years from the date of your last return. So, you need to keep records that relate only to the last three years. Bear in mind that tax returns may be based on financial records that date more than three years—for example, five-year depreciation on business equipment. So, keep records like these. For your personal income tax records, you will also need to hang on to information about capital gains and cost records for your house and improvements. There are some exceptions to the three-year rule—for example, you can be audited for six years if you fail to report more than 25% of your gross income, or you can be audited without any time limits if you file a fraudulent return.

How Likely Are You to Get Audited?

Partnership tax returns are audited less frequently than sole proprietorships (another advantage of filing a partnership tax return). Sole proprietorships with home business deductions are the number-one target for audits, especially if your business is claiming a loss.

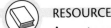
RESOURCE
A great source of information regarding business taxation is *Deduct It!*
Lower Your Small Business Taxes, by Stephen Fishman (Nolo).

Is Your Band a Hobby or a Business?

Remember, the only expenses that can be deducted from your income are business expenses. If the IRS doesn't believe that the deductions are business-related, then it will not let you take them. Therefore, if the IRS doesn't consider your band to be a legitimate business, band-related expenses will not be deductible.

So what criteria does the IRS use to determine whether an activity is a business or just a hobby? Basically, the criteria are whether you are operating like a business (for example, the level of expertise and record keeping) and whether you have shown a clear and reasonable intention to make a profit. Evidence such as advertising for gigs, a business bank account, efforts to sell merchandise, or other attempts to make money will help to show that your band is in fact a business, even if you aren't making any profit. Technically, there's no time limit for how long your band can lose money and still claim deductions.

However, you should be aware that the IRS does operate under a presumption that any business, including a band, that loses money for three out of any five consecutive years is a hobby, not a business, and thus cannot deduct expenses. This is known as the 3-of-5 rule. It is important to note that the 3-of-5 rule only creates a presumption that your band is a hobby, not a final conclusion. This means that even if you lose money three out of five years, you still can demonstrate that your band is a business with a clear and reasonable intention to make a profit. If you have been losing money for several years, an auditor will want to know what you are doing to turn the business around and make a profit.

Some good indicators that you are treating your band like a business are that you:

- maintain a separate checking account for your band
- keep good business records
- make some effort to market your band—for example, seek out shows or create a website
- have band stationery and cards printed
- obtain a federal Employer Identification Number
- secure all necessary business licenses and permits, and
- develop expertise in band business or in your field of music by attending classes and seminars.

The more time and effort you put into the band, the more it will look like you want to make money. So try to devote as much time as possible to your band, and keep a log showing the time you spend on it. If you cannot demonstrate an intention to make a profit, the band will be considered a hobby, and you will not be able to deduct your band's expenses from your personal tax return.

Payroll Taxes: When Your Band Hires Employees

If your band hires and pays someone for services (for example, a roadie, sound person, driver, or side musician), that person is either an employee or an independent contractor. Distinguishing between an employee and an independent contractor is very important for tax purposes. If your band hires employees, you will have to pay employment taxes (also called payroll taxes). No such taxes are required for hiring independent contractors. If you don't understand the difference between these two kinds of workers, you run the risk of miscategorizing your workers, which may land you in hot water for failing to pay the appropriate taxes.

Employee or Independent Contractor?

As a general rule, someone who receives a regular salary (for example, weekly or monthly payments) and must show up at all rehearsals and performances is probably an employee.

Some indicators that a person is an employee (not an independent contractor) are:

- the band tells the worker how to perform the job (this is one of the most important criteria!)
- the worker can quit at any time without any liability
- the worker can be hired or fired at will
- the worker receives employee benefits
- the band supplies equipment or facilities for the worker, or
- the band reimburses the worker for business and traveling expenses.

Workers who don't meet these criteria are probably independent contractors.

EXAMPLE: Bob and Mandy (a bass player and a drummer) are hired by the Velveetas, a nostalgia band. Bob and Mandy must practice with the band three days a week. They are paid $35 each for every practice. They bring their own instruments to band practices. Bob and Mandy receive $100 each for every show. For out-of-town shows, they travel on the band bus, and their hotel rooms are paid by the band. Bob and Mandy are given sheet music of what to play. Based on the degree of control and regular employment and pay, Bob and Mandy are employees.

The Employee/Independent Contractor Distinction Can Be Tricky

Making a distinction between employee and independent contractor can be difficult. The rules used by the government are discussed in detail in *Working With Independent Contractors*, by Stephen Fishman (Nolo). You may need to obtain the assistance of an accountant or tax preparer. You can also obtain advice from your state employment office, various government tax manuals, or the IRS.

Taxes for Employees vs. Independent Contractors

Your band must pay federal payroll taxes for every employee consisting of Social Security and Medicare payments (known as FICA) and federal unemployment taxes (known as FUTA). Your band will also have to deduct federal income taxes (known as FITW) from employees' paychecks. State payroll taxes consist of state unemployment taxes and state income taxes (except for Alaska, Florida, Nevada, South Dakota, Texas, Washington, and Wyoming, where there are no state income taxes). Five states (California, Hawaii, New Jersey, New York, and Rhode Island) also require that you pay state disability insurance. If you fail to pay payroll taxes or workers' compensation (see "Workers' Compensation," below), the owners/employers in the band may be personally subject to harsh fines and, on rare occasions, jail time.

Your band does not need to pay payroll taxes for independent contractors, because they pay income and self-employment taxes on their own. At the end of the year, your band gives a 1099 form to all independent contractors that it paid more than $600 that year. The independent contractor uses that 1099 form to pay his or her share of taxes.

Note,: You are *not* required to send a 1099 form to independent contractors if you paid them via PayPal (for business and services) or credit card (even if you paid the contractor more than $600 in the past year).

Workers' Compensation

Every state (except Texas) requires that most employers pay for workers' compensation insurance for employees (not independent contractors). In some states, workers' comp payments are not necessary if you employ fewer than a certain number of employees (usually two to four).

Usually, your band can acquire workers' comp insurance through private insurance carriers or from a special state fund (although in a few states, you must buy it from the state fund). Failure to pay for workers' compensation insurance can have very harsh repercussions for the employer, including potential lawsuits filed by injured employees and stiff fines for which the employers may be individually liable.

How to Get a Federal Tax ID Number (FEIN) for Your Partnership

A federal Employer Identification Number (FEIN) for a business is the equivalent of a Social Security number for an individual. You will need this number in order to file a partnership tax return, and you will probably need it to open a partnership bank account. (Record companies and music publishers may also request your FEIN before making payments to your band.)

In order to obtain a federal Employer Identification Number, the IRS has made it easy with an online "EIN Assistant" (simply type "EIN Assistant" into a search engine). A few things to keep in mind when using the EIN Assistant are that (1) you must complete this application in one session, as you will not be able to save and return at a later time, (2) your session will expire after 15 minutes of inactivity, and you will need to start over, and (3) you will receive your EIN immediately upon verification.

Using the EIN Assistant, you will first be asked what type of organization you are, then why you want an EIN (for example, you're hiring employees), who the principal officer or owner is (in the case of a band partnership, name any partner who wants handle the paperwork), where you are located, your accounting period, whether you have any employees, what type of business (list "Other: Musical Services") and whether you want to receive your confirmation by mail or online (you'll need Adobe *Reader*). Use the online help if you have questions.

You can also download a copy of Form SS-4 (*Application for Employer Identification Number*) from the IRS website (www.irs.gov). The downloadable version is in a PDF "fillable" format, which means that you can type in your information using Adobe *Reader*.

The form includes directions, but the following tips will help:

- **Space 1: Legal Name of Entity or Individual.** Insert the legal name of your partnership. This may be different from your band name. Usually, most bands take their band name and add the words "partnership" or "band partnership," for example, "Spyder Band Partnership." For more information on band names, see Chapter 9.
- **Space 2: Trade Name of Business.** Insert your band's name (for example, "The Spyders").

- **Space 7a: Name of Principal Officer, General Partner.** Someone in the band (one of the partners) must furnish their name and Social Security number. This person becomes the contact for the IRS.
- **Space 8a: Type of Entity.** Check the "Partnership" box.
- **Space 9: Reason for Applying.** Check "Started a New Business" and insert "Partnership" on the line.
- **Space 11: Closing Month of Accounting.** Usually this is December, but check with your accountant or tax expert in case you are using a different type of accounting year.
- **Space 12: First Date Wages Were Paid.** If you are not paying employees (see above), then write "Not Applicable."
- **Space 14: Principal Activity.** Check "Other" and write "Musical Services."
- **Space 15: Principal Line of Merchandise, Services.** Again, write "Musical Services."

After completing the form, you can get your band's FEIN right away by calling one of the TELETIN numbers on pages 2 and 3 of the form. If you cannot locate a number for your area, call 800-829-1040. The person who calls the IRS should be the person whose name is listed on Space 7a of the SS-4 form. The IRS operator will ask you questions about your completed SS-4 form and will then give you an FEIN number, which your band can use immediately. However, in order for the FEIN to remain valid, you must mail or fax your SS-4 form within 24 hours. Your FEIN is also used when filing your state tax return.

CANADIAN RULES

Canadian Income Taxes. Residents of Canada must file tax forms with Revenue Canada, the Canadian equivalent of the U.S. Internal Revenue Service (online at www.revcan.ca). Canadian residents must pay taxes by April 30 of each year and must have an SIN (Social Insurance Number) when filing. The SIN can be obtained from the Canadian government website (www.canada.ca). Click the "Jobs" tab, Click "Find a Job" from the drop-down menu. Then click "Social insurance number." Income tax packages are available from Revenue Canada income tax offices, online, or at post offices in the province or territory where you live. Note that many of the rules described in this chapter regarding U.S. corporate, partnership, and other business taxation may not apply for Canadian bands.

Using the Downloadable Forms

**Get Updates, Forms, and More at
This Book's Companion Page on Nolo.com**

You can download any of the forms and agreements in this book at:

www.nolo.com/back-of-book/ML.html

When there are important changes to the information in this book, we'll post updates on this same dedicated page as well as podcasts and videos from author Rich Stim.

Thisbook comes with downloadable files that you can access online at:
www.nolo.com/back-of-book/ML.html
You can view these files with Adobe *Reader*, free software from
www.adobe.com. Government PDFs are sometimes fillable using your
computer, but most PDFs are designed to be printed out and completed
by hand.

Editing RTFs

Here are some general instructions about editing RTF forms. You can open,
edit, print, and save these form files with most word processing programs
such as Microsoft *Word*, Windows *WordPad*, and recent versions of *Pages*
for Mac and iOS. Refer to this book's instructions and sample agreements
for help about what should go in each blank.

- **Underlines.** Underlines indicate where to enter information. After filling
  in the needed text, delete the underline.
- **Bracketed and italicized text.** Bracketed and italicized text indicates
  instructions. Be sure to remove all instructional text before you finalize
  your document.
- **Optional text.** Optional text gives you the choice to include or exclude
  text. Delete any optional text you don't want to use. Renumber
  numbered items, if necessary.
- **Alternative text.** Alternative text gives you the choice between two
  or more text options. Delete those options you don't want to use.
  Renumber numbered items, if necessary.
- **Signature lines.** Signature lines should appear on a page with at least
  some text from the document itself.

Every word processing program uses different commands to open, format,
save, and print documents, so refer to your software's help documents for help
using your program. Nolo cannot provide technical support for questions
about how to use your computer or your software.

CAUTION
**In accordance with U.S. copyright laws, the forms provided by this book
are for your personal use only.**

List of Forms

All the forms listed below are available for download at:
www.nolo.com/back-of-book/ML.html

The following files are in Rich Text Format (RTF):

Form Name	File Name
Artwork Agreement	ArtAgreement.rtf
(Abbreviated) Artwork Agreement	ArtAgreementShort.rtf
Band Partnership Agreement	Partnership.rtf
(Abbreviated) Band Partnership Agreement	PartnershipShort.rtf
Notice of Intention to Obtain Compulsory License for Making and Distributing Sound Recordings	LicenseNotice.rtf
Consignment Form	Consignment.rtf
Independent Distribution Agreement	Distribution.rtf
Mechanical License and Authorization for First-Time Recording of Song	FirstRecording.rtf
Independent Label Recording Agreement	LabelAgreement.rtf
Independent Label License Agreement	LabelLicense.rtf
Label-Shopping Agreement	Labelshopping.rtf
Management Agreement	Management.rtf
(Abbreviated) Management Agreement	ManagementShort.rtf
Model Release Agreement	ModelRelease.rtf
Musician Release Agreement	MusicianRelease.rtf
Performance Agreement	Performance.rtf
Budget for Recording Costs	RecordBudget.rtf
Agreement With Music Publisher for Use of Song Sample	SongSample.rtf

Form Name	File Name
Agreement With Record Company for Use of Master Recording Sample	MasterSample.rtf
Tour Budget	TourBudget.rtf
Master Use and Sync License (Short Form)	MusicSyncShort.rtf
Music Synchronization and Videogram License Agreement	SyncAgreement.rtf
Master Use and Videogram License Agreement	MasterUse.rtf

Index

C

© symbol, 278–279

Cable and satellite music subscriptions, 350, 469

California
booking agent licensing, 164
LLC taxes and fees, 62, 482
minors and agreements, 35
receiving stolen merchandise, 140
sales tax collection, 476
talent agent laws, 95
termination of attorney fee agreements, 112

California Lawyers for the Arts, 34

Canada
American Arbitration Association, 34
American Federation of Musicians (AFM) membership, 150
Canadian Music Reproduction Rights Agency (CMRRA), 229, 370
copyright laws, 170, 172, 173, 178
copyright registration, 351
fair dealing principle, 178
income taxes, 507
mechanical licenses, 370
moral rights principle, 173
musical contrivances/sound recordings, 351
performance royalties, 226
SOCAN, 315
Trade-Mark law, 247
trademark registration, 258
use of province name in agreements, 22

Canadian Application for Registration of Copyright, 351

Canadian Copyright Office/Board, 226, 351

Canadian Intellectual Property Office (CIPO)
Circular 2, *Musical Works and Mechanical Contrivances*, 178, 351
Trade-Mark law, 247
website, 178

Canadian Music Reproduction Rights Agency (CMRRA), 229, 370

Capital contributions, defined, 31

Capital expenses, 488

Car expenses, 493–496

Car insurance, 53, 162

Cash accounting method, 463

Cash flow, 464–465

Catalog numbers, 280, 360, 366

C Corporations, 481, 482–483

CD Baby, Inc., 230, 231, 253, 281, 370, 371, 379, 382, 467, 468

Cease and desist letters, 256, 312

Celebrity names, in trademark infringement, 268

Certificate of Organization, 57

Certificate of Registration (USPTO), 267

City sales taxes, 476

Clearance forms, 243, 244

Coauthorship and co-ownership of songs, 179–183
cowriters as co-owners, 180
evaluation of songwriting contributions, 180–182

Collaboration/cowriter agreements, 183

Commercially satisfactory, use in agreements, 401, 403

Commissioned music projects, 440

Commissioner for Trademarks (USPTO), 268

F

⚖ NOLO *Online Legal Forms*

Nolo offers a large library of legal solutions and forms, created by Nolo's in-house legal staff. These reliable documents can be prepared in minutes.

Create a Document

- **Incorporation.** Incorporate your business in any state.
- **LLC Formations.** Gain asset protection and pass-through tax status in any state.
- **Wills.** Nolo has helped people make over 2 million wills. Is it time to make or revise yours?
- **Living Trust (avoid probate).** Plan now to save your family the cost, delays, and hassle of probate.
- **Trademark.** Protect the name of your business or product.
- **Provisional Patent.** Preserve your rights under patent law and claim "patent pending" status.

Download a Legal Form

Nolo.com has hundreds of top quality legal forms available for download—bills of sale, promissory notes, nondisclosure agreements, LLC operating agreements, corporate minutes, commercial lease and sublease, motor vehicle bill of sale, consignment agreements and many more.

Review Your Documents

Many lawyers in Nolo's consumer-friendly lawyer directory will review Nolo documents for a very reasonable fee. Check their detailed profiles at **Nolo.com/lawyers**.